THE PRACTICE OF LIFE ASSURANCE

This volume forms part of a series of text-books published under the authority of the Institute of Actuaries and the Faculty of Actuaries and is designed to meet the needs of students preparing for the actuarial examinations.

THE PRACTICE OF LIFE ASSURANCE

A TEXT-BOOK FOR ACTUARIAL STUDENTS

BY

N. E. COE, F.I.A.

AND

M. E. OGBORN, F.I.A.

CAMBRIDGE

Published for the Institute of Actuaries and the Faculty of Actuaries

AT THE UNIVERSITY PRESS

1952

CAMBRIDGE UNIVERSITY PRESS
Cambridge, New York, Melbourne, Madrid, Cape Town,
Singapore, São Paulo, Delhi, Mexico City

Cambridge University Press
The Edinburgh Building, Cambridge CB2 8RU, UK

Published in the United States of America by Cambridge University Press, New York

www.cambridge.org
Information on this title: www.cambridge.org/9781107621824

First published 1952
First paperback edition 2013

A catalogue record for this publication is available from the British Library

ISBN 978-1-107-62182-4 Paperback

CONTENTS

Part III. Industrial Assurance

PREFACE

This book is one of a series commissioned jointly by the Councils of the Institute and the Faculty of Actuaries. It is designed as a text-book for the 'less advanced treatment' of life-office work in Part IV A of the revised Syllabus of the Institute; it is intended to be the sole reading for that stage of the Examinations. The student who elects to take the more advanced treatment of this subject in the 'specialized emphasis' of Part IV C should find the book useful by way of linking the various original papers which are set in the official List of Reading.

The reader of this book is assumed to have a thorough knowledge of compound interest and life contingencies, including the mathematics of the calculation of office premiums and of the valuation of assurances and annuities, and also a general knowledge of finance and investment. The standard is thus intermediate between the elementary treatment of premium calculations, valuation and so on in the earlier parts of the Syllabus and the more advanced treatment appropriate to 'specialized emphasis'.

The field which we have had to cover is a wide one, embracing all those practical applications of the theory of compound interest and life contingencies which are the concern of the life-office actuary. To encompass this within the covers of a single book has necessitated a fairly condensed treatment of the subject. The list of references which is appended to each chapter, except the first, will serve both as an indication of the sources that have been used and as a guide to further reading for those who desire a fuller knowledge of the subjects discussed. The references have been taken where possible from the *Journal of the Institute of Actuaries*, the *Transactions of the Faculty of Actuaries* and other sources readily accessible to British readers, but the references could, of course, be paralleled in many instances by reference to foreign sources.

The second chapter provides the historical background to many of the problems which arise in practice. Though it is not strictly necessary for the Institute Examinations we trust that it will be helpful to the student. In a few other places, for the sake of completeness, we have dealt with certain subjects in a rather fuller manner than is required for 'less advanced treatment'. Sections or passages of this nature have been marked with an asterisk, and these may be assumed to be outside the scope of Part IVA.

The line between 'less advanced treatment' and the more advanced treatment appropriate to 'specialized emphasis' is not an easy one to draw. In some instances it has led to a restriction of scope: for example, we have omitted reference to reassurances and to overseas life business and have made only passing references to the special problems of collecting friendly societies. More frequently, however, it has meant a reduction of emphasis. We have aimed at making the book reasonably comprehensive, though certain subjects which are dealt with in brief sketches would require much fuller study for 'specialized emphasis'. Perhaps the most striking example is in the treatment of valuation. The reader is assumed to have a thorough knowledge of the mathematics of the various formulae and, taking that knowledge for granted, the book endeavours to provide a guide through the maze of formulae produced by generations of actuarial effort. The subject has been disposed of in a single chapter which will, we hope, suffice to give the student an adequate view of the subject as a whole, although to form a mature judgment on valuation methods the student must go back to the original papers and discussions.

There is an essential unity of principle between ordinary and industrial life assurance which may be obscured by the very different practical circumstances in which the two types of life assurance operate. We have endeavoured to emphasize the unity of principle by including in Part I of the book those general principles which are common to both types, together with a sketch of the historical, legal and financial background. The aim has been merely to give sufficient background for the student to appreciate its bearing on the problems discussed in the later chapters.

Part II of the book deals with the various actuarial problems from the point of view of 'ordinary' life assurance and Part III from the point of view of industrial life assurance. This separation has been convenient in writing the book and will also, we feel, be helpful for purposes of reference. The student will probably find it best to continue his studies in parallel so that he reads at the same time the corresponding chapters in Parts II and III. The first chapter in Part III, Chapter 17, on 'Special features of industrial assurance', may be taken with Part I.

The word *Practice* in the title does not imply that we have concentrated on the practical to the exclusion of the theoretical, and certain practical aspects are, of course, outside our terms of reference. The word is rather to be understood in an older sense and is intended to convey a nice blend of the theoretical and the practical in the solution of those problems which come before the life-office actuary as such. In former years the student's reading has mainly consisted of Institute papers and discussions supplemented by the books prepared for the Consolidation of Reading series of the Institute of Actuaries Students' Society, to which we owe a considerable debt. One consequence has been that necessarily the course has been largely confined to British practice. In this book, we have taken the opportunity of presenting a wider view which embraces practice in other lands where this throws a fresh light upon the problems under discussion. We trust that actuaries overseas will feel that we have dealt fairly with their practice in these respects, and that such of them as read this book will find something of interest in it.

With a few exceptions, the following scheme of notation has been used in this book:

Pure-premium functions	Unaccented symbols
Office functions containing loading or other adjustments	Accented symbols
Functions on basis of actual experience	Symbols with double accent

The symbol π for a special valuation premium has not been used. It serves little purpose, especially when it appears in the place of the pure premium P which is normally employed in valuations in Great Britain.

The medical aspects of Chapter 11, 'Underwriting and extra risks', have been based on information given by John Forest Smith,

F.R.C.P. The tables and diagrams have been mostly prepared by G. V. Bayley, F.I.A., and C. M. O'Brien, F.I.A., whose criticisms have also been of assistance in the preparation of certain chapters. We are indebted to K. J. Britt, F.I.A., F.F.A., and R. K. Lochhead, F.I.A., for the careful scrutiny of the manuscript and for their many helpful comments and suggestions. The manuscript was duplicated for the use of students in advance of publication, and the opportunity has been taken to incorporate many suggestions of those who for various reasons have had occasion to read the duplicated version.

References in the text indicate those paragraphs or sections which have been incorporated with some modifications from the corresponding parts of the earlier Consolidation of Reading books.

N. E. C.
M. E. O.

May 1950

PART I

GENERAL

CHAPTER 1

INTRODUCTORY REVIEW

The purpose of this text-book is to outline the principles on which the business of life assurance is based. The student will have studied the mathematical basis for earlier parts of the examination syllabus and we now turn to the study of the practical application of the mathematics.

1·1. A continuing business.

Though the basis is mathematical the fundamental conception of life assurance as a business should be kept in mind. We are prone to think of our problems in abstract terms because the solution is mathematical. It is important to remember that the problems are rooted in actual business with actual policies on actual lives. The solution must take account of the past, the present, and as good an estimate of the future as can be made. It must further be such as can be applied in practice. For example, a decision about new business policy has to be made effective through the field staff. The actuary has not merely to convince himself: he has to carry others with him so that his solution can be put into force.

The business of life assurance is one of long-term financial contracts and the worth of the contract to any assured depends primarily on the stability of the corporation selling it. It is of the utmost importance that the life assurance fund should be founded on principles which will enable the fund to meet its contractual obligations in bad times as well as good.

Except where the fund is closed to new entrants, a life assurance fund is in a state of flux, new assurances coming into the fund and others emerging as claims, surrenders and so on. This state of flux forms the background to many actuarial problems which derive from it a special interest that would be lacking were the fund in a static condition.

These ideas are summed up in the statement that life assurance is a continuing business.

1·2. The pool of risks.

The fundamental principle on which insurance depends is the pooling of risks. Life assurance is founded on this principle but there are special features to be taken into account.

The conception of a pool of risks involves the principle of the selection of risks. Dividing lines have to be drawn between those risks which will be regarded as normal risks, those for which special terms will be required and those which will be excluded altogether. The selection of risks may take place in a variety of ways. What is generally termed class selection arises from the characteristics of a life assurance fund and of the connexions through which it obtains its business. Further selection may be exercised through the business organization of the fund and finally we have the medical selection of new entrants.

The individual risk is a complex of many factors and the normal effect of pooling the risks is to average the operation of the several factors. Assuming the risks to be well spread the factors would not generally affect all the risks at the same time. Certain of them, for example epidemics and wars, may have such a general effect on the pool of risks that special consideration should be given to them either by including a general margin for fluctuations in the financial basis or by limiting the extent of the assurance liability. Others, for example aviation and atomic energy, may introduce a new element to which past experience is no guide. Thus, in principle, the scope of the liability has to be considered as well as the selection of the risks to be assured.

1·3. Assessmentism.

Life assurance policies could be arranged as yearly contracts under which the premium charged for a given year is merely sufficient to pay for the risk incurred during that year. Such a practice is known as assessmentism. It has the advantage that the premiums are used to provide the maximum amount of assurance from the outset but it also raises difficulties which make the system impracticable. Though assessmentism has been tried from time to time, life assurance contracts have not generally taken this form.

Since assessmentism is based upon a yearly contract the office as well as the assured should, in principle, have the right not to renew the contract at the end of the year should either of them so desire. Some early life assurance contracts were in this form but a yearly contract which could be terminated by the office would be neither practical nor popular, for obvious reasons.

In theory the 1-year temporary assurance premiums could be so computed as to include the right of the assured to renew the contract at a premium appropriate to his attained age without evidence of health. This form of contract has also proved unsatisfactory and it is interesting to see why this should have been so.

One of the most important questions from the point of view of the policyholder is what would happen to the assurance should he be unable to continue paying premiums. With assessmentism, since each year's premium merely pays for the current year's risk, the premium must be paid within the days of grace without any of the reliefs, such as a loan or extended period of insurance, to which the policyholder is accustomed under the more normal forms of life assurance. Further, the premium payable for a given amount of assurance necessarily increases rapidly at the later ages and the burden of the larger premiums at those ages causes great disappointment.

From the point of view of the office the mortality experience under such contracts naturally depends upon which are, in fact, renewed and which discontinued. There is a tendency for contracts on unhealthy lives to be maintained at all costs and a larger proportion of healthy lives is found amongst the withdrawals than amongst those renewing their assurances. Though premiums were based on suitable average mortality the actual experience was found to be considerably higher than the average which had been expected under this class of assurance. In theory the contingency could have been provided for by a suitable charge for the option of renewal but in practice it is not possible to obtain a firm basis for assessing the cost of that option. Generally, therefore, we may say that assessmentism does not provide an adequate financial foundation for life assurance though such contracts may possibly be useful in special circumstances.

1·4. The accumulation of funds.

Life assurance policies are generally arranged as contracts under which the premium is assessed according to the period and the class of the assurance. Since the rate of mortality increases with age the practice necessarily involves the accumulation of funds to meet the claims of the later years.

With this form of contract the assured may, with safety, be left with the right of renewal of the contract because the fund normally has a balance in hand from the excess of the premiums over the cost of the risk in the earlier years of the assurance.

The scale of premiums to be charged for a given class and period of assurance has to allow for the expected average experience over that period. For some purposes it may be convenient to isolate a certain batch of contracts and to consider the average experience over the duration of the whole group. Thus in life assurance we must introduce the conception of averaging, as it were, in two dimensions—the average over the pool of risks and the average over the duration of the contracts.

A further consequence of the premiums being assessed at the outset according to the class and period of assurance is that we do not usually deal with one factor in isolation. The calculation of the premiums, for example, involves the interplay of several factors and the actuary is concerned with the combined effect, not with the effect of one alone.

The technical elements in a life assurance fund are normally five in number:

(*a*) Mortality,
(*b*) Interest,
(*c*) Expenses (and other loadings),
(*d*) Withdrawals,
(*e*) Investment profits and losses,

and taxation must also be taken into account.

1·5. The investment aspect.

In its investment aspect a life assurance fund is similar to an investment trust but there are important differences. Normally the life assurance fund is continuously open for new members.

Further, premiums are usually payable periodically, not in one sum at the outset, and the claim to the sum assured and declared bonus is, in effect, paid out at a parity with the sums invested by way of premiums, that is to say the assurance fund bears the cost of any depreciation in the market value of its securities that there may have been in the intervening time.

An investment trust is normally concerned only with income because each year it distributes to its members the bulk of the investment income for the year but leaves the capital untouched.

The income of a life assurance fund consists of premiums and investment income and the balance after paying current claims, expenses and other outgo has to be accumulated to meet later claims. It involves a process of converting income to capital. The fund is concerned not only with income but with both income and capital.

1·6. The premium scale.

The premium scale is the foundation of a life assurance fund. If the scale is inadequate the issue will be certain though it may be long delayed. For this reason it is generally held to be necessary that the bulk of the business should be on a participating basis. The premiums are computed on bases which appear to be more than adequate to meet any contingency that may arise—and as compensation the policyholder should be given the right to share in the profit.

A company that had shareholders could undertake the risks of a fund consisting wholly of non-participating business, but a large capital in proportion to the amount of the fund would be needed for the fund to be fully protected in bad times as well as good. It is more usual for non-participating business to be combined with participating business in a single fund and the participating policyholders take the risks of the non-participating business. As the participating policyholders bear the risks they also take their share of the profits (if any) of the non-participating business and the profits from such classes normally make a modest contribution to the bonuses of the participating policyholders.

1·7. The periodical investigation.

The condition of a life assurance fund must be kept under periodical review. The investigation should concern the working of the fund as a whole though it is often referred to as a valuation of the liabilities under existing contracts.

The premium scale should be kept under continuous review so that effect can be given to the trend of experience as early as possible. It may be convenient to make changes in the premium scale at the periodic valuation of liabilities; but, however this may be, the premium scale should be considered with the investigation of the liabilities at that time.

The valuation of the existing liabilities constitutes a test of the working of the fund and the bases and methods to be used depend upon the purpose of the investigation. For example, the valuation might be made (*a*) as a test of solvency, or (*b*) as a test of the premium basis, or (*c*) as an instrument for the division of surplus. This question of purpose is fundamental to the consideration of a valuation report and for the sake of clarity the report should open with a short statement about the purpose of the investigation.

The valuation balance sheet in its simplest form is as follows:

To present value of liabilities less value of future premiums	£	By value of assets	£
		By deficiency	£
To additional reserves	£		
To surplus	£		
	£		£

It will be seen that the valuation of the liabilities and of the assets must be considered together. One ought not to be considered apart from the other.

The value of the liabilities is often called 'the valuation reserve'. That expression is a loose one because it is actually the value placed upon the contractual liability, that is, upon the obligation that the fund will eventually have to meet. For the sake of clarity it is better to use the more correct expression 'present value of the liabilities' and to keep the word 'reserve' for any sum reserved in excess of that value.

The Companies Act, 1948, for example, includes a definition of 'reserve' which states that 'the expression *reserve* shall not... include any amount...retained by way of providing for any known liability'.

1·8. The nature of surplus.

In the working out of a life assurance fund it is not to be expected that the monetary effect of the factors entering into the premium scale will prove to have been precisely forecast even taking the average actual experience. The financial effect of the difference between the actual experience and that provided for in the premium scale represents the profit or loss to the fund.

Profit or loss, after provision has been made for taxation, may arise from any of the five factors mentioned in § 1·4. These five factors should be borne in mind though problems of surplus may be discussed in terms of the first three alone—mortality, interest and expenses.

Profit in this sense in respect of a group of assured lives can only be known precisely when the batch of contracts has run off. The profit in respect of a continuing business can never be known precisely though the accumulated amount of profit at any time could be estimated if the assets and liabilities were to be valued on suitable bases.

It rarely happens that the valuation basis is suitable for the purpose of estimating accumulated profit because the valuation is made with other purposes in view. For this reason the difference between the values of the assets and liabilities is termed 'surplus' or 'deficiency', as the case may be; the terms 'profit' and 'loss' are not used in this connexion.

Surplus is a balancing item and arises as the excess of the value of the assets over the value of the liabilities. Its amount depends upon the method of valuation both of the assets and of the liabilities but since the assets are often valued upon a conventional basis of book values we may say that surplus is a function of the basis of valuation of the liabilities.

It also follows that the working out of a fund could be ascertained by computing the monetary effect of the difference between each of the factors and the actual experience in respect of that factor. Such a computation is cumbrous and it is more usual to make the analysis of surplus as a supplement to the valuation itself. A rough calculation of the major elements making up the surplus can form a very useful guide to the progress of the fund during the valuation period.

The analysis of surplus does not purport to show the profit or loss in respect of any item. It shows the working out of the factors on the valuation basis between two dates, and valuations on the same basis at both dates are required. The analysis thus forms a check on the valuation but its usefulness for other purposes depends on the suitability of the valuation bases.

1·9. The constitution of the fund.

Before the distribution of surplus can be considered it is necessary to take into account the constitution of the fund. It may either be mutual or proprietary and there may be special provisions in the constitution of the fund particularly with regard to the distribution of surplus.

The assurance office may transact only life assurance and ancillary types of long-term business or it may transact all or many classes of insurance business. The latter type is known as a 'composite office'. Such an office maintains separate funds for the various classes of business and complies with the provisions of the Assurance Companies Act, 1909, with regard to the separation of funds. In some countries 'composite offices' are prohibited but separate proprietary offices for the various classes of business may be linked through shareholdings or in other ways. Some life assurance offices have a proprietary interest in other offices carrying on general insurance business. This is an example of an intermediate type between the life assurance society and the composite office.

The shareholders in a proprietary office generally take the interest on the amount of the shareholders' fund and a proportion of the surplus in the assurance fund. In British offices the proportion is usually small and the proprietors' share of surplus may be about equal to the surplus from non-participating business, leaving the participating policyholders to take their own surplus.

The surplus may be distributed among policyholders in many different ways, the principal methods being either by way of cash, a reduction in premium or an addition to the sum assured. The method of distribution of surplus has a powerful effect on the operation of the fund and the different effects of these methods of distribution have to be considered. The distribution of surplus in the form of an addition to the sum assured—a reversionary bonus—is the most gradual in its operation and was originally adopted for that reason but it presupposes that adequate reserves are built up for the purpose of maintaining the rate of the reversionary bonuses.

From what has been said about the distinction between profit and surplus it will be seen that the share of surplus arising in a valuation period, which might be apportioned to an individual contract, cannot necessarily be regarded as the proper share of profit earned in respect of that contract. The experience of the past and the decisions previously made have to be taken into account as well as the estimated future experience.

1·10. Competition and co-operation.

The problems which arise in a life assurance fund cannot usually be decided without reference to the experience of other similar funds. Healthy competition provides a means whereby the decisions in respect of one fund may be checked against similar decisions in respect of other funds.

Competition is also a reminder not to pay too great respect to the individual factors in a computation. The factors should be estimated as accurately as possible but it should be remembered that it is the final answer that matters. The answer may contain figures to many places, which are not significant. Thus the pence in the rate of premium per £100 assurance would not usually be significant nor would the last three figures be significant in a valuation, expressed to the nearest £, of liabilities totalling several million.

Though this practical side of actuarial work should be kept in view the element of competition should not override a sound policy. The personal and responsible judgment of the qualified actuary is necessary to the stability of life assurance. One purpose of the actuarial training is to develop and train the powers of judgment of the student.

1·11. The nature of the contract.

In concluding this introductory review we may note that the contract of life assurance is essentially a financial and a fiduciary one. It is financial because the contract s expressed in terms of currency, of money. It is fiduciary because a large part of the contract has to depend on the good faith of both parties.

As the liabilities are expressed in terms of currency the assets should normally consist of obligations of the same monetary character, i.e. the assets and liabilities should be matched in terms of currency. Such a policy assumes that the currency has sufficient stability, that suitable investments are available and that sufficient business can be transacted to form an average. If these conditions do not hold life assurance can be transacted on the basis of pooling risks in different currencies but the further uncertain factor of exchange has to be taken into account.

The assured receives a contract for the payment of money at a future date. A change in the price level may alter the real value of such a contract to the assured, but the insurance fund cannot vary the contractual liability to deal with such a change because its own assets are also expressed in terms of money. A suitable investment policy may afford some relief from the adverse effects of such changes by an increase in the distributable surplus.

CHAPTER 2

HISTORICAL BACKGROUND

2·1. The birth of life assurance.

It is helpful to look back to the origins of life assurance because we see the principles adopted by the pioneers and can review the changes that have taken place without the picture becoming clogged by the confusing detail of later years.

Until the eighteenth century life assurance was known only as a yearly contract developed probably from marine insurance. The business was confined to a limited age-group and a uniform rate of premium seems to have been charged for wide ranges of ages. For example, in 1755 a common premium for life assurance for one year was £5 per £100 for ages 20 to 50 and £6 per £100 for ages 50 to 60.† Small annuity societies also existed probably of benevolent character and of insecure foundation. The Amicable Society founded in 1705 had the character of a dividing society because the principle on which it was founded was that the premiums for the year should be divided among the claims for the year, though modifications were introduced later.

The story of the birth of life assurance as we know it to-day is the story of the Equitable Society founded in 1762. This was the first Society to be founded on a scientific basis with premiums computed according to the age and the period of insurance.

The principles upon which a life assurance society operates were investigated by James Dodson, F.R.S. He died in 1757 before the Society was actually established, but his principles were set out in the application for a charter by the nascent society. Though the charter was not secured the Society was established on Dodson's principles. The actuarial basis was as follows:

(*a*) the assurances to be mutual assurances on lives and survivorships;

(*b*) membership to be open and not limited in any way;

† *An essay on insurances*, by Nicolas Magus, 1755.

(c) members to share the profits or to bear their proportion of the losses;

(d) provision to be made for non-participating assurances (as we should now call them);

(e) extra premiums to be charged for special occupational risks and for female lives under age 50;

(f) the types of insurance to include temporary insurance for a single year and for a period of years and whole-life assurance.

James Dodson had a remarkably clear view of life assurance upon a mutual basis and it is not too much to say that his vision profoundly affected the whole development of the business.

Dodson's scale of premiums was based upon the deaths in London in 1728–50. These years included two years when the deaths were higher than the average by some 25%. They also covered what has been called 'the gin period', when the introduction and universal sale of gin in London created evil social conditions which were reflected in the bills of mortality. As a consequence the scale of premiums proved to be too high and in 1782 a new scale of premiums was adopted on the advice of Richard Price, D.D., F.R.S. This was based on the deaths in Northampton in 1735–80 and 3% interest (15% was added till 1786 to avoid too great a reduction at once). The table on p. 15 compares Dodson's and Price's scales of premiums and the last column gives the average current premiums for participating whole-life assurances according to *Whitaker's Almanack*, 1947.

In 1775 Richard Price gave three methods of determining the progress of the Society. These were (a) a comparison of actual and expected deaths, (b) a comparison of the actual claims with the whole of the premiums for temporary assurances for terms of less than 7 years and two-thirds of the premiums for assurances for the whole of life, and (c) a detailed valuation of the assets and liabilities. The comparison (b) was in effect a rough analysis of surplus.

The detailed valuation was to be made upon the same basis as the premiums, and the assets were to be brought in at market value at date of valuation. The summary of the valuation results and the valuation balance sheet were similar in form to those embodied in the Assurance Companies Act, 1909, but the values of the future premiums were added to the assets, not subtracted from the values of the sums assured.

Price suggested that the valuation might be made in 10-year groups, but his nephew, William Morgan, F.R.S., the Actuary of the Society from 1775–1830, who made the calculations, in practice worked out the value of each assurance separately, summarizing the results by years of entry in order to check his figures and to facilitate the calculation of the cost of bonus which depended upon the number of years' assurance.

Annual premium for £100 participating whole-life assurance

Age at entry under	Dodson's scale based on London 1728–50 and 3 % interest	Price's scale based on Northampton 1735–80 and 3 % interest	Average in Great Britain 1947
	£ s. d.	£ s. d.	£ s. d.
20	2 15 4	2 3 7	1 18 8
30	3 12 3	2 13 4	2 10 1
40	4 12 2	3 7 11	3 3 7
50	5 18 4	4 10 8	4 10 8
60	8 5 2	6 7 4	6 18 6

A major problem which was tackled by William Morgan was the equitable distribution of surplus. He took the rudimentary ideas of his predecessors and fashioned them into a simple method of distribution of surplus which fitted the scale of premiums and the method of valuation, and dealt equitably with the problem having regard to the large carry-forward of surplus which was then necessary for the general security of the Society. The fit was approximate, not exact, but he stated that it was not possible to distribute the exact share of surplus to each policyholder in a society which was continually open for new members. He also justified his method by reference to the large profits from lapses in the early years which could be used to level up the bonuses.

2·2. Progress in the nineteenth century.

In the years following the commencement of the Equitable Society a number of annuity societies were formed but they were not established on secure foundations and did not last. From 1792 onwards a steady stream of insurance offices opened for business. Francis Baily writing in 1813 states that there were then fourteen insurance offices in London of which half were composite and half transacted life and annuity business only. Three (Baily says two only) were mutual societies: the others were proprietary. Baily says that the newly established proprietary offices charged the same premiums as the Equitable Society based on Northampton 3% but did not give the assured a contractual right to a share in the profits. (This statement appears to need qualification in some cases.) Some of the proprietary offices had commenced to pay a commission of 5% of the premiums for the introduction of business.

David Jones, writing 30 years later than Baily, lists seventy-three offices of which thirteen were mutual societies. Of the others, seven offices reserved the profits for the proprietors and fifty-three divided the profits between policyholders and shareholders. The proportion allotted to policyholders was less than has since become customary but that may be partly explained by the smallness of the funds in proportion to share capital in those days.

By 1843 the Northampton Table had, for the most part, been abandoned for the calculation of premiums and the rates quoted varied considerably from office to office.

The original practice for the valuation of liabilities had been to value on the same basis as was used for the office premiums—the Northampton Table. With the abandonment of that table the practice had to be reconsidered and it became usual to value the liabilities upon the basis of a hypothetical table that would reproduce the actual rates of premium charged on the basis of the valuation rate of interest. This 'hypothetical' or 'reinsurance' method of valuation continued some of the features present in the Northampton valuations. The policy values would normally be understated but the values of bonuses would be overstated. The results might be reasonable for the purpose of distribution of surplus in suitable conditions but the method was too artificial to endure.

When suitable mortality tables based upon the experience amongst assured lives were introduced they naturally began to be used in the valuation of the liability. The premiums charged for the business of earlier date had been computed on bases not related to the new tables and it became necessary to decide what premiums should be valued. It became the accepted standard that the premium valued should be the mathematical (or 'pure') premium for the risk on the basis used for valuation and that the whole of the difference between that premium and the premium actually charged should be reserved for expenses and profits. G. H. Ryan dates this change to the years 1855–65.

The 'net premium method' which thus began its vogue was more in touch with reality as regards the mortality table but it was open to criticism because (*a*) the rate of interest commonly regarded as an adequate standard was much below the rate of interest earned on the funds, (*b*) the premium payable under the contract was ignored, and (*c*) no allowance was made for initial expenses.

The third criticism of the method was taken up by a German, Dr Zillmer, in 1863, on the grounds of the then newly adopted practice of paying a commuted commission for new business equal to 1 % of the sum assured. He suggested that the premium valued should be adjusted so that the premium for the first year would be less than the premiums for subsequent years by the amount of the first year's commission. The practice of paying commuted commission does not appear to have become usual in Great Britain until some years afterwards, but in 1870 T. B. Sprague took up the suggestion made by Zillmer and extended it to the whole cost of new business. Sprague suggested that the whole of the first year's premium should be allocated to claims and expenses and that the premium valued should be the pure premium at an age 1 year older than the true age. James Sorley in 1878 showed that allowance should be made for initial expenses and for initial selection in the mortality table and that the two adjustments tended to counteract each other. The full net premium valuation by H^{M} aggregate was about the equivalent of a valuation by $H^{[M]}$ allowing for one-half the first year's office premium as initial expenses. Sorley defended the net premium method 'on the broad principle of averages' and his view has prevailed in Great Britain.

It was contended by A. H. Bailey in 1878 that the rate of interest used for valuation should be as close an estimate as possible of the rate expected to be earned on the funds. He suggested 4% instead of the 3% stated to be used at that time in practice. The surplus shown by such a valuation would not necessarily be divisible in full but he regarded it as important that 'the object of every valuation ought to be, as far as practicable, to arrive at the truth'. He added: 'Do not necessarily divide the whole apparent surplus, but do look the facts in the face.'

The difficulties that the net premium method gives rise to because the office premium is ignored were discussed by S. G. Warner in 1902. At that time the pure premiums on the valuation bases then current left too little margin for expenses when compared with the premiums actually payable. The premium valued was sometimes taken as a percentage of the premium payable instead of the pure premium on the valuation basis and this constituted a departure from the net premium method which he regarded as unjustifiable.

Though the subject of the equitable distribution of surplus was also discussed it does not seem to us that the same progress was made as in the subject of valuation methods. The establishment of an adequate standard of valuation appears to have come before the equitable distribution of surplus.

The history of investment policies is, of course, outside the scope of this book but some of the special problems that have arisen in connexion with the investment of life assurance funds are of interest and we will attempt a brief sketch of them.

In the early days life assurance funds seem to have been invested in Government stock and mortgages. The fluctuations in the price of such stock caused embarrassment from time to time. For example, the relatively high prices touched by Government stock in the 1820's led ignorant people to absurd expectations of the profit that might be derived from them. Some advantage was taken of the situation by encouraging mortgages but only a gradual increase in the proportion invested in mortgages was possible. If Bailey's remarks in 1862 were indicative of the general view, mortgages were then regarded as a more suitable form of investment than Government stock because they were free from market fluctuations in price. Apart from other considerations, such a narrow view could not have been maintained in face of the increasing pressure of new money coming forward for investment with the growth of life assurance funds. By the end of the nineteenth century a much wider spread of investments in Stock Exchange securities had been accepted as permissible.

The growth of the practice of investing in ordinary shares since the 1914–18 war and the extension of the field of Government activity in economic affairs may indicate new trends which must be taken into account in life assurance problems but this is a topic which we cannot pursue in this book.

Life assurance in the twentieth century has to be viewed against the background of the two world wars, 1914–18 and 1939–45. Remarkable progress has been made in the development of new forms of assurance, perhaps the most outstanding growth being that of pension schemes and annuity business generally. Pension schemes date from the end of the nineteenth century but the main growth has occurred since 1918.

The general increase of life assurance business has been accompanied by a noteworthy expansion of business transacted by British offices overseas.

The legal control of British assurance business has always been light. It has been felt that as great a measure of freedom as possible should be given, subject to the publication of the relevant information. This is referred to in Chapter 3.

2·3. Industrial assurance.

The desire to provide a proper burial for the dead is older than civilization and in modern times this is the social motive which has been the principal stimulus to the growth of industrial assurance. In England the earliest recorded organizations to give expression to this motive were the guilds which are known to have functioned in Saxon times. The rules of one such guild provided for all members to come to the burying of a member, for relief in necessitous cases and for indemnity against the compensation required when one member killed another. In Norman times such guilds might become associated with trades, and this led naturally to the Livery Companies of the City of London.

With the decay of the guilds the function of providing for sickness, old age and death was taken up by friendly societies. These societies did not evolve out of the guilds but were voluntary associations for mutual assistance and assurance, and emphasized their local 'friendly' character. The movement became established in the seventeenth and eighteenth centuries but it received its main impetus from the Act of 1793 'for the encouragement and relief of friendly societies'. Large numbers of societies were formed in the early years of the nineteenth century and the movement received further encouragement from time to time, for example the power to deposit funds with the Bank of England at a good rate of interest.

Friendly societies are studied for a separate part of the examinations and in this book we wish to refer only to those special characteristics of friendly societies which have a bearing on the growth of industrial assurance. The underlying idea of the friendly society movement was that 'by the contribution of the savings of many persons to one common fund the most effectual provision can be made for casualties (liable to affect) all the contributors'. It was perhaps natural to proceed from this conception to the levy system though fixed contributions appeared at an early date. A main weakness in the early nineteenth century lay in the difficulty of providing for proper management both of the societies themselves and of their finances. Charles Ansell, in 1835, remarked on the comparatively high rates of lapse of membership in societies established in the large manufacturing towns compared with societies in rural districts where the population was less migratory and where employment was not so liable to sudden fluctuations. At that time the field of friendly societies was being extended, a popular new feature being endowments on the lives of children.

With the growth of life assurance business in the nineteenth century it was natural that some assurance societies should be attracted to the field occupied by the friendly societies. In his evidence to the Select Committee of 1853, G. P. Neison referred to 'a sort of intermediate business, something between the great majority of life assurance offices, and for small sums'. 'It consists', he said, 'of life policies effected by persons of a lower station in society than those who assure in the other life offices....' No reference is made here to the weekly collection of premiums, though some life offices had then recently adopted that practice which rapidly became the hall-mark of industrial assurance.

There were a number of attempts to establish industrial life assurance. The early experience was poor partly because industrial life assurance had to be established first in the towns where premiums could be collected at a reasonable cost and it was only possible at a later stage to extend the service to rural areas where the mortality was lighter and employment more stable. The high rates of mortality in the towns, and particularly in certain trades, posed some difficult administrative problems.

The oldest of the large industrial assurance institutions are collecting friendly societies, the Liverpool Victoria Friendly Society, which was founded in 1843, and the Royal Liver Friendly Society, founded in 1850.

However, the successful development of industrial life assurance is principally due to the Prudential Assurance Company, Limited, which was founded in 1848 (as the Prudential Mutual Assurance Investment and Loan Association) and which commenced to grant industrial life assurances in 1854. The first tables provided for whole-life and joint-life assurances and for endowment assurances maturing at ages 65, 60, 55 and 50. Examples of the sums assured under whole-life assurances are given in the following table:

Age at entry	Sum assured for 1*d.* weekly £	*s.*
10	11	9
20	8	11
30	6	6
40	4	11
50	3	3

At first, assurances were only granted on lives between the ages of 10 and 60 years. In 1856, however, the minimum age was reduced to 7 years and the maximum age was abolished: a year later the Company took the revolutionary step of granting assurances on the lives of infants from birth onwards.

The nature of industrial life assurance made it essential to build up a large business as rapidly as possible. There were several reasons for this. The collection of premiums weekly from the homes of policyholders, an integral part of the business, was an expensive service which could only be provided at all on the basis of a large business.

Since the industrial life assurance policyholders were drawn from the artisan and labouring classes, it frequently happened that a policyholder removed from one place to another because of economic or other conditions. Such a removal would have no significance if premiums were collected, for example, by post but with industrial life assurance the policy would lapse unless the assurance office could continue in the new area the same service of collection of premiums weekly from the home as it gave in the original area. It has, in fact, been held that there is an implied obligation to collect premiums. Thus the transaction of industrial life assurance requires the provision of 'home service' in as many areas as possible. In a general business it is of little use to provide the service in a restricted number of areas though there are, of course, a large number of local friendly societies which cater for limited areas only.

In the early days the part of the population served by industrial life assurance was largely illiterate and, since the field staff of the various companies was necessarily only a little removed from that class of the population, the unscrupulous and the careless might abuse their positions; added to this there was the friction which must spring from the complications of a specialized business such as life assurance when transacted largely with ignorant people.

When a company or society opened up business in a new town the agent would at first be employed spare-time on commission reckoned largely on new business. He might, for example, receive 50% of first years' premiums though in spite of the high rate of commission his actual remuneration would be small because of the smallness of the sums to be collected. That practice was bound to lead to a proportion of undesirable business which would quickly lapse and the lapses were accentuated both by the 'friendly society' background and by fluctuations in employment amongst the industrial policyholders. Such lapses profited neither the policyholder nor the office and the history of industrial life assurance is largely the history of efforts to improve the status and quality of the business.

For many years it was the practice to pay a comparatively high rate of commission on first years' premiums and a comparatively low rate on subsequent premiums though the rate might be varied from time to time, for example with the introduction of new tables. At a later stage the remuneration of the field staff was changed to a salary depending on the amount of the 'book' of premium collections so that lapses were set off against new business; and tables were introduced which provided for monthly collections with larger benefits and lower rates of commission. Particularly in the collecting societies the system of 'book interest' has hampered the efforts to reduce commissions and to put the business on a more satisfactory basis. Where 'book interest' does not exist it has been possible to reduce expenses substantially by concentrating the business in areas under a 'block system' the first steps towards which were taken in 1912.

Some of the collecting societies have, since the earliest times, paid increased claims by the allocation of surplus and the first step to a regular profit-sharing arrangement was taken by the Prudential in 1908, a reversionary bonus system following in 1923. What is practicable by way of profit-sharing depends very much on the individual circumstances of the office, and generally, we think, the attainment of an adequate valuation standard has been regarded as a prerequisite to a profit-sharing scheme.

The cost of collecting premiums has led to various alternative methods being tried. Where the business can be linked to a trade and premiums can be collected by the employer by deductions from wages, assurances for small sums can be transacted at a relatively low cost, but this is obviously practicable only in a strictly limited class of case.

Since 1833 depositors in savings banks have been enabled to buy restricted amounts of Government annuities, whether immediate or deferred. In 1864 a life assurance scheme was instituted, under which sums from £20 to £100 were insured for ages 17 to 60 by single, annual or monthly premiums. The insurances carried the right to a surrender value after 5 years. The limits were extended from time to time and in 1884 endowment assurance tables were issued. However, the scheme was unsuccessful, either because the business was not sold or because there was no 'home service' and the grant of insurances was discontinued in 1929.

New business of seven large companies

Year	Number of new policies	New sums assured	Average sum assured
	(mill.)	(mill. £)	(£)
1910	7·0	66·8	9·61
1920	5·8	107·1	18·51
1928	6·5	133·0	20·35
1938	7·3	155·5	21·37
1946	5·6	201·4	35·76
1948	4·8	183·8	38·01

Note: The figures for industrial assurance business as a whole are not available for the earlier years. The inclusion of the collecting societies would reduce the average amount of the new assurances.

The great bulk of industrial life assurance has always been transacted by a few large units because it requires such an extensive organization. At the present time the bulk is transacted by nine companies and three societies which each have a premium income in excess of £1 million. As a consequence of the large masses of statistics to be dealt with, the industrial assurance offices have been pioneers in the application of punched-card systems to assurance business. The marked improvement that has taken place in the character of the business is perhaps best illustrated by the above table which compares for various years the numbers and the aggregate and average amounts of new assurances. Premiums under industrial assurance policies are now collected in about nine-tenths of all working-class households in this country.

The improvement in the character of the business has to be viewed against the background of much public criticism exemplified by the following Committees: the Parmoor Committee whose report in 1919 prepared the way for the Industrial Assurance Act, 1923; the Cohen Committee of 1931; and the Beveridge Committee on Social Insurance and Allied Services whose report was published in 1942.

2·4. The development of life assurance in Europe.

Various forms of life assurance and provident institutions can be traced back to the Middle Ages, for example in France, Belgium and Holland. These were mainly concerned with pensions, and the theory of life annuities was first developed in the Netherlands. Pension funds for government servants in Belgium and a widows' fund in Denmark were types of institutions prevalent before the advent of life assurance.

A life assurance company was started in France in 1787 (with the help of advice from Richard Price) but it came to an end six years later in the troubled times of the Revolution. Life assurance really began in Holland in 1807, followed by France, Belgium, Germany and Austria all in the 1820's. Denmark, Norway, Sweden and Switzerland entered the field later—about the middle of the century.

A detailed history of life assurance in Europe would be out of place in this book but practice in these countries is so different from British practice that a short section comparing the two will, we think, be helpful to the student.

Perhaps a main factor in Europe has been political and economic instability, particularly in the twentieth century. The State takes a much larger part in supervision and, in varying degrees in the different countries, regulates the calculation of premiums and reserves, the policy conditions, the choice of assets, the rights and duties of agents, the rates of commission payable to them, the surrender and paid-up policy values and the transfer of business and reassurance contracts.

The depreciation of currencies has meant that established offices have had, in effect, to start afresh incurring the new business strain with all that that implies. Rates of commission are frequently considerably higher than in Great Britain. Consequently, the valuation liability cannot reasonably be computed on the full net premium method and has to be adjusted by the method suggested by Zillmer.

Accounts of European life assurance companies do not usually show the balancing item of the 'assurance fund' which is customary in Britain. The valuation liability is computed each year and entered in the balance sheet with any additional reserves. The 'valuation balance sheet' and the ordinary balance sheet of British practice are thus, in effect, combined in one document to show the actual position from year to year.

Since the valuation liability has often to be computed on a basis fixed by the State it has become necessary to depart from the 'market value' basis for the valuation of the assets. An amortization basis is often permitted to redeem the securities on the basis of a yield comparable with the rate of interest used for the valuation liability.

We may illustrate some of our remarks by a brief reference to the experience of one country, Belgium. Life assurance began in Belgium in 1824 and in its early days passed through the difficult years of the 1830's when Belgium separated from Holland with which it had been united since 1815. Belgium emerged from the war of 1914–18 bruised in all respects. Though both new business and business in force increased rapidly in amount, that was not so much the sign of a reviving prosperity as of a monetary situation which was out of order. One of the difficulties of such an experience is that the capital becomes insufficient and as an example of what became necessary we may remark that the capital of one company which had been 1¼ million francs in 1855 was increased to 9 millions in 1927 and to 36 millions in 1941.

The years of occupation during the war, 1939–45, raised formidable administrative problems because of the difficulty of keeping in touch with branches and policyholders. These years were characterized by an uninterrupted rise in the monetary circulation which brought in its train a continuous increase in the expenses of management. The increase in expenses bore hardly upon life assurance funds because the premiums on contracts in force could not be increased. During this period, too, the investment of funds was made more difficult by the large scale repayment of existing loans. That the offices have been able to surmount the difficulties of the times is a tribute to the resilience of a well-managed life assurance business.

Experience of the two world wars has led to interesting experiments in several European countries in the field of war risks. In many European countries there are interesting examples of co-operation between the offices. In Holland, for example, the insurance offices have combined to form a subsidiary company to insure those lives which are considered uninsurable by the other offices. The transaction is by way of reassurance—the principal office grants the insurance but cedes the risk to the subsidiary. The offices thus pool the worst risks, and share the liability and any profits through the subsidiary company.

Perhaps the most complete form of co-operation has been developed in Norway. There each company quotes the same scale of premiums by agreement, not by compulsion, and a central statistical bureau has been developed for the following common purposes:

(*a*) joint mortality investigations;

(*b*) other special investigations, such as disability, withdrawals and causes of death;

(*c*) calculation and publication of tables based on the offices' experience including both the pure premiums and the premium rates actually to be charged and tables for the calculation of the premium reserves;

(*d*) calculation, on the common basis, of any special tables of premiums required by any individual office;

(*e*) reports on special problems of an actuarial or statistical nature;

(*f*) registry of applicants for insurance who are under-average risks.

2·5. United States of America.

It is interesting to compare the development of life assurance in the United States of America with that of Great Britain. Sometimes a similar end is reached by a different road and sometimes the development is in strong contrast to its British counterpart.

The annuity societies that sprang up in Britain in the eighteenth century had their counterparts in the United States of America. One such, the Presbyterian Ministers' Fund, started in Pennsylvania in 1759 and has had a continuous existence to the present time. It now grants life assurance within the limited class of life that it serves. The first joint stock company to specialize in life assurance business and to transact it on scientific lines was formed in 1809, also in Pennsylvania. It based its premiums on the Northampton Table. The first proprietary company in the U.S.A. to allow its policyholders to participate in the profits was organized in Philadelphia in 1836. The early companies, though not the Presbyterian Fund, ultimately discontinued their life assurance for their trust business or went entirely out of existence.

Thus by 1840 life assurance business had become organized but the typical American contribution to life assurance had not appeared. Shepard B. Clough lists fifteen companies still in active operation that started business in the years 1843–51. These were mostly on a mutual basis partly because of a lack of confidence in joint stock companies due to failures in fire insurance and partly because the aftermath of the depression at that time made it difficult to raise capital for life insurance. The success of mutual assurance in Great Britain and the introduction of profit-sharing in 1836 would have been contributory factors.

The starting of the Mutual Life Insurance Company of New York in 1843 opened a new era in American life insurance. The charter clearly lays down the basis of mutual assurance. Every policyholder was to be a member. The members were to elect the trustees who in turn elected the president. The powers of investment of the trustees were limited to mortgages on unincumbered real estate in the State of New York and to the bonds of the United States, New York State or any incorporated city of New York State. A financial statement was to be prepared every 5 years and the surplus distributed to members. The wording of this section clearly pointed to the contribution method of distribution.

The original premium scale was based on a mixture of the Carlisle and Northampton Tables with 4% interest and a loading of 35% of the net premium. After 10 years a new scale was introduced which allowed roughly for the experience of the Equitable (of London). The same rate of interest of 4% was assumed with a loading of 25% of the net premium. The first valuation fell to be made in 1848. The liability was computed by the formula $(P_{x+t}-P_x)(1+a_{x+t})$. This was reminiscent of the 'reinsurance' method but as the premium used was the unloaded premium the valuation was, in effect, a net premium valuation.

The contribution method of distribution of surplus, as it is known to-day, was introduced in 1863 by Sheppard Homans, the actuary of the company. This brought to birth the ideas that had been latent in the charter:

> The principle is that the share of any policyholder in a given amount of surplus is in the proportion which the excess of his payments over and above the actual cost of insurance (as determined by experience) bears to the total contributions to this surplus.

When the Mutual of New York was founded it was necessary for the new company to obtain a considerable amount of business fairly rapidly in order to establish itself since it was mutual and had no working capital. This was achieved by a person-to-person solicitation of business which has become a characteristic of American life assurance.

As more and more companies came to be established competition for business grew more keen. The use of a contribution method with annual dividends (adopted by the Mutual of New York in 1866) was too high a standard for the newer companies to attain. This led to the introduction of tontine and deferred dividend plans (by the Equitable of the United States in 1868) which were widely used until 1905. In its original and extreme form the idea of the tontine plan was that dividends were to be paid only at the end of specified periods and to those policyholders whose policies were still in force. Those who died earlier received no share and no surrender values were paid. Provision was made for surrender values in later plans. From the point of view of the company, the accumulated surplus at any time was not a legal liability and sometimes no provision was made for it in the accounts.

An experiment to which reference may be made was the introduction of renewable term insurance. Sheppard Homans founded a new office in New York in 1875 to popularize this form of life insurance. Much literature was prepared to convince the public that the savings element in the traditional forms of life assurance ought to be eliminated and 200 million dollars' worth of insurance was granted within 20 years. However, by 1890 the mortality experience had begun to prove unexpectedly heavy and in 1900–4 the actual mortality was about two-thirds greater than had been assumed in the original premium scales. Attention was called to the great disappointment of the older assured lives whose premiums had been raised to the full cost of insurance at their attained ages. The company went out of existence in 1911.

The pressure for new business made for high costs of acquisition and some undesirable practices. The rapid growth of funds posed an investment problem which took the companies into entrepreneur business and to activities not strictly within the life assurance field. In 1905 the State of New York appointed a committee 'to investigate and examine into the business and affairs of life insurance companies doing business in the State of New York, with reference to the investments of said companies, the relation of the officers thereof to such investments, the relation of such companies to subsidiary corporations, the government and control of said companies, the contractual relations of said companies to their policyholders, the cost of life insurance, the expenses of said companies and any other phase of the life insurance business deemed by the Committee to be proper, for the purpose of drafting and reporting to the next session of the Legislature such a revision of the laws regulating and relating to life insurance in this State as said Committee may deem proper.'

The Armstrong Committee as it is known proved a turning-point in American life assurance business. Great reforms resulted within the companies and abuses were stopped. The activities of the companies were henceforth restricted to life assurance business and the management was on more conservative lines. The effect on the growth of the business was only temporary and there has since been a very considerable growth. The business in force increased more than sevenfold in the 35 years from 1907 to 1942.

The legal background to life assurance in the United States is confusing to the non-American actuary because each of the States of the Union has its own laws with its own superintendent of insurance. Effectively, the American life assurance company has to deal with as many different 'countries' as there are States in which it transacts business. The laws prescribe much that affects the day-to-day conduct of business and vary widely from State to State.

The laws may, for example, deal with:

(*a*) *Investments.* Those permissible or those not permissible.

(*b*) *Contractual rights.* Types of assurance, terms of non-forfeiture and of reinstatement, incontestability, and so on.

(*c*) *Valuation liability.* Minimum standard basis of valuation.

(*d*) *Distribution of surplus.* Some States require distribution to be on an equitable basis and most provide for annual distributions of surplus.

There is considerable variation in the permitted investments between the various States and some of the laws have kept to a narrow field of investment. Of recent years, as in the United Kingdom, the question of the suitability of equities as investments for life assurance funds has been discussed: and in America there has also been an interest in real estate.

It is perhaps typical of the American conception of mutual life assurance that each policyholder is regarded as having a share in that part of the total funds which has been built up out of his accumulated premiums after paying for the cost of assurance. This conception—Maclean strongly criticizes it—colours many of the practices of American life assurance.

New business has expanded rapidly by means of active salesmanship backed by such features as guaranteed cash surrender values and optional modes of settlement, and by new types of assurance such as group insurance and the inclusion of disability benefits in life assurance contracts. The large volume of business led to new methods of organization such as the use of modern machinery and the adoption of the numerical rating system for the underwriting of new assurances.

In 1944, reversing a decision of 1869, the Supreme Court of the United States decided that fire insurance—and hence other classes of insurance also—was inter-state commerce, the power to regulate which was reserved to the Federal Government. The decision challenged the right of the various states of the Union to make their own laws regulating insurance but it is too early to say what the outcome will be.

2·6. The British Dominions.

Dominion students will perhaps forgive us if we deal with their countries in a rather summary fashion. British offices operated in the Dominions from an early date. For example, certain Scottish offices had agencies in Canada about 1840. Dominion life assurance offices opened in South Africa in 1845, Canada in 1847, and Australia in 1849. Both legislative and administrative practice in South Africa and Australia have tended on the whole to conform to British practice whereas in Canada they have tended more to the United States model. This was perhaps natural because Canadian offices do a considerable business in the United States.

Perhaps the outstanding feature of Canadian life assurance is the way in which the Canadian offices (in contrast to their United States counterparts) have spread their operations throughout a large part of the world.

In both Australia and South Africa the business has been influenced by the fact that the earliest life assurance societies were established on a mutual basis and many of the assurance societies have extensive operations outside their own countries. The oldest Australian office is, in fact, the largest mutual life assurance society in the British Commonwealth.

BIBLIOGRAPHY

The following is a list of the more important (mainly secondary) sources that have been used in the compilation of this chapter.

General

Reviews of the history of actuarial science in the various countries. *Trans. Third Int. Congress* (Paris, 1900), pp. 674–1006.

Great Britain

F. Baily (1813). *The doctrine of life annuities and assurances, analytically investigated and practically explained.*

Charles Babbage (1826). *A comparative view of the various institutions for the assurance of lives.*

H. W. Manly (1868). A comparison of the values of policies as found by means of the various tables of mortality and the different methods of valuation in use among actuaries. (Messenger Prize essay.) *J.I.A.* vol. XIV, p. 249.

G. H. Ryan (1900). Methods of valuation and distribution of profits in the United Kingdom. *J.I.A.* vol. XXXVIII, p. 69. Reprinted from the *Transactions* of the Third Int. Congress, Paris, 1900.

W. P. Elderton (1918). Investments a hundred years ago. *J.I.A.* vol. LI, p. 32.

W. P. Elderton (1931). William Morgan, F.R.S. (1750–1833). *T.F.A.* vol. XIV, p. 1.

M. E. Ogborn (1948). The actuary in the eighteenth century. *Proc. Cent. Assembly Inst. Act.* vol. III, p. 357.

Charles Ansell (1835). *A treatise on friendly societies.*

This book gives a picture of friendly societies just before the advent of industrial life assurance.

R. W. Barnard (1948). *A century of service: the story of the Prudential, 1848–1948.*

K. J. Britt (1948). The development of industrial assurance in Great Britain since 1928. *Proc. Cent. Assembly Inst. Act.* vol. III, p. 3.

The *Proceedings* of the Centenary Assembly also include papers on Industrial Assurance in Canada (by J. D. Buchanan) and in the United States (by M. E. Davis).

United States of America

M. A. Linton (1937). *Life insurance speaks for itself.*

This book deals with the arguments for accumulation of funds and against assessmentism.

J. B. Maclean (1945). *Life insurance*, 6th ed. McGraw Hill Publishing Co. Ltd.

This book contains a chapter on the historical development of life insurance in the United States.

Shepard B. Clough (1946). *A century of American life insurance.*

J. B. Maclean (1948). Some recent actuarial developments in the United States of America. *T.F.A.* vol. XVIII, p. 281.

Bruce E. Shepherd (1948). Insurance supervision in the United States. *Proc. Cent. Assembly Inst. Act.* vol. III, p. 144.

Europe

Many of the older European life assurance offices have issued booklets dealing with their histories. The remarks about Belgium were based on *Compagnie Belge d'Assurances Générales sur la vie, les fonds dotaux et les survivances, 1824–1949.*

CHAPTER 3

THE LEGAL BACKGROUND OF LIFE ASSURANCE IN THE UNITED KINGDOM

3·1. List of principal Acts.

The purpose of this chapter is to bring together by subjects the various provisions of the law so that the student may obtain a clearer view of the whole structure. The Acts and Bills mentioned in this chapter need not be referred to by the student for the 'less advanced treatment' of Part IVA of the examinations.

Name of Act	*Institutions to which it is applicable*
Assurance Companies Acts, 1909 and 1946	All assurance offices (not being registered friendly societies) which transact any of the specified classes of assurance within the United Kingdom or which, being registered under the Companies Acts, transact any such business in any part of the world
Industrial Assurance Act, 1923 Industrial Assurance and Friendly Societies Act, 1929 Industrial Assurance and Friendly Societies Act, 1948	All assurance companies and societies which transact the defined class of industrial assurance business
Assurance Companies (winding up) Acts, 1933 and 1935	Assurance companies under 1909 Act which may be wound up by the Court under the Companies Acts

Certain assurance companies also have to comply with the Companies Act, 1948. Collecting friendly societies come under the Friendly Societies Act, 1896, and the law relating to them is different in some respects from that relating to companies.

The law relating to life assurance was considered in the *Report* of the Departmental Committee of 1927 which included a draft

Insurance Undertakings Bill. This Bill never became law but it is of interest as showing what changes in the law were then considered to be necessary. The student is not required to have a detailed knowledge of this Bill.

In the 1909 Act, the definition of life assurance business† is:

the issue of, or the undertaking of liability under, policies of assurance upon human life, or the granting of annuities upon human life.

In the 1923 Act, the definition of industrial assurance business is:

the business of effecting assurances upon human life premiums in respect of which are received by means of collectors,

but there is a proviso which excepts policies where the premiums are payable at intervals of two months or more and certain other assurances.

3·2. The basis of the contract.

A life assurance is a contract between the proposer and the assurance office. The office relies upon the facts stated in the proposal or to the medical examiner and the proposer looks to the office to redeem its promise to pay the claim in due time, always assuming, of course, that the proposer keeps his part of the bargain by paying the necessary premiums. Thus life assurance requires the utmost good faith between the contracting parties.

The proposal will usually contain a declaration that the facts stated in it or to the medical examiner are true and complete, and the policy will be granted on the basis of this declaration. The declaration may be limited to facts within the knowledge or belief of the proposer. Since, however, the precise form of the declaration is of importance only in the very exceptional case when the facts have to be contested the simpler and more usual form seems to be preferable.

† This definition excludes capital redemption insurances and some kinds of disability insurance business.

3·3. Insurable interest.

One of the characteristics of the eighteenth century was the gambling mania and the possible use of insurance on lives as a means of gambling was clearly one to be guarded against. This was effected by the Life Insurance Act, 1774. Under this Act a claimant under a life assurance policy must show that the original grantee had, in fact, an interest in the life for an amount at least equal to the sum assured. This Act gave legal effect to what was the practice of the Equitable Society which had required a declaration of insurable interest by all proposers who insured the lives of others.

Life assurance policies are not contracts of indemnity and it is not necessary to prove that the insurable interest still subsists at the time of the claim. In this respect the Act fell short of the Equitable practice because that Society had required an assurance to be surrendered when the insurable interest ceased.

The interest must be a definite and legal pecuniary interest except that, under English law, a person is presumed to have an interest in his or her own life and in the life of his or her spouse of unlimited amount.

This aspect of the law has had an important bearing on the development of industrial assurance. From the earliest times there has been a demand for policies on the lives of children and also for policies on the lives of various relatives where the proposer expected to have to meet the funeral expenses. In general it was held that, under English law, a parent had no insurable interest in the life of his or her child: and also that the expectation of having to pay funeral expenses was not sufficient to establish insurable interest.

Insurances, for limited amounts, by parents on the lives of their children were permitted by the Friendly Societies Act, 1896.

The 1909 Act permitted both collecting societies and industrial assurance companies to grant insurances for the purpose of paying the funeral expenses of a parent, grandparent, grandchild, brother or sister. The Act did not define what constituted 'funeral expenses' and this has given rise to some difficulty.

The 1923 Act added 'child' to the permitted relationships and the maximum amounts insurable on the life of a child were increased. Neither the 1909 Act nor the 1923 Act made clear what classes of assurance could be granted for the purpose of paying funeral expenses, nor whether returns of premium were to be included in the maximum amounts assurable. The 1929 Act gave specific permission to the issue of endowments and endowment assurances within the permitted relationships provided that the sum payable on death did not exceed a reasonable amount for funeral expenses. For the purpose of calculating the maximum sum insurable, no account was to be taken of any repayment of premiums paid under any endowment policy. Policies granted under the 1929 Act were to have special rights with regard to free policies and surrender values.

When the National Insurance Act, 1946, became law the general provision of £20 at death necessitated a reconsideration of the whole problem of funeral expense policies.

The 1948 Act terminated the power both to issue policies for funeral expenses and to issue policies on the lives of children. However, recognition was given to a legitimate demand for the insurance of lives closely related to the proposer. The 1948 Act permits a maximum of £20 (inclusive of all relevant assurances) to be insured by a person on the death of each of his or her parents (including step-parents) and grandparents.

3·4. Evidence of financial stability.

From what has been said it will be clear that an essential part of an assurance contract is the stability and integrity of the insurance undertaking. In some countries the State seeks to achieve this objective by detailed regulation and control of assurance funds. In this country the aim has been to preserve as much freedom as possible in day-to-day operations subject to publication of sufficient information about each insurance undertaking to enable others to judge of its progress.

The 1909 Act provided that every assurance company should deposit £20,000 with the Paymaster-General in respect of certain classes of assurance business (later extended to other classes,

[cont. p. 42]

SCHEDULES TO THE ASSURANCE COMPANIES ACT, 1909

IN SO FAR AS THEY RELATE TO THE STATUTORY RETURNS TO BE MADE IN RESPECT OF LIFE ASSURANCE BUSINESS

FIRST SCHEDULE

N.B. Where...sinking fund or capital redemption insurance business is carried on, the income and expenditure thereof to be stated in like manner in separate accounts.

(A)—*Form applicable to Life Assurance Business*

Revenue Account of the........................for the Year ending........................in respect of Life Assurance Business

	Business within the United Kingdom	Business out of the United Kingdom	Total		Business within the United Kingdom	Business out of the United Kingdom	Total
	£ s. d.	£ s. d.	£ s. d.		£ s. d.	£ s. d.	£ s. d.
Amount of life assurance fund at the beginning of the year	—	—		Claims under policies paid and outstanding:			
Premiums . . .				By death . . .			
				By maturity . . .			
Consideration for annuities granted . . .				Surrenders, including surrenders of bonus .			
				Annuities . . .			

Interest, dividends and rents . .	£ s. d.				Bonuses in cash . .			
					Bonuses in reduction of premiums . . .			
					Commission . . .			
					Expenses of management	—	—	
Less income tax thereon		—	—		Other payments (accounts to be specified) . .	—	—	
Other receipts (accounts to be specified) . .		—	—		Amount of life assurance fund at the end of the year, as per Third Schedule . . .	—	—	
£					£			

NOTE 1. Companies having separate accounts for annuities to return the particulars of their annuity business in a separate statement.

NOTE 2. Companies having both Ordinary and Industrial branches to return the particulars of the business in each department separately.

NOTE 3. Items in this Account to be net amounts after deduction of the amounts paid and received in respect of re-assurances of the Company's risks.

NOTE 4. If any sum has been deducted from the expenses of management account, and taken credit for in the Balance Sheet as an asset, the sum so deducted to be separately shown in the above Account.

NOTE 5. Particulars of the new life assurances effected during the year of account to be appended to the above Account showing separately, as respects business within and business out of the United Kingdom, the number of policies, the total sums assured, the amount received by way of single premiums, and the amount of the yearly renewal premium income, the items to be net amounts after deduction of the amounts paid and received in respect of re-assurances of the company's risks. The particulars as to yearly renewal premium income need not be furnished in respect of Industrial business.

NOTE 6. The columns headed 'Business out of the United Kingdom', in the case of companies having their head office in the United Kingdom, apply only to business secured through Branch Offices or Agencies out of the United Kingdom

SECOND SCHEDULE

Profit and Loss Account of the......................for the Year ending......................19....

	£ s. d.		£ s. d.
Balance of last year's account . . .		Dividends and bonuses to shareholders .	
Interest and dividends not carried to other accounts . . . . . £ s. d.		Expenses not charged to other accounts .	
Less income tax thereon . . .		Loss realised (accounts to be specified) .	
Profit realised (accounts to be specified) .		Other payments (accounts to be specified) .	
Other receipts (accounts to be specified) .		Balance as per Third Schedule . . .	
	£		£

THIRD SCHEDULE

Balance Sheet of the....................................on the..............................19.......

LIABILITIES	£ s. d.	ASSETS	£ s. d.
Shareholders' capital paid up (if any) . £ s. d.		Mortgages on property within the United Kingdom	
Life assurance funds:*		Do. do. out of the United Kingdom	
Ordinary branch		Loans on parochial and other public rates . .	
Industrial do.		Do. Life interests	
Annuity fund*		Do. Reversions	
Fire insurance fund		Do. Stocks and shares	
Accident insurance fund . . .		Do. Company's policies within their surrender values	
Employers' liability insurance fund .		Do. Personal security	
Bond investment and endowment certificate fund		Investments:	
Marine insurance fund		Deposit with the High Court (securities to be specified)	
Sinking fund and capital redemption fund		British Government securities	
Profit and loss account		Municipal and county securities, United Kingdom	
Other funds (if any) to be specified .		Indian and Colonial Government securities .	
		Do. provincial securities . .	
		Do. municipal do. . .	
£		Foreign Government securities . . .	

Liabilities	£	Assets	£
Claims admitted or intimated but not paid†		Do. municipal do.	
Life assurance		Railway and other debentures and debenture stocks—Home and Foreign	
Fire insurance		Railway and other preference and guaranteed stocks	
Bond investment		Do. ordinary stocks	
£		Rent charges	
Annuities due and unpaid†		Freehold ground rents	
Other sums owing by the company† (to be stated separately under each class of business)		Leasehold do.	
		House property	
		Life interests	
		Reversions	
		Agents' balances	
		Outstanding premiums†	
		Do. interest, dividends, and rents†	
		Interest accrued but not payable†	
		Bills receivable	
		Cash:	
		On deposit	
		In hand and on current account	
		Other assets (to be specified)	
£		£	

* Life companies having separate annuity fund to show amount thereof separately.

† These items are or have been included in the corresponding items in the First Schedule.

Note 1. When part of the assets of the company are specifically deposited, under local laws, in various places out of the United Kingdom, as security to holders of policies there issued, each such place and the amount compulsorily lodged therein must be specified in respect of each class of business, except that, in the case of fire, accident, or employers' liability insurance business, it shall be sufficient to state the fact that a part of the assets has been so deposited.

Note 2. A Balance Sheet in the above form must be rendered in respect of each separate fund for which separate investments are made.

Note 3. The Balance Sheet must state how the values of the Stock Exchange securities are arrived at, and a certificate must be appended, signed by the same persons as sign the Balance Sheet, to the effect that in their belief the assets set forth in the Balance Sheet are in the aggregate fully of the value stated therein, less any investment reserve fund taken into account. In the case of a company transacting life assurance business or bond investment business, this certificate is to be given on the occasions only when a statement respecting valuation under the Fourth Schedule is made.

Note 4. In the case of a company required to keep separate funds under section 3 of this Act, a certificate must be appended, signed by the same person as signed the Balance Sheet and by the auditor, to the effect that no part of any such fund has been applied, directly or indirectly, for any purpose other than the class of business to which it is applicable.

sometimes with smaller deposits). This system has been swept away by the 1946 Act except that some companies which had previously complied with the 1909 Act may find it convenient, for example in connexion with overseas business, to maintain their deposits under the 1909 Act rather than to qualify under the 1946 Act for the withdrawal of the deposits.

By § 2 of the 1946 Act

no person shall carry on in Great Britain assurance business of a class to which the principal Act [the 1909 Act] applies except a company incorporated, whether under the Companies Act, 1929, or otherwise, and having a paid-up share capital of not less than fifty thousand pounds.

This requirement does not apply to assurance companies which, immediately before 29 October 1945, were carrying on assurance business of a class to which the 1909 Act applies. The Board of Trade also has power to exempt any mutual association established after that date for the purpose of carrying on long-term business but such an association must make the deposit under the 1909 Act.

By § 3 of the 1946 Act, with certain reliefs and exemptions, an assurance company which carries on general business is deemed to be unable to pay its debts if the value of its assets does not exceed the amount of its liabilities by a defined amount. Should the company be unable to show this margin of solvency the 1933 and 1935 (winding up) Acts would apply accordingly. For the purposes of this test it is sufficient for the actuary to give the following statutory certificate in respect of long-term business.

I certify that in my belief the liabilities in respect of long-term business do not exceed the amounts of the respective funds and all other liabilities in respect of long-term business as shown in the balance sheet.

The 'margin of solvency' test does not affect the manner in which the assets and liabilities are to be dealt with when an assurance office is wound up.

[cont. p. 50]

FOURTH SCHEDULE

N.B.—Where sinking fund or capital redemption insurance business is carried on, a separate statement signed by the actuary must be furnished, showing the total number of policies valued, the total sums assured, and the total office yearly premiums, and also showing the total net liability in respect of such business and the basis on which such liability is calculated.

(A)—*Form applicable to Life Assurance Business*

Statement respecting the Valuation of the Liabilities under Life Policies and Annuities of the ...., to be made and signed by the Actuary.

(The answers should be numbered to accord with the numbers of the corresponding questions.)

1. The date up to which the valuation is made.

2. The general principles adopted in the valuation, and the method followed in the valuation of particular classes of assurances, including a statement of the method by which the net premiums have been arrived at, and whether these principles were determined by the instrument constituting the company, or by its regulations or byelaws, or how otherwise; together with a statement of the manner in which policies on under average lives are dealt with.

3. The table or tables of mortality used in the valuation. In cases where the tables employed are not published, specimen policy values are to be given, at the rate of interest employed in the valuation, in respect of whole-life assurance policies effected at the respective ages of 20, 30, 40, and 50, and having been respectively in force for five years, ten years, and upwards at intervals of five years respectively; with similar specimen policy values in respect of endowment assurance policies, according to age at entry, original term of policy, and duration.

4. The rate or rates of interest assumed in the calculations.

5. The actual proportion of the annual premium income, if any, reserved as a provision for future expenses and profits, separately specified in respect of assurances with immediate profits, with deferred profits, and without profits. (If none, state how this provision is made.)

6. The consolidated revenue account since the last valuation, or, in case of a company which has made no valuation, since the commencement of the business. (This return should be made in the form annexed. No return under this heading will be required where a statement under this schedule is deposited annually.)

7. The liabilities of the company under life policies and annuities at the date of the valuation, showing the number of policies, the amount assured, and the amount of premiums payable annually under each class of policies, both with and without participation in profits; and also the net liabilities and assets of the company, with the amount of surplus or deficiency. (These returns to be made in the forms annexed.)

8. The principles upon which the distribution of profits among the shareholders and policyholders is made, and whether these principles were determined by the instrument constituting the company or by its regulations or byelaws or how otherwise, and the number of years' premiums to be paid before a bonus (*a*) is allotted, and (*b*) vests.

9. The results of the valuation, showing

(1) The total amount of profit made by the company allocated as follows:

(*a*) Among the policyholders with immediate participation, and the number and amount of the policies which participated;

(*b*) Among policyholders with deferred participation, and the number and amount of the policies which participated;

(*c*) Among the shareholders;

(*d*) To reserve funds, or other accounts;

(*e*) Carried forward unappropriated.

(2) Specimens of bonuses allotted to whole-life assurance policies for 100*l*. effected at the respective ages of 20, 30, 40, and 50, and having been respectively in force for five years, ten years, and upwards at intervals of five years respectively, together with the amounts apportioned under the various modes in which the bonus might be received; with similar specimen bonuses and particulars in respect of endowment assurance policies, according to age at entry, original term of policy, and duration.

Note. Separate statements to be furnished throughout in respect of Ordinary and Industrial business respectively, the basis of the division being stated.

(Form referred to under Heading No. 6 in Fourth Schedule (A))

Consolidated Revenue Account of the........................for...........years....................commencing........................and ending........................

	£ s. d.		£ s. d.
Amount of life assurance fund at the beginning of the period		Claims under policies paid and outstanding:	
Premiums		£ s. d.	
Consideration for annuities granted . . .		By death	
£ s. d.		By maturity	
Interest, dividends, and rents . .		Surrenders	
Less income tax thereon . . .		Annuities	
		Bonuses in cash	
		,, ,, reduction of premiums . . .	
Other receipts (accounts to be specified) . .		Commission	
		Expenses of management	
		Other payments (accounts to be specified) . .	
		Amount of life assurance fund at the end of the period, as per Third Schedule	
£		£	

NOTE. If any sum has been deducted from the expenses of management account and taken credit for in the Balance Sheet as an asset, the sum so deducted to be separately shown in the above Statement.

(Form referred to under Heading No. 7 in Fourth Schedule (A))

Summary and Valuation of the Policies of the..............................as at......................19.......

Description of transactions	Particulars of the policies for valuation				Valuation: Value by the........table, interest....per cent			
	Number of policies	Sums assured and bonuses	Office yearly premiums	Net yearly premiums	Sums assured and bonuses	Office yearly premiums	Net yearly premiums	Net liability
ASSURANCES								
I. *With immediate participation in profits*								
For whole term of life . . .								
Other classes (to be specified) . .								
Extra premiums payable . . .								
II. *With deferred participation in profits*								
For whole term of life . . .								
Other classes (to be specified) . .								
Extra premiums payable . . .								
Total assurances with profits .								

III. *Without participation in profits*								
For whole term of life								
Other classes (to be specified)								
Extra premiums payable								
Total assurances without profits								
Total assurances								
Deduct re-assurances (to be specified according to class in a separate statement)								
Net amount of assurances								
Adjustments, if any (to be separately specified)								
ANNUITIES ON LIVES								
Immediate								
Other classes (to be specified)								
Total of the results								

NOTE 1. The term 'extra premium' in this Act shall be taken to mean the charge for any risk not provided for in the minimum contract premium. If policies are issued in or for any country at rates of premium deduced from tables other than the European mortality tables adopted by the company, separate schedules similar in form to the above must be furnished.

NOTE 2. Separate returns and valuation results must be furnished in respect of classes of policies valued by different tables of mortality, or at different rates of interest, also for business at other than European rates.

NOTE 3. In cases also where separate valuations of any portion of the business are required under local laws in places outside the United Kingdom, a summary statement must be furnished in respect of the business so valued in each such place showing the total number of policies, the total sums assured and bonuses, the total office yearly premiums, and the total net liability on the bases as to mortality and interest adopted in each such place, with a statement as to such bases respectively.

(Form referred to under Heading No. 7 in Fourth Schedule (A))

Valuation Balance Sheet of..................................as at.........................19........

Dr.	£	*Cr.*	£
To net liability under Life Assurance and Annuity transactions (as per summary statement provided in Fourth Schedule (A))		By Life Assurance and Annuity funds (as per balance sheet under Schedule 3) . . .	
To surplus, if any		By deficiency, if any	
£		£	

FIFTH SCHEDULE

N.B. Where sinking fund or capital redemption business is carried on, a separate statement, signed by the actuary, must be furnished showing the total sums assured maturing in each calendar year and the corresponding office premiums.

(A)—*Form applicable to Life Assurance Business*

Statement of the Life Assurance and Annuity Business of the.................... on the..............................19 to be signed by the Actuary.

(The answers should be numbered to accord with the numbers of the corresponding questions. Statements of re-assurances corresponding to the statements in respect of assurances are to be given throughout.) Separate statements are to be furnished in the replies to all the headings under this schedule for business at other than European rates. Separate statements are to be also furnished throughout in respect of ordinary and industrial business respectively.

1. The published table or tables of premiums for assurances for the whole term of life and for endowment assurances which are in use at the date above mentioned.

2. The total amount assured on lives for the whole term of life which are in existence at the date above mentioned, distinguishing the portions assured with immediate profits, with deferred profits, and without profits, stating separately the total reversionary bonuses and specifying the sums assured for each year of life from the youngest to the oldest ages, the basis of division as to immediate and deferred profits being stated.

3. The amount of premiums receivable annually for each year of life, after deducting the abatements made by the application of bonuses, in respect of the respective assurances mentioned under Heading No. 2, distinguishing ordinary from extra premiums. A separate statement is to be given of premiums payable for a limited number of years, classified according to the number of years' payments remaining to be made.

4. The total amount assured under endowment assurances, specifying sums assured and office premiums separately in respect of each year in which such assurances will mature for payment. The reversionary bonuses must also be separately specified, and the sums assured with immediate profits, with deferred profits, and without profits, separately returned.

5. The total amount assured under classes of assurance business, other than assurances dealt with under Questions 2 and 4, distinguishing the sums assured under each class, and stating separately the amount assured with immediate profits, with deferred profits, and without profits, and the total amount of reversionary bonuses.

6. The amount of premiums receivable annually in respect of each such special class of assurances mentioned under Heading No. 5, distinguishing ordinary from extra premiums.

7. The total amount of premiums which has been received from the commencement upon pure endowment policies which are in force at the date above mentioned.

8. The total amount of immediate annuities on lives, distinguishing the amounts for each year of life, and distinguishing male and female lives.

9. The amount of all annuities on lives other than those specified under Heading No. 8, distinguishing the amount of annuities payable under each class, and the amount of premiums annually receivable.

10. The average rate of interest yielded by the assets, whether invested or uninvested, constituting the life assurance fund of the company, calculated upon the mean fund of each year during the period since the last investigation, without deduction of income tax.

It must be stated whether or not the mean fund upon which the average rate of interest is calculated includes reversionary investments.

11. A table of minimum values, if any, allowed for the surrender of policies for the whole term of life and for endowments and endowment assurances, or a statement of the method pursued in calculating such surrender values, with instances of the application of such method to policies of different standing and taken out at various interval ages from the youngest to the oldest. In the case of industrial policies, where free or paid up policies are granted in lieu of surrender values, the conditions under which such policies are granted must be stated, with specimens as prescribed for surrender values.

3·5. Classes of insurance business.

The following are the classes of assurance business within the scope of the Assurance Companies Acts, 1909–46.

(*a*) Life assurance and annuity business.
(*b*) Industrial assurance business (by the 1923 Act).
(*c*) Fire insurance business.
(*d*) Accident insurance business.
(*e*) Employers' liability insurance business.
(*f*) Bond investment business.
(*g*) Motor vehicle insurance business (Road Traffic Act, 1930).
(*h*) Marine, aviation and transit insurance business (1946 Act).

Where a company carries on both employers' liability and any other class of assurance business to which the 1909–46 Acts apply, the employers' liability insurance business, by virtue of an Order, 1948, No. 1839, need no longer be treated as a class of business to which those Acts apply.

Sinking fund and capital redemption insurance business is not one of the defined classes and therefore has to be treated as miscellaneous business not within the 1909–46 Acts but separate accounts have to be prepared for sinking fund and capital redemption insurance business by virtue of the headings to the forms of account in the Schedules to the 1909 Act.

The 1909 Act provides that separate funds shall be kept in respect of each class of assurance business (modified in respect of certain classes). Section 3 reads:

(1) In the case of an assurance company transacting other business besides that of assurance or transacting more than one class of assurance business, a separate account shall be kept of all receipts in respect of the assurance business or of each class of assurance business, and the receipts in respect of the assurance business, or, in the case of a company carrying on more than one class of assurance business, of each class of business, shall be carried to and form a separate assurance fund with an appropriate name: Provided that nothing in this section shall require the investments of any such fund to be kept separate from the investments of any other fund.

(2) A fund of any particular class shall be as absolutely the security of the policyholders of that class as though it belonged to a company carrying on no other business than assurance business of that class, and shall not be liable for any contracts of the company for which it would not have been liable had the business of the company been only that of assurance of that class, and shall not be applied, directly or indirectly, for any purposes other than those of the class of business to which the fund is applicable.

Taken in conjunction with the proviso that investments need not be kept separate the meaning of the section is obscure. The word 'fund' may mean actual cash or other resources or it may merely be a description of an account. The definitions of the various assurance funds clearly indicate that they are to be regarded as accounts and, in fact, they appear as liabilities in the balance sheet. No accountancy figure, however, can be a 'security'.

The 'fund' which is to form a 'security' ought to mean a collection of assets.

The whole question was fully investigated by the Departmental Committee of 1927. In § 34 of the Report which deals with the separation of funds and assets, the Committee says:

> It seems clear that the policyholders were intended to have rights of the nature of a security as against such parts of the assets as correspond to the 'fund' arising from the business with which they are concerned, but these rights would appear to be effective only in liquidation; and upon liquidation Section 17 of the Act operates, under which the policyholders' rights are to be estimated in manner provided in the Sixth Schedule. Reference to that Schedule shows that the rights of the policyholders in question are to be measured on a basis which, in practice, as seems to be admitted on all hands, would in most cases (i) give the policyholders a sum less than the value which their policies would have if the Company, being solvent, continued as a going concern; and (ii) might fail to give policyholders any benefit in respect of unallocated surplus derived from business of their class. Two points of difficulty emerge. In the first place, if a solvent Company goes into liquidation a question arises whether the policyholders would not find themselves, by reason of Section 17, and notwithstanding Section 3, deprived of a great part of the real value of their policies, the shareholders being correspondingly benefited. In the second place, in the case of a composite company, where the Company is forced into liquidation by a serious loss on (e.g.) fire business, it may well be that, notwithstanding that the life business has been highly successful and that a large Life fund has been built up which ought to have increased the security for and the value of their policies, life policyholders may find their rights limited to a proof on the footing of a valuation under the Sixth Schedule of the Act, and thus may see a large part of the Life fund which they have helped to build up made available to meet fire losses, while they are left with assets which fall far short of the value which their life policies would bear if assets equal to the Life fund were definitely allocated to secure to them the payment of their claims on maturity of their policies.

The Committee reported in favour of the separation of the assets in respect of insurance contracts which are of a permanent character and suggested that the directors of an insurance company should be put in the position, as regards responsibility, of trustees in relation to the separated assets. It is perhaps a reflection on our parliamentary system that time has never been found for putting these proposals into effect although the Committee itself drafted the necessary Bill with a wide measure of agreement among the various interests concerned. The 1933, 1935 and 1946 Acts have left unresolved the ambiguity of the 1909 Act in this important respect and these Acts give the impression of being a patchwork rather than the fundamental treatment that is required.

The 1946 Act adds to the confusion because in § 4 it refers to 'the value of the assets of the fund or of each such fund'. What construction is to be placed on these words when assets are not segregated?

3·6. Accounts and statements.

The forms of the periodical accounts and statements are laid down by the 1909 Act. They consist of:

Account or statement	Schedule to 1909 Act*	How frequently to be prepared
Revenue account	First	Yearly
Profit and loss account	Second	Yearly
Balance sheet	Third	Yearly
Abstract of actuarial report	Fourth	At least once in every 5 years and whenever valuation made for bonus or results made public
Statement of assurance business	Fifth	Whenever foregoing valuation made or (if valuation annually) at least once in every 5 years

* The Schedules, in so far as they relate to life assurance business, are reprinted on pp. 38–50.

The form of the accounts may be affected by the Companies Act, 1948. Provision is made for the audit of the accounts and for the deposit of the accounts and statements with the Board of Trade.

The 1923 Act provides that the accounts and statements of industrial assurance companies shall be sent to the Industrial Assurance Commissioner as well as to the Board of Trade, and provides for returns by collecting societies. The Commissioner may require additional particulars with regard to industrial assurance valuations (see the Second Schedule, p. 59).

The 1909 Act lays down the procedure for the amalgamation and transfer of assurance companies which must be by sanction of the Court on the petition of the directors. The Act provides that:

Before any such application is made to the Court—

(*a*) notice of the intention to make the application shall be published in the *Gazette*; and

(*b*) a statement of the nature of the amalgamation or transfer, as the case may be, together with an abstract containing the material facts embodied in the agreement or deed under which the amalgamation or transfer is proposed to be effected, and copies of the actuarial or other reports upon which the agreement or deed is founded, including a report by an independent actuary, shall, unless the Court otherwise directs, be transmitted to each policyholder of each company in manner provided by section one hundred and thirty-six of the Companies Clauses Consolidation Act, 1845, for the transmission to shareholders of notices not requiring to be served personally: Provided that it shall not be necessary to transmit such statement and other documents to policyholders other than life, endowment, sinking fund, or bond investment policyholders, nor in the case of a transfer to such policyholders if the business transferred is not life assurance business or bond investment business; and

(*c*) the agreement or deed under which the amalgamation or transfer is effected shall be open for the inspection of the policyholders and shareholders at the offices of the companies for a period of fifteen days after the publication of the notice in the *Gazette*.

The 1909 Act also provides in relation to life assurance business that the Court shall not sanction an amalgamation or transfer of such business when life policyholders representing one-tenth or more of the total amount assured dissent from the amalgamation or transfer.

Within ten days from the date of the completion of the amalgamation or transfer, there must be deposited with the Board of Trade:

(*a*) certified copies of statements of the assets and liabilities of the companies concerned in such amalgamation or transfer, together with a statement of the nature and terms of the amalgamation or transfer; and

(*b*) a certified copy of the agreement or deed under which the amalgamation or transfer is effected; and (*c*) certified copies of the actuarial or other reports upon which that agreement or deed is founded; and

(*d*) a declaration under the hand of the chairman of each company, and the principal officer of each company, that to the best of their belief every payment made or to be made to any person whatsoever on account of the amalgamation or transfer is therein fully set forth, and that no other payments beyond those set forth have been made or are to be made either in money, policies, bonds, valuable securities, or other property by or with the knowledge of any parties to the amalgamation or transfer.

The procedure for amalgamation and transfer, including the stringent provisions for the transmission of reports to each policyholder of each company, applies—by virtue of the 1946 Act—only where long term business (life, industrial and bond investment business) or employers' liability business is concerned. Also, the Court sometimes exercises its discretion to relax those provisions, subject to suitable safeguards.

A curious weakness in the statutory provisions with regard to amalgamation or transfer was disclosed by a legal case† in 1939 when it was held that the provisions apply only to an arrangement by way of amalgamation or transfer between companies all or both of whom are companies to which the 1909 Act applies. The Court has no jurisdiction to sanction, and the statutory provisions do not apply to, an arrangement where any of the companies is, for example, a foreign assurance company carrying on no assurance business in the United Kingdom, and such an arrangement may be made without the sanction of the Court.

Where industrial assurance is concerned, and at least one of the offices is a collecting society, the approval of the Industrial Assurance Commissioner is required under the 1896 Act; if all the offices are companies under the 1909 Act, he is entitled to be heard by the Court.

3·7. Provisions regarding valuations, including solvency.

The 1909 Act lays down no standard basis or method of valuation but the form of the Fourth Schedule suggests a net premium valuation and that of the Fifth Schedule, a prospective

† *J.I.A.* vol. LXX, p. 407.

method. Bonus reserve valuations have been accepted under the 1909 Act, the reserve for future bonus being included with the value of sum assured and existing bonus.

The 1923 Act lays down that:

The basis of valuation adopted shall be such as to place a proper value upon the liabilities, regard being had to the mortality experience among the persons whose lives have been assured in the society or company, to the average rate of interest from investments and to the expenses of management (including commission), and shall be such as to secure that no policy shall be treated as an asset.

Thus negative values must be excluded from industrial assurance valuations.

The Court may order the winding-up of an assurance company on the petition of (*a*) ten or more policyholders owning policies of an aggregate value of not less than £10,000 (1909 Act), (*b*) the Industrial Assurance Commissioner (1923 Act), (*c*) the Board of Trade (1933 and 1935 Acts).

In the winding-up of an assurance company the policies are to be valued by the rules stated in the Sixth Schedule to the 1909 Act. The rule for valuing a life assurance policy, which is reproduced below, indicates a net premium valuation. This is the amount in respect of which the policy ranks in a winding-up and the aggregate of these values would be compared with the aggregate of the available assets. It is in no sense a solvency valuation.

Rule for valuing an Annuity

An annuity shall be valued according to the tables used by the company which granted such annuity at the time of granting the same, and, where such tables cannot be ascertained or adopted to the satisfaction of the Court, then according to such rate of interest and table of mortality as the Court may direct.

Rule for valuing a Policy

The value of the policy is to be the difference between the present value of the reversion in the sum assured according to the contingency upon which it is payable, including any bonus or addition thereto made before the commencement of the winding up, and the present value of the future annual premiums.

In calculating such present values interest is to be assumed at such rate, and the rate of mortality according to such tables, as the Court may direct.

The premium to be calculated is to be such premium as according to the said rate of interest and rate of mortality is sufficient to provide for the risk incurred by the office in issuing the policy, exclusive of any addition thereto for office expenses and other charges.

The 'margin of solvency' under the 1946 Act relates to general insurance business and does not affect life assurance provided that the actuary can give the statutory certificate about the adequacy of such long-term funds.

The 1923 and 1929 Acts include rules for valuing policies on forfeiture but these provisions are referred to in Chapter 22 which deals with surrender values and paid-up policies of industrial assurance business.

3·8. Powers of the Industrial Assurance Commissioner.

The powers of the Board of Trade are limited and include little direct control of assurance business. However, the 1923 Act gives the Industrial Assurance Commissioner wide powers of control of industrial assurance business. The main powers of the Commissioner are as follows:

(*a*) He may refuse to issue a warrant for a deposit under the 1909 Act if he thinks fit. The office may appeal to the Court.

(*b*) He may reject any return which he considers does not comply with the Act, and require such modifications as he may direct to be made. He must consider representations by the office concerned, but there is no appeal.

(*c*) If he considers that an offence has been or is likely to be committed he may order an inspection of the company's business and may petition the Court for its winding-up. In the case of a society he may award that it be dissolved and its affairs wound up. There is no appeal.

(*d*) He may reject a valuation on the grounds that it does not comply with the requirements of the Act. The office may appeal to the High Court.

(*e*) He may call for additional information regarding the valuation in the form set out in the Second Schedule to the

Act and such further explanations as he may consider necessary (see p. 59).

(*f*) He may award the winding-up of a society, or petition the Court for the winding-up of a company, if a deficiency is disclosed and he considers the financial position is unsound.

(*g*) Disputes may be referred to him for settlement, subject to certain restrictions.

(*h*) Amalgamations or transfers of societies are not effective unless sanctioned by him, and he is entitled to be heard by the Court when industrial assurance companies amalgamate with or transfer to other companies.

(*i*) He may make regulations for carrying into effect the provisions of the Act. Such regulations are subject to the approval of the Treasury and must be submitted to Parliament, which may annul them.

(*k*) He may (under the 1948 Act) make regulations regarding premium receipt books which must include reprints of certain statements.

(*l*) He may also (under the 1948 Act) make regulations requiring statements of the movements of assurances 'on' and 'off', reconciling the business in force at the beginning and end of the year separately for premium-paying and free policies.

3·9. Statutory duties of an actuary.

The student is referred to the *Institute of Actuaries Year Book* for a list of the statutory duties of an actuary.

Industrial Assurance Act, 1923

SECOND SCHEDULE

Additional particulars as to valuations

1. An analysis as near as may be of the premium income of each of the five years preceding the valuation date into income arising from

(*a*) policies which were not of more than one year's duration at the date such income arose; and

(*b*) policies which were of more than one year's duration at the date such income arose.

Note: This analysis to be given separately for policies with weekly premiums and for policies with premiums payable at longer intervals than one week.

2. The amount, if any, by which the value of the Office Yearly Premiums as shown in respect of each item in the Form referred to under Heading No. 7 in the Fourth Schedule (A) to the Assurance Companies Act, 1909, has been reduced in order to secure that no policy shall be treated as an asset.

3. If the proportion of the annual premium income reserved as a provision for future expenses and profits as stated in answer to question 5 of the Fourth Schedule (A) to the Assurance Companies Act, 1909, is not uniform for all policies of the same class, specimens of the proportion so reserved in respect of policies effected at such ages and having been in force for such periods as the Commissioner may select.

4. Specimen values of the net liabilities under policies (exclusive of any bonuses added) according to the basis of valuation adopted, in respect of each of the principal classes of assurances for policies effected at such ages and of such durations as the Commissioner may select.

5. A statement of the actual number of deaths at ages over ten years in the five years preceding the valuation date under policies for the whole term of life in comparison with the number of deaths which would have occurred if the mortality experience had been in exact agreement with the table of mortality employed for the purpose of the valuation, to be given separately for decennial groups of ages.

BIBLIOGRAPHY

1. Acts and Orders

Life Insurance Act, 1774.
Assurance Companies Acts, 1909–46.
Industrial Assurance Acts, 1923–48.
The Assurance Companies Rules, 1950. (*S.I.* 1950, No. 533 *as amended by* No. 643.)

2. Other references

J. Murray Laing (1923). Notes on the Industrial Assurance Act, 1923. *J.I.A.* vol. IV, p. 27.

Clauson Report (1927). *Report of the Departmental Committee appointed to inquire and report what amendments are desirable in the Assurance Companies Act, 1909.* Cmd. 2820.

K. J. Britt (1931). Amalgamations of life assurance companies. *J.I.A.* vol. LXII, p. 276.

K. J. Britt and B. C. Lucena (1934). The duties and powers of the British Industrial Assurance Commissioner. *Trans. Tenth Int. Congress*, Rome, vol. II, p. 365.

D. Houseman (1947). A note on the Assurance Companies Acts, 1909 to 1946. *J.I.A.* vol. LXXIII, p. 113.

K. J. Britt (1948). A note on the Industrial Assurance and Friendly Societies Act, 1948. *J.I.A.* vol. LXXVI, p. 164.

CHAPTER 4

THE INVESTMENT OF LIFE ASSURANCE AND ANNUITY FUNDS

The student is assumed to be familiar with investment and financial conditions, and this book deals only with the principles which need to be considered in connexion with life assurance and annuity funds.

4·1. The nature of the investment problem.

The general nature of the problem can perhaps be seen best by analogy with a form of investment trust. Let us suppose that an investment trust is established under which the capital subscribed to the trust is repayable at par either at the subscriber's death or at the completion of an agreed period of years and suppose also that the trust is continually open for new members.

Such a trust would have to choose its investments so that they would be redeemed at about the time the trust would be liable to repay the subscribers' capital. The business would be considered as a whole and the matching of assets to liabilities would be general rather than particular because the time for repayment of an individual subscription would not be a definite date; it would depend upon the date of that subscriber's death.

The equitable distribution of the income of the trust would also have to be considered, because (*a*) the investments made at different times would show different interest yields, (*b*) the accumulation of reserves would mean that earlier subscriptions would be entitled to a rather larger share of the total investment income than the later subscriptions, and (*c*) new subscriptions might to some extent be set against repayments of old subscriptions thus enabling a portion of the investments to be in long-term securities with a rather higher yield than if the investments were precisely matched to the current liabilities.

The analogy is incomplete and must not be pressed too far. For example, in life assurance the investment is not made in one sum at the outset. The premiums under life assurance policies are usually payable over the duration of the contract or for an agreed period of years. Further, the new money available for investment is not the premium income but the balance of the premium and investment income after paying claims, expenses and other outgo.

The sale of immediate annuities gives rise to an investment problem which is different in many respects from the life assurance problem. The consideration is received in one sum at the outset and the fund is liable each year for a payment consisting of three parts: (*a*) a repayment of principal, (*b*) interest on the principal outstanding, (*c*) a payment by way of compensation because the balance of the principal is not to be returned at death. The item (*c*) should be merely a balancing item because the total payable under (*c*) each year would equal the total amounts of principal which would fall in by reason of the deaths for that year if the assumed mortality experience were to work out exactly. As part repayments of principal have to be made each year the mean period of investment is comparatively short.

4·2. Mean period of discount.

An estimate of the mean period for which investment is actually required may be obtained in the following manner. Suppose we compute the premium at a suitable rate of interest and also the corresponding premium when $i=0$. The proportion of the one to the other will be, in effect, a mean discount factor and the period corresponding to this mean discount factor may be taken as an estimate of the mean period for which investment is required. The mean period so found on the basis of $2\frac{1}{2}\%$ and A1924–29 for assurances, *a* (*m*) for annuities, is set out in the table on p. 63 and compared with the expectation of life.

The mean periods set out in the table may seem shorter than would have been expected. The reason is that the investment does not commence until the premium is paid. Essentially, an assurance contract (excepting single premium assurance) is one to invest future excess income in the early years to provide for future excess outgo in the later years.

The mean periods set out in the table do not tell the whole story because a fund can normally expect to continue to receive new business. The mean periods would be materially increased by aggregating new business over a period of years and dealing only with the aggregate income and outgo. Further, the computation is based on the assumptions at the inception of the assurance by averaging the weighted discount factors. The 'mean' is not therefore a true mean based on the spread of investments.

Class of policy	Age at entry	Expectation of life	Mean period of discount (years)
Whole-life assurance	25	45·3	22
	40	31·9	15
	55	19·4	8
Endowment assurance at 60	25	—	17
	40	—	10
	50	—	5
Limited-premium life assurance—premiums ceasing at 60	25	45·3	28
	40	31·9	22
	50	23·4	18
Immediate annuity—male life	50	23·8	13
	65	13·5	8
	80	6·2	5

Note. The mean period would be slightly shortened if expenses were to be allowed for, and the effect of withdrawals should also be kept in mind.

When we consider the actual periods for which the funds must be invested in order that the assets may match the liabilities in respect of existing business we find that the periods may be chosen in different ways according to different 'plans of investment'. (New business is ignored because that is assumed to enter on terms appropriate to the experience.)

It has been suggested that investments should be so chosen as to produce the amounts required to pay the expected claims of each year after allowing for the premiums to be received in respect of those expected claims. This 'plan of investment' produces a specific distribution of assets matched to liabilities. But it segregates each year's expected claims and, consequently, the expected claims in the early years will be provided for by maturing investments, notwithstanding that during those years there will be in the aggregate an excess of income over outgo.

It is sounder to consider the fund as composed of two parts. The one part is fed by the contributions each year to expected death strain and the actual death strain is paid out of this fund. The other part is fed by the balance of the premium and investment income after paying expenses and other outgo and is the part which has to be invested to meet the claims by survival and the excess of the expected death strain over the premium income in the later years of whole-life and other similar assurances. During the time that this fund is increasing the investment periods may be chosen in different ways, provided that by the time the fund reaches its peak the investments have been so chosen as to produce the sums required each year thereafter to meet the excess of outgo over income. The conception of 'assets matched to liabilities' in this sense may thus contain an ambiguity which should be borne in mind in discussions of the subject.

There is a further complication. The new business for any year will no doubt comprise endowment assurances for various terms as well as whole-life assurances and the 'investment pattern' for the various classes of assurance would be very different, were they in separate funds. It is possible and generally desirable, we think, to consider the fund as one whole. The short-period assurances may thus derive some advantage from being combined with long-period assurances in a fund invested mainly in long-dated securities.

The following numerical example is taken from Suttie's paper† and the discussion on it. The assumptions are that the fund comprises 40-year endowment assurances effected at age 25; that the new business has been constant for at least 40 years; and that the experience has been in accordance with the life table. We then reach the investment pattern given on the next page.

*4·3. Notes on the available types of investment.

It is not necessary to review in detail the various types of investment available but some notes may be added on them.

† *J.I.A.* vol. LXXII, pp. 204 and 228.

(*a*) *Loans and mortgages*

Generally speaking, the period for which the money is invested is not a long one. Though a mortgage may be nominally arranged for a long period it is not customary for the equity of redemption to be deferred. The loan may be repaid or called in after a short period of notice and the interest yield tends to follow (with a time-lag) the current market yield for such securities. Mortgages are usually taken at face value in a valuation but it should be remembered that the actual value depends upon the underlying value of the security. Certain types, for example loans on rates, do not wholly conform to these characteristics.

Investment pattern

No. of years to maturity of investment	Percentage of total investments	
	(*a*) When matched to expected claims (%)	(*b*) When matched to excess of outgo over income (%
1– 5	31	1
6–10	24	4
11–15	17	7
16–20	13	10
21–25	8	14
26–30	5	18
31–35	2	21
36–40	—	25
	100	100

(*b*) *Government securities*

Generally speaking, Government securities are readily realizable whatever economic conditions may prevail at the time. Exceptionally this may not be true as, for instance, when minimum prices were imposed after the outbreak of war in 1939. For a given purchase price such securities yield a fixed rate of interest over a period of years—often a long one—and the periods may be chosen to accord roughly with the periods of the liabilities. The market prices may fluctuate widely from time to time. The security depends on the credit of the debtor Government.

(*c*) *Other securities*

The general characteristics of other types of fixed-interest securities are similar to those of Government securities but the stocks may not be readily marketable and the yield would reflect the nature of the security. The group includes a wide range of types.

(*d*) *Equities*

There is a difference of opinion about the suitability of equity stocks for the investment of life assurance funds. This is discussed in the text-book on investments. There may be wide fluctuations both in price and in interest yield but such securities may form a useful hedge against inflation. Over a long period the equity stocks should produce both a larger income and a larger capital value than fixed-interest stocks.

(*e*) *Properties*

In general, investments in property are not so readily realizable as investments in securities and yield a higher rate of interest. Those that give the right to occupation of property may form a useful hedge against inflation. Reserves must be built up, out of income, for repairs and replacement of buildings and, in respect of leasehold and other temporary interests, to redeem the capital.

(*f*) *Reversions and life interests*

The market in reversions is limited and the yield is normally higher than for a direct investment in the same securities. Such investments provide a suitable set-off to the mortality risks assumed by a life assurance fund.

(*g*) *Subsidiary companies*

For some reasons it is convenient to invest in or to operate certain types of business through subsidiary companies. They are of such diverse types that little can be said here but investments in subsidiary companies may have a substantial influence on general office policy.

Where such an investment has turned out to be very profitable, problems of the equitable distribution of surplus may be raised in an acute form (and this, of course, may apply to other investments of a limited character besides subsidiary companies). Should such an investment be treated as having been made by the policyholders at that time or should later policyholders be admitted to a share in it? Suppose the fund has expanded very considerably. Generally, we think that life assurance should be considered as a continuing business and the investments ought not to be allocated to a particular generation of policyholders.

4·4. Changes in interest levels.

We may now consider in a general way the effect on the working of a life assurance fund of changes in the general level of prices of securities, that is to say, in the market rate of interest.

For various reasons, such a change in the general market level does not affect all stocks to the same extent even allowing for differences in redemption dates. A change would probably affect some funds more than others though all of them would normally be affected in the same direction.

The principal reason for the difference in effect is that changes in prices are brought about by the operations of many individuals in a free market. Buyers, when prices are falling, naturally search for those investments which, they hope, will minimize the fall and, when prices are rising, for those investments which will yield most advantage from the rise. The spread of investments differs from fund to fund and thus it comes about that all funds would not necessarily be affected to the same extent by a change in the market level.

Suppose we were to compute on a suitable basis the emerging income and outgo of a life assurance fund on the assumption that no more new business was to be granted after a certain date, the valuation date. If the amount of new business had been stable for a long period before that date the outgo on claims, etc. would exceed the premium and investment income and the fund would decrease as the business ran off. If the amount of new business had been increasing in the years preceding the valuation date the income would exceed the outgo at first and the fund would increase for a time.

The effect of a change in the general level of prices of securities depends on whether the life assurance fund is increasing or decreasing and also on what steps have been taken to provide for such a possible change.

Where the fund is decreasing investments will have to be realized to meet the excess of outgo over income. The primary concern is, therefore, the price at which the investments can be realized. A considerable loss would be incurred if long-term securities had to be sold at depreciated prices. Such a possibility could have been provided for by choosing investments to mature at about the dates required; there would then have been no loss.

Where the fund is increasing the position is more complex because the excess of income over outgo has to be invested until the time when the position is reversed. The new investments would be made on the basis of the new level of prices and would act as a set-off to the effect of the change on the fund. If the general level of prices rises to a higher level the nominal profit on the increased prices will be offset by the lower rate of interest on new investments and on the conversion of old investments. If the general level of prices falls to a lower level the nominal loss on the lower prices will be offset by the higher rate of interest on new investments.

From what we have said it will be apparent that the distribution of the investments by redemption date is probably more important at present than the geographical distribution. The argument may be taken a step further on lines suggested by Kirton.†

As a simple numerical example, consider 20-year capital redemption assurances granted 5 years earlier on the basis of 3% without loading, expenses being ignored for simplicity. Suppose that, at the end of the 5 years, there is a sudden change in market levels to a basis of (*a*) 2½%, (*b*) 3½%. If the valuation liability at 3% be 1,000 the corresponding values of the liability at 2½% and 3½% would be (*a*) 1,076, (*b*) 930 for single premium assurances and (*a*) 1,174, (*b*) 841 for annual premium assurances.

In order to provide for the liabilities when they fall due the funds should have been invested in stocks redeemable after a further 15 years, that is at the maturity date of the assurances. Had

† *J.I.A.* vol. LXIV, p. 423.

such investments been made at 3% the market value at the 3% level would be 1,000 and the corresponding values at the $2\frac{1}{2}$% and $3\frac{1}{2}$% levels would be (*a*) 1,062, (*b*) 942. The single premium valuation shows (*a*) a small deficit, (*b*) a small surplus, which arises from the reinvestment of interest income in the presumed new conditions. The annual premium valuation produces a larger (*a*) deficit, (*b*) surplus, because the premium income as well as the interest income has to be invested in the new conditions.

Suppose that the funds were, in fact, invested in stocks redeemable 5 years earlier than the maturity date of the assurances. The market value of the stocks at 3% would be 1,000 as before but the corresponding values at the $2\frac{1}{2}$% and $3\frac{1}{2}$% levels would be (*a*) 1,044, (*b*) 958. It will be seen that the deficit or surplus is swollen.

Let us now suppose that the funds were, in fact, invested in stocks redeemable 5 years later than the maturity date of the assurances. The market value of the stocks would still be 1,000 at 3% but the corresponding values at the $2\frac{1}{2}$% and $3\frac{1}{2}$% levels would be (*a*) 1,078, (*b*) 929. The deficit or surplus is diminished and, as regards the single premium assurances, eliminated.

The liabilities of an assurance fund, of course, will not all mature on one day. The fund will be increased by premium and interest income and decreased by claims, surrenders, expenses and other outgo; sooner or later the outgo will exceed the income at which time investments must be realized to provide the necessary cash.

Should the existing investments be so chosen as to be redeemable at precisely the times and in precisely the amounts required to meet the excess outgo, intervening fluctuations in the market values of the investments can be ignored except for the profit or loss in respect of any new investments that may have to be made. A fall in market values would produce a profit by reason of the higher rate of interest on new investments and, correspondingly, a rise would produce a loss.

Should the existing investments be invested to redemption dates earlier than the required times for the liabilities, the value of the investments would be affected to a less extent by a fall in market values. The profit from the better rate of interest on new investments would be increased by a further profit on the 'short' investments which would reflect the better rate of interest expected between the redemption of the investments and the maturing of the liabilities. Similarly, if prices rise the loss on new money would be increased by the loss on 'short' investments. Thus it happens that a 'short' position tends to exaggerate the profit or loss from changes in price levels.

Should the existing investments be invested to redemption dates later than the required times for the liabilities the value of the investments would be affected to a greater extent by a fall in market values. The profit from the better rate of interest on new investments would be diminished by the loss on 'long' investments which would reflect the depreciation expected when the investments came to be sold to meet the liabilities. Similarly, if prices rise the loss on new money would be diminished by the profit on 'long' investments. Thus it happens that a 'long' position tends to minimize the profit or loss from changes in price levels and may turn a profit into a loss and vice versa.

The conclusion seems to be that the redemption dates of investments should be chosen so far as possible to correspond with the times when the existing liabilities mature and since only a rough correspondence can be achieved in practice the redemption dates should be chosen 'long' rather than 'short' in normal circumstances.

In this discussion we have ignored the effect of new business because we were considering the effect of changes in the price level upon the existing business. The terms for new business can, presumably, be adjusted to the new conditions. Since changes in experience are often gradual rather than abrupt the flow of new business provides an important bridge from the old to the new conditions.

It also follows that the valuation of the liabilities must be considered in conjunction with the valuation of the assets. The valuation is customarily expressed in terms of the amount of the fund and the value of the liabilities: but the real comparison is between the expected income and the expected outgo of the fund. The assets may be valued upon a conventional basis such as market value but the reality is the comparison of expected income and expected outgo and we have to consider the relationship of our conventions to that reality.

4·5. The valuation of the assets.

When considering the valuation of the assets we have to take account both of the capital value placed on the assets and the yield of the assets on the basis of that capital value.

In Great Britain the published yield of the funds is usually derived from the formula

$$2I/(A+B-I).$$

Here A and B are the account figures for the funds at the beginning and the end of the year. I in the denominator is the interest taken into account in arriving at B (usually the net interest after deduction of income tax). I in the numerator is the gross or net interest according as it is the gross or net yield that is sought. B would normally be taken before deduction of any transfer to reserve.

The interpretation of the published yield depends to some extent on the treatment of redeemable securities. Since, in normal circumstances, more securities are bought at prices below than above their redemption prices there is perhaps some justification for ignoring both profits and losses on redemption, and where this practice obtains, any premium on redeemable securities would be written off out of realized profits as soon as possible. The published yield would thus represent an average running yield based on book values, subject to any adjustments in the accounting.

An alternative practice is to adjust the interest in the accounts by the sums required for amortization of the premiums or discounts contained in the purchase prices compared with the redemption prices of redeemable stocks. If the securities were valued in the books at cost price the published yield would be a kind of average redemption yield; but since the securities will probably have been written down from time to time it becomes rather difficult to say what the published yield represents.

The expenses of purchase and sale of investments may be charged to interest income. Profits, after deduction of losses, on sale and realization of securities may be credited to investment income but such profits should, we think, be accounted for separately. In the United Kingdom it is customary for such profits to be used to write down the book values of the assets (and not to be brought into account) or to be credited to an investment reserve fund.

When a valuation has to be made of the assets and liabilities of the fund the published figure for the yield based on the amount of the funds must be used with caution.

It would be possible to select an appropriate rate of interest and to value both assets and liabilities at that rate. This would put the valuation on a real basis if the valuation rate of interest were suitably chosen but several objections may be made to the method as regards the assets. It would be necessary to assume a period for the investments where the period is not definite (e.g. a mortgage which can be redeemed or a security which can be called for repayment). As all the investments would be valued at one average rate of interest, those investments which yield more than the average would be given a high value. It would, we think, sometimes be necessary to value rather less than the full nominal rate of dividend or interest because of the possibility of default. The method would not, we think, be applicable to the valuation of properties nor of shares in the equity of industrial companies.

The investments could be valued at two rates of interest, so chosen that the figures for the aggregate value of the investments would be on either side of the aggregate market value. A figure for the mean yield of the assets taken at market value could then be computed by interpolation. This method would avoid some of the objections referred to in the previous paragraph. It would not get over the artificiality of the method in some respects. Further, the use of such a mean yield for valuing the liabilities would imply that the same mean rate could be obtained on such new investments as might be required.

An alternative approach suggested by Whyte is that each security should be valued at a 'notional price' based on a particular assumption regarding gilt-edged prices. Each security would be valued at a rate of interest which would reflect (*a*) the basic rate of interest assumed for gilt-edged securities of a similar date, and (*b*) the margin required above gilt-edged having regard to the nature of the security. The method of 'notional prices' avoids the difficulties we have mentioned which arise where the assets are valued at one rate of interest, and is an attempt to apply actuarial principles to the valuation of the assets. Combined with an estimate of future investment income the method would yield a good deal of information about the assets. The notional prices would, however, depend upon individual appraisement of the securities and there does not seem to be any guiding principle which would enable a valuation by one person to be compared with a similar valuation by another person.

When a valuation of assets and liabilities is to be made we feel that it is best to take the assets at market value unless market conditions happen to be passing through what is believed to be a temporary abnormal phase. 'Market value' provides a basis which is independent of personal idiosyncrasies and which is freely accepted by the public. The assets would not, of course, be capable of being realized in bulk at market value but that contingency should not arise and the 'market value' basis does seem to keep in touch with reality. Since, however, the market values will fluctuate from time to time the method may cause some inconvenience and must be combined with a willingness to vary the basis of valuation of the liabilities correspondingly.

An attempt is being made in America to eliminate the extreme fluctuations of a market value basis by using a kind of 'moving average' so that the book values of stocks will always be moving in the direction of current market values though not to such a large extent.

The 'market value' basis is suitable when it is desired to investigate the position of the fund as fully as possible. Where a series of valuations is made—as for example in the periodic valuations of a life assurance fund—it may be felt that continuity is more desirable than a striving after an unattainable accuracy. It may be desired to maintain a particular basis for the valuation of assets and liabilities without allowance for a variation in conditions which may prove to be merely a temporary fluctuation. This consideration is of special importance where the bonus allotted is a function of the valuation basis. In such circumstances it may be necessary to ignore the market price and to value the assets by an amortization method. Redeemable securities would be valued by writing the purchase price up or down out of income to the redemption price. A sudden fall in Stock Exchange prices may, however, absorb the whole of the published, and any hidden, investment reserve and when such a fall occurs it seems a questionable practice to maintain book prices of securities at a level above the market prices. [See Note 3 to the statutory balance sheet (p. 41).]

4·6. Investment policy and the legal framework.

The general considerations of investment policy are, of course, outside the scope of this book. There are, however, certain special considerations arising out of life assurance business with which we now propose to deal.

The principal aim of the investment policy is to invest the funds in such a way as to ensure the due fulfilment of the contractual obligations. Since these obligations are of a long-term character the investments should be such as will make available the money needed when the liabilities become payable, possibly many years later. As with all investors those responsible for the investment of life assurance funds will look for a satisfactory increment but, apart from questions of income tax, it does not matter to the fund whether that increment is by way of interest or capital appreciation so long as the money becomes available at about the required times.

The principal aim we have stated does not preclude a 'short' view being taken when circumstances justify it but what can be achieved in this way is limited by practical considerations.

Investment policy has to take account of legal requirements and of any special features of the fund. Certain types of investment, for example Government securities, may be prescribed either by legislation or the threat of legislation or by the constitution of the assurance fund. The general purpose of restrictions on investment is no doubt to improve the security of the policyholders. Such limitations tend to reduce the yield obtainable on the funds and in the event the additional security may prove to be illusory.

Investment policy has also to take account of the types of assurance comprised in the liabilities, particularly having regard to their probable duration; the rate of expansion of the fund; its policy with regard to guaranteed surrender values, and so on. Where the flow of new business is considerable a portion of the fund may be invested in securities of a longer term than would otherwise be regarded as desirable.

The basis and weight of taxation may have a considerable bearing on investment policy. An investment bought at a given price produces very different net yields according to the basis of taxation of the particular fund. Thus it happens that certain types of investment may be suitable and other types unsuitable, having regard to the basis of taxation. (See § 5·2.)

4·7. Currency and life assurance.

Life assurance contracts are money contracts and investments should normally be made in the currency in which the contracts are expressed to be payable. Such a policy is the ideal and it assumes that suitable investments in that currency are available. The liabilities under the contracts in a particular currency would then be precisely matched by assets in the same currency and there would be no risk of financial loss to the fund because of a change in the rates of exchange between different currencies.

Where the amount of business is small or where suitable investments are not available the method of the preceding paragraph cannot be followed. The question arises whether life assurance is possible at all in such circumstances. Experience has shown that a life assurance fund may assume liabilities in a number of different currencies and keep investments in one currency which should be chosen for its stability and convertibility. A charge should be made for the risk assumed and the practice should, we think, be limited strictly to the cases where it is not practicable to invest in the same currency as the liabilities.

The premiums and the sum assured are both normally expressed to be payable in terms of a particular currency and if the currency depreciates the loss necessarily falls on the policyholder. This is an illustration of the truth that the essence of an assurance contract depends upon the nature of the assets which form the security for the due performance of the contract. Where the investments are in money obligations of a particular currency the investments depreciate with the currency and there would be no fund out of which to reimburse the policyholder for the loss in purchasing power.

A hedge against depreciation in currency may be provided by investing part of the funds in real estate or in the equity of industrial companies where the necessary powers exist. Such investments tend to maintain their value when a currency depreciates. Though the nominal amount of the contract would still be expressed as the same sum in the depreciated currency the investments in real estate and in the equity of industrial companies would show profits in terms of the depreciated currency which should enable the position to be partly rectified by allocations of profit. Such a hedge is only partial at best and may prove unfounded because the values of these investments may not follow the course of the purchasing power of money. The values may, for example, be affected by limitation of dividends or control of rents.

It is not essential for a contract to be expressed in terms of currency: it could be expressed, for example, in terms of gold. It would be necessary for both premiums and sum assured to be payable in gold or in its equivalent at time of payment. Theoretically, the assets of the fund should be held in gold and the policyholder would apparently have complete protection against depreciation in currency. The protection is more apparent than real because the price of gold does not necessarily move in step with the prices of commodities, in which the policyholder is primarily interested, and also because Governments tend, as in the United States of America in 1933, to abrogate such 'gold-clauses' in contracts at the time when they would be of most assistance. A disadvantage would be that the expenses of keeping the gold would be exceptionally heavy. The amount of the premium payable by the policyholder in terms of currency would depend upon the price of gold and a change in the price might cause considerable inconvenience. Though such contracts have been tried in special circumstances it is not surprising that the vast majority of contracts are expressed in terms of currency.

The ideas we have been discussing may be summed up in the phrase that the assets should be matched with the liabilities. They should be matched both as regards their term and their nature; and the basis of valuation of the liabilities should have regard to the basis of valuation of the assets.

Such a matching of assets and liabilities is an ideal which can only be approximated to in practice. There are severe limitations on what is practicable in this respect.

BIBLIOGRAPHY

W. PENMAN (1933). A review of investment principles and practice. *J.I.A.* vol. LXIV, p. 387.

A. C. MURRAY (1937). The investment policy of life assurance offices. *T.F.A.* vol. XVI, p. 247.

T. R. SUTTIE (1944). The treatment of appreciation or depreciation in the assets of a life assurance fund. *J.I.A.* vol. LXXII, p. 203.

L. G. WHYTE (1947). Life office investments in a planned economy. *T.F.A.* vol. XVIII, p. 215.

J. B. H. PEGLER (1948). The actuarial principles of investment. *J.I.A.* vol. LXXIV, p. 179.

G. H. RECKNELL (1949). Insurance against inflation. *T.F.A.* vol. XIX, p. 17.

The student must be referred to other parts of the syllabus for an adequate course of reading on investments. The general background to investment policy in the United Kingdom, Canada and the United States of America is dealt with in three papers to the Centenary Assembly of the Institute of Actuaries, 1948.

The subject of currency depreciation as affecting life assurance is discussed in papers submitted to the Eighth International Congress of Actuaries, London, 1927.

CHAPTER 5

SOME IMPLICATIONS OF UNITED KINGDOM INCOME TAX

The student is not expected to have a detailed knowledge of United Kingdom income tax but we propose to consider in a general way in this chapter the bearing which United Kingdom income tax may have upon investment policy and upon actuarial calculations. The statement is general and glosses over many details because the full implications of income tax can only be comprehended against the background of the actual provisions of the Income Tax Acts and the Finance Acts.

5·1. The general basis of the charge to tax.

Effectively, there are four different bases of the charge to tax.

Basis I. The fund may not be taxed, either temporarily or because it is exempted by law.

Basis II. The fund may be taxed upon profits.

Basis III. The fund may be taxed upon investment income but not upon profits.

Basis IV. The fund may be taxed both upon investment income and, in respect of certain taxes, upon profits.

A fund may be charged on one only of these bases or it may be charged upon alternative bases, whichever yields more tax.

In general the investment income is taxed by deduction at source and the bases we have set out are produced by means of rebates and reliefs of various kinds or by direct assessment where necessary.

Where the assurance office is proprietary, the proprietors' fund is, of course, taxed upon profits at the full standard rate of income tax and the fund also bears such other taxes as may be levied upon profits (Basis II). The proprietors' fund is deemed to include profits of the life assurance fund except such part of those profits 'as belongs or is allocated to, or is reserved for, or expended on behalf of policyholders or annuitants'.

A life assurance fund, generally, is taxed (at a maximum rate of 7*s*. 6*d*. in £) upon investment income subject to a rebate in respect of management expenses (Basis III). The effective rate of tax depends upon the relationship of the management expenses to the investment income. Thus if the management expenses amount to one-third of the interest income the effective rate corresponding to 7*s*. 6*d*. in £ would be 5*s*. in £.

The limitation of income tax to a maximum rate of 7*s*. 6*d*. in £ applies to the policyholders' share of the investment income after allowing for the appropriate reliefs in respect of expenses and so on. It does not apply to the proprietors' share.

The amount of management expenses on which relief is given is reduced by the amounts of fees and fines and profits on reversions and on annuities.

Where a mutual life assurance fund incurs management expenses which exceed the investment income the fund is temporarily relieved of income tax (Basis I). A similar position arises in a proprietary fund where the rebate of tax on management expenses would reduce the total tax to a lesser amount than tax on the proprietors' share of the profits. In such circumstances the repayment is restricted to such an amount as will leave the actual tax equal to the tax on the proprietors' share; the life assurance fund is thus temporarily relieved of income tax.

The industrial and ordinary life funds of industrial assurance offices are treated as separate businesses for purposes of taxation. In respect of industrial assurance, proprietary offices are generally taxed upon the alternative basis of proprietors' profits, the policyholders' fund being temporarily relieved of tax (Basis I), whereas mutual offices are taxed upon the excess, if any, of interest over expenses (Basis III). Registered collecting friendly societies are exempt from tax by law (Basis I).

In a composite office the life assurance fund pays income tax as a separate business and the foregoing paragraphs apply to the life assurance funds of composite offices.

A Dominion or foreign assurance office which transacts business in the United Kingdom is taxed upon the proportion of its total investment income and total management expenses which is deemed to arise from United Kingdom business.

Where a British assurance office which is taxed on Basis III transacts life assurance through overseas branches, the part of its investment income which arises from its 'foreign life assurance fund' is relieved of income tax *provided* that the fund is either invested abroad, the investment income not being remitted to the United Kingdom, or invested in certain securities, such as $3\frac{1}{2}\%$ War Loan, on which the interest is payable free of tax to non-residents. A proportionate reduction is made in the rebate on the management expenses of the life assurance business as a whole. Thus the 'foreign life assurance fund', representing the valuation liability in respect of foreign business, can be rendered exempt from tax (Basis I) by taking the appropriate action.

The definition of life assurance business in the Assurance Companies Act, 1909, includes annuity business and consequently a combined life assurance and annuity fund is regarded as one business by the Income Tax Act, 1918. It follows that the separate parts of a combined life assurance and annuity fund cannot, under British income tax law, be separately assessed.

However, the annuity fund differs from the life assurance fund because the income tax suffered by deduction from the investment income of the annuity fund is largely or wholly recouped by the income tax retained on the annuities paid out. Where the combined life assurance and annuity fund is taxed upon proprietors' profits, the profits will include those derived from the annuity business as well as those from the life assurance business. Where the combined life assurance and annuity fund is taxed upon 'interest less expenses', the taxation of the annuity fund depends upon whether the annuities exceed or fall short of the investment income of the annuity fund.

Where the annuities exceed the investment income, the income tax suffered by deduction is wholly recouped and any excess of tax retained on annuities over and above the tax suffered by deduction must be paid to the Inland Revenue. (This type of fund is called by Rowland and Wales, Type A.) Since the annuity business forms part of the combined life assurance and annuity fund, the profit on the annuity business cannot be separately assessed to tax. However, the combined fund has to make a claim for the repayment of income tax in respect of its management expenses and the amount of this claim is reduced by the annuity profit, thus securing indirectly that the profit shall be taxed.

Where the annuities fall short of the investment income, income tax suffered by deduction is not wholly recouped. In these circumstances, the annuity fund, effectively, pays income tax on 'interest less annuities'. The excess interest so taxed may be less than the profit (Type B fund) or may be larger than the profit (Type C fund). The income tax which has been paid on 'interest less annuities' is regarded as discharging the liability for tax on a corresponding part of the profit. With the Type B fund the remainder of the profit is deducted from management expenses; with the Type C fund the payment of tax on the excess of interest over annuities and profit is regarded as having discharged the liability for tax on a corresponding amount of profits in later years (though of course it may be many years before sufficient profits are made and the rate of tax may be different).

Sinking fund business, in so far as it relates to policies effected before 1 January 1938, is taxed upon profits at the full standard rate of income tax, together with such other taxes as may be levied upon 'profits' computed on income tax principles with the required adjustments (Basis II).

Sinking fund business, in so far as it relates to policies effected after 31 December 1937, is taxed upon investment income at the full standard rate of income tax and also, in respect of certain taxes, upon 'profits' computed in the highly arbitrary income tax sense with the required adjustments (Basis IV).

Annuities-certain are included with sinking fund business in the capital redemption fund but the effect of taxation is somewhat different. As is explained in § 10·14, each instalment of an annuity-certain is divided into principal and interest, income tax being deducted from the interest portion. Thus the income tax deducted from the office's investment income is partly recouped by the tax retained by the office on the interest portion of the instalments: only the excess interest—that is to say the profit—is taxed (Basis II).

5·2. The bearing of U.K. income tax on investment policy.

Since an assurance office may have several funds subject to various bases of taxation the income tax payable by the assurance office as a whole will be an amalgam of taxes at different rates and on different bases. Where the assets of the several funds are effectively segregated they may be considered as separate entities and a suitable investment policy may be chosen for each fund: but where the assets are not effectively segregated it is not possible to keep distinct investment policies and a middle course must be followed. The following notes assume that assets are segregated.

Where Basis I applies, that is to say with a life assurance fund which is temporarily relieved of tax and also with a registered collecting friendly society, the yield of investments applicable to the life assurance reserves may be computed on a gross basis.

Where Basis II applies, that is to say with the proprietors' fund, the Type A annuity fund and the pre-1938 sinking fund, the yield of investments applicable to the various funds may be computed on a gross basis since only the profit is taxed.

Where Basis III applies, that is to say in general with the life assurance fund, the yield of investments applicable to the life assurance reserves should be computed net by deduction of income tax from the dividends or interest. The deduction is made at the standard rate of income tax (maximum rate 7*s*. 6*d*. in £) and not at the effective rate because the calculation is concerned only with the tax on investment income and not with the management expenses rebate. Since on Basis III capital gains are not taxed, the full equivalent of such gains may be added to the net income but any loss on redemption must be met out of net income.

The Type C annuity fund is in a similar position to the life assurance fund taxed upon investment income but the capital gains may or may not be taxed and there are endless complications into which we need not enter in this book.

Where Basis IV applies, that is to say with the post-1937 sinking fund, the yield of investments must be computed by deduction of income tax (at the full standard rate) from the dividends or interest and by the provision for income tax and for such additional taxes there may be upon 'profits' as computed in the highly artificial income tax sense. The tax position may be complicated by annuity-certain business, to which Basis II is applicable.

5·3. The bearing of U.K. income tax on actuarial calculations.

It is, of course, obvious that actuarial calculations must take into consideration the tax expected to be payable. Where Basis I or Basis II applies it is sufficient to adopt a gross rate of interest in actuarial calculations. Any tax that is payable in respect of profits may be left to be set against the profits when they arise.

The only qualification to this statement is when bonus calculations are being made. Since, however, such calculations are usually made only in connexion with life assurance business and since tax is not charged upon policyholders' profits in a life assurance fund we do not have to make any provision for tax on policyholders' profits and the remainder of tax may be left to be set against the profits when they arise.

Where Basis III applies, that is to say in general with the life assurance fund, the actuarial calculations must allow for the income tax payable in respect of investment income. The tax may be given effect to in alternative ways. Either the interest may be reduced by the effective rate of income tax or the interest and expenses may be both reduced by the standard rate of income tax (with a maximum of 7*s*. 6*d*. in £). These alternatives are discussed in § 6·3.

The Type C annuity fund poses an interesting problem because presumably there will come a time when, apart from new business, the fund must necessarily alter to Type A. There may be more than one change, but for convenience we may assume that there will be only one change and that that will occur n years later than the date of valuation or other calculations. Strictly the calculations should allow for tax on Basis III during the period of n years, all items for interest, annuities and expenses being taken net of income tax during that period, and for tax on Basis II after the n year period, all items for interest, annuities and expenses falling due thereafter being taken gross. Though this is the strict theoretical position, in practice some more or less arbitrary assumption would have to be made.

Where Basis IV applies, that is to say with the post-1937 sinking fund, the actuarial calculations must allow for the income tax payable in respect of investment income. Since expenses are small it is probably sufficient to reduce the interest by income tax at the full standard rate. Provision must also be made for such other taxes as may be levied upon 'profits' computed according to income tax principles.

Before we leave this subject we may illustrate one of the effects of the income tax system by a simple numerical example.

Suppose that there are two offices which both earn 4% gross interest and experience A 1924–29 select mortality but that one office incurs expenses, and charges for them in its premium scales, at a rate five times higher than the other. For purposes of illustration consider a 20-year endowment assurance effected at age 40 and assume that Office A incurs 5% expenses on premiums whereas Office B incurs 25% expenses.

With income tax at 5*s.*, 7*s.* 6*d.* and 10*s.* in £ the corresponding net rates of interest will be 3, 2½ and 2% respectively and we may assume for simplicity that a corresponding relief is obtainable on the expenses in the particular circumstances.

On these assumptions Office A might charge what are considered suitable premiums to maintain a simple reversionary bonus of 20*s.*% per annum when income tax is 5*s.* in £ but should the tax be increased to 7*s.* 6*d.* in £ the same scale would only support a bonus of 14*s.* and should the tax be further increased to 10*s.* in £ the same scale of premiums would only support a bonus of 8*s.* 4*d.*

The corresponding figures for Office B would be 20*s.*, 18*s.* 5*d.* and 16*s.* 8*d.*% per annum respectively, though the premiums would, of course, be on a much higher scale.

These figures illustrate the fact that Office B, which conducts its business on the basis of a comparatively high rate of expense has a substantial protection from the effects of changes in the rate of income tax by reason of the rebate that is given in respect of management expenses. Office A with a comparatively low rate of expense is in a much more vulnerable position and the effect would have been even more striking had we taken our illustration from policies in force rather than from new business. By a sufficiently large increase in the rate of income tax, Office A could, in fact, be rendered unable to meet its engagements and no doubt this was in the minds of the legislators when fixing the maximum rate of income tax at 7*s*. 6*d*. in £ for life assurance funds.

BIBLIOGRAPHY

1. Acts

The Income Tax Act, 1918, and Finance Acts so far as they relate to income tax (including sur-tax) with Statutory Regulations and Orders and cross-references. [H.M. Stationery Office, 1949.]

2. Other references

S. J. Rowland and F. H. Wales (1937). The taxation of the annuity fund and some practical points arising therefrom. *J.I.A.* vol. LXVIII, p. 447.

A. H. Shrewsbury (1943). Income tax as affecting life assurance offices. *J.I.A.* vol. LXXII, p. 35.

M. E. Ogborn (1947). The taxation of annuities. *J.I.A.* vol. LXXIV, p. 31.

E. E. Spicer and E. C. Pegler (1948). *Income tax.* H. F. L. (Publishers) Ltd.; 18th ed. by H. A. R. J. Wilson.

G. V. Bayley (1950). The taxation of annuity funds. *J.I.A.* vol. LXXVI, p. 237.

CHAPTER 6

THE ELEMENTS

In Chapter 1 we discussed the fundamental principles of life assurance and we saw how the actuarial structure is built of certain elements. In this chapter we shall consider those elements in more detail, but before doing so it may be helpful to consider the various uses to which the actuarial structure is put because the purpose for which it is employed naturally colours the choice of basis. What are the actuary's objectives?

6·1. The objectives.

The first objective must be to collect from the body of assured lives such periodic sums as will, with the interest earned by investing them, suffice to meet the claims as they arise, pay the expenses of the office, provide bonuses for the participating policies (if any) and, in the case of a proprietary office, leave a margin for profits to the proprietors. Since the premium is usually fixed at the inception of the assurance this objective requires, for any given batch of entrants, an estimate of the average future experience amongst those entrants as regards mortality, interest, expenses and so on.

Now we cannot predict the future, nor can we make a close estimate of future experience, except fortuitously. We can only examine past experience and form an opinion of the extent to which it is likely to be repeated in the future. Where past experience discloses a marked trend it may be appropriate to assume that the trend will continue: but extrapolation is hazardous and particularly so in connexion with the experience of a fund which is in a state of flux. Thus the assessment of the scale of premiums requires the exercise of a high degree of individual judgment after a careful appraisement of the relevant facts. Even so, the assessment may prove to be wrong. Who, for example, in the year 1900 could have correctly forecast the course of interest rates over the first half of the present century? Some buffer is therefore required against the possibility of adverse experience.

A second objective is the maintenance of equity as between different generations of policyholders, different classes of assurance and different groups of assured lives. What can be done in this respect is limited by practical considerations. It is usually not possible, and it is probably undesirable, to attempt to segregate different sections of the business into separate funds (apart, possibly, from such major divisions as ordinary and industrial life assurance business). Some attempt should, however, be made to allow for variations in experience where they seem to be of sufficient importance. Failure to do so might lead to selection against the office because business would probably be attracted from those groups where the premiums were relatively too cheap and discouraged where the premiums were too dear.

The theoretical considerations which affect the choice of the actuarial basis for the premium scale can be reduced to a statement of principle which would, we think, be generally acceptable to actuaries. The actuarial basis for the premium scale for new business should be so chosen as to provide for the expected average experience of that new business, not as a separate entity but as an integral part of the fund. The new business should, in fact, be self-supporting within the framework of the fund as a whole. In this manner the expected average experience of the whole liabilities of the fund will be continuously adjusted to provide for the inclusion of new business.

The application of this principle helps, for example, to clarify our ideas with regard to expenses. While the new business should be self-supporting in this as in other respects there is no need to treat the new business as if it were a separate fund. The real question is what additional costs will be incurred by the existing fund because of the transaction of the new business.

The actuarial basis is required not only for the premium scale but also for office calculations of all kinds such as surrenders, alterations and so on. For such calculations the actuarial basis should, in principle, be so chosen as to leave the remaining business in the same relative position as before the change. Thus the emphasis is on the experience of the fund at the time the surrender or alteration takes place. This assumes that the office has the right to change the basis of such calculations from time to time and has not guaranteed the surrender values or terms of alteration in the original contracts.

Perhaps the main use of the actuarial basis is for the purpose of testing the financial condition of life assurance funds from time to time. Clearly such a test may be required for a variety of different purposes and the purpose of the test will colour the choice of basis. The customary purpose of a valuation is the distribution of surplus but valuations may also be required, for example, for the purpose of testing solvency, for settling the terms of an amalgamation, for complying with statutory requirements, and so on.

At any given time the fund will comprise a mass of assurances of different classes, effected at different times for different periods and on different terms. That circumstance would cause no embarrassment if the experience in respect of each batch of assurances had been correctly anticipated because each batch would be valued on its appropriate original basis and the experience of the mass as a whole would be properly provided for. Such a state of affairs is unlikely to occur in practice and we have to consider what is the best approach to the valuation of the mass of contracts having regard to the variations in experience and to the purpose for which the valuation is required.

In the exceptional case where a fund is likely to prove insolvent or nearly so, the actuarial basis would reflect the average experience expected having regard to the measures which the actuary proposes to recommend for the purpose of dealing with the situation. For example, a stronger basis would probably be required if the fund is to remain open for new business than if it is to run off as a closed fund.

Generally, however, the fund which is to be valued has a surplus and the effect, if not the actual purpose, of the valuation is to determine what part of the surplus shall be disclosed at the date of valuation and what part left to arise at later date from the margins in the actuarial basis or, in a bonus reserve valuation, from the explicit provision for future bonus. The choice of the actuarial basis, other things being equal, determines the strength of the valuation. It would not be appropriate for the actuarial basis to reflect the expected average experience because thereby the whole of the surplus would be anticipated, a result which would be undesirable except in a bonus reserve valuation. Thus it comes about that the actuarial basis is chiefly determined by considerations of the strength which is appropriate in all the circumstances, especially having regard to the particular bonus system by which surplus is distributed.

The five elements mentioned in § 1·4 were:

(*a*) Mortality,
(*b*) Interest,
(*c*) Expenses (and other loadings),
(*d*) Withdrawals,
(*e*) Investment profits and losses,

and taxation and competition must also be borne in mind. We now propose to review these elements.

6·2. Mortality.

The mortality experience of the population of a particular country is a broad average based on a heterogeneous body of lives. The total experience may hide some very considerable variations between various sections of the population and the question is to what extent those variations should affect the actuarial basis for life assurance. The lives assured by a life office may be regarded as a selection from the whole population of the country and the decision about the mortality basis must rest, first of all, upon a consideration of the way in which the lives are selected.

The primary basis of selection is to be found in the characteristics of the particular fund, the sources from which it draws its business and the type of organization it employs. These characteristics may lead to a special selection, for example with regard to occupation, race or residence. The business may be developed mainly in one area or occupation, or in the towns or in the country, or among the professional, the commercial or the industrial classes. This may be called 'class selection' and it largely determines the mortality experience. If it is practicable to use a mortality table based on the actual experience of the fund the 'class selection' is automatically provided for. In general, however, it is both customary and probably more practical to adopt a standard published mortality table which reflects the actual experience sufficiently closely.

A second basis of selection is to be found in the medical assessment of the risk, usually called 'initial selection'. Different offices have different standards of selection, depending to some extent upon the type of business being transacted. No doubt these differences are reflected in the mortality experiences. Premiums for assurances with medical examination should always be based on a select mortality table where a suitable experience is available. It is not so clear whether premiums for assurances without medical examination should also be based on a select table. The evidence suggests that non-medical assurances experience the higher mortality during the select period and, theoretically at least, the mortality basis should reflect such a difference in experience. Where, however, an office transacts assurances both with and without medical examination amongst the same class of life it may be reasonable to set the excess mortality on non-medical assurances against the saving in expenses on that class of business, thus enabling the same scale of premiums to be charged for assurances with and without medical examination.

It is a common feature that the mortality experience differs according to the class of assurance though the evidence is neither so clear nor so conclusive as could be desired. There may be many contributory explanations of this feature and it is not easy to determine which is the most important. For example, there may be 'self-selection' by the proposer which has an effect on the mortality experience. Temporary, whole-life and endowment assurances tend to appeal to proposers in different circumstances of life and the less expensive forms of assurance may appeal to those sections which have a comparatively high mortality experience. Annuities generally and the forms of assurance where the rate of premium is high seem to appeal to those sections of the population which have a light mortality experience. Self-selection operates most clearly, perhaps, in annuity business and this class of business should be based on its own mortality experience.

A possible explanation of the difference between the experience of the various classes of assurance may lie in differential rates of withdrawal. The less expensive forms of assurance usually experience comparatively high rates of withdrawal, not only because more of the assurances may lapse or be surrendered but also because a proportion of the assurances will be altered to other types of assurance at higher rates of premium. Such withdrawals and transfers may have a selective effect so that the remaining assurances have a higher mortality than they otherwise would have experienced. Where this feature is present the terms for withdrawals and transfers should include an appropriate allowance; no charge is required in the premium scale.

It is a more difficult question whether differences in experience should be reflected in the mortality basis for whole-life and endowment assurances. There is commonly a well-marked difference in experience, yet it is also common for both classes of assurance to be held by the same proposer and the use of separate tables might make it difficult to preserve equity between, say, limited-premium life assurances and endowment assurances. The practical advantages of using the same mortality table for all the principal types of assurance seem far to outweigh any theoretical advantage there may be in discriminating between them.

Generally speaking, too, there is little need for discriminating between participating and non-participating assurances. There is not such a well-marked difference in experience; in fact the evidence is conflicting, and any difference there may be can be left to emerge in the bonus.

Female lives experience a lighter mortality than male lives at most if not all ages and where there is a substantial amount of business on female lives, as for example with annuity business, appropriate mortality tables should be used based on the separate male and female experiences. Except in industrial assurance, there is usually only a small amount of life assurance on female lives, consisting mainly of endowment assurances. Since such assurances probably cover the period when the two experiences most nearly approximate to each other it is justifiable as a practical measure to charge the same premiums for female as for male lives. This is the usual practice in Great Britain.

So far it has been assumed that the mortality table will reflect the past experience. It is well to remember that mortality in Great Britain has been improving at all ages material to life assurance since the beginning of the business in the eighteenth century. Since premium scales have been based on past experience the actual mortality experience has tended to be better than was assumed in the premium scales. This has provided a useful margin for life assurance but from the earliest times it has been recognized that the opposite is true for annuity business. In Great Britain, in the United States of America and in certain other countries, the mortality table for annuity business has had to be based on an extrapolation in order to provide for the improving vitality of annuitants.

6·3. Interest.

It is difficult to imagine life assurance upon a scientific basis without the foundation of a mortality table but it is quite possible to envisage life assurance without the interest income of invested funds. The structure would be much the same with a zero rate of interest though life assurance would be more costly than if the funds earned interest.

Now the interest income can be dealt with in alternative ways. Either it can be ignored in the actuarial basis and so treated as a profit when it is earned; or it can be anticipated in the actuarial basis, thus making an appropriate reduction in the cost of life assurance. Life assurance has developed along the lines of the second of these alternatives but it so happens that the reduction in some of the sources of profit, particularly in the interest surplus, has led in the United Kingdom to average scales of premiums for participating assurances which effectively ignore interest: the scales could more or less be reproduced on a basis of $i=0$ with a correct provision for the other elements of mortality and loading. However, the surplus is usually distributed by some form of reversionary bonus, a system which requires an estimate, a conservative estimate, of the rate of interest.

The amount to be invested each year is the excess of income over outgo and this is equal to the amount of the increase in the valuation liability plus the valuation surplus for the year (before any adjustments for investment and other reserves and accounting items). Taking the new business fund alone we see that this will require new investments each year for a number of years depending on the composition of the business but thereafter the investments will begin to be realized to meet the excess of outgo over income as the claims become more numerous. The position in the existing fund will depend upon the composition and average duration of the business but whether the fund is increasing or decreasing the effect of transacting new business is to defer or to slow down the decrease in the fund.

For purposes of analysis we require to translate the earned interest income of the fund into an average yield. This was discussed in § 4·5. The yield may be computed in several ways, for example by reference to the mean fund at (*a*) book values, (*b*) current market values, (*c*) amortized value, or purchase price where irredeemable. Further, the yield will be an average based on the spread of existing investments. Clearly the use of such an average must be restricted to those circumstances in which the particular method of computation of the average is appropriate.

Where the fund is increasing we shall have to consider how the current average yield is likely to be affected by the new investments. We think that this problem will be simplified if the yield is based on current market values and, whenever it is necessary to make a full investigation on a basis as close to the facts as possible, we consider that assets should be taken at market values.

In accordance with the principle enunciated at the beginning of this chapter the rate of interest to be assumed for new business would be based primarily on the expected yield of new investments. Since, however, the new business is to be regarded as an integral part of the whole fund we must allow both for the spread of the new investments and the effect, if any, of the transaction of new business on the existing fund.

It is virtually impossible to make an estimate of the yield of future investments because the rate of interest is subject to social, economic and political forces which may be quite unforeseeable for more than a very short time ahead. The rate of interest may be subject to governmental action as may be seen, for example, by a comparison of the market rates of interest in London during the wars of 1914–18 and 1939–45. Reference to past experience is of little value as a guide to the future. All it can do is to indicate the current trend. How long such a trend, if apparent, will continue is a matter for speculation. But some estimate must perforce be made and the actuary must reach a conclusion based on the best assessment he can make of the various operative forces which affect the rate of interest.

The difficulty might seem to be insuperable but for the mitigating circumstance that new trends in the experience usually develop slowly over a period of years. For example, a new trend in the market rate of interest in Great Britain was inaugurated by the War Loan Conversion of 1932 when the market level of the rate of interest for Government stocks was reduced suddenly, almost overnight. The average rate of interest at which new money of assurance funds could be invested was not at once affected to the same extent because new investments are not all made in Government stock—there is some time-lag in the spread of the lower level to other forms of investment. The trend to a lower level was intensified during the war of 1939–45 by governmental action. The increase in the rate of income tax from 5*s*. 6*d*. in £ in 1939/40 to 7*s*. in £ in 1940/41 and to 10*s*. in £ in 1941/42 was an example of a sudden and arbitrary reduction in the net rate of interest whose effects were all the more serious because the change was so sudden.

So far, we have assumed that, in calculating the premium for a particular new entrant, a fixed rate of interest will be used throughout the whole term of the contract. But where the opinion is formed that the rate of interest will vary in a certain way, for example, continuously increase or decrease throughout the term, it may be suggested that such variation should be allowed for in the premium basis. There is no theoretical reason why this should not be done, but it is not common practice to do so. It greatly complicates the calculations to very little purpose, for there is no particular reason to suppose that the resulting premiums will be any nearer to those which subsequent experience shows should have been charged than the rates based on a level rate of interest.

Variations in the rate of interest are, however, sometimes made for contracts of different terms. There are two reasons for this. First, the yield on long-term securities may differ from that on short-term securities, and if the view is held that the assets purchased by the premiums should be matched with the terms of the several contracts, there is clearly a justification for varying the rate of interest used in the premium bases. Secondly, if it is thought that the rate of interest earned will, say, decrease steadily for a number of years, it is obvious that the average rate over a short term will be higher than that over a long term, while if it is thought that the earned rate will increase the converse will apply. On these grounds it is sometimes felt justifiable to use a rate for short-term endowments different from that used for whole-life assurances. A logical development of this principle would require, however, the use of a different rate for each term of endowment assurance, and to avoid this complication it is often the practice to use the same rate throughout and to make the necessary adjustments in the loadings.

The foregoing discussion is based on gross rates of interest, no reference having yet been made to the question of taxation. In Chapter 5, we discussed the basis on which life offices are taxed in Great Britain and we saw that, broadly speaking, tax is payable either on 'interest less expenses' or on the 'profits not allocated to nor reserved for policyholders', whichever is the larger amount. Now this tax is part of the outgo of the fund just as much as claims or expenses, and it must be taken into account in determining the premium basis. It could, in theory, be treated simply as an additional form of expense, and allowed for as such in the expense loadings. This treatment would be appropriate where, for example, the tax is based on premium income. Where, however, the tax is based on interest income it seems more suitable to regard it as a deduction from that item.

Where the tax is based on profits the amount of tax paid may be deducted from the item of interest income in the accounts but it may usually be ignored in the actuarial basis; this would depend to some extent on the precise definition of 'profits'.

The British system of income tax presents some interesting problems because some types of business may be taxable on alternative bases. As has been mentioned, life assurance business is so taxable and where the 'profits' basis of taxation is applicable the actuarial basis of the fund can allow for full gross interest; but there will be a marginal point where a block of new business of a certain type might be just sufficient to put the fund on to the alternative basis of taxation. Under the general principle referred to in §6·1, the actuarial basis for such new business should, in theory, provide for the increase in tax to which the new business gives rise.

Where the basis of taxation is 'interest less expenses' there are alternative ways of dealing with the charge to income tax. Either the income tax may be set against the separate provisions for interest and expenses in the actuarial basis or the net amount of tax on 'interest less expenses' may be set against the provision for interest.

Supposing the chargeable rate of income tax were assumed to be 7*s.* 6*d.* in £, the first method means that the rate of interest and the loading for expenses would each be reduced by a rate of 7*s.* 6*d.* in £, that is to say they would be multiplied by ·625. This may be called the 'true net interest' method.

Supposing, also, that the expenses were assumed to amount to one-third of the interest income the income tax of 7*s.* 6*d.* in £ on 'interest less expenses' would amount to an effective rate of 5*s.* in £ on the interest item alone. By the second method the rate of interest would be reduced by the effective rate of tax, 5*s.* in £ in the example, and the loading for expenses would be charged in full. This may be called the 'effective net interest' method.

The difference between the two methods is best seen by a simple numerical example which is chosen solely to illustrate the two methods and not because the bases would necessarily be suitable in practice. The standard and effective rates of tax are assumed to be 7*s.* 6*d.* in £ and 5*s.* in £ respectively. The gross rate of interest is assumed to be 4% so that the effective net rate is 3% and the true net rate is 2½%. Table 6·1 compares the premiums by A 1924–29 select with loadings of 5% of the premiums and ·3% of the sum assured—less tax on the true net interest basis.

The practical effect of the two methods depends upon the relationship of the interest element to the expenses element of the premium. Though whole-life and endowment assurances may not be much affected by the two methods, the difference for other classes may be substantial. It seems that limited premiums would be raised by the 'true net interest' method to a level consonant with the facts. The reduction in temporary assurance premiums seems less justified because it arises from the relief on expenses which is really earned by the invested funds of other classes of business.

TABLE 6·1

Table showing the computed premiums for 1,000 *assurance at age* 40 *at entry*

Class of assurance	Effective net interest method	True net interest method	On the basis of gross interest
Whole life assurance	24·21	24·09	21·52
Whole life, premiums limited to 20 years	32·51	33·71	27·48
Endowment assurance, 20 years	44·60	44·64	40·65
Temporary assurance, 20 years	10·92	9·69	10·63

The true net interest method keeps the facts clearly in view so long as the basis of taxation is 'interest less expenses'. However, it assumes that there is a sufficient quantum of interest against which the expenses may be set and this may be an objectionable assumption for classes of business, such as temporary assurance, with only a small interest element. The assumption may also be objectionable when allowance is made for initial expenses because, in relation, for example, to surrender values, it would credit the man who surrenders his assurance with the rebate of tax on the initial expenses, a rebate which is really earned by the invested funds of existing, not new, business.

The effective net interest method has little to commend it theoretically. The method assumes a certain composition and rate of expansion of business because the relationship of expenses to interest income is assumed to be stable, and this assumption may be unjustified. However, it can be said for the method that it is probably incorrect to separate the rebate of tax on expenses from the income tax which has been paid by deduction from interest income because the authorities would no doubt consider the two together. We feel that there is much to be said for keeping the actuarial basis as free as possible from assumptions about the basis and the rate of income tax, arbitrary changes in which are bound to occur from time to time.

The final column of the table shows the computed premiums on the basis of gross interest and a comparison of this column with the other two columns gives an idea of the burden imposed by the British income tax system in the particular circumstances. It is interesting to notice that the temporary assurance premium is actually less on the 'true net interest' method than upon the gross interest basis.

6·4. Loadings.

The business of life assurance cannot be conducted without incurring expense and the expenses are met out of the premiums paid by policyholders. Also, since future experience cannot be estimated accurately, it is desirable that the premiums should include a margin for fluctuations and profits (or a specific provision for bonus where the assurance is participating). It is customary for the pure premiums to be increased by certain 'loadings' to provide for expenses and for fluctuations and profits.

The expenses comprise, for example, commissions, salaries of staff, travelling expenses, medical fees, stamp duties, stationery and postages, brokerage and other investment expenses, office expenses such as rent, heating and lighting, cleaning and repairs, cost of maintenance of office equipment and so on. It is clear that the management can exercise a fair degree of control over most of these items and that their level will be materially affected by the efficiency with which the office is managed. Should extravagant administration lead to an increase in expenses beyond the amount provided for, the position could probably be rectified fairly speedily by the introduction of a policy of retrenchment.

The foregoing remarks are subject to one qualification. Unpredictable events, such as currency inflation, may seriously affect the relationship of the expenses to the loadings in the premiums.

The premiums, and therefore the loadings, are fixed at the inception of assurance whereas the expenses of management follow the trend of current costs. This suggests that the estimate of expenses should include a margin.

As has been mentioned in § 6·1 the expense loadings of each batch of new business should, in principle, be sufficient to pay the additional costs to which the new business gives rise. In this manner the total expense loadings for the whole business will be continuously accommodated to the total expenses, assuming of course that the required provision in the loadings is in fact correctly forecast. This structure depends upon a correct analysis of expenses between new and old business and between the various classes of assurance.

Some reference may be made to the analysis of expenses though the general subject of costing need not be studied for the purpose of the examinations. There are three general processes used in analysing expenses:

(*a*) A subjective classification according to the kind of goods or services purchased.

(*b*) An objective classification according to the purpose for which the expenses were incurred.

(*c*) An analysis according to the revenues from which the expenses are ultimately paid.

Classification (*a*) follows the usual items in the expenditure accounts, e.g. salaries, rent, advertising, printing. Examples of classification (*b*) would be analyses by geographical area of origin of business, by class of assurance, or by department. Classification (*c*) might provide an analysis suitable for assessing the charges to be made according to the type of expense, e.g. investment expense assessed against surplus interest income, initial expenses against the new business, renewal expenses against the renewal premium income, overheads against the business in force.

The apportionment of expenses between the major classes of assurance business is of considerable importance particularly where separate statutory funds are required to be kept. The statutory form of accounts in Great Britain under the Assurance Companies Acts, 1909–46, provides practically no information on this subject.

Before deciding on premium loadings it may be decided to analyse the expenses into *first year* and *later years*. This will involve a rough apportionment of those items, and they are many, which are not directly attributable to one or the other. The test to be applied in this apportionment is the actual strain on surplus caused by the acquisition of new business. Other considerations may play a part at a later stage when we are concerned with the methods of financing the expenses by premium loadings.

Now the analysis of expenses has to be related to the various factors that enter into the premium and other calculations. Broadly speaking, the various items of expenses of management must be related either to the premium or to the sum assured though some rough allowance may be made for those items which are more or less constant per policy whatever the size of the assurance and certain items of expense, for example investment expenses, may be dealt with in special ways.

It is probably best to keep commission separate in the analysis,† so that the proper provision for commission can be included in the loadings for each class of assurance. The other expenses can then be put into some such scheme as the following:

Method of allocation of expenses	Expenses of first year of assurance	Expenses of subsequent years of assurance
Per cent of sum assured		
Per cent of annual premium		
Per policy		

The aggregate expenses would be the total of the six items when related to the actual figures of new business and business in force.

The average sum assured varies with the class and period of assurance. The following table is an example of the kind of variation that may occur, though the figures relate to endowment assurances effected in a single year in a particular office and would not necessarily be applicable to other offices.

It will be seen from the table that the average sum assured increases with the period of assurance but that the average annual

† The same is true of other items, e.g. *m*thly premiums.

premium tends to decrease as the period lengthens. Thus it comes about that those expenses which are constant per policy are probably best allocated partly in proportion to the sum assured and partly to the premium rather than wholly in proportion to one or the other of the items.

TABLE 6·2

Averages per policy issued

Period of assurance	Average sum assured	Average annual premium
	£	£
10 years	332	37·8
15 ,,	300	22·2
20 ,,	442	24·2
25 ,,	516	22·3
30 ,,	573	20·3
35 ,,	604	18·1
All periods	500	24·3

The fact that certain expenses are more or less constant per policy whatever the size of assurance suggests that some adjustment should be made in the rate of premium according to size of assurance. A rough adjustment is commonly made in the United Kingdom by quoting separate rates for two or three broad ranges of sum assured. But it should be remembered that large assurances may entail special problems and expenses, which are not present with the smaller assurances, and that they probably also require a rather larger loading for fluctuations. The question of how to devise a system of loadings from this analysis of expenses is dealt with later in the appropriate chapters of this book.

In addition to the loadings for expenses there should be included either a loading for fluctuations and profits or, for participating assurances, a provision for bonuses. Since it is not possible to estimate the future accurately it is necessary to make specific provision for fluctuations in the actuarial basis of non-participating assurances, and should the experience work out as expected this provision will fall into surplus. This surplus may go to increase the bonus on participating assurances or, where the office is proprietary, to the proprietors or it may go partly to one and partly to the other, depending on the constitution of the fund. The loading for fluctuations and profits is commonly made by adding to the annual premium a uniform percentage of the sum assured with a suitable adjustment for limited-premium assurances.

The position of the participating assurance fund is rather different. The effects of adverse experience would fall in the first place upon the divisible surplus and would thus result in a smaller allocation of bonus. It is generally considered desirable that the premiums for participating assurances should be specifically loaded for the type of bonus it is expected to declare and a further loading for fluctuations would not be required. The valuation position is not so clear because the valuation basis frequently does not include a specific provision for future bonus. The position is rather complicated and discussion of it must be left to the chapters on valuation.

We have already referred to the possible deduction of the income tax relief from the expense loadings where the basis of taxation is 'interest less expenses'. We may notice here that the deduction should be made only from that part of the expense loadings which represents allowable expenses for income tax.

6·5. Withdrawals.

It is not customary to provide for lapses and surrenders in the actuarial basis of life assurance because they are less susceptible to mathematical treatment than the three main elements we have discussed and provision for withdrawals would complicate the calculations without much practical advantage. However, the effect of lapses and surrenders should not be ignored and we propose to refer briefly to some of the questions which arise in connexion with them.

Lapses and surrenders are generally assumed to have some effect on mortality though the precise effect is not clear because it is rarely possible to trace the mortality experience amongst lives whose assurances have lapsed or have been surrendered. The assumption is that lives in poor health will tend to withdraw proportionately less frequently than lives in good health. Since the mortality table would be based on the experience of those whose assurances were continued, the use of a mortality table based on assured lives will make some, though not necessarily an appropriate, allowance for the selective effect of the withdrawals.

A high rate of withdrawal alters the relative importance of the other elements of the actuarial basis. It means that a considerable proportion of the assurances terminate early, thus lessening the practical importance of the interest element and increasing the importance of the loading element.

Lapses must be considered carefully in connexion with expenses. Since a considerable part of the expenses are incurred at the inception of the assurance, an early lapse may mean that part of the initial expenses is not covered by the premiums received, less the contribution to expected death strain. Such a possible source of loss may usually be avoided (for example by paying the initial commission in two instalments) without any special provision in the actuarial basis. Circumstances may require some special provision to be made with a specific allowance for lapses but it is preferable to restrict the initial expenses.

Since an office usually looks to make a margin of profit on surrenders for the benefit of the continuing assurances, the introduction of a rate of withdrawal in conjunction with the surrender value scale would often result in a reduction in the pure premium. The corresponding valuation liability might, however, be increased because most surrenders occur in the earlier years of assurance and the profit on these surrenders would have to be accumulated to make good the reduction in premium in the later years of assurance. Withdrawals are not usually allowed for in a valuation because the net premium method assumes a balance of conflicting forces in which such profits as surrender profits are set against the cost of new business.

Where the surrender value scale is guaranteed in the assurance contract consideration must be given to that scale when the actuarial basis is decided upon. The scale would usually be within the valuation liability but specific provision for the scale might be necessary in special circumstances. Statutory provisions for minimum scales of surrender or paid-up-policy values may create a similar problem.

6·6. Investment profits and losses.

So far we have considered a fund which receives increments by way of premiums and interest, and suffers decrements by way of claims, expenses and other outgo. The true amount of the fund may, however, vary from time to time by reason of changes in the values of the investments of the fund. Such changes in the values of the investments represent a further source of increment or decrement, as the case may be. But while some of them may be real and permanent, others are only apparent and temporary. We must now discuss the question whether such changes should constitute an element in the actuarial basis.

If an investment has appreciated in value so that it can be realized at a higher price relatively to other comparable investments than it could have been when the investment was made, the excess constitutes a real investment profit. (This definition is not complete nor watertight but it is sufficient for the purposes of our discussion.) The profit is an addition to the yield of the investment and is probably best dealt with in the actuarial basis by an adjustment to the rate of interest. Such profits are fortuitous and must be averaged over a considerable period of years.

When the values of the investments merely change in accordance with general market conditions there may be an apparent profit or loss on investments but it will not be a real profit or loss unless investments have to be realized to pay the claims and other outgo. So long as the fund has an excess of income over outgo there will be no need to realize investments, and changes in the values of existing investments in accordance with general market conditions have no immediate significance. Such changes may have an ultimate significance in the indication that they may give of the ultimate price at which the investments may be realized when the outgo exceeds the income of the fund. Supposing, however, that the assets have been matched to the liabilities, the redemption price is the only price that matters and intervening changes in value have no significance at all. These remarks assume that the change in value is in accordance with general market conditions and does not portend a deterioration in quality of the investment and a prospect that payment of interest or principal may not be forthcoming.

Market fluctuations in the values of the assets need have no effect on the actuarial basis at a valuation except to the extent (*a*) that such fluctuations have been reflected in the book values of the assets, (*b*) that new investments are required because the fund is increasing. The subject is discussed in § 4·5.

It might be thought that market fluctuations should affect the actuarial basis for surrenders and similar calculations. Though the basis must to some extent reflect current market conditions (where the basis has not been guaranteed at the inception of the assurance), there is no need for the basis to be in close correspondence with those conditions because surrender values are normally paid out of the income of the fund and not out of realized investments. The actuarial basis should, however, be such as can be maintained in bad times as well as good times so that frequent changes in basis may be avoided.

6·7. Competition.

The student may wonder why this item is included in a discussion of the elements. He may feel that when the other elements have been assessed to the best of the actuary's ability, and the premium scale produced on the basis of them, the fact that the premiums prove to be out of line with the rates charged by other offices does not justify modifying the premiums. He may argue that in such circumstances the actuary should have the courage of his convictions, even though he seems to be the only one in step.

This is partially true, but it is by no means the whole truth. For the elements will be affected by the amount and nature of the business written, which are in turn affected by the degree of competition encountered. Thus, although competition is not itself an element in the calculation, it may have a marked influence on the provisions for the basic elements. For example, the amount of business written by a particular office in certain areas or of a particular type, will be affected by the way in which its premium rates compare with those charged by other offices and will in turn affect the office's over-all mortality experience. Or again, the investment opportunities may depend on the amount of money available for investment, which will be affected by the amount of business written. But perhaps the item most affected by the question of competition is that of expense loadings. As we have seen, some of the expenses of the office will be largely independent of the amount of business written, so that the proportion to be allocated to each policy is determined by the volume of new business. This, in turn, depends to some extent on the competitive level of the premium rates.

Thus we see that competition enters implicitly into the equation. It is not possible to make any precise allowance for it, but the actuary must keep it constantly in mind in assessing the scale of premiums to be charged, and must endeavour, as far as possible, to ensure that it does not invalidate any of the assumptions made in the premium basis.

Even in choosing the valuation basis the element of competition may make itself felt. A strong valuation basis is undoubtedly a good 'selling point' and may materially affect the amount of business sold. It is probably true to say that the possibility of adverse comparison with a net premium valuation by members of the public has deterred many actuaries from publishing a bonus reserve valuation, even though such a comparison is quite unsound.

Competition is also a useful corrective. Much of the actuary's work depends upon individual judgment, and competition provides a test of his decisions by reference to those made by other actuaries in similar circumstances. It should thus tend to restrain both excessive optimism and unnecessary caution.

BIBLIOGRAPHY

Mortality of assured lives, 1924–29 (Extracts and Discussions), pp. 54–119.

D. G. Kellock (1933). The mortality of female assured lives. *T.F.A.* vol. xiv, p. 269.

W. Palin Elderton, H. J. P. Oakley and H. B. Smither (1936). Some points that have arisen out of the continuous investigation into the mortality of assured lives 1924–29. *J.I.A.* vol. lxviii, p. 54.

E. H. Lever (1937). Some reflections on long-term investments with particular reference to the business of life assurance. *J.I.A.* vol. LXIX, p. 10.

I. A. Miller and C. F. B. Richardson (1937). Expense investigation and kindred problems. *J.I.A.* vol. LXIX, p. 50.

L. S. Vaidyanathan (1938). Mortality of Indian assured lives. *J.I.A.* vol. LXX, p. 15.

Continuous mortality investigation: assured lives (1924–38), *J.I.A.* vol. LXXI, p. 259.

P. H. Hammon and R. S. Skerman (1948). Ordinary assurance premium bases in the United Kingdom with particular reference to interest, expenses and taxation. *Proc. Cent. Assembly Inst. Act.* vol. II, p. 232.

The mortality of annuitants (1950). *J.I.A.* vol. LXXVI, p. 130.

CHAPTER 7

WAR AND LIFE ASSURANCE

The student is not expected to study those problems of a temporary character which arose out of the recent war. The purpose of this chapter is to outline some of the problems of a permanent character that war gives rise to. The problems may be conveniently grouped under the headings:

Mortality of lives assured.
Effect on investments and investment income.
Depreciation in currency.

7·1. Mortality of lives assured.

We may take first the problems of war mortality. Can it be measured statistically? Can the experience of the past be useful as a guide to the future? With certain qualifications, it is possible to measure war mortality once a war has ended but the evidence collected from one war is not necessarily a guide to what may be expected in a possible future war. The two wars of 1914–18 and 1939–45 provide a sufficient example of this fact. The potentialities of the atomic bomb merely underline what has been true of many wars in the past—that changes in methods of warfare may invalidate the experience of one war as a guide to what may be expected in a later war.

The excess mortality to be measured may be considered under four heads: the excess amongst combatants and civilians respectively and, within each group, the deaths from the direct and indirect effects of war. The indirect effects of war would include disease of all kinds through abnormal war conditions, epidemics and starvation and exposure. Amongst funds with a world-wide spread of risks, the influenza epidemic of 1919 probably had a greater effect than the direct war mortality of 1914–18.

The measurement of excess war mortality presents certain statistical difficulties. First, there is the difficulty of definition.

The direct war deaths may be classified fairly accurately but there will be a proportion of cases where the classification is uncertain. The fact of death may be probable but not definitely established; or the life assured may have been killed in circumstances which might have happened in peace-time but which actually occurred in war conditions. The deaths from the indirect effects of war can be classified only partially at best and some will not occur until several years after the war has ended.

The second statistical difficulty is that the exposed to risk to which the deaths relate cannot be accurately measured so far as life assurance statistics are concerned. An alternative would be to use statistics derived from the aggregate data for the population, but that does not wholly dispose of the difficulty.

A third statistical difficulty is that war may have an effect on the mortality amongst nationals of a country that is neutral. The effect may be direct or indirect, for example by lowering of vitality through lack of food. The neutral countries must be included in a complete account of the effects of war.

It will be apparent that no useful statistics can be obtained from past wars on the basis of which adequate provision may be made for possible future wars.

7·2. Special conditions in life assurance policies.

Because adequate provision cannot be made in the statistical basis of life assurance, it is perhaps natural to assume that the scope of the assurance liability should be restricted by the exclusion of war deaths. This was attempted in Great Britain in 1939–45 by the inclusion in new assurances of special conditions which varied from office to office but which took the following general form:

> If the death of the life assured shall arise either directly or indirectly from any war (whether war be declared or not) the amount payable under this policy shall be limited to....

Such a condition takes care of the main mortality risks but it can only provide a partial protection. The word 'indirectly' might be thought to sweep into the net many deaths only remotely attributable to the war. Actually, a count of the war deaths might show about seven-eighths as 'direct' and one-eighth as 'indirect'. If the condition were to be interpreted in the widest possible sense it might make the whole contract void for uncertainty, because almost any claim in war-time might be held 'to arise directly or indirectly' from war. The use of the phrase 'directly or indirectly' gets rid of the burden of proof that death in a particular case is directly due to war.

Such a condition discriminates against those who serve or live in the war areas. For this reason some Governments have prohibited the use of such conditions. Although there may be no prohibition, when war breaks out the assurance fund may be deprived of the protection of the condition either by governmental action or by pressure of public opinion.

There are usually some proposals which contain a request for full war cover. Such a request might be refused on principle but it is perhaps more usual to endeavour to meet the public demand. These special quotations are, however, troublesome. Any extra premiums that may be quoted would be arbitrary and in peace-time, when the possibility of war may seem remote, the extra premium would be so small that it would seem preferable to include the charge in the tabular premiums and to give full war cover to the whole body of the assured lives.

An alternative approach to the problem is to provide for an assessment on the whole body of the assured lives in wartime. The method has the advantage that the fund is protected from the effects of war however long it may last though we think that special arrangements would be required for new business in war-time. Where the assured cannot meet his assessment it would form a charge on the surrender value and it, or its equivalent, could be deducted from the sum assured when payable.

The following notes on practice in various countries in the war of 1939–45 may serve to indicate some of the methods that have been adopted to deal with war risk.

In Canada and the United States of America some companies excluded war deaths in new assurances but the majority—ultimately about six-sevenths—excluded (*a*) deaths during or as a result of military service, (*b*) deaths from civilian foreign travel, and (*c*) deaths due to aviation. Thus combatants could only secure assurance cover in war-time by the payment of comparatively high extra premiums.

In the United States, the National Service Life Insurance Act, 1940, enabled persons serving in the Armed Forces to obtain $10,000 unrestricted life insurance cover from the Government at a very low premium rate. Under this Act, claims traceable to the war and all expenses of administration were to be borne by the Government and this was additional to the usual arrangements for war pensions for dependants.

In the Netherlands new assurances after 1 September 1939 included a '90% clause' which specified that, at the outbreak of war in the Netherlands, all sums assured would be reduced to 90% of the amounts shown in the policies. Later this was altered to a similar reduction at such time as an 'active state of war' might be proclaimed. The 'active state of war' was deemed by the Government Insurance Board to have lasted from 15 September 1944 to 5 May 1945 and the ultimate reduction determined upon was 3%.

In Belgium, assurances before the war included full war cover for civilians but not for participants in the war. Several companies provided for a maximum extra premium for participants of from 4 to 6% of the sum at risk. The extra premiums were modified from time to time during the course of the war and in July 1946 it was decided to return the extra premiums for civilian war risk cover in so far as they were not absorbed by war losses.

In France, by an Act of Parliament of 1940, life assurance companies were not allowed to cover, at their own expense, any war risk on new business, nor to offer war risk cover under current policies. Where war risk was to be covered the risk had to be reassured with a pool. Under the Act war deaths included deaths of military men and of deportees and internees, whatever the cause of death, and also deaths of civilians caused directly by the action of any armed force. An extra premium was charged but the results were so favourable that the extra premiums paid were returned to the policyholders.

In Denmark, new assurances included a provision for an annual extra of ·6% of the sum assured to commence at the outbreak of war and after the war an account of the extra premiums received and of the claims paid was to be made up and the balance, if any, to be returned to the policyholders. The condition was not in fact applied in practice.

7·3. The effect on investments and investment income.

The investment problems that war gives rise to are more serious in many respects than the mortality problems. The value of the investments may decrease or be lost, there may be a loss of investment income, and there may be increased taxation on capital or investment income.

The depreciation in the value of investments may be the result of actual loss by physical destruction of the security or by default. The physical loss may be spread over all owners of property as was provided, in effect, by the War Damage Act, 1941. It would be interesting to compare the aggregate of contributions paid by insurance companies under that Act and of other capital losses with the aggregate loss on mortality in war-time.

The decrease in the value of investments may, however, be a book item arising from a change in market values and the general rate of interest. Such a decrease is only important where securities have to be realized; where the fund is increasing, the decrease in value of the existing investments is to some extent offset by the higher rate of interest obtainable on new investments.

There may be a loss of investment income in war-time because of temporary or permanent default in interest payments or of reductions in dividends or of governmental restrictions on interest and dividends or because it becomes impossible to remit interest payments from overseas.

The financial policies of the Government in war-time have a considerable effect on the problems. Throughout the war of 1939–45, except during its early stages, the British Government had strict control over the investment market. Life assurance funds had the (somewhat doubtful) benefit of the high prices of securities but the investment of a large part of the funds in British Government stocks at low rates of interest must have placed a considerable burden on the funds.

There may be a loss of income through increased taxation. After 1941, the rate of income tax borne by the investment income of life assurance funds in Great Britain was 2*s.* in £ higher than the rate before the war (7*s.* 6*d.* in £ instead of 5*s.* 6*d.* in £). This reduction in investment income has had a most serious effect and is more far-reaching than the relatively small losses by default and otherwise in respect of capital and interest. Moreover it is clear that the burden is not equally shared by the various offices because the tax on investment income is offset by the relief on expenses. The strain falls most heavily on those old-established and economically managed funds whose expenses are a relatively small proportion of their investment income.

Arising out of the thought that investment losses may be as serious as excess mortality, it has been suggested that all such losses should be averaged over the claims of those that die in war-time whatever the cause of death. A proportion only of the sum assured would be payable at death in war-time and, as the initial proportion would have to be fixed in advance, provision should be made for settling the exact proportion after the end of the war, should the experience prove more favourable than was expected. This type of condition is easily understood and is simple to operate. It deals with a number of troublesome special risks. It saves reference to the circumstances of each individual claim. The condition does not, however, deal satisfactorily with a loss, for example increased taxation, which may continue long after the war has ended; also the possibility of a further payment after the war would entail keeping estates open for the time being.

A war condition on the lines of the preceding paragraph was operated by two offices during the war of 1939–45, two-thirds of the sum assured being payable (one-half for men of military age).

7·4. Depreciation of currency.

The effect of currency depreciation on life assurance has been dealt with in § 4·7 and little more need be said here. Where the assets and liabilities are in the same currency, the loss falls on the assured except to the extent that the particular investments provide a hedge against inflation. The fund does not escape all consequences because the new business will be inflated in terms of money units compared with the old business. In the extreme case the existing business is wiped out and the fund has to recommence as a new fund with all that that entails.

A further effect of currency depreciation is that prices rise and with them wages and salaries. Thus, even if the new business is placed on a self-supporting basis, the office will incur losses due to a higher wage bill and increased costs of stationery, equipment, etc., a large proportion of which is attributable to the existing business. If this occurs, the policyholder may not only suffer from receiving a sum which is less, in terms of real goods, than he expected, but participating policyholders may also receive less in hard cash, owing to a reduction in bonus rates.

7·5. Practice of offices.

The general practice in Great Britain is not to impose any special condition with regard to war risk except for young lives, for group insurance, for industrial assurance and for the ordinary life assurance transacted by industrial assurance offices. Though this is the general practice there is no standard practice and widely different views are held about war risks.

We have dealt at some length with various special conditions that may be imposed but there is much to be said, on grounds of simplicity, for contracts which have no special conditions attached to them. It should be remembered that the effects of war are not to be disposed of by ignoring them and omitting any reference to war risk in life assurance policies. Where no special condition is made the effects of war will fall first on the general reserves and on the bonuses. Perhaps the best that can be done, in face of the unascertainable losses that may be incurred, is to build the business on as sound a foundation as possible with ample reserves, and to trust to those reserves and the margins for fluctuations and bonuses to carry the fund through evil times.

This has the justification that it does not discriminate against those who are called on to bear the greatest risk. In modern warfare there is inevitably great inequality of sacrifice. For example, the man who is called up for the forces and engaged in active fighting runs a far greater risk than another who follows a 'reserved' occupation in a safe area. It seems unfair that the former should have his insurance cover greatly reduced by reason of a special condition attached to his policy, and any method which avoids this seems preferable.

The attempt to deal with one unfairness may create another as between policies effected during a war and the pre-war policies under which full war cover has been granted. Persons who effect policies in war-time will be called upon to pay premiums on at least as high a scale as pre-war policies, though their bonuses are likely to be reduced by the war claims on the pre-war policies.

We may close with a suggestion arising out of the thought that the burden should be carried as far as possible by the general reserves. Where it is necessary to impose a special condition with regard to war risk, the operation of the condition should, perhaps, be limited to the first 15 or 20 years of assurance. That would give time for the necessary reserves to be built up.

BIBLIOGRAPHY

W. Palin Elderton (now Sir William Elderton, K.B.E.) (1937). War risk in life assurance. *The Review*, 5 November 1937.

G. Harbitz (1947). The mortality amongst industrial insured lives in Norway during the war. *Skand. Act.* (1947), p. 167.

H. R. Bassford (1948). War mortality among life insurance policyholders in the United States. *Proc. Cent. Assembly Inst. Act.* vol. II, p. 297.

Jhr. G. M. M. Alting von Geusau (1948). War risk cover in life assurance. *Proc. Cent. Assembly Inst. Act.* vol. II, p. 320.

Papers on this subject were also submitted to the Twelfth International Congress, Lucerne, 1940.

CHAPTER 8

ACTUARIAL INVESTIGATIONS

The student will appreciate how necessary it is that the financial condition of assurance funds should be kept under periodical review and we now turn to discuss the considerations that would guide the actuary in such a review. The discussion is of general principles: suitable bases are suggested in Parts II and III.

8·1. The purpose of the investigation.

First, it is of importance to appreciate how fundamental to the problem is the purpose for which the investigation is made. The purpose of the investigation necessarily colours the choice of the actuarial basis and may also affect the methods to be used. For example, an investigation for the purpose of testing solvency would obviously require a different approach from one for the purpose of distributing surplus. Yet another approach might be required for a valuation to comply with statutory requirements or to provide a basis for amalgamation with another assurance fund. As has been said in Chapter 1, the question of purpose is fundamental to the consideration of a valuation report and for the sake of clarity the report should open with a short statement about the purpose of the investigation.

Secondly, the actuarial investigation should not be confined to one aspect of the problem; the investigation should be treated as a whole. It is often thought of in terms merely of a valuation of the liabilities, possibly because this normally constitutes the greater part of the arithmetical work. The full report should deal with the following investigations:

(*a*) A review of the past experience of the fund.

(*b*) A valuation of the assets.

(*c*) A valuation of the liabilities.

(*d*) An investigation into the adequacy of the premium rates (where the fund is to remain open for new business).

(*e*) Recommendations, including those about the amount of divisible surplus and its equitable distribution (where the valuation is for that purpose).

Thirdly, the methods and processes employed should be adapted to suit the circumstances of the case. This is perhaps a truism but it may serve as a warning to the student that normally there is no single *best* method of procedure and that the actuary must choose whatever seems most appropriate out of the methods available to him, having regard to the form in which the valuation particulars have been prepared or are needed for the purpose of complying with statutory or other requirements.

8·2. The valuation process.

The value of the liability under assurance contracts may be determined by a number of different processes, for example:

(*a*) by a prospective process;
(*b*) by a retrospective process;
(*c*) by means of prepared tables of policy-values;
(*d*) by an accumulative process from the valuation liability at an earlier valuation.

By the prospective process we have, on the one hand, the value of the contractual liability and, on the other hand, the value of future premiums less the assessed expenses and the provision for profits, the excess of the one over the other being the value of the net liability. This is known as the 'gross premium' method of valuation because the premium that is valued is the gross or office premium actually payable.

For various reasons discussed in § 8·5 the premium that is valued may be not the office premium but the pure premium that would have been charged for the contractual liability on the basis of the interest and mortality assumed in the valuation. This is known as the 'net premium' method of valuation. The name 'net premium' method is somewhat unfortunate because the *net premium* that is valued is not derived from the *gross premium* as might be thought from the customary sense of the words 'net' and 'gross'. However, the expression has been established by common use and is used in this book.

The pure premium that is valued has regard only to the valuation basis and not to the basis on which the office premium was originally computed; it is, in fact, unrelated to the office premium and may, possibly, even be inconsistent with that premium. The important question is whether the value placed upon the net liability is reasonable and adequate.

The student will see that the prospective process of valuation requires a decision about the premium to be valued as well as about the basic elements of the valuation.

When the prospective process is applied to whole life assurances the valuation factors take a simple form, being dependent only upon attained age. For limited-premium and endowment assurances the valuation factors depend upon the two variables of attained age and unexpired period of assurance and there may be further variables for other classes of assurance. Some approximation may be necessary and the methods of valuation are discussed in Chapter 12.

From a retrospective point of view, the funds in hand represent the accumulation of the premiums paid less the actual cost of assurance. This is to be compared with the theoretical accumulation of the pure premiums at the valuation rate of interest less the provision for the expected claims. For a wide variety of classes of assurance the valuation formula may be written

$$S \times V(t) = S\{P(N_x - N_{x+t}) - (M_x - M_{x+t})\}/D_{x+t}. \quad (8\cdot1)$$

The pure premium P is assumed to be annual and the duration t is assumed to be integral. Small adjustments would be required to deal with special circumstances.

By a simple transformation (8·1) reduces to

$$S \times V(t) = S\{A_{x+t} - P\ddot{a}_{x+t}\} + S(P \times N_x - M_x)/D_{x+t}. \quad (8\cdot2)$$

If, therefore, $S(P \times N_x - M_x)$ be tabulated for each assurance as a 'valuation constant' the remaining factors will depend solely upon attained age and we shall have reached a simple formula of wide applicability. This type of formula is called after its originator, Karup, and the student will find further examples of the method with a description of its use in Chapter 12. The same type of formula may be used with a prospective process. It is in fact usually applied in that form and the valuation constant is related to the age at maturity.

The retrospective and the prospective processes must yield identical results by the net premium method of valuation provided that consistent assumptions are made about the ages, durations and so on. The retrospective process is not suitable for a gross premium valuation because the process would accumulate the surplus or deficiency in the gross premium.

The value of the net liability for an assurance of a particular class depends upon a number of variables: for example, age at entry, duration since entry, original period of assurance, original period of premium payments, and so on. If the records for each class of assurance are so arranged as to isolate those assurances which have all characteristics in common, the valuation can evidently be made by using prepared tables of the valuation liability per unit of assurance. These tables would be prepared earlier in readiness for the valuation. Thus we should have tables of ${}_tV_x$, ${}^n_tV_x$ and ${}_tV_{x\overline{n|}}$ or similar values adjusted for any special features arising from the method of tabulation. This process has the advantage of extreme simplicity but it involves extensive tabulation of factors and extensive classification of data. It is referred to further in Chapter 12 together with the accumulative process.

In Great Britain, the valuation of the main classes of assurance is usually made by a prospective process because the prospective values of sums assured and bonuses, and of future premiums have to be separately stated in the returns to the Board of Trade under the Assurance Companies Act, 1909, Fourth Schedule.

In America, the valuation of the main classes of assurance is commonly made by means of prepared tables of policy-values. Here the determining factor is the contribution method of distribution of surplus which is in general use. This requires the tracing of the contribution of each assurance to the surplus (though on fairly broad lines) and the work is facilitated by the tabulation of the assurances in force by year of entry and age at entry as well as by class and period of assurance.

8·3. The mathematical analysis of policy-values.

The student is assumed to be familiar with Lidstone's Equation of Equilibrium which expresses the relationship between pure-premium policy-values. Suppose that unaccented symbols represent one basis and accented symbols another basis, the Equation of Equilibrium is (in the form in which it is usually stated):

$$(i'-i)(V+P)+(P'-P)(1+i')=(q'-q)+(p'-p)V_1, \quad (8\cdot3)$$

where V and V_1 are the policy-values at the beginning and end of the year.

This equation assumes equal policy-values but Lidstone goes on to consider the case where the two sides of the equation are not equal. He shows how the algebraic value of the inequality may be accumulated separately as the Variation Fund which represents the difference between the policy-values on the two bases.

In the form stated, the equation is restricted to the year's working of assurances subject to annual premiums, though it can easily be generalized. The equation deals with pure-premium policy-values and does not take account of expenses and withdrawals. This could be done as was shown by Lidstone, but for this purpose it is probably simplest to put all items on a continuous basis in a form of the equation which goes back to the Danish mathematician, Thiele.

Suppose we consider a group of assurances all of the same type, effected at the same time and at the same age at entry. Suppose, also, that accented and unaccented symbols represent computations on two different bases. We may then write down the following differential equation:

$$S\times\frac{d}{dt}V(t)=S\{\delta(t)V(t)+P-\mu(t)-\nu(t)R(t)+[\mu(t)+\nu(t)]V(t)\}. \quad (8\cdot4)$$

Premiums are assumed to be payable continuously though (8·4) may be applied to annual premium assurances provided that the discontinuity at the time of each premium payment is allowed for. The symbols $\delta(t)$, $\mu(t)$ and $\nu(t)$ are the forces of interest, mortality and withdrawal at time t; $S\times R(t)$ is the payment on withdrawal.

Expenses are not taken into account because it is assumed, in dealing with pure values, that they are exactly met by the loadings. Where the uneven incidence of expenses is provided for, there must be a corresponding adjustment of P and $V(t)$.

The integration of (8·4) produces $V(t)$. Now $V(t)$ commences with $V(0)$ at the inception of the assurance and ends with $V(n)$ at duration n, where n is the period of the assurance or $(\omega - x)$ for assurances which continue for the whole of life. $V(0)$ is zero with the pure-premium policy-values that we are considering and $V(n)$ takes a definite value according to the type of assurance, for example:

Temporary assurance	$V(n)=0$;
Whole-life and endowment assurance	$V(n)=1$;
Double endowment assurance	$V(n)=2$.

Suppose that we are considering the pure-premium policy-values of two similar assurances on different bases. It is clear that $V(0)$ and $V(n)$ will be identical on both bases: should the values of $\frac{d}{dt}V(t)$ by (8·4) also be identical on both bases, the policy-values will be equal at all durations.

Now the differential coefficient, $\frac{d}{dt}V'(t)$ on the 'special' basis may at some durations exceed and at other durations fall short of the differential coefficient, $\frac{d}{dt}V(t)$, on the 'normal' basis. Since, however, $V(0)=V'(0)$ and $V(n)=V'(n)$ the integration of (8·4) over the whole period of n years must yield identical results. The positive items of the excess of the 'special' values of (8·4) over the 'normal' values must be balanced by other negative items, that is to say the deficiency when the 'special' values of (8·4) fall short of the 'normal' values.

Suppose, for simplicity of analysis, that there is only one such change from positive to negative or vice versa.

Should the special values at first exceed the normal values but afterwards fall short of them, the special policy-values will be built up at a higher rate until at the later durations the excess over the normal policy-values begins to diminish, and ultimately both sets of policy-values tend to $V(n)$. Thus the special policy-values must exceed the normal policy-values at all durations.

Should the special values of (8·4) at first fall short of the normal values but afterwards exceed them, the special policy-values must similarly be less than the normal policy-values at all durations.

This line of argument may be pursued to yield useful results in a number of special instances. Let us first consider a change in the rate of interest, the other elements being the same on both bases. From the special and normal values of (8·4), we have

$$\frac{d}{dt} V'(t) - \frac{d}{dt} V(t) = [\delta'(t) - \delta(t)]\, V(t) + (P' - P) + [\delta'(t) + \mu(t) + \nu(t)]\, [V'(t) - V(t)]. \quad (8\cdot5)$$

If the difference between the policy-values on the two bases be regarded as a 'variation fund' the last term of (8·5) merely arises from the accumulation of the 'variation fund' with interest and benefit of survivorship. This may be regarded as taking place within the separate 'variation fund' and we are then concerned solely with the relationship of the first two terms.

Assuming that $V(t)$ increases continuously with duration from zero to unity, a constant increase ϵ in the force of interest will lead to a reduction in the premium and the negative value of $(P' - P)$ will be offset by the positive increasing values of $\epsilon \times V(t)$. Thus $(P' - P)$ will lie between the extreme values of 0 and ϵ and the special policy-values will be less than the normal policy-values. A similar argument applies to a reduction in the rate of interest which, in general, leads to an increase in the premium and in the policy-values.

Now consider a change in the force of mortality, the other elements being the same on both bases. From the special and normal values of (8·4), we have

$$\frac{d}{dt} V'(t) - \frac{d}{dt} V(t) = (P' - P) - [\mu'(t) - \mu(t)]\, [1 - V(t)] + [\delta(t) + \mu'(t) + \nu(t)]\, [V'(t) - V(t)]. \quad (8\cdot6)$$

The last term of (8·6) arises from the accumulation of the 'variation fund' with interest and benefit of survivorship and we are concerned with the relationship of the first two items.

If the policy-values on the two bases are to be the same at all durations, (8·6) must reduce to zero, that is to say:

$$(P'-P) \equiv [\mu'(t)-\mu(t)]\,[1-V(t)].$$

Thus the condition for equal policy-values is that the excess mortality shall be inversely proportional to the death strain at risk. Hence, also, if any given difference in the force of mortality leaves policy-values unchanged, any multiple of that difference, whether added to or subtracted from the normal force of mortality, will leave policy-values unchanged.

Assuming that $1-V(t)$ decreases continuously with duration from unity to zero, a constant increase of ϵ in the force of mortality leads to a negative second term of (8·6) which decreases numerically from ϵ to 0. Thus $(P'-P)$ is positive and lies between ϵ and 0, and the special policy-values will be less than the normal policy-values. A similar argument applies to a constant reduction in the force of mortality which, in the circumstances mentioned, leads to an increase in the policy-values.

Combining a constant increase of ϵ in the force of mortality with a constant decrease of the same amount in the force of interest, we see that the policy-values will be unchanged but the normal premium is increased by ϵ.

If the special mortality represents a proportionate increase in the normal force of mortality of k say, the second term of (8·6) is proportionate to $\mu(t)\,[1-V(t)]$. This term is positive (save for the special classes of assurance where $V(t)$ may exceed unity) and $(P'-P)$ is also positive and lies between the maximum and minimum values of $k\mu(t)\,[1-V(t)]$.

Where this expression is continuously increasing, the special policy-values will be larger than the normal; and where it is continuously decreasing, the special policy-values will be less than the normal. It is, of course, theoretically impossible for the expression to be increasing continuously throughout the period of assurance unless $\mu(t) \to \infty$ when $V(t) \to 1$.

When $k=1$ the force of mortality is assumed to be doubled, that is to say the special basis is effectively a joint-life assurance on two lives of equal age. Should the joint-life policy-values be larger (smaller) than the single life policy-values, the policy-values for any number of lives of equal age will also be larger (smaller) than the single life policy-values.

When $k = -1$ the special basis effectively assumes zero mortality, that is to say it becomes a sinking fund contract. This can be considered as a special limiting case of the series of assurances on 0, 1, 2, 3, ..., r, ..., lives of equal age.

Let us now consider the pure-premium policy-values when the special basis is the same as the normal basis except that it includes an allowance for withdrawals which is not made in the normal basis. Then (8·4) leads to

$$\frac{d}{dt}V'(t) - \frac{d}{dt}V(t) = (P' - P) + \nu'(t)\,[V(t) - R(t)] + [\delta(t) + \mu(t) + \nu'(t)]\,[V'(t) - V(t)]. \quad (8\cdot 7)$$

The last term of (8·7) arises from the accumulation of the 'variation fund' with interest and benefit of survivorship.

So long as the payment at withdrawal is within the amount of the valuation liability, the second term of (8·7) will be positive. $(P' - P)$ will be negative and will lie between the maximum and minimum values of $\nu'(t)\,[V(t) - R(t)]$. This expression probably decreases continuously because of the rapid fall in the rate of withdrawal and in these circumstances the special policy-values will exceed the normal policy-values.

If the special policy-values are to be equal to the normal policy-values the force of withdrawal must be inversely proportional to the excess of the valuation liability over the payment at withdrawal.

In practice a withdrawal soon after entry may entail a loss because of the unrequited balance of initial expenses. This loss may be analysed on similar lines to the foregoing discussion but we do not pursue it here because we have confined our remarks to pure-premium policy-values.

8·4. The valuation basis.

The considerations affecting the choice of the interest and the mortality basis have been dealt with generally in Chapter 6. There are only a few further considerations which we wish to emphasize here, but these remarks should be read in conjunction with the remarks in the next chapter about office premiums.

In the first place, since valuations are usually made with a view to the distribution of surplus from time to time, continuity is probably of more importance than a striving after extreme accuracy. Thus it is usually more important that the mortality basis should be a standard one, which may be maintained from valuation to valuation and which will give a basis of comparison with other similar funds, than that the mortality basis should represent precisely the expected experience. The mortality table chosen should represent the best and most appropriate estimate of the expected experience but extreme accuracy is unnecessary, especially in view of the large probable error in the other estimates of future experience.

Secondly, though a select table is, on the face of it, more appropriate than an aggregate or ultimate table, the use of a select table may complicate the calculations to an extent which may not be justified by the gain in accuracy. Where the valuation is made with a view to the distribution of surplus, the main consideration is the release of surplus at an appropriate rate, having regard to the method of distribution of surplus, and this may be achieved without the use of a select table of mortality.

Various approximations have been suggested to overcome the difficulty of valuing by a select table, though these approximations need not be studied for the purpose of the examinations. The greater part of the difference in the value of the liability computed on the basis of a select table of mortality arises from the use of select net premiums.

The student will notice that an aggregate table may be used for valuation, though it is regarded as unsuitable for the calculation of office premiums.

Since the course of experience cannot have been foreseen with any precision, it will usually happen that the assurances in force at any valuation will have been granted at varying times on differing assumptions regarding the rate of interest. The question arises whether these contracts should each be valued on the original premium basis or whether they should all be valued on the basis of one rate of interest considered to be appropriate in all the circumstances.

A similar question arises for the future. Where a definite trend is expected in the future rate of interest, should that trend be allowed for explicitly in the interest basis?

Both these questions are intimately related to the purpose for which the valuation is being made. Where the valuation is made with a view to the distribution of surplus the main consideration is the release of surplus at an appropriate rate having regard to the method of distribution of surplus. The method may require us to trace the contribution of each assurance to the total surplus and the use of the original premium basis is appropriate in such circumstances, subject to the provision of any contingency reserves necessary where a fall in the rate of interest may be expected. On the other hand where the uniform reversionary bonus system is in use it is more important to look to the future so that provision may be made for future bonuses, either explicitly in the valuation basis or implicitly in the margin between the rate of interest assumed in the valuation and that actually earned on the funds.

The remarks made about the use of a select table of mortality are also apposite to the use of a varying rate of interest. It would be a striving after an accuracy which is both unattainable and, normally, inappropriate to the problem in hand.

8·5. The provision for future expenses and profits.

The question of the proper provision to be made for future expenses and profits is one of the most intricate and interesting questions that has to be dealt with in the consideration of a valuation basis. It is a pity that, under the net premium method of valuation commonly used in Great Britain, the question has been side-tracked because the premium valued is not the actual premium payable but the pure premium on the valuation basis, and the provision for expenses and profits arises merely as a margin, the margin between the premiums valued and those actually payable. The following discussion is intended to deal with the subject fully, as far as possible from first principles.

It is suggested in Chapter 9 that the office premium should be computed from the pure premium by the addition of a loading for expenses and profits by a formula of the following type:

$$P' = \frac{1}{(1-p)} \cdot [P + I/\ddot{a} + c].$$

It is also suggested that c might consist of f for expenses and g for fluctuations and profits. Correspondingly it might be expected that the provision for future expenses and profits at the time of valuation would be the values of the loadings p and c. The initial expenses would have been spent but would be compensated for by the provision for their redemption in the premium scale. The whole of c might be expected to be reserved, not merely the part f attributable to expenses, because normally it is regarded as inadmissible to anticipate profits.

This approach to the problem is not the usual one for various reasons and not least because the provision in a valuation for future expenses should be related to the expenses of conducting the business at that time rather than to the provision originally made for expenses in the premium scales.

Since the division of expenses between the first year and the later years of assurance is to a considerable extent a matter of opinion rather than of strict accounting, it will be apparent that the determination of the proper allowance for future expenses in a valuation is a question of some considerable difficulty and, moreover, one which may lend itself to abuse in unscrupulous hands.

Should the provision for future expenses be merely that part of expenses which is represented in the premium formula by the loadings p and c, the implication would be that the part represented by initial expenses would be wholly borne by the new business. This may be reasonable, but it may serve as a warning not to over-estimate the allowance for initial expenses. It seems desirable to limit its amount to the actual out-of-pocket expenses of new business, which would be automatically reduced were the quantity of new business transacted to fall. Such remaining part of the expenses, which might in some circumstances be deemed to be initial expenses, may be regarded as a provision for the continuance of the fund, for which purpose an adequate flow of new business on proper terms is essential.

†This kind of approach to the problem leads directly to the gross premium method of valuation, which may be said to be the obvious and logical way of valuing non-participating policies, as it seeks to take account of the actual facts and to give due effect to them. To extend the principles to participating policies, it is merely necessary to remember that the office premiums include a bonus loading in addition to provision for expenses, and that if credit is to be taken for the office premiums less a percentage for expenses, then a *pro forma* liability of the present value of the future bonus that it is expected to declare must be set up. In other words, to the gross premium value of the policy should be added the present value of the future bonus on the same bases of interest and mortality. To the extent that some small margin of safety must in prudence be retained on the rates of interest and mortality used, a small profit may be expected from these sources, and it therefore arises that the full rate of expected bonus need not be treated as a specific liability nor need so full a percentage be thrown off the office premiums for expenses. This method is known as the bonus reserve method of valuation. It has many ardent advocates but also some hostile critics. It has been strongly attacked because it treats future bonus as a liability, in complete contradiction of the true nature of bonus; but on the other hand it has been stoutly defended for the way in which it keeps the true facts in view, in contrast to its chief competitor for favour, the net premium method, which keeps none of the facts in view, although making indirect provision for future bonus by the use of an artificially low rate of interest, as will be discussed in a later chapter.

It was partly the difficulty of determining the proper allowance for future expenses that led to the general adoption in Great Britain and elsewhere of the net premium method of valuation. Under this method the premium valued is the pure premium on the valuation basis and the provision for future expenses and profits is the difference between the premium valued and the office premium actually payable.

† Lochhead.

At this point it may be helpful to the student to refer again to the historical survey included in Chapter 2. In particular, the student should notice that there are two important questions which should be distinguished but are often confused, namely (*a*) what premium should be valued? and (*b*) should the provision for future bonus be explicit or arise from the margins in the valuation basis?

In the valuation of an office which is open for new business, continuity in practice is of considerable importance. Fluctuations in experience occur from time to time and if such fluctuations were to result in a complete recasting of the valuation system on each occasion a considerable amount of work would be entailed. The net premium method of valuation is a useful standard with just that possibility of continuity from valuation to valuation, provided that fluctuations in market values of assets can be ignored, or dealt with by investment reserves. The actuary who makes a net premium valuation does not attempt an accurate estimate of the valuation liability. The method depends upon a balance of conflicting tendencies which experience has confirmed as appropriate in suitable conditions. The net premium method may, perhaps, be best regarded as showing the changes in the amount of surplus from time to time and it is the changes that are of most importance when decisions have to be made about bonus policy.

8·6. The treatment of recently effected business.

Where it is both appropriate and convenient to value recently effected assurances on the basis assumed in the premium scales, there is no special valuation problem. This fortunate state of affairs rarely obtains in practice and we have to consider the special problems inherent in the valuation of such business.

Where the actual experience is more favourable than was assumed in the premium scales, a valuation upon a prospective basis corresponding to the actual experience will produce negative values of the liability at the early durations (unless the bonuses which that improved experience gives rise to are also brought into the valuation); that is to say, the recent assurances will be treated as an asset not a liability. Such negative values are generally regarded as inadmissible and should be excluded. The 'asset' is the value placed upon the expected future profit but it will be realized only if the assurance is maintained and may be further jeopardized should surrender values be paid in respect of such assurances.

Since the assured is not concerned with the value placed upon the assurance in the actuarial valuation, theoretically the problem could be suitably met by providing in the actuarial basis for the probability of withdrawal. This, however, would complicate the calculations and it seems better merely to exclude the negative values. The question of adequate provision for any surrender values that may be payable should also be considered but it may be sufficient to have regard to the composition of the surrender values as a whole in recent years so that any deficit on recently effected assurances may be offset to some extent at least by any valuation surplus that there may be from the surrender of earlier assurances.

The problem of negative values that we have been discussing is obviated by the use of the net premium method of valuation and this has been claimed as one of its advantages. Under this method of valuation the pure premiums that are valued are necessarily equivalent to the contractual benefits at the inception of the assurance. The method, however, gives rise to another problem which must now be discussed.

Under the net premium method of valuation the premium that is valued is the theoretical or pure premium for the contractual benefits on the basis of interest and mortality adopted for the valuation. Since this pure premium makes no allowance for the uneven incidence of expenses, the method must involve a strain in respect of new business.

Suppose that the provision for initial expenses in the premium scale was $I/\ddot{a}_x$. If the valuation is made by the net premium method on the same basis there will be an initial strain of I but in later years $I/\ddot{a}_x$ will fall into surplus each year. The value $I\ddot{a}_{x+t}/\ddot{a}_x$ is the unrequited balance of the initial expenses on the original premium basis. The initial expenses constitute a strain on surplus at the inception of the assurance which is recompensed in the later years of assurance by the provision for initial expenses in the premium scale.

Zillmer suggested that the commuted commission in respect of new business should be spread over the duration of the assurance in a manner corresponding to the provision in the premium scale but on the valuation basis. This method has regard to the actual strain on surplus arising from new business. It may have the disadvantage, more especially with whole-life assurances, that the deduction in the first year may exceed the valuation liability, so producing a negative value for the liability at the earliest durations unless some further adjustment is made.

Sprague suggested that the whole of the first year's premium should be regarded as having been absorbed by the cost of assurance (including both expenses and risk) and that the assurance should be treated as having been effected one year later at an age one year older than the true age at entry. This method obviates the danger of negative values but it departs from the principle of relating the allowance for initial expenses to the actual strain on surplus and, when applied to limited-premium and endowment assurances, may easily lead to extravagance. A compromise adopted in Canada is to limit the allowance to that under a corresponding whole-life assurance at the same age at entry.

Sprague's method, when applied to all classes of business, is known as the 'preliminary term' method of valuation. The various modifications of it, to limit the provision for initial expenses where the rate of premium is high, are known as 'modified preliminary term' methods. Sprague's method provides, for initial expenses, a sum equal to the excess of the office premium over the cost of the risk. This sum is assumed to be spread over the whole of the later premium payments and it has been suggested that it would be preferable to spread the same sum over a shorter period, for example 5 years.

A net premium valuation is usually made by an ultimate mortality table and not by a select table. The ultimate policy-values are less than the select policy-values and the deficiency may be regarded as some offset to initial expenses. When the duration exceeds the select period the difference between the select and ultimate policy-values is the present value of the difference between the corresponding pure premiums: this difference may, for certain mortality tables, be about equivalent to the unrequited balance of initial commission. This, however, is fortuitous and provides an illuminating example of the way in which the net premium method achieves a balance of contrary errors, producing an appropriate result although the facts are ignored.

It will be seen that the precise provision for initial expenses depends upon the age of the business. Where the assurances comprised in the fund are of sufficient average age, the fund should be able to bear the strain of a reasonable amount of new business without embarrassment. Where the fund comprises more recently effected business some—strictly limited—adjustment of the liability by the net premium method will be appropriate.

Both the methods of Zillmer and Sprague have the disadvantage that the deduction from the valuation liability is permanent. Since the problem is one which tends to disappear as the business ages it would be better in some respects to base the allowance in some way on the duration of the business as a whole, so that the allowance would automatically disappear as the need for it got less. This could be effected, for example, by making an allowance in the aggregate based on the average value of the total valuation liability compared with the total sums assured. No doubt, however, such a practice would give rise to other difficulties particularly with regard to determining the precise amount of the liability under individual assurances.

8·7. Valuations of funds in deficiency.

An interesting question that needs some care is the proper allowance for expenses, where past extravagance has weakened the fund so that a normal valuation cannot be made. Here the recommendations of the actuary with regard to the actuarial basis cannot be separated from his recommendations of remedial measures, the principal one of which must be the ending of the extravagance. We will assume for the purposes of this discussion that the deficiency is caused only by the extravagance and not by investment losses nor by inadequate actuarial bases apart from expenses.

For a solvency basis we may turn for a definition to the draft Insurance Undertakings Bill, Seventh Schedule, Part I:

> The liabilities of an insurer in respect of current contracts effected in the course of life business...shall...be calculated upon the basis of the rate of interest and rates of mortality...upon which...the like calculation could properly be based if the obligations under the contracts were to be fulfilled as and when they became due, taking into account the premiums which would be received under the contracts and such sum as...is the lowest that could properly be assumed in respect of the office expenses and other charges which would be incurred in respect of the contracts.

Thus the allowance for expenses in a solvency valuation would be merely for those expenses incidental to the fund running off as a closed fund. Clearly this type of basis is inappropriate for a fund which is to remain open for new business. We may, as has been stated earlier, divide the expenses into three parts: (*a*) the minimum expenses assuming the fund to be closed, (*b*) the additional general expenses if the fund is to continue open for new business, and (*c*) the initial expenses attributable to the new business. The valuation for a continuing fund cannot be regarded as satisfactory unless provision is made for both (*a*) and (*b*).

The first step, after recommendations for the ending of the extravagance, is to investigate the premium rates for new business. If, as is probable, the premium scale is inadequate the scale must be put upon an adequate basis; no juggling with the valuation basis can avoid this necessity. The new business can then be accepted without affecting the existing business.

The next step is to value the existing business, making allowance for items (*a*) and (*b*) of the expenses, which are the necessary expenses for the business to operate as a continuing business. It may be found that this valuation reveals a deficiency, whereas the solvency valuation allowing for item (*a*) alone would have shown a surplus. It is extremely unlikely that such a position would obtain in Great Britain, but the problem is a practical one in, for example, India where life assurance is in its infancy. It seems to us that an adequate actuarial basis should be regarded as a necessary condition for a fund to remain open for new business and that the minimum standard should be a valuation allowing for items (*a*) and (*b*) of the expenses, after eliminating extravagance. This standard might be attained either by a further pruning of expenses or by other measures.

†8·8. The origin and nature of surplus.

The valuation of a fund in deficiency is of a special character. The normal problem is the valuation of a fund with a view to the distribution of surplus. This will be assumed in the remainder of the book, but before we turn to such problems we must consider the origin and nature of surplus.

The following elementary facts will clear the ground for our discussion and will assist the student to preserve a proper perspective:

(*a*) Broadly speaking, profit originates because the premiums charged prove to be more than sufficient for the cost of assurance, including both risk and expenses, as determined by the experience of the fund.

(*b*) Surplus arises primarily as a cash sum and is the difference between the amount of the life assurance fund and the amount of the valuation liability. Surplus may or may not be divisible as bonus, depending on the circumstances at the time, and since its amount depends upon the valuation basis the two must be considered together in problems of the equitable distribution of surplus.

(*c*) Investment and contingency reserves and the excess (if any) of the market values over the book values of the assets constitute additional reserves for the security of policyholders: but the excess over book values should not be treated as additional surplus because some alteration in the valuation basis might be required, should the margin be taken into account.

(*d*) When a bonus is declared, a certain part of the surplus is converted into a definite liability to the policyholders. Improper bonus allotment may transform a surplus into a deficiency, though the effect may not be immediately apparent where the valuation basis is inadequate.

† This section closely follows Lochhead.

(*e*) A life insurance institution (unless it be a closed fund) does not exist solely for the benefit of the existing assured. It must be considered as a continuing business which should be treated as a trust for posterity as it has been a heritage from the past. The existence of shareholders, where the institution is proprietary, does not affect this argument though the claims of policyholders, whose assurances may mature by the death or the survival of the life assured, should be carefully weighed against the claims of shareholders, whose stake in the business may be treated as having a continuing existence though they themselves may not survive.

(*f*) It has been said†

> The value of life assurance depends entirely upon the absolute and permanent stability of the corporation selling it.

The security of the fund must be the primary aim; questions of equity and other refinements must be subordinate to that aim. As a consequence it has become the traditional policy to face a loss immediately but to reveal a profit slowly.

It has been mentioned above that surplus is the difference between the life assurance fund and the valuation liability. It is usual to look upon surplus as a function of the valuation liability only in considering its amount and its proper apportionment, but it can also be greatly influenced by the treatment of the assets constituting the fund. This fact should always be kept in mind. The established practice of British offices is to write down security values when prudence dictates such a course and only in very exceptional circumstances to take credit for capital appreciation apart from actual realized profits on maturity or sale. The justification for this procedure lies in the necessity for creating a reserve against adverse movements in the value of the assets, so endeavouring to secure that the life assurance fund shall be represented by assets of equal value. From this point of view the treatment of the assets arises from a distinct consideration and should be kept apart from the question of what is the proper value of the liabilities. The two ideas cannot, however, be kept entirely in

† See Guthrie's remarks, *T.F.A.* vol. XII, p. 77.

watertight compartments and, in all reading bearing on the subjects under discussion, the possible influence of the treatment of the assets must be kept in mind.

Reference has been made to surplus and to profit and it is important to have clear ideas of what is intended by these terms. Surplus is dependent on the amount of the life assurance fund and the valuation liability and, granting that any special treatment of the assets must be looked upon as investment reserve, it may be said that surplus is a function of the valuation basis.

Profit, on the other hand, is the result of charging a higher premium than the subsequent experience merits. It is therefore independent of the valuation basis but, apart from saying this, it is extremely difficult to say what it is. If a fund consisting of certain policies issued at certain ample rates of premium were allowed to run off as a closed fund, then the balance remaining after the last claim had emerged would represent the accumulated profit of the fund. To be able to say what is the present value of the potential profit when the fund commences, it would be necessary to have precise knowledge of the future experience of the fund. Only an estimate can be made of this. At any intermediate point of time a valuation on bases similar to those on which the premiums were fixed would show the accumulated profit to date of valuation, provided either that no distribution of profit had been previously made or that it had been distributed in cash.

Consideration will show that this 'accumulated profit' (whether it relates to the period since business was commenced or only to the last valuation period) is not necessarily the best measure of what can properly be distributed to policyholders. It will be observed that the valuation would have to be made on the bases underlying the office premiums and, apart from other objections, the persistent use of such bases in defiance of changing experience might result in the emergence of a 'negative profit', i.e. a loss. As it is impracticable to increase premiums, this deficit would have to be met by a reduction in the sum assured and this is the logical outcome of the attempt to distribute the real profit. The sum assured must be secured against reduction and so it may be imperative to retain some of the profit earned against possible adversity. This is accomplished by strengthening the valuation basis when the necessity for such a course becomes apparent (or gradually over a period to avoid violent upheaval), but as soon as this is done the valuation ceases to reveal true profit but valuation surplus instead.

No mention has here been made of the fact that specific bonus loadings may be contained in the premium scale, because it is important to realize that the necessity for adequate reserves exists independently of provision for any bonus system which may be superimposed on the main contract.

*8·9. The mathematical analysis of experience.

The student needs to have a firm grasp of the relationship between the actual experience of a fund and the mathematical assumptions made in the computation of premiums and of valuation liability. This section is inserted for those students who prefer a mathematical approach but it is not necessary to study this section in detail.

Suppose that symbols with a double accent represent the actual experience, symbols with a single accent represent the office premium basis, and unaccented symbols represent the valuation basis, which is assumed to be a net premium valuation. Consider a fund which consists of assurances all of the same type, effected at the same time and at the same age and assume for simplicity that all functions are to be taken on a continuous basis.

The revenue account of such a fund may be stylized in the following form, where the symbols have similar meanings to those in § 8·3 and $F(t)$ represents the fund at time t.

$$\frac{d}{dt}F''(t)=\delta''(t)\,F''(t) + S.l''(t)/l''(0)\,\{P'-\mu''(t)-\nu''(t)\,R(t)-p''\,P'-c''\}. \quad (8\cdot8)$$

Now the fund, $F''(t)$, must consist of the valuation liability in respect of the survivors *plus* the surplus, say $Z''(t)$. Whence

$$F''(t)=Z''(t)+S.l''(t)/l''(0)\times V(t)$$

and

$$\frac{d}{dt}F''(t)=\frac{d}{dt}Z''(t)+S.l''(t)/l''(0)\left\{\frac{d}{dt}V(t)-[\mu''(t)+\nu''(t)]\,V(t)\right\}. \quad (8\cdot9)$$

Substituting in (8·8) we have, after rearrangement,

$$\frac{d}{dt} Z''(t) = \delta''(t)\, Z''(t)$$
$$+ S.l''(t)/l''(0) \Big\{ \delta''(t)\, V(t) + [(1-p'')P' - c''] - \mu''(t) - \nu''(t)\, R(t)$$
$$+ [\mu''(t) + \nu''(t)]\, V(t) - \frac{d}{dt} V(t) \Big\}. \qquad (8\cdot 10)$$

We may now substitute in (8·10) the expression

$$\frac{d}{dt} V(t) = \delta(t)\, V(t) + P - \mu(t) + \mu(t)\, V(t).$$

Thus

$$\frac{d}{dt} Z''(t) = \delta''(t)\, Z''(t)$$
$$+ S.l''(t)/l''(0) \{ [\delta''(t) - \delta(t)]\, V(t) + [(1-p'')P' - P - c'']$$
$$- [\mu''(t) - \mu(t)] - \nu''(t)\, R(t) + [\mu''(t) - \mu(t) + \nu''(t)]\, V(t) \}. \quad (8\cdot 11)$$

This equation is basic to the analysis of surplus, showing how it is built up from the several items.

Now if the differential equation (8·10) be integrated from $t=0$ to t the result, $Z''(t)$, is evidently the accumulated surplus to time t. At the limit of life or at the expiry of the period of the assurance the remaining balance of the fund after paying claims then due must be the accumulated surplus. Hence, for n-year assurances,

$$F''(n) = Z''(n) + S.l''(n)/l''(0) \times V(n), \qquad (8\cdot 12)$$

where $V(n)$ equals unity or zero according to the type of assurance. Looking back to (8·8), it is clear that the ultimate surplus, $Z''(n)$, is independent of the valuation basis though the intervening values of $Z''(t)$ will, of course, be affected by the valuation basis. This is referred to again in the next section.

The student should notice that the interest yield has been defined in relation to the amount of the fund. Fluctuations in market values have no mathematical significance and do not affect the calculations until securities have to be realized to pay claims or other outgo.

So far we have ignored the element of bonus. The surplus $Z''(t)$ thus comprises: (*a*) the accumulated value of bonus paid away before duration t; (*b*) the value at duration t of bonus allocated but not paid away; (*c*) unallocated surplus. Where a cash bonus system is in operation the second item will usually be negligible. Where a reversionary bonus system is used the second item will represent the value at duration t of the bonuses declared up to that time in respect of those then surviving.

The value of the unallocated surplus obviously depends upon the valuation basis. If the valuation liability were to be computed on a basis as close to the experience as possible, the unallocated surplus would comprise the whole of the surplus carried forward at duration t and practically the only source of surplus thereafter would be the difference between the pure premium valued and the office premium payable, less the actual expenses. This was the type of valuation advocated by Bailey in 1878. This is not the usual practice. Normally, the valuation basis contains considerable margins so that in fact only part of the real surplus is disclosed by the valuation.

Though the published valuation is usually upon a conservative basis the type of calculation we have been discussing is sometimes useful for testing the fairness of the bonus distribution. Thus, in America the bonuses may be tested by the computation of 'asset-shares'. This computation is essentially of the nature of an analysis of the type of differential equation (8·10) though of course the asset-shares are not computed in that form.

The unallocated surplus should tend to zero at the expiry of the period of assurance and this might provide a mathematical definition of equity in bonus distribution. We have, however, over-simplified the problem because in practice a fund consists of many different types of assurance and generations of assured lives. It is only possible to do rough justice, having regard to the main sources of surplus in the different sections of the business.

It is also clear that the accumulated amount of the aggregate surplus for a particular class of assurance and generation of assured lives is represented by $Z''(n)$. This amount may be spread over the n-year period in many different ways each of which, in suitable circumstances, may be considered to be fair. Thus, one type of reversionary bonus is not necessarily more fair than another type; the surrounding circumstances must be considered. The student should notice (*a*) that the valuation basis and the system of distribution of surplus must be considered together, and (*b*) that, where the system requires the distortion of surplus, the more marked the distortion the more difficult it is to maintain equity between the different classes and generations.

8·10. The emergence of surplus.

Were the experience of the fund to be foreknown, the premium P'' required on the basis of that experience could be computed to provide the precise cost of the assurance, including both risk and expenses. The excess of the actual premium, P', over the required premium, P'', would represent the profit. The accumulated amount of these items of profit must equal $Z''(n)$ as defined in §8·9 and is independent of the valuation basis. Should the liabilities be valued on the basis of the actual experience the surplus would be uniformly released over the duration of the assurances as loading surplus. Should the liabilities be valued on any other basis the apparent sources of surplus would be changed and the rate of release of surplus would be affected, save in the exceptional circumstances discussed by Lidstone for equal policy-values.

It is important to grasp this fact. The valuation basis may have to be modified from time to time but whether the modification be small or large it cannot affect the real profit, only the rate of release of surplus. Thus the choice of valuation basis is intimately linked to the rate of release of surplus which is considered appropriate for the particular system by which surplus is distributed.

Since the fund usually comprises a mass of assurances of different types and durations in force, the choice of valuation basis may affect the share of surplus attributed to the various sections of the business, though the real profit of the fund as a whole would be unaffected. While, therefore, it may be deemed necessary to strengthen the reserves for particular reasons, it is also necessary to guard against excessive caution. Either excessive caution or unjustified optimism may lead to inequitable results.

Changes in the experience, however abrupt, need cause no embarrassment so long as they are foreknown. The value of $Z''(n)$ evidently shows the final effect of such changes and the valuation basis can be so arranged as to produce sufficient surplus as may be required from time to time to provide bonuses at the appropriate rates. A numerical illustration of this was given by E. H. Lever at the Ninth International Congress of Actuaries. Such a happy state of affairs does not exist in the real world. Changes in experience occur, sometimes gradually, sometimes abruptly, but generally in unexpected ways. We have to provide for such changes to the best of our ability and Lever's work shows that minor fluctuations may be smoothed out.

Suppose that such a change in experience has occurred. So long as the valuation basis remains unchanged the effect of the altered basis of experience will appear in the changes in the sources of surplus shown by differential equation (8·11). This might be suitable where the experience is favourable and it is not desired to anticipate profit. Where, however, the experience is unfavourable the loss arising from that unfavourable experience should be faced at once and not left to appear as a deficiency or strain on the surplus from time to time.

The loss arising from unfavourable experience may be faced by an alteration in valuation basis. Suppose for simplicity that the rate of interest earned on the funds is suddenly reduced at time τ but that, in other respects, the experience conforms to the valuation basis. The differential equation (8·11) shows how the reduction in the rate of interest will appear as a negative item of surplus, that is to say a deficiency from time to time. If the valuation basis is altered to conform to the reduced rate of interest, the valuation liability will be increased, producing an equivalent strain on surplus at time τ. Thereafter there will be no deficiency on interest in the differential equation but there will be a deficiency on loading, because the new valuation basis will, under the net premium method, require a higher pure premium to be valued.

If the loss is to be completely faced at time τ it is necessary both to alter the valuation basis to conform to the reduced rate of interest and to add to the valuation liability so found the value of the difference between the two pure premiums, that is to say, it is necessary to depart from the strict net premium method of valuation and, effectively, to value the premium on the original basis, not the premium on the new basis.

It is important to keep clearly in mind the different procedures that we have been discussing. There may be occasions when it is appropriate to maintain the valuation basis in the face of changing experience, leaving that experience to be reflected in the emerging surplus; on the other hand there may be occasions when it is appropriate to alter the valuation basis and even to depart from the net premium method, for example in order to face the loss arising from an adverse trend in experience. The decision about the change in valuation basis would have to take account of the circumstances at the time and the security of the fund as a whole would have to be considered, as well as questions of equity between different classes and generations of policyholders.

8·11. Influence of the bonus system upon the valuation basis.

If it were possible to foresee the future experience it would be possible to distribute the whole of the surplus as it arises from time to time and there would then be no 'problem' in the distribution of surplus. Since, however, the future experience cannot be foreseen accurately, it is not practicable to distribute the whole of the apparent surplus. The security of the fund as a whole must come first and, generally speaking, an adequate valuation basis has been regarded as of primary importance, the question of equity in bonus distribution being regarded as subordinate to that primary aim.

If, too, we were dealing with closed funds, each batch of assurances constituting a self-contained unit, the problem would be simplified, because an inequity at one distribution could be made good to the survivors at a later distribution. Where different generations are combined in one fund it may not be possible to correct an inequity in that way.

In a fund which is continually open for new business there must be some carry-forward of surplus, whether explicit or implicit in the valuation liability, which will serve to maintain the stability and credit of the fund. As Morgan said:

> It is, I believe, impossible to devise any method of giving each member his exact share of the profits of a Society which is always open for the admission of an unlimited number of persons to partake of them.

These facts form the background to the development of life assurance. Attention has been focused more perhaps upon the other elements in a valuation than upon the valuation rate of interest, but the student should not be misled by this into thinking that those other elements are the more significant. The original scale of premiums scientifically computed for life assurance as we know it today was computed in 1756 upon the assumption of a rate of interest of 3% per annum. The rate of interest actually earned was considerably higher than that and there was also a large margin in the mortality; it was natural, however, to make the same assumptions in the valuation basis. As other assurance funds became established a similar caution might be displayed, and where less cautious counsels prevailed the original example provided a standard towards which others would wish to strive.

Technical progress has in some degree lessened the importance of the elements other than the rate of interest, because it has become possible to make estimates of those other elements with some degree of confidence. The course of the rate of interest, complicated now by the further element of the rate of income tax at its present high level, remains impossible to foresee for even a short period ahead and this element in the computations must be treated with as much caution as in the past.

Now from what has been said it will be evident that the conservative practices adopted with a view to the welfare of the business of life assurance must have delayed the emergence of surplus. When it became possible to distribute surplus as bonus it was generally recognized that the earlier assurances were entitled to a larger share of the divisible surplus than the more recently effected assurances. It was, perhaps, easier to say that the earlier assurances should have a larger share of the divisible surplus, than it was to devise a suitable system of distribution of surplus. From the earliest times the problem was tackled in two main ways.

First, there were those who, recognizing that only rough justice could be done, decided to allocate some form of reversionary bonus, preferring its simplicity to the complications of more refined methods.

Secondly, there were those who attempted in some way or other to relate the surplus distributed to the sources from which it was derived. The early methods of this kind did not attempt more than rough justice, though some of these methods have survived and are still in use. The method attempts a precision which other methods cannot presume to attain.

In Great Britain it began to be recognized that a uniform reversionary bonus system gave just such an increasing share of the surplus to the earlier assurances as was required. The share of surplus represented by the value of the reversionary bonus allotted also seemed to be roughly what might be considered equitable, especially when the premium scales were suitable for that type of distribution and the margin between the valuation rate of interest and the yield of the funds was sufficiently wide to provide for the emergence of surplus at about the right rate.

When suitable mortality tables became available it was found that they could properly be used for the valuation of existing business, provided (*a*) that only the pure premium on the valuation basis was valued, and (*b*) that the same conservative view of the rate of interest was maintained in the valuation basis. In the circumstances in which it came to be used the method had the advantages of being more in touch with reality than earlier methods so far as mortality was concerned, and of making automatically a proper provision for future expenses. Later, when it became the custom to pay initial commission, the longer established offices were able to bear the strain without adjustment of the valuation basis.

From what has been said it might seem that this section should have been called 'Influence of the valuation basis upon the bonus system'. This is not so. Rather have the twin problems of valuation and surplus developed side by side and the ideas we have been discussing have crystallized over a long period of time.

The modern view, we think, would be that the system of distribution of bonus should be fitted to the premium scale and to the methods and bases of valuation. For various practical reasons bonuses may be desired of a certain type or on a certain scale and the premium and valuation bases must be chosen correspondingly.

BIBLIOGRAPHY

S. G. WARNER (1902). Some notes on the net premium method of valuation, as affected by recent tendencies and developments. *J.I.A.* vol. XXXVII, p. 57.

This is the classic paper on the net premium method and refers to the methods of Zillmer and Sprague.

G. J. LIDSTONE (1905). Changes in pure premium policy-values consequent upon variations in the rate of interest or the rate of mortality, or upon the introduction of the rate of discontinuance. *J.I.A.* vol. XXXIX, p. 209.

C. R. V. COUTTS (1907). Bonus reserve valuations. *J.I.A.* vol. XLII, p. 161.

E. H. LEVER (1930). Fluctuations in life office profits (their origin and method of treatment). *Trans. Ninth Int. Congress*, Stockholm, vol. I, p. 181.

W. P. ELDERTON (1931). Valuations in modern conditions. *J.I.A.* vol. LXII, p. 62.

R. K. LOCHHEAD (1932). *Valuation and surplus.* Cambridge University Press.

T. R. SUTTIE (1944). The treatment of appreciation or depreciation in the assets of a life assurance fund. *J.I.A.* vol. LXXII, p. 203.

E. ZWINGGI (1948). The principle of equivalence, central principle of valuation. *Proc. Cent. Assembly Inst. Act.* vol. II, p. 208.

K. G. HAGSTROEM (1948). Hypothetical expenses adopted in valuations in Sweden. *Proc. Cent. Assembly Inst. Act.* vol. II, p. 219.

PART II

'ORDINARY' LIFE ASSURANCE BUSINESS

CHAPTER 9

OFFICE PREMIUMS

The preceding chapters have dealt with the background to the operation of a life assurance fund and we now turn to the application of that knowledge to the actuarial calculations required for the purposes of such a fund.

It should be remembered that each fund presents a unique problem. What is applicable to one fund is not necessarily applicable to another. We can only suggest suitable lines of approach. There are considerable variations between the experiences of such funds and the bases and formulae that we suggest should be understood as indicating what we consider suitable in average circumstances for British offices transacting 'ordinary' life assurance in Great Britain.

The basic elements have been reviewed in Chapter 6 and in this chapter we deal with those elements in relation to the calculation of premiums.

9·1. Mortality.

The mortality table should be derived from the actual experience of the individual fund or from the combined experience of similar funds. A select table should normally be used for the calculation of office premiums, though sometimes it may be necessary to adopt an ultimate table. An aggregate table is unsuitable except in special circumstances.

In Great Britain we are fortunate in having a range of tables based on the combined experience of British assured lives and annuitants and one of these standard tables should normally be used for the calculation of premiums.

The latest table derived from the experience amongst assured lives is the A 1924–29 table with the Light and Heavy tables also produced in connexion with that experience. These tables are somewhat out-of-date but until tables based on recent experience are made, the improvement in vitality that has occurred and may be expected to continue may be regarded as a provision for fluctuations and profits.

The latest tables derived from the experience amongst annuitants are the *a* (*f*) and *a* (*m*) tables. They were derived from the experience in 1900–20 but the rates were extrapolated to approximate to what might have been expected amongst annuitants who bought annuities in 1925.

The experience amongst annuitants since 1920 is conflicting and difficult to interpret, but it seems likely that a new downward trend may have commenced since the war 1939–45 and a deduction† of, say, one to two years should be made from the age by the *a* (*f*) and *a* (*m*) tables. These tables were based on immediate annuities and do not necessarily apply to deferred annuities. On the other hand, deferred annuities do not commence to be payable until many years after the date when the contract is made, and there seems some grounds for regarding the pension date, not the entry date, as the 'date of purchase' when considering what the mortality experience may be.

The *a* (*f*) and *a* (*m*) tables were derived from the mortality experience of immediate annuities and a peculiarity of the table is that the rates of mortality at the younger ages are rather high. The tables are not suitable for estimating the cost of survival benefits on young lives such as are met with in deferred annuity business.

9·2. Interest.

A fundamental question is whether the yield of the existing investments of the fund should be taken into account or whether the rate of interest obtainable on new investments only should be considered when calculating premiums for new business. This question has been discussed in § 6·3.

The spread of the yield of new investments is illustrated in Table 9·1 by figures taken from the Actuaries' Investment Index.

† The suggested deduction is arbitrary and does not accurately reflect the trend of the experience. The book was written before the new annuity experience became available.

The spread is as important as the actual level of interest rates though both will vary from time to time. It is suggested that the student should insert the current figures in the final column which has been left blank for the purpose.

TABLE 9·1

Actuaries' Investment Index

Class of security	Approximate yield per cent at the end of year		
	1948	1949	
2½% Consols	3·14	3·56	
Home Corporations	3·23	3·76	
Debentures	3·74	4·10	
Preference shares	3·98	4·90	
Ordinary stocks and shares:			
(*a*) Banks	3·71	4·15	
(*b*) Insurance	3·62	4·01	
(*c*) Investment trusts	4·33	5·24	
(*d*) Industrials	4·74	5·58	

We may notice that the dated Government stocks would have yielded less than 2½% Consols; also that greater weight should normally be given to the top half of the table because the proportion invested in ordinary shares is usually comparatively small.

It is difficult to give comparative figures for investments not in the Actuaries' Investment Index. As a rough indication for comparative purposes we may put the yield of well secured ground rents without an early reversion to rack rent, at about that of good class debentures. Mortgages might yield up to, say, ½% more with reasonable security and property would probably yield 1–2% more, depending upon the nature of the investment. The relationship may vary from time to time because the property market does not necessarily move in step with the stock market which, generally speaking, is more susceptible to day-to-day influences on values.

The yields must be reduced somewhat to allow for costs of investment. As a rough guide for examination purposes it seems reasonable to take the yield of long-term British Government securities as representing a suitable 'safe' rate of interest, before allowing for tax, for the purpose of calculating premiums for non-participating assurances and annuities. There is less need to keep a margin in the rate of interest assumed for participating business because the bonus loading provides a buffer against adverse experience: a somewhat higher rate of interest, for example $\frac{1}{2}\%$ higher, might be assumed, depending on the spread of the investments.

Income tax must be provided for where the fund is taxed upon interest less expenses. The present rate of income tax for life assurance funds is 7*s.* 6*d.* in £ which is considerably below the standard rate of income tax and a provision for income tax at the rate of 7*s.* 6*d.* in £ seems suitable for examination purposes. Thus, either the rate of interest and the loading for management expenses may be both multiplied by ·625, or the rate of interest may be reduced by the effective rate of tax which would depend upon the relationship of the expenses to the interest income. (See § 6·3.)

The rate of interest suggested for participating assurances assumes that an attempt is to be made to keep as closely as possible to the facts. Though we think it is desirable to make this attempt, it may not be considered proper actually to use such a basis for calculating tables of premiums because the assumptions may soon become obsolete, and the tables would be constructed on a basis which could reasonably be expected to be maintained for some time so far as could be foreseen. In such circumstances specimen values of the premiums required would be computed on a basis as close to the facts as possible, and then a scale would be fitted to those specimen values on a more conservative basis as regards interest, and with a smaller provision for bonus.

9·3. Loading.

The purpose of the loading is to provide for commission and expenses of management and either a margin for fluctuations and profits, or a specific loading for bonus where the assurance is to participate in profits.

It is a common practice to treat both the initial expenses and the general expenses of management as being proportionate to the sum assured and the renewal expenses as being proportionate to the premium. This treatment of the initial expenses seems appropriate where the initial commission is itself proportionate to the sum assured: in other cases the practice may be less appropriate but may be adopted for convenience. Renewal commission is commonly based on the premium and a small amount should be added for other renewal expenses. There may be more difference of opinion about the allocation of the general expenses of management but it appears to be the modern tendency to treat them in the manner suggested.

Thus for whole life and endowment assurances we reach a formula of the general form

$$P' = \frac{1}{(1-p)}[P + I/\ddot{a} + c]. \tag{9·1}$$

In this formula, I is usually referred to as the 'initial loading', c as the 'constant', and p as the 'percentage'. The terms do not indicate that I and c are proportionate to the sum assured, and p to the gross premium, but they are traditional, and are adopted here. The student should notice that the constant and percentage loadings are made in respect of the first year's premium as well as of subsequent premiums, the total amount provided by the formula for initial expenditure being therefore $(I+c)$ per unit of the sum assured, plus p per unit of the gross premium.

The 'constant' c would provide for the general expenses of management and for the margin for fluctuations and profits. Where the assurance participates in profits the latter item would be omitted and P would include the provision for bonus.

The use of formula (9·1) for limited-premium assurances would imply that c is no longer required after premiums have ceased. It is probable that some part, say c_0, will be required and the balance c_1 will not be required. The formula then becomes:

$$_nP' = \frac{1}{(1-p)}[{}_nP + I/\ddot{a}\,(n) + c_1 + c_0\ddot{a}/\ddot{a}\,(n)], \tag{9·2}$$

where $\ddot{a}\,(n)$ is the temporary annuity value.

The complication may be avoided by commuting the whole of the office premium at a somewhat higher rate of interest than is assumed in the premium calculations. The problem is particularly acute when only one premium is to be paid, that is to say a single premium policy. Other considerations arise, such as the rate of interest, since the money has to be invested at once. Beyond stating the problem little useful guidance can be given here.

We may now consider the relationship of the provision for expenses in the premium formula to the actual expenses shown in the accounts. Suppose the premium formula is

$$P' = \frac{1}{(1-p)}[P + I/\ddot{a} + c],$$

and suppose that c consists of f for expenses and g for fluctuations and profits. It will be apparent that we can compute the total provision for expenses by the premium formula from the total sums assured and premium income from existing business and the amount of the new business. This computation is unlikely to give a figure comparable with the actual expenses, for example, because (*a*) the existing business may have been written on different terms from those considered suitable for new business, and (*b*) both the existing and the new business will comprise many different types and the premium formula may not be applicable to some of them.

The crude ratio of expenses to premium income, after making such adjustments, will depend on the proportion of new business to existing business. A few numerical tests will convince the student that the total expenses to be provided for may be divided in different proportions between the initial and the continuing expenses without greatly affecting the premium scale. When, however, we turn to consider the valuation of the liabilities and the computation of surrender values the relative amount of the initial expenses will be the determining factor in the values placed on the assurance in its early years. It is important that the provision for expenses should be appropriately apportioned between the initial and the continuing expenses.

The values to be placed on I, c and p would vary widely from office to office but for examination purposes the values suggested by Gunlake still seem suitable, namely

$$I = \cdot 03,$$

$$c = \cdot 0025,$$

$$p = \cdot 04.$$

The values are *before* deduction of income tax recovery.

The values of the various items of loading are affected, amongst other things, by the average size of the assurances as we have explained in § 6·4. It is a question of policy whether the larger assurances should be encouraged by reducing the rate of premium as the size of the assurance increases. A common custom is to quote different rates for, say, three separate ranges of sum assured. Thus the rates for assurances up to £500 might be more than those for assurances from £500 to £2,000 which might themselves be more than those for assurances over £2,000. It is doubtful whether it would be practicable to make any further reduction in the rate per cent for very large assurances, because the incidence of expenses may be affected by the necessity to cede part of the risk to other offices and possibly also by higher commissions: and it seems desirable to keep a larger margin for fluctuations because of the smallness of the numbers of such large assurances.

The amount of the variation according to size of assurance could be determined from the analysis of expenses. Such a course would not be convenient, because it might entail separate scales of premium for each range of sums assured. It is preferable, and customary, to make a more or less arbitrary adjustment to the rate of premium per cent. For example, the rates of premium per cent in the middle range of sums assured might be 2*s*. less than those in the lowest range and 2*s*. more than those in the highest range.

9·4. Assurances participating in profits.

The basis for the computation of premium rates for participating assurances depends to some extent on the purpose for which the computation is being made. The problem of computing a scale of premium rates for a new fund or a new participating class is obviously different from the problem of computing such rates for new entrants to an existing fund: the latter problem may also be distinguished from that of testing the suitability of such a scale in the consideration of the equitable distribution of surplus.

Taking the last problem first, we may notice that each element in the calculation should be estimated as nearly as possible to the expected future experience so that we may obtain a clear view of the prospective position. We may rely upon the bonus loading to provide a buffer against adverse experience and the margin for fluctuations and profits is not required.

The premium scale should include a provision for bonus of the type expected to be declared. This provision should also include an allowance for the proprietors' share of profits where the fund is proprietary. Thus if the proprietors are entitled to one-tenth of the profits the provision for bonus should—theoretically—be increased by one-ninth to provide their share. On the other hand, part of the bonus comes from miscellaneous sources of profit, including profits from other classes of business. That part of the bonus must be excluded when computing the premium scale, unless it is desired to provide for the maintenance of the bonus without the aid of such sources of profit. It may happen that the miscellaneous profits can be equated to the proprietors' share of profits, and both would then be ignored.

Such a basis as we have outlined would be suitable for testing a premium scale in the course of considering the equitable distribution of surplus, but it would not necessarily be suitable for computing a new scale of premium rates. In the first place a scale of rates for participating assurances is rarely considered in isolation. More usually it has to be considered in conjunction with corresponding scales for non-participating assurances and also, perhaps, with scales for assurances with different participating rights. Secondly, it is customary with participating assurances to maintain a given scale of rates in force for as long as possible, leaving changes in the actual experience to be reflected in the bonuses allotted from time to time. This course is convenient and tends to simplify problems of equity between successive generations of policyholders.

Thus it comes about that the scale of rates for participating assurances often remains on an out-of-date basis apparently unrelated to current experience.

From the point of view of consistency between premium rates for participating and non-participating assurances it would appear to be simplest to compute the former by adding to the latter a bonus loading to provide a bonus of the right type but necessarily at a lower rate than that expected to be declared. It is necessary to exclude from the expected bonus, both that part expected to be provided out of miscellaneous sources and that part expected to be provided by the margins in the elements of the premium basis. These two parts might provide as much as half of the expected bonus, leaving only half to be provided for in the bonus loading.

In modern times the element of the premium basis which has been most susceptible to fluctuation is the interest element, and another point of view is provided by excluding this element altogether. As has been mentioned in § 6·3 the average scale of rates for participating assurances in Great Britain does not differ much from a scale based on $i=0$, both bonus and interest being ignored. Such a scale may have the advantage of permanency in varying circumstances and might be suitable for whole-life and long-term endowment assurances. We think that the premium scale for short-term endowment assurances on such a basis would need some adjustment where a uniform reversionary bonus system is in operation.

Continental actuaries have introduced the two terms 'basis of the first order' and 'basis of the second order' which are helpful in clarifying our ideas when dealing with problems of premium rates, valuation and distribution of surplus. A basis of the first order is one which is suitable for the computation of office premiums for participating assurances because the basis provides adequate margins compared with the expected experience. A basis of the second order is one which is as close to the actual experience as may be estimated and which is thus suitable for the consideration of problems of distribution of surplus.

American actuaries tend to approach the problem of computing scales of premium rates for participating assurances from yet another point of view because for them the problem is conditioned by the contribution method used for the distribution of surplus. It is customary in America to compute the rates for participating assurances on very broad lines without attempting any accurate assessment of experience. There can be little objection to this practice because the actual experience is reflected in the cash bonuses (or dividends as they are termed) which are calculated as a proportion of the individual assessed contributions to surplus.

Under the system of loading quoted by Maclean, the loading for whole-life assurances is a percentage of the net premium and for other types of assurance is a percentage of the net premium plus a percentage of the corresponding premium for whole-life assurance at the same age at entry. Suppose, for example, that A, B and C respectively represent the pure premiums, at a given entry age, for whole-life assurance, limited-premium life assurance of a certain period of premium payments and endowment assurance for the same period. Suppose also that 25% loading is suitable for the whole-life assurance. The following scheme might be adopted for the other classes.

For whole-life assurance

$$\tfrac{1}{4}A.$$

For limited-premium life assurance

$$\tfrac{1}{8}A+\tfrac{1}{8}B=\tfrac{1}{4}A+\tfrac{1}{8}(B-A).$$

For endowment assurance

$$\tfrac{1}{8}A+\tfrac{1}{16}B+\tfrac{1}{16}C=\tfrac{1}{4}A+\tfrac{1}{8}(B-A)+\tfrac{1}{16}(C-B).$$

Thus the limited-premium life assurance carries the same loading as the corresponding whole-life assurance with a smaller percentage of the excess of the limited-premium over the whole-life pure premium. Similarly, the endowment assurance carries the same loading as the limited-premium life assurance with a still smaller percentage of the excess of the endowment assurance over the limited-premium pure premium. Rough justice is done by such expedients and any injustice is left to be corrected in the distribution of surplus.

9·5. Annuities.

For various reasons the formulae for premiums for annuities give rise to different considerations from those for assurances. The subject is treated here in a general way. The special considerations relating to pension schemes are discussed in Chapter 16. Further, it is assumed that the annuity fund is taxed upon profits so that it is appropriate to base the actuarial calculations upon a gross rate of interest. The special considerations which arise when the annuity fund is taxed upon 'interest less annuities' are discussed briefly at the end of this section.

It is as well to remember that the British Government sells annuities through the National Debt Commissioners and the Post Office as a means of reducing the National Debt. Thus it competes with life assurance offices as a vendor of annuities. The purchase prices are tabulated according to the price of $2\frac{1}{2}\%$ Consols at the time of purchase to make allowance for variations from time to time in the market rate of interest.

The loading formula used by life assurance offices for annuities is generally simpler than for assurances. In Great Britain a heavy stamp duty, 2% of considerations after 1 August 1947, has to be paid, and commission would take another 1%. For examination purposes, the student may assume the other expenses to be 1% of the consideration and $1\frac{1}{2}\%$ of the annuity as suggested by Gunlake. These loadings would, we think, assume that a good margin for profit is to be kept in the rate of interest.

The stamp duty is payable at a lower rate if the purchase price is less than £2000, but the small margin provided by the formula in such a case may be set against the proportionately greater expense of granting small annuities. An additional loading may be desirable if payments are made frequently, e.g. monthly, but the considerations for quarterly annuities often include the same expense loadings as those for half-yearly annuities.

Thus for immediate annuities, curtate, we might reach a formula of the form:

$$96/(1{\cdot}015)\,\{a_{[x-k]}+(m-1)/2m\}. \qquad (9{\cdot}3)$$

Here m represents the frequency of payment and k is the deduction from the age for improvement in vitality of annuitants.†

The investment problem arising from the sale of immediate annuities may be regarded as a loan of capital by the annuitant to the assurance office which is to be redeemed by equal instalments of principal and interest. It is true that, for any individual annuitant, the instalments cease at death, but taking the body of annuitants as a whole the transaction is effectively a loan of capital repayable by instalments. Thus it seems suitable to assume a rate of interest approximating to the gross yield of medium-term Government stock.

It has been the common experience both in Great Britain and the United States of America and also in other countries that there has been a large and rapid growth in the volume of annuity business in force since the war of 1914–18. The causes of this growth are partly to be found in sociological factors which do not concern us here, but we propose to consider in a general way the special problems arising from the rapid growth of this business.

The growth of annuity business has happened to be contemporaneous, both in Great Britain and in the United States of America, with a steep fall in the rates of interest earned on the assets of assurance and annuity funds and with a persistent though irregular improvement in the vitality of annuitants. It is this combination of circumstances that has given the problems their special character.

The trend in the mortality of annuitants will be familiar to the student from his reading for other parts of the examinations. The trend suggests that a mortality basis which is a conservative one for annuities commencing at once or in the near future cannot necessarily be assumed to be conservative for annuities whose commencement is deferred for long periods. Various assumptions may be made about the trend of mortality with a view to facilitating the calculations, but whatever assumption is made prudence suggests that the longer the term of deferment the more conservative should be the mortality assumption.

† The deduction of k is only an artifice; other adjustments may be more suitable.

From this point of view the various types of annuity may be conveniently considered in three groups:

(*a*) immediate annuities,

(*b*) deferred annuities,

(*c*) annuities at guaranteed rates on maturity of endowment assurances.

The first and third groups are clearly defined and entail similar types of formula. In the third group, purchase of the annuity is deferred until the maturity of the endowment assurance and some allowance may be made for this by a more conservative assumption about mortality. The annuities in the third group are bought at younger ages on the average than the immediate annuities in the first group which would include a proportion of annuities bought on old lives, but otherwise little difference may be expected in the mortality experience.

The second group, of deferred annuities, is heterogeneous. It would consist of individual deferred annuities with and without return of premiums at death and of similar contracts effected under pension schemes, and also of survivorship and other special classes of annuity. The association of deferred annuities with pension schemes may lead to a rather long period of deferment which should receive recognition in the premium basis. On the other hand the members of the pension schemes may be drawn from a different class of life than annuitants and the mortality of pensioners may be higher than the contemporaneous mortality of annuitants.

Deferred annuities by single premium are charged the same stamp duty as immediate annuities, 2% of the consideration, but deferred annuities by annual premium are charged in proportion to the amount of the annuity, the proportion depending on whether the premiums are payable up to pension age or are limited to a shorter period. Such a nicety can hardly be reflected in the premium basis and it is usually sufficient to load the premium with a percentage for expenses. The percentage might be somewhat higher in the first year than in subsequent years because commission is often calculated in that way. There should be a margin in the assumed rate of interest to make a provision for fluctuations and profits.

So far we have assumed a gross rate of interest, but the position in Great Britain is clouded by differences in the way in which individual annuity funds are taxed. Where the annuity fund is effectively taxed upon profits it is appropriate to assume a gross rate of interest. Where the annuity fund is effectively taxable upon 'interest less annuities' for a period, say n years, after which it may be assumed that the fund will become effectively taxable upon profits, the premiums for new business should, in theory, provide for net interest and net annuities only during that period of n years, and for gross interest and gross annuities thereafter. In practice it is doubtful whether the theoretical position would be followed through in the formula for the premium scale because competitive and other practical considerations would have to be taken into account. So far as deferred annuities are concerned it would probably be sufficient to assume net interest up to pension age and gross interest thereafter, the gross annuity payments being valued.

The greater part of annuity business is non-participating, but the uncertain nature of some of the elements of the actuarial basis for annuities suggests that it may be worth reconsidering this practice. It seems desirable to incorporate in the premium basis a substantial provision for future improvement in vitality of annuitants which may, of course, not eventuate, or not eventuate to the anticipated extent. Should such a provision be made and the experience prove to be more favourable than expected, a share of profits could be given by way of compensation.

9·6. Consistency.

The considerations affecting the various classes of assurance are so different in many respects that it is not surprising that different bases may come to be used for the several classes. Thus it becomes important to test the scales for anomalies between the various classes.

This problem has been tackled in Sweden, where a common basis for all companies was required on a 'basis of the first order'. The formula

$$\bar{P}' = \frac{1}{(1-p)}[\bar{P} + I/\bar{a} + c]$$

was assumed to be appropriate and was transformed by replacing the loadings by a 'symmetrical mortality and interest' loading ϵ applied to the force of mortality as an addition and to the force of interest as an equal deduction. Such a transformation leaves the annuity-values unchanged but affects the assurance values. It enables a uniform and unambiguous basis to be adopted for assurances for both capital sums and annuities.

Let

$$(I.\delta + c)/(1+I) = \epsilon.$$

Where

$$\bar{P} = 1/\bar{a} - \delta,$$

we may transform the formula for the office premium into

$$\bar{P}' = \frac{1+I}{1-p}\cdot\left[\bar{P} + \frac{I.\delta + c}{1+I}\right]$$

$$= \frac{1+I}{1-p}\cdot(\bar{P}+\epsilon). \qquad (9\cdot4)$$

$(\bar{P}+\epsilon)$ is of course the pure premium with a 'symmetrical mortality and interest' loading equal to ϵ. The formula for the office premium thus reduces to the pure premium, including the 'symmetrical mortality and interest' loading, with a uniform percentage addition to the premium.

The formula assumes that premiums payable for a limited period are obtained by commutation of those payable for the whole duration of the contract without any relief for saving in expenses after premiums have ceased.

If the formula were to be applied to temporary assurances it would assume that ϵ constitutes a suitable loading. This cannot be justified theoretically and is simply a practical question whether the loading happens to be appropriate for that class of business.

†9·7. Premiums payable more often than once a year.

The premium that is payable m times a year must exceed the corresponding annual premium on account of the loss of interest, the possible loss of premiums (unless they are instalment premiums) and the additional expense of collecting m renewals each year

† Gunlake.

instead of one. The surcharge is commonly expressed as a percentage of the annual premium irrespective of class of policy, age, or term, favourite additions being $2\frac{1}{2}\%$ for half-yearly and 5% for quarterly payments (true premiums). The theoretical additions for the first two items mentioned above are derived in Chapter 7 of *Life and other contingencies* by Hooker and Longley-Cook; the following numerical examples are interesting:

TABLE 9·2

Approximate additions (apart from extra expenses) to annual premiums to obtain mthly *premiums (basis* A1924–29 $3\frac{1}{2}\%$*)*

<table>
<tr><th rowspan="2">Class of policy</th><th rowspan="2">Age at entry</th><th colspan="3">Instalment premiums (addition to cover loss of interest)</th><th colspan="3">True premiums (addition to cover loss of interest and premium)</th></tr>
<tr><th>$m=2$ (%)</th><th>$m=4$ (%)</th><th>$m=12$ (%)</th><th>$m=2$ (%)</th><th>$m=4$ (%)</th><th>$m=12$ (%)</th></tr>
<tr><td>Whole-life assurance</td><td>20</td><td rowspan="6">$\frac{3}{4}$</td><td rowspan="6">$1\frac{1}{4}$</td><td rowspan="6">$1\frac{1}{2}$</td><td>1</td><td>$1\frac{1}{2}$</td><td>2</td></tr>
<tr><td></td><td>35</td><td>$1\frac{1}{4}$</td><td>$1\frac{3}{4}$</td><td>$2\frac{1}{4}$</td></tr>
<tr><td></td><td>50</td><td>$1\frac{1}{2}$</td><td>$2\frac{1}{4}$</td><td>3</td></tr>
<tr><td>Endowment assurance at 60, or whole-life assurance with payments ceasing before 60</td><td>20</td><td>1</td><td>$1\frac{1}{2}$</td><td>$1\frac{3}{4}$</td></tr>
<tr><td></td><td>35</td><td>1</td><td>$1\frac{1}{2}$</td><td>$1\frac{3}{4}$</td></tr>
<tr><td></td><td>50</td><td>1</td><td>$1\frac{3}{4}$</td><td>2</td></tr>
</table>

The payment of premiums by monthly instalments by means of a banker's order is now a well-established scheme, the addition to the annual premium being a percentage, e.g. $2\frac{1}{2}\%$, or perhaps waived altogether. The last practice can hardly be justified theoretically unless the cost to the office of collecting premiums twelve times a year in this special way is less than the cost of collecting once a year in the ordinary way to a sufficient extent to neutralize the loss of interest, but the banker's order scheme may produce larger assurances, on the average, than the ordinary direct-payment plans, or the scheme may stimulate new business sufficiently to justify some concession because of the expenses being spread over a larger volume of business.

BIBLIOGRAPHY

J. H. Gunlake (1939). *Premiums for life assurances and annuities.* Cambridge University Press.

J. B. Maclean (1945). *Life insurance.* McGraw Hill Publishing Co. Ltd., 6th ed.

P. H. Hammon and R. S. Skerman (1948). Ordinary assurance premium bases in the United Kingdom with particular reference to interest, expenses and taxation. *Proc. Cent. Assembly Inst. Act.* vol. II, p. 232.

W. A. Jenkins (1948). The problem of annuity premium rates in the United States. *Proc. Cent. Assembly Inst. Act.* vol. II, p. 254. See also the discussion in vol. I, pp. 106–116.

CHAPTER 10

PREMIUMS FOR SPECIAL CLASSES OF ASSURANCE

There are a wide variety of special classes of assurance to meet special needs. They can usually be reduced to some combination of the standard forms of whole-life, endowment assurance, temporary assurance and pure endowment. The considerations affecting them will now be reviewed.

†10·1. Joint whole-life and endowment assurances.

Full-term, limited or single premiums for assurances on two or more joint lives can be calculated upon the same basis as the corresponding single-life rates. It is a matter of opinion whether an additional loading should be included to allow for the small extra management expense that may arise, and the greater margin for fluctuations that is sometimes thought desirable in dealing with 'special' classes.

When two lives are concerned it is not necessary to prepare rates for every reasonable combination of ages, as it is found quite practicable to publish rates for equal ages only, coupled with a rudimentary uniform seniority table. In the 'number of years to be added' fractions can be dispensed with for endowment assurances, but it may be thought necessary to retain half-years for whole-life assurances.

The pure premium for a joint-life endowment assurance can be obtained by a simple formula of Lidstone's:

$$P_{xy\overline{n}|} = P_{x\overline{n}|} + P_{y\overline{n}|} - P_{\overline{n}|}. \qquad (10{\cdot}1)$$

The formula can be extended to any number of lives. The same formula is not applicable to office premiums because the loading should be included in respect of only one of the premiums.

Joint-life policies sometimes include the option to split the assurance at any time into two separate single-life assurances, each

† Section largely based on Gunlake.

for one-half of the sum assured. No special allowance need be made for this option in calculating the joint-life premiums. For whole-life assurance, since the reserve that has accumulated under the joint-life contract up to the time of the alteration is generally not less than the sum of the reserves that would have been accumulated under the two separate single-life contracts, the premiums payable after division can be those corresponding to the original entry-ages. In the case of an endowment assurance, however, these would often be insufficient and a special calculation might have to be made.

†10·2. Temporary assurances.

If the standard type of formula, with the loadings that have been used earlier in this book as examples, were to be applied to temporary assurances it would be found that in proceeding from the longest terms to the shortest the resulting rates of premium would first diminish, but after a certain point would begin to increase again. The last-mentioned feature, which is of course due to the initial loading, is quite inadmissible, for it is contrary to common sense and would enable proposers requiring cover for short periods to make a better bargain by effecting policies for longer periods and allowing them to lapse when they are no longer needed. It is true that for temporary assurances it is the general practice to make a large reduction in the usual agency commission (for example, to 10% of the first year's premium, or even less for the shortest terms) and to curtail or withhold any overriding commissions normally payable, but even if the initial loading of 3% referred to in § 9·3 were correspondingly reduced, the difficulty would still persist.

The orthodox solution of this problem is to abandon the standard type of formula and to use an entirely different basis for temporary assurances, for example a formula of the type:

$$P'^{\,1}_{[x]\overline{n}|} = \frac{1}{(1-p)}\left(P^{\,1}_{[x]\overline{n}|} + c\right). \qquad (10·2)$$

In this formula the net premium would be calculated by an

† Section largely based on Gunlake.

appropriate table showing considerably heavier mortality than that used for whole-life and endowment assurances and the values of p and c would probably be different from those suggested for the principal classes of assurance. Though this method may be suitable for the normal range of the periods for which temporary assurances are required, there would probably be some inconsistency between the premiums for the longer periods. An alternative approach to the problem was therefore suggested by Gunlake.

An investigation into the mortality experience of forty-eight offices during the period 1924–34 relating to medically examined† lives assured under ordinary temporary assurances indicated that the mortality rates were about 25% in excess of those by the A1924–29 table and very slightly in excess of those of the A1924–29 Heavy table. Suppose that the A1924–29 table is suitable for the main classes of assurance and that the loading is calculated by a formula of the type suggested in § 9·3. Suppose also that the saving on commission makes it appropriate to reduce the temporary assurance initial loading to, say, half the general initial loading. The following formula might be considered appropriate for the longer periods:

$$P'^{\,1}_{[x]\overline{n}|}=\frac{1}{(1-p)}\,[P^{\,1}_{[x]\overline{n}|}+\tfrac{1}{2}I/\ddot{a}_{[x]\overline{n}|}+c], \qquad (10{\cdot}3)$$

with the net premium based on the A1924–29 Heavy table. Owing to the incorporation of an initial loading into the formula, it will produce absurd results for the shorter periods because in passing from the longer to the shorter terms for a given age at entry there will be a point at which the premiums begin to increase. For shorter periods than this the premiums can be obtained by interpolation, so that they run smoothly into the premiums for assurances for one year which would be fixed independently on suitable assumptions.

The premiums for assurances for 1 year must be fixed on more or less arbitrary principles. The net premium is the select q less perhaps some discount, but it is not practicable to add a full share

† Medical examination is usually insisted upon for temporary assurances. The fee is often payable by the proposer if the sum assured is small (say, less than £500) and this helps to ease the difficulty of the initial loading.

of expenses because of the difficulty of constructing a suitably graded table of rates increasing with the period of assurance. A value of $c = \cdot 0025$ was suggested for whole-life and endowment assurances and it seems doubtful whether the value of c for 1-year temporary assurances should be less than ·005. The fact that a stage has been reached at which it is necessary to proceed upon arbitrary lines is no doubt responsible for the remarkable differences in premiums that are found to exist. It would be a useful exercise to tabulate the premiums for 1-year assurances for a few offices so as to obtain an idea of the variation.

TABLE 10·1

Rate of mortality by A1924–29 *select*

Age at entry $[x]$	$q_{[x]}$	$q_{[x]+1}$	$q_{[x]+2}$	Mean of three q's
50	·00455	·00663	·00832	·00650
52	·00535	·00786	·00993	·00771
54	·00632	·00941	·01199	·00924
56	·00757	—	—	—

An examination of the variations will probably disclose that some offices base temporary assurance premiums upon a select table of mortality whereas others use an ultimate table. There is a difference of opinion on this question. Theoretically there seems no reason why the 1-year assurances should not be based on select mortality. In practice, however, offices exercise a proper caution in quoting for such assurances and the use of ultimate mortality provides a margin for fluctuations and tends to offset initial expenses. It also reduces the possibility of selection against the office in the last few years of an assurance, when a life who is in good health might lapse his assurance and re-enter for the remainder of the period at the lower select premiums. Taking for example an entrant at age x, the rate of mortality in successive years will be $q_{[x]}$, $q_{[x]+1}$ and so on. The pure premium for a temporary assurance for r years must approximate to the mean of these q's over the r years. How this works out can be seen from the simple example in Table 10·1.

Should a pure premium of ·00650 be charged for 3 years

assurance at age 50, the third year's assurance could be obtained for a pure premium of only ·00535, supposing the life still to be assurable at normal rates. It has been suggested that the premium for the 3 years assurance should be calculated on the assumption that the proportion of lives who remain select will, in fact, pay only the select premium, but this seems both artificial and unduly complicated. The use of ultimate mortality obviates the difficulty.

A further practical consideration to be borne in mind is that, since temporary assurances are usually arranged for comparatively short periods of years, there may be some adverse selection by reason of such assurances becoming popular when the risk is temporarily raised, and it is probably as well to include a rather larger margin for fluctuations than would be incorporated in the loading for whole-life and endowment assurances.

Enquiries are occasionally made for rates for periods less than 1 year, e.g. 3 or 6 months, and there may often be some extra risk involved—the enquirer may be going abroad on a business trip, perhaps by air. A practical method which is sometimes adopted is to charge the appropriate fraction of the net premium, together with the whole of the loading included in the 1-year rate. This, however, can lead to unreasonable results in some circumstances, and an alternative would be to quote, say, two-thirds or three-quarters of the 1-year rate for 6 months, and one-half or a little less for 3 months—a practice similar to that current in some other branches of insurance business. It is obvious that for such a short period the risk cannot much exceed the ordinary fatal accident risk.

Joint-life temporary assurances though unusual are by no means unknown. The student will be aware that unless the term is long the pure premium may with sufficient accuracy be taken as being equal to the sum of the pure premiums for two single-life assurances, but it would obviously be incorrect analogously to add the two gross premiums together, as the effect would be to double the loading. The rate can therefore be arrived at by combining the gross single-life premium in respect of one life, the net single-life premium in respect of the other, and a further small loading if need be, to provide for commission on the increased premium and for contingencies.

10·3. Varying temporary assurances.

Temporary assurances with decreasing sums assured are usually required to cover the capital outstanding from time to time under loans repayable by instalments. The sum assured thus diminishes by unequal decrements if the loan is repayable by an unvarying annuity, or by equal decrements if a fixed part of the capital is paid off periodically, but there is no distinction between these two plans so far as the basis for the premiums is concerned. The temptation to take the net present value of the assurance under the former scheme as

$$C\,[a^{(m)}_{\overline{n}|} - a^{(m)}_{x\overline{n}|}],$$

where C is the annual amount of the service of the loan, must be resisted because loans are not often granted at the rates of interest that are suitable for premium calculations. They are, in fact, usually granted at higher rates of interest and it can be shown that the foregoing value should be reduced by a factor $f(n)$ which is nearly independent of age (McAlpin, 1932). We thus reach the formula:

$$C\,[a^{(m)}_{\overline{n}|} - a^{(m)}_{x\overline{n}|}] \times f(n). \tag{10·4}$$

However, it is sufficient and probably more usual to adopt the arithmetical method described in the next paragraph.

Commonly, the repayments will be made more frequently than once a year, but this need not complicate the problem of the calculation of the premium, which may with sufficient accuracy be based upon the average sum at risk during each successive year of the policy's duration. If these sums are listed, one obvious method (and that often used) is to difference them, to multiply the differences by the normal office rates of premium for terms of 1 year, 2 years, 3 years, ..., and to sum the products continuously. This will give a series of decreasing premiums having the advantage of complete consistency with the rates for ordinary temporary assurances, but the disadvantage of perhaps proceeding irregularly, even when the sum assured diminishes steadily. This could be avoided if desired by multiplying the annual premiums, before they are continuously summed, by the appropriate annuities-due, adding the products together and dividing the total by the decreasing annuity-due. If a constant annual premium were wanted, this would have to be limited, to say two-thirds of the full term of the policy, in order that it might suffice to cover policy-stamp, commission and risk in the first year. The amount can be arrived at by dividing by the temporary annuity-due, instead of the decreasing annuity-due, as the last step in the method outlined above.

As an alternative it is clearly easy to obtain the net single and (level or diminishing) annual premiums by combining the sums at risk in the successive years of the policy's duration with the appropriate values of C_x, or, when the sum assured decreases steadily, by the use of R's, but it is less easy to decide upon suitable loadings. Subject always to the avoidance of anomalies, it would probably be satisfactory to make use of the office's ordinary temporary-assurance loadings, calculated by reference to the mean sum at risk throughout the whole duration of the varying assurance.

Most policies of this kind are called for in connexion with mortgages granted by building societies for the purchase of private dwelling-houses, and they are then generally effected by single premium. The borrower is, however, rarely in a position to pay this himself, and the Society will usually be willing to add it to the loan (the amount of the periodical repayment being proportionately increased) if the policy carries a surrender value that it considers satisfactory. Quotations for such an arrangement are clearer to Society and borrower if the special single premium, which is required to cover the outstanding portions of both itself and the normal loan, is expressed as a percentage of the latter alone; if £A is the ordinary gross single premium for a normal loan of £100, the special gross single premium is obviously £$A/(1-\cdot 01A)$.

The need for limiting the number of constant annual premiums that can be accepted for a decreasing temporary assurance has just been mentioned. With the object of avoiding this need, decreasing temporary cover is sometimes combined under one policy with another kind of assurance—such as, for example, whole-life or endowment—and since the two benefits may be expected to be a little less troublesome administratively in combination than apart, a small relaxation of the loading normally added for one of them is perhaps permissible. The use of two mortality tables in one calculation is not really defensible, and if the two premiums taken singly are based upon different tables, it might be better to calculate the premium for the contract as a whole on one uniform suitable basis, subject always to the avoidance of anomaly with published premiums—which may prove difficult.

This difficulty arises generally with all 'combination' policies, but particularly with the type of assurance known as 'family income benefit'. This consists of a decreasing temporary assurance providing for the payment, in the event of the death of the life assured during a selected period (frequently 20 years) of a fixed income (say £100 a year) during the remainder of the period. The benefit is occasionally granted by itself but is usually fused with a basic whole-life or endowment assurance, with the object of avoiding the limitation of the premiums to a part only of the selected period; sometimes indeed the payment of the premiums for the decreasing temporary assurance is spread over the whole term of the basic policy—which may, however, give rise to difficulties in other directions. The formula for the net supplementary premium naturally depends upon the precise conditions governing the payment of the income; the expression

$$B\,(\bar{a}_{\overline{n}|} - \bar{a}_{[x]\overline{n}|})/\ddot{a}_{[x]\overline{n}|}, \tag{10.5}$$

where B is the annual income and n the selected period, is applicable to the contract granted by many offices. The principal considerations to be borne in mind in choosing a basis are: (i) it may be prudent to anticipate rates of mortality heavier than normal, even though extra care in selection is taken; this of course applies equally to the basic policy, but as the premium for that will be a tabular one the situation can best be met by basing the supplementary premium on an especially stringent mortality table or by including an additional loading on this account; (ii) the administration of a claim would cause much more work than the payment of the sum assured under an ordinary temporary assurance; (iii) since the benefits are granted as an addition to a basic policy with normal loadings, and usually form a comparatively large sum assured, some relaxation of expense loadings may be permissible. The formula for the loading for the supplementary premium would probably dispense with the initial loading because initial expenses would be borne by the basic assurance. The other loadings might be suitably taken as the same as in § 9·3, the 'constant' being based on the mean sum at risk during the *n* year period.

It will be seen that this basis is considerably more generous than those previously indicated in connexion with ordinary temporary assurances. This may be due to the removal of a part of the loading on the grounds that the income benefit is granted in conjunction with a basic assurance, and in this connexion it must be remembered that the smaller the ratio of income to basic sum assured, the larger the reduction in the rate of loading included in the supplementary premium may be; many offices associate an income of £120 a year with a sum assured of £1000. If, as is often the case, the capital sum of £1000 may be retained by the office until the end of the selected period in the event of a claim arising, an additional income can be granted in respect of interest. Care must be taken in consenting to issue these policies for premiums payable more often than annually; the first premium must not on any account fall short of the premium the office would charge under an ordinary temporary assurance for the sum at risk until the first renewal date, after adjustment to allow for any difference in the amounts of commission paid and for the cost of the option of continuance.

†10·4. Convertible temporary assurances.

Commission must also be taken into account in deriving the premium for a convertible temporary assurance—that is, a temporary assurance that, without evidence of good health and at any time during the policy's currency (or possibly at any time except during the last few years), the life assured may convert the assurance into a whole-life or endowment assurance, usually at the tabular rate of premium in force at the time of conversion. Some offices pay only the ordinary temporary-assurance commission at the outset followed by the full 'main class' commission

† Gunlake.

when conversion takes place, and there is clearly no need to add anything to the temporary-assurance premium on this account. Those offices, however, that pay more at the outset and perhaps less on conversion ought to protect themselves against the loss that they would suffer if the policy were not converted; this could only be done by making an appropriate addition to the normal temporary-assurance premium, but it is hardly practicable to grant a compensatory reduction in the tabular premiums subsequently payable by those who convert. If these are the premiums in use at the time of conversion, provision is automatically made for any changes that may occur in the interest or mortality basis, and the only feature, apart from commission, that calls for an addition to the ordinary temporary-assurance premium is the option. Such an addition is obviously necessary on the grounds of consistency, although it may be mentioned that the investigation referred to in § 10·2 revealed materially lighter mortality among the holders of convertible temporary assurances than among the holders of ordinary temporary assurances.

The theory of options, for all its complexity (see § 16·5), is largely unhelpful, for it is based on probably fallacious assumptions. Moreover, option premiums when calculated on the usual formulae by different mortality tables are found to exhibit remarkable variations, due to the arbitrary treatment of the select period. Statistics of the mortality of lives assured under converted policies are not available, and at present there is nothing for it but to make a quite arbitrary charge. The annual addition per £100 assured should be greater for the older ages and possibly for the shorter terms. The reserve that accumulates under the temporary assurance, which is not usually taken into account in the premium payable after conversion, makes a contribution towards the cost of the option that may be considerable if the term is long and the option is exercised near the middle of it. The practice, which is not followed by all, of barring the exercise of the option during the last few (often five) years of the policy's term, seems to curtail the force of the option against the office substantially.

†10·5. Ascending-scale assurances.

Ascending-scale assurances are contracts whose character (e.g. whole-life or endowment assurance) is determined at the outset, but for which the premiums during a short initial period (generally 5 years) are a proportion (often one-half) of the premiums payable thereafter. The rates can be calculated from the corresponding gross level premiums by making an equation of payments upon the same basis of interest and mortality, but care must be taken to ensure that the 'high' premium does not exceed the tabular premium for the age attained at the end of the initial period, that the 'low' premium is not less than the ordinary temporary-assurance premium for that period including the option of continuance, and that the contract as a whole is not inconsistent with a convertible temporary assurance. As there is no particular virtue in the ratio of one-half, or indeed in any fixed ratio, there is something to be said for this type of policy giving place to the more flexible convertible temporary assurance.

†10·6. Pure endowments with return.

It is the general and obviously justifiable practice in calculating premiums for pure endowments, with return of premiums in the event of death, to dispense with mortality and to use compound-interest functions only; it is also a fairly common but less easily justifiable practice to dispense with loadings and to use a rate of interest lower than that used for the main classes. The commission payable is often upon a considerably reduced scale, and the basis for the premiums must allow for this; as an illustration take the case of an office that pays no overriding or renewal commissions for pure endowments, and limits the agent's initial commission to n% of the first year's premium (n being the term), and assume that the formula normally used by the office is

$$[100P+3/\ddot{a}+0{\cdot}3]/{\cdot}975.$$

† Gunlake.

Then, modifying the formula, we have:

TABLE 10·2

Term n	Annual premium by the formula	
	$\dfrac{100P_{\overline{n}\vert}+1\cdot5/\ddot{a}_{\overline{n}\vert}+\cdot3}{1-\cdot01n/\ddot{a}_{\overline{n}\vert}}$ at $3\frac{1}{4}$ %	$P_{\overline{n}\vert}$ at 2 %
40 years	1·61	1·62
25 ,,	3·00	3·06
10 ,,	8·93	8·95

The rates of interest of $3\frac{1}{4}$ % and 2 % were those adopted by Gunlake: they are used solely for purposes of illustration.

It will be seen from the last column that even when the commission is thus restricted the unloaded premiums must be based upon a rate of interest at least 1 % lower than that normally employed if these policies are to avoid being subsidized by the other classes. Strictly, the benefit payable at death should not exceed the premiums paid, less expenses, accumulated at the rate of interest ($3\frac{1}{4}$ % in the above example) upon which the premiums are in reality based, and, as a practical approximation to this, it is sometimes taken as the accumulation at interest of all premiums paid after the first year. A benefit amounting to the whole of the premiums paid, together with interest at the alternative lower rate (2 % in the above example), has the advantage of greater simplicity, whilst running with equal smoothness up to the sum assured at maturity, and will not generally lead to much loss except in the event of an early death. This benefit should therefore probably be modified if such a policy is granted to an old life, even though evidence of good health (which is not usually asked for in connexion with this type of contract) be obtained.

Single premiums can be ascertained according to the principles previously described. If the commutation method is used, the rate of interest should be that considered to be suitable for single-premium commutations generally, and not necessarily the special rate at which the annual premiums must be calculated if they are unloaded. The effect of making allowance for any curtailment of the commission payable may be to magnify the natural difference between the single premiums for pure endowments and ordinary endowment assurances to an extent that appears unreasonable.

Pure endowments are sometimes issued, particularly on the lives of children, with a provision for the cessation of the annual premiums after the death of a nominated life, usually the father. The special premium for an assurance of this kind could be obtained by multiplying the ordinary annual premium by the annuity-certain and dividing by the temporary life annuity. To base these on the lower and not the higher rate of interest would provide a small margin which, seeing that the special provision is one that does not justify the expense of elaborate medical selection, it may be advisable to provide otherwise, or even to augment, by the addition of a precautionary loading or the use of a stringent mortality table. The additional benefit of cessation of premiums is akin to the family income benefit, and comparison could be made with the appropriate proportion of the supplementary premium under that table.

†10·7. Pure endowments without return.

Annual and single premiums for pure endowments, without return of premiums, can also be calculated by means of the standard formulae used by the office for the main classes, adjusted for any difference there may be in the commission payable. It is customary to take the age of the life as the age last birthday, and some actuaries might prefer to use a light mortality table, or to make a small addition to the loading, to guard against exceptional longevity. Obviously, the premiums for pure endowments without return must be less than those for pure endowments with return. The latter is the more satisfactory contract; the former is apt to lead to disappointment in the event of the life failing to survive the term.

Since under both of these tables the full sum assured is not payable in certain contingencies, there may be something to be said on the grounds of equity for making a small reduction in the loadings (as well as the adjustment for commission), and the premiums quoted by many offices suggest that this view is widely held.

† Gunlake

†10·8. Double endowment assurances.

Double endowment assurance can be regarded as a combination of endowment assurance and pure endowment, but for various reasons it is not desirable to compute the premiums by adding those for the separate contracts. For example, that would assume that the combined contract needed the combined loadings for expenses.

The rate of premium for double endowment assurance for a given period does not vary much with age and may, indeed, theoretically reduce as the age increases. For this reason the same rate of premium would be quoted for a wide range of age-groups.

As will be seen in § 11·5 it is often possible to accept a double endowment assurance at normal rates on an under-average life where the impairment would make an extra premium necessary for normal types of assurance. We do not think that this should affect the mortality basis for this class of assurance. The terms should be fixed for normal lives and the table applied to under-average lives only where it seems appropriate to the particular circumstances.

The same type of loading formula as for whole-life and endowment assurance may also be applied to double endowment assurance, but the amounts of the loadings need further consideration. A double endowment assurance may be compared with several combinations of contract, for example an endowment assurance *plus* a pure endowment, or an endowment assurance for the amount on survival *minus* a temporary assurance. If the loadings for an assurance for £1,000 at death or £2,000 on survival were to be taken as the full endowment assurance loadings for £2,000, the deduction from the endowment assurance premium because one-half of the sum assured only was to be payable at death would merely be the pure premium for the temporary assurance with the percentage loading.

The initial commission on double endowment assurance is usually restricted to the commission on the sum at death and it seems best to charge the initial expenses on this sum only or as

† Section largely based on Gunlake.

Gunlake suggests on this sum *plus* part only of the pure endowment. The charge c for general expenses and fluctuations and profits may be based on the sum assured on survival (though perhaps at a lower rate) or this charge may be omitted and the premium for the pure endowment portion of the contract may be computed at a suitably lower rate of interest than the endowment assurance portion.

In Sweden an assurance, such as a double endowment assurance, under which the death strain at risk assumes both positive and negative values during the period of assurance, is known as a 'combined life assurance'. It often happens that a lighter mortality is used for assurances of the pure endowment type than for ordinary assurances and it is important to consider what basis would be suitable for 'combined life assurance'.

Suppose that the table of mortality used for ordinary assurance is defined by accented symbols and for pure endowments by a double accent. Esscher shows that any table of mortality defined by

$$\mu = \mu'' + k(\mu' - \mu''),$$

where k is a positive fraction less than unity, will produce a lower premium for double endowment assurance than whichever is the larger,

$$(P'_{x\overline{n}|} + P'^{\;1}_{x\overline{n}|}) \quad \text{or} \quad (P''_{x\overline{n}|} + P''^{\;1}_{x\overline{n}|}).$$

Esscher also considers the case where

$$\mu = \mu'' + k(\mu' - \mu'') + l,$$

both for positive and negative values of l.

On the basis of this theoretical work he suggests 'the method of the highest premium', using whichever alternative table gives the highest premium. This has something to commend it, though the somewhat arbitrary character of the premium scale when age is ignored suggests that refinements are out of place.

†10·9. Debenture assurances.

These are simply policies under which the sum assured takes the form of a debenture—that is, the sum assured is payable at the

† Gunlake.

end of an agreed period after a claim arises, interest at a guaranteed rate being paid in the meantime. On the face of it, this class of assurance does not seem to present much difficulty, because, assuming that the expense of making the periodical interest-payments is inappreciable, it is merely necessary to multiply the ordinary gross premium for the class of assurance concerned by $v^n + ja_{\overline{n}|}^{(m)}$, where j—the rate of interest allowed—can be any rate within reason that the office likes to offer. If the sum assured could be taken only in this form, the problem of the rate of interest for the valuation of the special benefit need not be differentiated from the general problem of the rate of interest for the premium as a whole, but if as is usual the claimant is given the right to an alternative cash payment, and the amount of this is determined at the outset, a 'financial' option is introduced. The office which is charging a premium estimated to be sufficient on the average to produce the cash sum assured, is in effect undertaking to carry out a fresh transaction when a claim is made, namely the grant of a debenture, on terms prescribed at the outset. The office is therefore likely, in theory at all events, to have the money left in its hands, if ruling rates of interest are low when a claim arises, at a time when it will be experiencing difficulty in finding remunerative investments and would be glad to pay the cash sum, whilst being deprived in the opposite event of the chance of retaining the money and earning some interest profit upon it. The value of the debenture upon which the premium is based should therefore be calculated at the lowest rate of interest that it is considered the office is ever likely to use for premium calculations.

†10·10. Instalment assurances.

The 'financial' option is, in fact, of frequent occurrence. It arose in § 10·3 in connexion with the deposit until the end of the selected period of the sum assured under a family income policy, although attention was not there drawn to it; it occurs in connexion with optional annuities (see § 9·5), and in the instalment assurance. This is an assurance under which the sum assured may

† Gunlake.

be paid in instalments over an agreed period of years, and the premium may, in a similar way to that for the debenture assurance, be derived from the ordinary gross premium by multiplying it by

$$a_{\overline{n}|}^{(m)} (1+i)^{1/m}/n,$$

although if the commission payable is based on the total of the instalments and not on the alternative cash sum an adjustment is obviously necessary. This expression also should be calculated at a low rate of interest. It is however, doubtful whether this is always done, and the omission is perhaps of little consequence where the policy takes the form, as many do, of an instalment endowment assurance for educational purposes, when n is often as small as 4 or 5, and the term of the policy covers at most the period from birth until school or university fees begin to be payable.

10·11. Contingent assurances.

Contingent assurances usually arise in connexion with reversionary transactions and it is the usual custom to assume that the counter life (whose age is generally taken as the age last birthday) is subject to mortality of the life-tenant type. The latest available table of annuitant mortality is therefore called for, and it will make a desirable simplification if the relatively few male counter lives are treated as female. The failing life (whose age is generally taken as the age next birthday) may perhaps not unreasonably be assumed to experience adverse mortality, but little, if at all, more adverse than that of the proposer for a temporary assurance. The mortality table used for the latter may therefore be adopted for the failing life under a contingent assurance, the premium for which could embody the same loadings as would be used for a temporary assurance of a term roughly equal to the expectation of life of the counter life.

In practice this type of assurance frequently gives rise to troublesome calculations because the necessary functions have not been tabulated, particularly where the assurance depends upon a complicated age-status involving several lives. If the mortality table has been graduated by Makeham's law it will usually be possible to compute the premium exactly or approximately by reference to the Makeham constants or derivatives of them. With other tables it may be sufficient to derive the premium by a process of approximate integration by one of the well-known formulae. It is probably best to use repeated applications of a simple short-range formula rather than a more complicated formula covering the whole range of the status. There are alternative approximations which may be used, for example the substitution of a term-certain for an age-status (A. W. Evans [1931], *J.I.A.* vol. LXII, p. 126). A rather larger margin for fluctuations should be added to premiums which have been calculated by approximate methods, unless the approximation can itself be relied on to give that margin.

A practical difficulty may be found where a level annual premium is quoted for certain types of contingent assurance. For example, suppose that a level annual premium is quoted to assure (x) against the survivor of (y) and (z) and that (y) or (z) dies soon after the assurance is effected: if (x) is then in good health he would be able to lapse the assurance, and take a fresh policy against the survivor at a lower annual premium. This option should be guarded against by quoting in the first place for an annual premium which decreases to, say, one-half at the first death of (y) and (z).

A little consideration will show that contingent assurances may range from what is effectively short-period temporary assurance, where a young assured life is associated with an old counter life, to what is effectively whole-life assurance, where an old assured life is associated with a young counter life. It is helpful to bear this in mind in considering what approximation would be suitable in given circumstances. Before making elaborate calculations it is desirable to examine the chance of the event on which the sum assured is to be payable, making the computation on broad lines without allowance for interest. For example, consider an assurance payable if r lives (x), all die within the lifetime of (y), and let us suppose that the chance of (x) dying before (y) is approximately 0·1. The chance of the assurance becoming payable may be assumed to be $(\cdot 1)^r$ or ·01 for $r=2$, ·001 for $r=3$, and so on. It will be apparent that the assurance on two lives should be paid for by a comparatively small single premium, rather than by an annual premium, and that the risk where more than two lives are involved is nominal, so that the smallest practicable single premium should be quoted. In such circumstances it is important to ensure that the actual premium for the amount of assurance required is sufficient to cover the necessary medical fees, which may be comparatively heavy unless some of the lives can be accepted without medical examination.

†10·12. Children's deferred assurances.

A type of contract that, despite certain legal difficulties, has achieved marked popularity is that known as the child's deferred assurance. Until the child reaches a selected age (usually 21 or 25) the contract is merely a kind of 'savings bank' assurance, but thereafter the policy, without any evidence of health being required, may be continued in the form of an ordinary assurance. There are usually a large number of options available at the selected age: the payment of premiums may go on or stop; the assurance may begin to participate in profits or remain non-participating; the policy may be continued in the form of a whole-life assurance (full-term or limited-premium), or endowment assurance of selected term. The amounts of the various alternative sums assured under such of these options as the office cares to offer are set out in the policy and must be calculated at the outset. There are a great many variations of practice in connexion with this type of policy—for instance the options are sometimes exercisable on the policy anniversary preceding the attainment of the selected age, sometimes on the succeeding policy anniversary, and sometimes on actually reaching age 21 or 25 (the first premium then possibly applying to a year and a fraction, and renewal premiums falling due on each birthday)—and one scheme is therefore taken here as an example. Consider the case of a policy issued by an office under which the options are exercisable on the policy anniversary immediately prior to the 21st birthday. In broad outline the method of procedure is to apply the accumulated premiums, less expenses, at age 21 as a single premium, and if annual premiums

† Gunlake.

are to be continued after that age to add the sum assured in respect of them. Until age 21 the policy is similar in character to the pure endowment with return (see § 10·6), and subject to certain considerations mentioned later the cash sum available as a single premium at age 21 might be assumed to be equal to the sum assured which would be secured under that table by the annual premium that is being paid. For quotation purposes this annual premium is usually taken as £10 (or some multiple thereof) and the formula for the corresponding sum assured that suggests itself as suitable on this basis is thus

$$\frac{10\,\ddot{s}_{\overline{21-x}|}}{P'_{[21]}\,\ddot{a}_{[21]}}+\frac{10}{P'_{[21]}}, \qquad (10{\cdot}6)$$

where x is the child's age next birthday and $P'_{[21]}$ is the ordinary gross premium per unit for a whole-life assurance at age 21 next birthday. The annuity value would be calculated upon the same basis of interest and mortality as the premiums for whole-life and endowment assurances but the accumulative factor would be calculated on the pure endowment basis. The formula is subject to obvious modifications for an endowment-assurance option. The amount of the benefit payable on death before age 21 will be subject to the same considerations as arise with the pure endowment, and should not conflict with the surrender value.

Although this formula would probably be regarded as not unreasonable in its general effect, objection could be made to it on several points of detail:

(i) By taking the sum available at age 21 as the same as the sum assured under a pure endowment, we are assuming that the initial and renewal expenses before that age are the same for the child's deferred assurance. In practice the initial commission for the latter is very generally larger (as is also the stamp duty), and it might also be argued that as the sum assured becomes much increased in the event of the policy being continued it would be only fair to make some addition to the initial and constant loadings provided by the premium-basis for pure endowments. In order to give effect to either of these considerations, an appropriate deduction should be made from the amount of the premiums accumulated to age 21 and applied as a single premium in the first term of the formula. If deductions were made from the gross premiums of £10 corresponding to the provision considered necessary for all expenses and commission before age 21, the residual premiums could of course be accumulated at the same rate of interest as the annuity value.

(ii) On the other hand, the premium $P'_{[21]}$ which appears in both terms of the formula, includes the full normal loading for initial expenses and commission. Part of this might thus be considered to cover the two considerations of heading (i), and part might be needed to provide the further commission that is sometimes paid if the policy is continued at the end of the period of deferment. The extent of these parts would be a matter for investigation in any particular case, and it might be that some deduction could be made in $P'_{[21]}$.

(iii) It must, however, be borne in mind that the formula embodies no specific provision for the cost of the option of continuance without evidence of health, and some of the initial loading that is included in $P'_{[21]}$ and is not otherwise required must therefore be preserved for this purpose. What the cost of this option is, is not known. A limited investigation disclosed rates of mortality which were nearly 10% higher in the age-group 21–35 in this class as compared with the ultimate table. To set part of the initial loading included in the $P'_{[21]}$ of the formula against this option is not merely to provide an arbitrary sum but also to use a method that is in some respects unsatisfactory; for (*a*) the single-premium part of the sum assured really requires a smaller sum per cent for the option than the annual-premium part; and (*b*) it seems reasonable to suppose that the option bears chiefly, if not indeed solely, upon the class of assurance offering the largest sum assured at age 21, namely the non-participating whole-life assurance, and this would invalidate the adaptation of the formula to an endowment-assurance option by the mere replacement of $P'_{[21]}$ and $\ddot{a}_{[21]}$ by $P'_{[21]\overline{n}|}$ and $\ddot{a}_{[21]\overline{n}|}$. If the initial loadings included in $P'_{[21]}$ and $P'_{[21]\overline{n}|}$ were regarded as being fully absorbed in other ways, specific provision for the cost of the option would be necessary.

It will be observed that the formula as it stands provides exactly the same sum assured as would be obtained if the contract were treated (*a*) up to age 21 as a pure endowment at that age and (*b*) after age 21 as an assurance effected at that age for an annual premium of £10 and a single premium equal to the sum assured by the pure endowment—provided that the life assured remains in good health and the office's tabular rates of premium are not changed in the meantime.

The cash option generally granted at the end of the period of deferment will usually be somewhat less than the sum assured that could be obtained by means of a pure endowment, chiefly as a result of the difference in commission, but also because all those who withdraw, having had an option open to them, ought to leave something behind as their contribution towards the cost of covering the impaired lives who continue. Also, the 'educational option' sometimes granted at age 15 or thereabouts—which consists of a cash sum, or equivalent periodical payments for 3 or 4 years—should not exceed the amount that the office may properly grant as a surrender value. The various sums assured after age 21 under a policy effected by a single premium of £10 could be determined merely by differencing the sums assured per £10 of annual premium corresponding to the age at entry in question and the next higher age; it is a matter for decision whether these could be used for quotation, or whether some more accurate but less consistent method, taking all the facts into consideration, should be used. The provision for the cessation of premiums until age 21 on the death of a nominated life is sometimes applied to children's deferred assurances, and the extra premium payable during the period of deferment can be obtained as described in § 10·6.

†10·13. Assurances with guaranteed bonuses.

It is in some ways a pity that the word 'bonus' should have come to be used in the description of these policies, which are simply non-participating whole-life or endowment assurances with increasing sums assured. The supplementary premium for the 'bonus' can be calculated on the same basis of interest and

† Gunlake

mortality as the premium for the normal assurance to which it is added, and the only problem is the determination of the extra loadings that should be imposed. The suggestion, previously made in § 10·8 on double endowment assurances, of applying one-half of the normal rates of initial and constant loadings to the additional sum assured, could be adopted by taking this as equal to the extra amount payable by way of 'bonus' at maturity in the case of an endowment assurance, or at death after a period roughly equal to the expectation of life in the case of a whole-life assurance. It is, of course, only reasonable that if the bonuses distributed in the office's with-profit section happen to be at the same rate as the 'guaranteed bonus', the owner of a policy of the latter kind should pay more than his participating counterpart for the same benefit, for his benefit is guaranteed. The increases in the sum assured take place sometimes with the payment of each annual premium, and sometimes with the completion of each year of assurance, and allowance should be made for this in the premiums.

10·14. Special types of annuity.

In order to avoid the disappointment that is often felt in the event of the early death of an annuitant, various special types of annuity have been devised. Among these may be mentioned:

(i) Annuities payable for a selected period and continuing during the remainder of life if the annuitant survives the period.

(ii) Annuities payable until the total of the payments made equals the purchase price, and continuing until the subsequent death of the annuitant.

(iii) Annuities under which the amount, if any, by which the total of the payments made up to the date of the annuitant's death falls short of the purchase price is then refunded.

(iv) Annuities under which an amount equal to a selected proportion (e.g. one-half, or one-third) of the purchase price is refunded on the death of the annuitant. This sometimes takes the form of a scheme providing a fixed rate of annuity (e.g. £4 for each £100 of purchase price), coupled with the return of a proportion of the purchase price varying according to age and sex.

These schemes appear to call for little comment as regards basis, it being obviously desirable to maintain consistency between them and the ordinary immediate annuities. It may be mentioned that type (iv) can also be regarded as an ordinary immediate annuity coupled with the deposit at interest of the sum to be refunded at death, or alternatively as a whole-life assurance for that sum effected by a single premium, the balance of the purchase price being applied towards an ordinary immediate annuity, and it may be helpful to bear both of these aspects in mind when selecting a basis.

The annuities we have mentioned are true annuities though of special types. Under British income tax law an annuitant is liable for income tax on the whole amount of the annuity notwithstanding that each instalment of annuity includes a provision for the redemption of the original purchase price. Of recent years a special form of contract has become popular under which the interest content only of each instalment of annuity is taxable. This type of contract is not a true annuity but is an annuity-certain combined with a deferred annuity to commence at the expiry of the annuity-certain.

The annuity-certain part of the contract is based on interest alone; there is, of course, no provision for mortality and the cost would be increased by a suitable percentage loading. Since for income tax purposes the charge to tax is based upon a schedule showing the amounts of interest and of principal contained in each instalment, the schedule has to be calculated on an assumed 'effective' rate of interest so chosen as to reproduce the actual cost on the basis of the true rate of interest with loading.

The deferred annuity part of the contract is simply a deferred annuity by single premium without return of the premium at death and the basis would be chosen conformably with that for other deferred annuities. The premium is sensitive to the mortality assumption because the annuity may be deferred to a late age. For example, an annuity purchased at age 70 might be arranged as an annuity-certain for 10 years and the deferred annuity would commence at age 80 years. For this reason the mortality assumption should be a conservative one.

A reversionary or survivorship annuity—a contract which provides an annuity to commence on the death of one life, the life assured, should another life, the annuitant, be then living—gives rise to similar considerations to a contingent assurance (see § 10·11).

BIBLIOGRAPHY

J. H. Gunlake (1939). *Premiums for life assurance and annuities.* Cambridge University Press.

H. Moir (1904). Office premiums. *T.F.A.* vol. II, p. 207.

A. W. Evans (1925). On the calculation of contingent assurances and the compound survivorship annuity when Makeham's law holds. *J.I.A.* vol. LVI, p. 220.

R. R. McAlpin (1932). Valuation of policies assuring the amount outstanding under a loan. *J.I.A.* vol. LXIII, p. 437.

W. K. Bowie (1937). Temporary assurance mortality, 1924–34. *T.F.A.* vol. XVI, p. 285.

Sir William Elderton (1945). Mortality options in life assurance, *T.F.A.* vol. XVIII, p. 12.

CHAPTER II

UNDERWRITING AND EXTRA RISKS

11·1. The standard of selection.

In Chapter 1, we have referred to the standard of selection applied to assurances within the normal rates class. This standard is the result of a decision of policy which affects and is affected by the constitution of the fund and determines some of its fundamental characteristics. The standard will be determined to some extent by the type of connexion from which the business is drawn. For obvious practical reasons the standard should be such that the normal rates class will comprise the majority of the assurances so that those requiring special treatment are comparatively few in number.

The standard for a particular fund should be reflected in the mortality table adopted as its technical basis.

It should be remembered that the desire to maintain a high standard of selection must be balanced against the desire to cater as widely as possible for the needs of the assuring public. Those funds which maintain the highest standards of selection mostly draw their business from a comparatively limited range of the population, comprising the professional and managerial classes. Other funds which draw their business from wider sections of the population cannot maintain so high a standard of selection, yet may, by the width of their appeal, serve a useful purpose for which the other type of fund does not cater.

Life assurance is based upon averages. The normal rates class comprises a diversity of risks and there must, naturally, be a number of borderline cases where it is difficult to decide whether to include the proposal in the normal rates class or to require special treatment. Opinions differ about the magnitude of certain risks. Medical opinion may differ about the prognosis, or actuarial opinion may differ about the interpretation of statistical and other evidence. Since the proposer will have the choice of terms offered by various offices the element of competition provides a healthy corrective to excessive caution in underwriting practice.

The question of what is a 'normal' life needs some consideration especially from a medical point of view. Statistically there is a fair degree of variation between individuals all of whom may be classed as 'normal' and the student may think that these statistical variations may have a bearing on the mortality. This is not so: the variation in a particular case needs to be interpreted in the light of clinical experience.

To take an example, a group of 265 'normal young men' at Harvard were found to have systolic blood pressures which ranged from 98 to 146 with a mean of 114·9 and a standard deviation of 9·6. Such variations form part of the mechanism whereby the body adjusts itself to the changing conditions of life and should not be thought of as being necessarily associated with corresponding variations in mortality. They may have no medical significance at all.

11·2. The means of selection.

The proposal for life assurance is usually completed by the proposer in the presence of the agent or inspector. In addition the office will obtain reports from the following persons:

(i) The medical examiner.
(ii) The agent (if any).
(iii) A salaried representative of the office, if the life proposed for assurance has been seen by him.
(iv) One or two intimate friends of the life proposed.
(v) The proposer's own doctor (if the circumstances require it).

Where the proposal is to be considered without medical examination the report from (i), the medical examiner, may be replaced by a series of additional questions in the proposal form and an interview by a salaried representative of the office would generally be insisted upon. The report from (v), the proposer's own doctor, does not take the place of medical examination but may give useful additional information.

The medical examiner should be chosen partly by his age and qualifications but more for his experience either in general practice or as a consulting physician to a general hospital. The general practitioner and the consultant have a wide variety of experience of all sorts of conditions that is useful for the purpose of assessing a risk. The specialist or the surgeon is not so suitable as a medical examiner unless a special condition has to be investigated.

The report from (v), the proposer's own doctor, is required as a matter of routine where the sum assured exceeds, say, £5000. It is also required for smaller assurances where the personal medical history contains some point that needs to be cleared up.

Special reports may also be required, for example, blood-sugar-tolerance tests, X-ray reports and electrocardiograms. Certain of these may be required for all proposals for more than, say, £10,000 assurance.

The information obtained from the various papers may be grouped under the following heads:

(*a*) Age and (possibly) racial origin.
(*b*) Occupation.
(*c*) General health and habits.
(*d*) Personal medical history.
(*e*) Build and appearance.
(*f*) Family history.
(*g*) History of other proposals for assurance.
(*h*) Prospect of residence in unhealthy climates.
(*i*) Aviation.

The medical examiner, in addition to commenting on some or all of these particulars, will also give the results of medical examination.

11·3. The methods of giving effect to extra risks.

Where a proposal is subject to extra risk so that it cannot be included in the normal rates class, it may be dealt with in one of three ways. The proposal may be declined or postponed or special terms may be quoted.

Terms should be quoted whenever possible so that the number of declined proposals is kept as small as possible. There will remain a proportion of cases which have to be declined because the risk is so hazardous or the prognosis so uncertain that it is not possible to arrive at a reasonable assessment of the risk.

A proposal should be postponed where the assessment of the risk is uncertain at the time but where the prognosis should be clearer after the lapse of, say, 6 months or 1 year. Such proposals might include, for example, those with a history of recent illness or operation or those with unexplained blood-pressure changes.

When it has been decided to impose special terms the method of giving effect to the extra risk must be considered. There are five main methods:

(i) An increase in the premium, whether for one year or a limited time or for the period of extra risk or for the whole duration of the assurance.
(ii) A decrease in the amount of the assurance at early death.
(iii) A limitation of the scope of the assurance.
(iv) An adjustment of the bonuses (where the assurance participates in the profits).
(v) A change in the type of assurance.

Some of these methods may be employed in combination with each other. The fourth method is not very suitable except perhaps for a limited class of extra risks; it tends to be rigid in operation and the charge varies with the amount of the bonuses from time to time. It is of little importance in Great Britain. The third method is not suitable for medical conditions except for certain special clearly defined risks.

Which of the other three methods is most suitable for a particular proposal depends on the type and amount of extra risk. Before we turn to consider the theoretical aspects of the subject it will be helpful to review some practical aspects of medical selection.

*11·4. The underwriting of extra risks.

For examination purposes the student does not need to be familiar with medical terms and this section is included merely to give him a practical background to the treatment of extra risk.

It will be convenient to group our remarks under the various headings of the medical report form reproduced on pp. 196–7. There is considerable variation in the medical report forms used by the various offices and the report form which is reproduced in this book is given for purposes of illustration only.

Family history

There is considerable confusion of thought about the significance of the family history of a proposer. The student may think that certain infections are inherited but this is not so. If a parent has suffered from a particular infection the child might inherit the ability to resist that infection.

There is no doubt that certain constitutional defects are inherited. Under this heading we may note insanity and epilepsy. There is also a tendency for certain forms of blood-pressure changes to run in families and this may also be due to the inheritance of a constitutional defect.

The view has been widely held that tuberculosis is inheritable. Medical opinion would, we think, nowadays regard that as a mistake. The earlier view probably arose because a tuberculous mother or father may infect the child at a very early age, though the fact of the infection may not be at once apparent. An alternative view is that some predisposition to this disease may be inherited. We think that there would be a conflict of opinion on this point, but if a predisposition to tuberculosis is inheritable, it seems to be the only infective disease of which that is true. Tuberculosis is of course associated with dirt, poverty and exposure and the general surrounding circumstances of life have a considerable bearing on the incidence of the disease.

From the underwriting point of view the family history has to be weighed against the personal history of the applicant and the results of medical examination. The family history is generally of less significance in the older lives though even at such ages it may be helpful in building up a picture of the prospects of longevity of a proposer.

Personal history

Little that is useful can be said on this point in this book. The interpretation of the personal history of the applicant is very much a matter which must be dealt with by the medical officer. In

Information to be obtained from the proposer

1. (a) Name (b) Residence (c) Profession or occupation (d) Is the proposer married or single?	(e) Age next birthday

2. Family history	Age approximately	If living State of health	Age at death approximately	If dead Cause of death (Precise information is necessary: such terms as childbirth, dropsy, accident being avoided)
Father				
Mother				
Brothers				
Sisters				
Have any of the above persons suffered from insanity, epilepsy or tubercular disease other than those (if any) stated to have died therefrom? If so, give full particulars				

3. For what illnesses or injuries, and from whom, has the proposer required medical assistance?	
4. Has the proposer had any form of venereal disease?	
5. (a) What kind and amount of alcoholic stimulant does the proposer take? (If an abstainer state for how long: if not, state the daily or average weekly consumption). (b) Has the proposer ever taken narcotics or other drugs: if so, for what reason?	

I declare that the foregoing answers are true and complete and I agree that they shall be held to form part of the proposal for an assurance on my life with the Life Assurance Society.

Date........................19 *Proposer's Signature*..

Confidential Medical Report to the Life Assurance Society, on the life of

General:	Appearance Any suspicion of bad habits		
Measurements:	Height Weight		
Circulation:	Pulse Heart		
	Blood pressure	Systolic	Diastolic
Respiration:	Girth at nipple Chest	Inspiration	Expiration
Digestion:	Tongue Bowels Appendix Hernia Abdomen Umbilical girth		
Genito-Urinary system:	S.g. of urine Albumen Sugar Venereal disease		
Nervous system:	Sleep Headache Tremors Reflexes	Knee Jerks	Pupils
Special circumstances (e.g. points arising out of past illnesses) If female, what is state of uterine functions?			
(*a*) Do you think the proposer will live to extreme old age? or (*b*) Do you think he is a normally healthy subject? *If the proposer does not come within either of these categories please indicate your general impression of his prospects of longevity.*			

Examiner's Signature..

Qualifications ....

Date....................19 *Address* ....

See other side for information to be supplied by the proposer.

dealing with non-medical proposals, the actuary will have to make himself familiar with those diseases which can be ignored. For example, one attack of pneumonia would probably be ignored, but a history of several attacks might be significant.

The personal history must be looked at carefully because some diseases have associations or after-effects which are important for underwriting. Thus, a history of one attack of pleurisy associated with pneumonia might be ignored, but pleurisy by itself might be tubercular in origin. Medical examination should always be required where there is a history of rheumatic fever because it frequently leaves the subject with a damaged heart.

The student will notice that a specific question is asked with regard to venereal disease.

Build, appearance and habits

The information obtained under the heading of build, appearance and habits is basic to the underwriting of the proposal because it gives general information which is useful in building up a picture of the proposed life.

A table of average weight in relation to height and age will be found in *J.I.A.* vol. LIV, p. 215. This table must be used with caution. There is obviously a considerable range on either side of the average weight where the variation would be considered of no medical significance. Further, the weight must be considered in relation to the bone structure and the general build and habits of the proposer. Some persons have a large bone structure, and such cases must be distinguished from those where the excess weight is due to fat.

Weight should also be considered in relation to the habits and the general muscular development of the proposer. His mode of life might be important and the quantity of alcohol he consumes as a regular practice. The facts stated in the proposal cannot always be taken at face value when considering the mode of life of the proposer. For example, when the proposed life is stated to be a total abstainer we need to know for how long he has been an abstainer. If he has previously suffered from alcoholism, the risk is one of a return to alcoholic excess.

Underweight is of less significance than overweight. Generally, underweight of itself would only be considered of significance in young lives where the proposer is of the weedy type with poor muscular development, or where there is a family history of, for example, tuberculosis. Underweight should be regarded as a decreasing extra risk and it is of little significance after, say, age 40.

Overweight is generally significant at all ages and is regarded as an increasing extra risk. It is of less importance in the younger lives, particularly where it is combined with good muscular development as in an athlete, but it should be remembered that the excess weight will involve a strain on the circulatory system when the proposer attains the later ages. The condition of overweight may also be regarded with less severity where the tendency to a large build runs in the family and the family history is good.

Overweight combined with high blood pressure is an adverse feature and the extra premium for the combined risk should be greater than for either of them separately.

Circulation

In healthy adults the pulse rate is about 70–75 per minute but there may be considerable variation, especially for example due to nervousness.

The blood pressure measures the strength of flow of the blood from the heart. In non-technical language, we may regard the systolic pressure as measuring the pressure of blood in the arteries at the period of maximum flow; the diastolic pressure measures the pressure at the period of steady flow in between the heart beats, and thus provides some measure of the elasticity of the tissue of the arteries. The difference between the two is often referred to as the pulse pressure and in healthy adults the three measures should be approximately in the relationship of 3:2:1 respectively. Thus the systolic pressure might be 120, the diastolic pressure 80, and the pulse pressure 40.

Tables of average blood pressure should be used with caution. The real question is not the amount of any particular variation from the average, but whether that variation is clinically significant. In healthy adults the systolic pressure may vary from 100 to 150 mm.

of *mercury* on the standard scale. Generally speaking a systolic blood pressure of more than 150 mm. would be regarded as clinically significant, though regard should be had to the age and other circumstances disclosed by the medical examination. The systolic pressure may be temporarily raised because of the nervousness of the proposer. A diastolic pressure up to 90 mm. would not be regarded as clinically significant, but special consideration must be given to cases where the diastolic pressure exceeds 90 mm.

Changes in blood pressure may be of an intermittent and transient character. For example, a proposer aged 50 years was found to have a blood pressure of 171/100 on the average of four readings. Six months later the pressure was 150/90 which was regarded as being normal for his age. The evidence in this type of case is difficult to interpret, because the pressure may settle down to normal or may become fixed at too high a level. A precautionary extra premium would be required.

Where the diastolic pressure is too high in relation to the systolic pressure, it means that the action of the heart is too weak. The student should, however, be warned that the diastolic pressure is often stated at a higher figure than the true figure because the exact point at which the pressure is taken is not so clearly marked as for the systolic pressure. Further readings would be required where the diastolic pressure is believed to have been overstated.

Where the systolic and diastolic blood pressure are too far apart it means that the heart is having to act too vigorously, either because a defect in the aortic valve allows blood to return into the heart or because of certain other conditions. The condition is associated with an enlarged heart, and such cases would usually have to be declined.

From an underwriting point of view the extra risk arising from high blood pressure is generally small until after age 50. It is of greater significance when associated with overweight or with the presence of albumen in the urine, and it will also have to be considered in relation to the other results of medical examination, for example, the state of the blood vessels in the eye as seen through the ophthalmoscope. The extra risk increases very rapidly after age 55.

Low blood pressure is not usually of as much significance as high blood pressure.

The statement that the extra risk arising from high blood pressure is small until after age 50 needs qualification in one respect. A high blood pressure in a young proposer may be of much greater significance than in an older proposer. For example, readings of 200/100 for a proposer aged 25 years would carry a much worse prognosis than similar readings in a proposer aged, say, 55 years. The former would probably be declined whereas the latter may be acceptable on special terms. This indicates a difficulty in the analysis of sub-standard risks. Care must be taken to see that only those cases which have a similar prognosis are grouped together.

Electrocardiograms may help in the assessment of the heart risk. They record the electrical discharges set up in the heart muscle. It is the general practice, we believe, in America, though not in Great Britain, to require electrocardiograms for all proposals for very large assurances. The electrocardiogram does not provide a sure diagnosis of all heart conditions. For example, a proposer whose electrocardiogram is normal may die a few months later of coronary thrombosis. The electrocardiogram would not detect the condition.

Respiration

The measurements of chest at inspiration and expiration should be taken into account with the other measurements and need not be further referred to in this section. We propose to refer here to a few of the main medical conditions.

The student may not be aware how widespread is the disease of tuberculosis. If X-ray photographs were taken of the chests of any group of healthy adults, it is probable that a large proportion would show traces of healed tuberculosis, though none would have had any clinical symptoms of the disease. There are many forms of tuberculosis, and a person who has suffered from one of the milder forms is protected to some extent against the more serious manifestations of the disease.

Where there is a personal history of pulmonary tuberculosis it is possible to consider assurance on special terms, provided the disease has been quiescent for some years. X-ray photographs would be available. The terms would depend upon the extent of the disease as shown by the X-ray photographs, and upon the build and family history of the proposer. The age of the proposer at the onset of the disease is of importance, and his conditions of life. The risk is of a decreasing character and may be suitably met by a reduction in the sum assured at early death.

Where there is a family history of tuberculosis, the important points are contact, build, chest and personal history. Such a proposer can frequently supply an X-ray photograph. A history of tuberculosis in brothers and sisters is generally more serious than in father or mother. Where there is a family history but not a personal history of tuberculosis, the main risk is before the age of 45 years and can often be ignored after that age.

Unless pleurisy is associated with pneumonia, it is almost certainly tubercular in origin. However, this is one of the milder manifestations of tuberculosis and carries only a comparatively small risk of recurrence. The risk decreases with the time elapsed since the date of the attack.

A personal history of asthma in childhood can usually be ignored. There is a form of asthma which the child grows out of at about the age of puberty. Asthma in adults is serious because it puts a strain both on the heart and lungs which increases with age. The risk is thus of the increasing type and the assurance cover should not extend to the older age-groups.

An isolated attack of bronchitis is of no significance for underwriting. Chronic bronchitis returning most winters is similar in effects and significance to asthma.

Emphysema refers to the loss of elasticity in the tissue of the lungs. The condition is thus one of the problems of 'ageing' and imposes a progressive strain on the heart. It may result from bronchitis or asthma or from the occupation of the subject.

Digestion

A personal history of indigestion needs to be carefully investigated because a proposer who has suffered from a peptic ulcer may omit to refer specifically to that fact.

The prognosis of peptic ulcer (whether gastric or duodenal) is too uncertain to permit of assessment for life assurance until at least 2 years after cessation of symptoms. Thereafter the prognosis improves with the length of the period free from symptoms. Thus the risk is a decreasing one and may be ignored after 10 years' freedom. The condition is commoner in males than in females and the period of maximum risk would fall in the age-group 45–55.

Periodic remissions and relapses are characteristic of peptic ulcer. A period of freedom from symptoms may lull both the proposer and the assurance society into a false sense of security. X-ray reports would generally be available and should be obtained to show the end results of the disease.

Peptic ulcers arise from the effect of mental or emotional disturbances on the functioning of the stomach. It is coming to be recognized as a constitutional defect and, since it tends to run in families, the family history is important.

Genito-urinary system

There has been considerable progress in the testing of renal function and tests have clarified the significance of findings which formerly would have led to the rejection of lives for assurance. About 10–15% of healthy lives aged up to 30 years would show the presence of albumen in the urine but the albumen may be of no importance for life assurance. For all age-groups, the clinical significance lies not so much in the finding of albumen in the urine as in the associated findings in the urine, the blood vessels, etc. The evidence needs to be interpreted by the medical officer. It is not possible to classify the risks in a simple way.

The presence of sugar in the urine may or may not signify diabetes. A blood-sugar tolerance test would generally be required. Medical opinion, we believe, would regard the condition of renal glycosuria as being of no significance for life assurance.

Diabetes properly controlled with insulin carries an increased mortality, partly because the patient's resistance to other diseases is lowered. Diabetes is more severe in young subjects than in older lives and, in the absence of suitable statistics, the risk might be considered as roughly a constant addition to the rate of mortality.

It is not practicable to assess the risk for the longer period assurances because insulin has only been used for the control of diabetes since 1921 and there may be long-term effects from its use which are not yet apparent.

There has been an enormous improvement in the treatment of venereal diseases in their acute stages. Thus, where the disease has been adequately treated, a personal history of venereal disease is not so important as formerly. The risks really arise from the possible sequelae from the disease. The modern methods of treatment have not yet been used long enough to say with certainty whether they prevent the sequelae or whether the immediate infection only is cured. Thus the risk may be regarded as a late risk.

Nervous system

Two conditions should be distinguished. The first is psychosis or mental change. It is almost impossible to insure this risk.

The second condition is neurosis. The condition may interfere with the patient's joy of life but medical opinion would not, we think, regard it as having any effect on the expectation of life. It may be ignored for life assurance unless it is very severe.

Where there is organic disease of the nervous system there is a marked risk because the condition is often progressive. It is an increasing risk.

A personal history of infantile paralysis may be significant. It would, however, be ignored in a proposal where the life had suffered from the condition as a young subject and the disease had not been widespread. Infantile paralysis may be classed as a medium rather than a late risk.

Female lives

The underwriting of proposals on female lives is different in some respects from that of male lives. Some conditions have a less significance and some a greater significance for female than for male lives.

It also used to be customary to charge an extra premium for the risks of childbirth. The very considerable reduction in maternal mortality, particularly in recent times, makes this practice less justifiable and it is doubtful whether the mortality of young married women is any greater than that of men of the same age-group.

11·5. Theoretical aspects of extra risks.

The student will appreciate from his earlier studies of the theory of life contingencies that the incidence of extra risk can be shown to be at least as important as the amount of extra risk in the calculation of extra premiums. The mathematics provide the background to the assessment of extra risk, though our knowledge of the factors is not usually sufficient for a full mathematical treatment.

The student should keep in mind the conception of early, medium and late risks to which we have referred in the previous section. That is fundamental to the assessment of extra risk. But he should also try to free his mind from too mathematical an interpretation in a particular case. There is an infinite variety of extra risks. The aim should be to assess the risk in a manner appropriate to the individual circumstances.

There has been a tendency to equate the conception of early, medium and late risks with mathematical expressions for decreasing, constant and increasing additions to q. We feel that this is a mistake, though the mathematical expressions may be useful in analysing particular cases. We should recognize that the problem is essentially one of assessing a particular life aged x, say, and we have to assess both the amount of the extra risk and the ages at which that extra risk will probably be incurred.

First, notice how important is the influence of the age of the proposed life on the problem of extra risk. Many forms of impairment affect only a limited range of ages. We must therefore consider whether the proposed life is near the age of maximum risk for that impairment or whether the period of maximum risk has passed or is still to come. If that period is still to come, is the age of maximum risk beyond the age up to which assurance is required? Fig. 11·1 will help to fix this idea. It shows the curve of deaths by the A 1924–29 table and on the assumption of various percentage additions to the rate of mortality.

Fig. 11·1 illustrates the kind of picture that a doctor might have in mind when considering the period of maximum risk. It must be remembered that the doctor is expressing a clinical judgment based on his valuation of the significance of certain facts. Where an impaired life has passed the modal age for that impairment the doctor may feel that the prognosis is too uncertain to admit of assessment for life assurance.

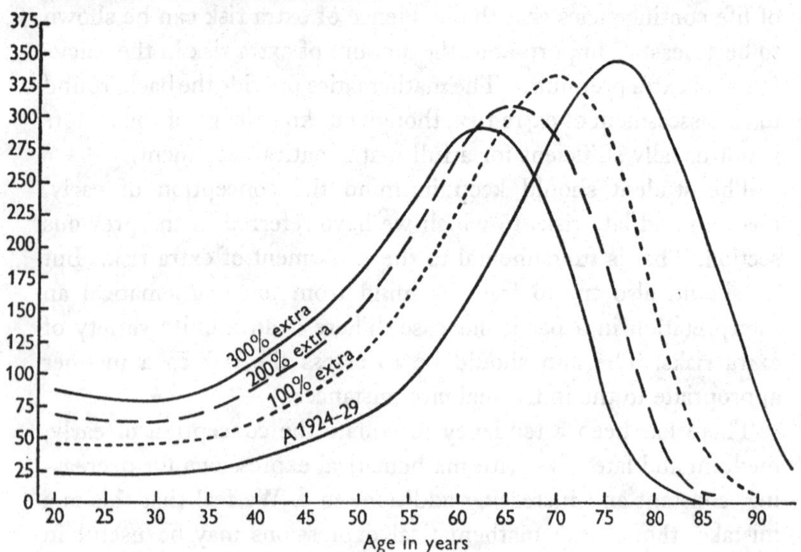

Fig. 11·1. The curve of deaths by the A1924–29 table and allowing for certain percentage additions to mortality. The radix has been taken as $l_{10} = 10{,}000$ in each case.

Secondly, notice the importance of the incidence of extra risk in relation to the extra premium to be charged. Suppose that unaccented symbols represent values on the normal basis, and that accented symbols represent the values on the basis of the expected special mortality for a particular type of extra risk; also that E is the required extra premium. Then

$$(1+i)\,E = (q'-q)\,(1-V_{+1}) + p'\,(V'_{+1}-V_{+1}) - (1+i)\,(V'-V). \tag{11·1}$$

This equation follows from the 'equation of equilibrium'. It expresses the fact that the extra premium is equivalent to (i) the excess expected death strain on the basis of normal policy-values plus or minus, (ii) the increase or decrease in the reserve in respect of the extra risk. (Remember that $V' - V$ is the algebraic reserve for the extra risk.)

Where $V' = V$ the second and third terms vanish and the extra premium is equal to the excess expected death strain.

Where the special policy-values are zero the extra premium is equal to the excess expected death strain minus the provision for normal policy-values in respect of the expected survivors on the special basis. In these circumstances the net premium merely covers the risk for the year.

It sometimes happens that the excess expected death strain is negative at certain durations. This may happen either because the special mortality is less than the normal at those durations or because the policy-values exceed unity, the sum at death. Credit may be given to a group of lives, which are subject to extra risks, for the fact that those lives are a specially select group which would, apart from those extra risks, show a lighter mortality than the normal. This argument must be used with caution though it is sometimes justified by the facts. The other case, where V exceeds unity, is dealt with later.

The cost of the excess expected death strain may be

(*a*) within the amount of the current provision by way of extra premium, or

(*b*) in excess of that amount but within the sum of that provision and of the amounts provided for the normal policy-values, or

(*c*) in excess of the extra premium plus the provision for normal policy-values.

Where position (*a*) obtains, no difficulty arises. It is generally best to arrange the charge for extra risk so that position (*a*) is reached.

Where position (*b*) obtains, the normal premium plus the extra premium is insufficient to provide the policy-values on the normal basis. Suitable deductions should be made both from the surrender value scale and from the valuation liability. The practices of offices vary: some would accept the position (*b*) but some would insist that the extra premium itself must be sufficient to pay for the current extra risk.

The extra premium should not be quoted in such a form that position (*c*) obtains. The normal premium plus the extra premium would, in this case, be insufficient to pay the expenses and the current normal and extra risk and there would be a considerable risk of loss from withdrawals. Where position (*c*) might hold, a single extra premium should be quoted or an extra premium payable for a limited period so chosen that position (*a*) or (*b*) is arrived at instead of (*c*).

Where the extra risk is decreasing the values of $(q'-q)(1-V_{+1})$ necessarily decrease because $(1-V_{+1})$ is also decreasing. If a level extra premium were to be payable for the whole duration of the assurance, either position (*b*) or (*c*) would be reached. The extra premium should be payable in one sum or for a limited period.

Where the extra risk tends to be constant the values of

$$(q'-q)(1-V_{+1})$$

decrease because $(1-V_{+1})$ is decreasing. If a level extra premium were to be payable for the whole duration of the assurance, position (*b*) would hold. The amount of the extra premium might be fixed according to the first year's extra risk and the period for which the extra premium is to be payable would have to be chosen correspondingly.

Where the extra risk tends to be increasing, the progression of the values of $(q'-q)(1-V_{+1})$ depends on the relationship between the rate of increase of $(q'-q)$ and the rate of decrease of $(1-V_{+1})$.

Thirdly, in addition to the age and the incidence of the extra risk, we must notice how important is the influence of the class of assurance upon the treatment of extra risk. It frequently happens that the medical officer feels he can assess the extra risk for a certain period or up to a certain age but that after that period or that age the prognosis is so uncertain that he cannot make any reliable assessment of the extra risk. Should this happen, an assurance might be considered within that period but an assurance for any longer period would probably be declined.

Sometimes it may be felt that the extra risk is wholly deferred beyond the period of the assurance, or that during that period the extra risk is minimal and may be ignored. Such a special extra risk is suitably met by the offer of an assurance for a period which would expire before the onset of the extra risk and an endowment assurance might be acceptable at the normal rate of premium.

The considerations that apply to endowment assurances in such circumstances apply also to some extent to temporary assurances for similar periods but much more caution is necessary with this class of assurance. The premium rates are very sensitive to changes in the mortality basis and an extra that is negligible for endowment assurances would not necessarily be negligible for temporary assurances. The death strain at risk under a temporary assurance is practically equal to the sum assured throughout the period of assurance; where the period is a long one the risk is at least as great as under a whole-life assurance and should be underwritten with just as much caution as for that class.

Decreasing temporary assurances are more nearly akin to endowment assurances with the 'savings element' removed but the relatively small premium for decreasing temporary assurances suggests that care should be exercised when dealing with extra risks.

Double endowment assurances, and similar types of assurance, have the peculiarity that the death strain at risk is positive at the early durations and negative at the later durations of the assurance. Considering a group of lives subject to a particular type and amount of extra risk, the excess deaths expected within the period of the assurance may fall in the 'positive' or the 'negative' parts of the period and the one tends to offset the other. Whether the positive and negative items will balance depends upon the incidence of the extra risk within the period of the assurance. It is tempting to assume that the values of the positive and negative items will be equal so that normal rates may be charged. Such an assumption is usually justified where the extra risk is of an increasing type and it may also be made as a practical measure where the extra risk is approximately constant provided that the period of the assurance is fairly short. The assumption is not justified where the extra risk is of the decreasing type, nor where the extra risk is approximately constant and the period of the assurance is a long one.

The values of the positive and negative items depend upon the incidence of the excess deaths rather than upon the incidence of the excess rate of mortality. For this reason it is important that the assumption of equivalence between the positive and negative items should be made only where the double endowment assurance matures not later than the modal age of the curve of deaths for the particular type of extra risk. Where the maturity age is later than the modal age the double endowment assurance premiums tend to be higher on the special than on the normal basis because the negative death strain falls at a time when there are fewer excess deaths.

The argument with regard to double endowment assurances may be illustrated by the following figures based on A 1924–29 select $2\frac{1}{2}\%$ unloaded. The modal age of the curve of deaths by the A 1924–29 table is 75 years.

Age at entry	$100\, P_{[x]\overline{10}\vert}$	$100\,(P_{[x]\overline{10}\vert} + P_{[x]\overline{10}\vert}^{\;\;1})$
40	8·907	17·3
50	9·132	17·2
60	9·841	16·9
70	11·83	16·9
80	16·20	18·4

Though for a given double endowment assurance, it may be legitimate to charge the same premium on the special mortality basis as on the normal mortality basis, there would not be the same equivalence between the policy-values on the two bases. Thus the scale of surrender values should be adjusted to provide for the type and amount of extra risk and the question whether the valuation liability should be modified should also be considered.

For limited-premium policies the extra risk may continue after premiums have ceased and a reserve must be built up from the extra premiums received during the premium paying period to provide for the extra risk during the remainder of the assurance. The death strain at risk under a limited-premium policy is larger than the death strain at risk under an endowment assurance for the same sum assured for a term equal to the premium paying period. The extra premium for that period must, therefore, be larger for the limited-premium policy than for the endowment assurance.

To illustrate these remarks we include Fig. 11·2 which shows the death strain at risk by A1924–29 3% for various classes of assurance.

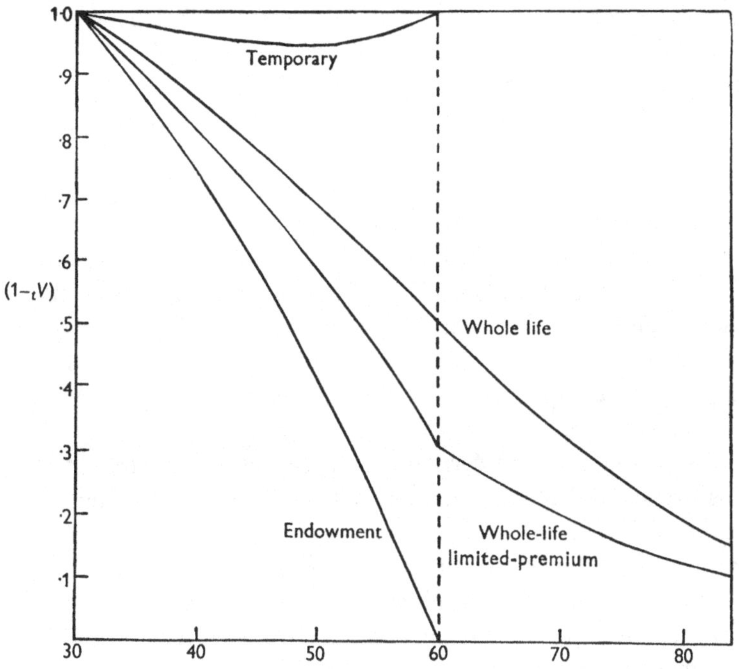

Fig. 11·2. Graph showing the death strain at risk for assurances effected at age 30.

Let us now consider method (ii) of § 11·3, where the extra risk is met by a decrease in the amount of the assurance at early death. The expected death strain on the normal basis is $q\,(1-V_{+1})$ and on the special basis is $q'\,(1-D-V'_{+1})$ where D is the decrease for the year. We have a relationship corresponding to equation (11·1), thus:

$$q'\times D=(q'-q)\,(1-V_{+1})+p'\,(V'_{+1}-V_{+1})-(1+i)\,(V'-V). \tag{11·2}$$

Suppose that the incidence of the extra risk is such that the main weight falls in the early years of assurance and that the decreases in the amount of the assurance in those years are insufficient to recompense the fund for the extra risk. The special policy-values will then be less than the normal policy-values and the surrender values should be correspondingly adjusted. Further, the amounts of the decreases required in the later years will be correspondingly larger. The relative amounts of the decreases will depend to a considerable extent on the relative size of the factor q'.

Suppose, on the other hand, that the incidence of the extra risk is such that the main weight falls in the later years of the assurance but that the decrease in the sum assured is to be made in the early years when the extra risk is light. The amount of the special reserve required for the extra risk will be determined very largely by the main weight of the risk which falls to be met in the later years of the assurance, but the decrease in the amount of the assurance in the early years to finance that special reserve will appear heavy because the value of the decrease is relatively small owing to the comparatively light special mortality q' operative during those years.

Thus it is important to arrange the decreases in the amount of the assurance so that the extra risk shall be met at about the time it is incurred. In fact, we may say that the purpose of the arrangement is to limit the liability at about the time that the extra risk is likely to be incurred. This result will be automatically produced by making the special policy-values equal to the normal. Formula (11·2) then reduces to

$$D=\frac{q'-q}{q'}(1-V_{+1}). \tag{11·3}$$

This is an important formula which should be memorized because it forms a useful standard by which to judge the amounts of the decreases in practice. It is true that the decreases are of irregular amounts but it is simple to adjust the figures as may be deemed necessary.

Arising out of the thought that the liability is to be limited by a decrease in the sum assured at the time when the extra risk is incurred, it may be suggested that, for such a purpose, the extra risk may be assessed on a less conservative basis than would be considered appropriate in the computation of an extra premium.

Comparing the two contracts, we see that the extra premium is effectively paid for a temporary assurance for varying amounts equal to the decreases in the amounts of the basic assurance and should include a considerable margin for contingencies. In our opinion the extra premium should include a margin of, say, at least 50%. Thus, where the extra risk is assessed directly for the extra premium, only two-thirds at most of that extra risk need be assumed in the computation of the corresponding decreases in the amount of assurance at early death.

One further practical consideration may be mentioned in connexion with endowment assurances. Where the reduction in sum assured decreases by equal amounts each year over the period of the endowment assurance the reduction is about the same for a given extra premium whatever the incidence of the extra risk. Fig. 11·3 shows how the initial debt varies with the extra premium on two extreme assumptions, taking an endowment assurance to mature at age 60 and A1924–29 $2\frac{1}{2}\%$ for the three terms, 10, 20 and 30 years.

*[There is a simple explanation of the phenomenon illustrated by Fig. 11·3 and we believe it to be of sufficient interest to discuss it at length.

Consider an endowment assurance for n years effected at age x and a sinking fund assurance for the same period of n years. The difference between the pure premiums for the two contracts, $P_{x\overline{n}|} - P_{\overline{n}|}$, will be equal to the level pure premium required for a decreasing temporary assurance for $n-1$ years, the sum assured under which is, in any year say t, equal to an amount $a_{\overline{n-t}|}/a_{\overline{n}|}$ just sufficient to make up the sinking fund policy-value to the full sum assured under the endowment assurance. Since the decreasing temporary assurance is assumed to be paid for by a level annual premium, the policy-values under that part of the contract would generally be negative, that is to say the endowment assurance policy-values would be less than the sinking fund policy-values.

Now suppose that the endowment assurance premium is increased by an additional pure premium, l, because of the presence of extra risk whatever may be the incidence of that extra risk. Then again the difference between the endowment assurance premium, so increased, and the sinking fund premium, namely $P_{x\overline{n}|}+l-P_{\overline{n}|}$, is the level pure premium on the special basis for the decreasing temporary assurance referred to.

Thus if, on the special basis, the premium to be paid for the endowment assurance is the normal premium, $P_{x\overline{n}|}$, the sum assured must be reduced by a proportion of the sums assured under the decreasing temporary assurance. Whence

$$D(t)=\frac{l}{P_{x\overline{n}|}+l-P_{\overline{n}|}}\times\frac{a_{\overline{n-t}|}}{a_{\overline{n}|}}. \qquad (11\cdot4)$$

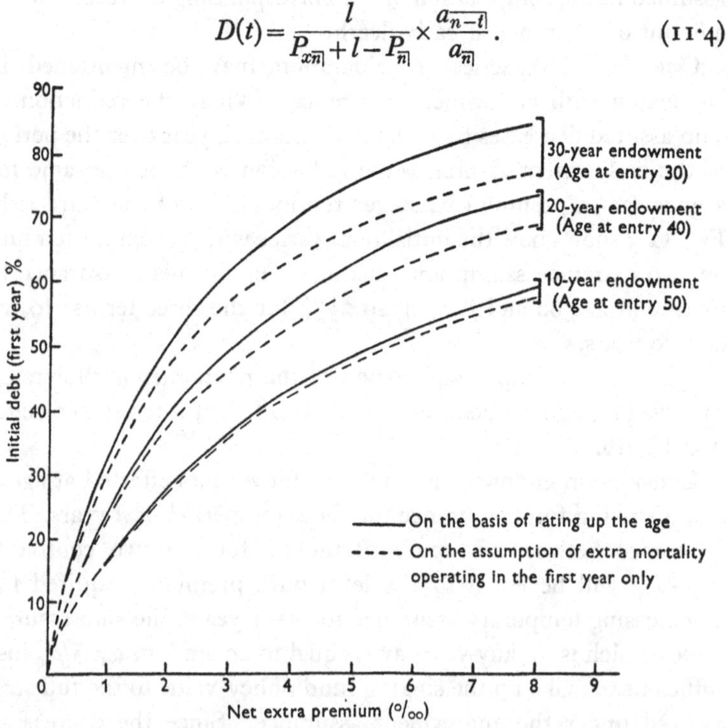

Fig. 11·3. Graph showing initial debt corresponding to fixed net extra premium on the assumption of: (1) Rating up in age. (2) Extra risk confined to first year only.

This expression depends only on the extra premium and is not affected in any way by the incidence of the extra risk. We may notice that it assumes that the reduction in sum assured in year t is proportionate to $a_{\overline{n-t}|}/a_{\overline{n}|}$. However, that series of reductions is not very different from the more usual assumption of a reduction decreasing by equal amounts each year over the period of the endowment assurance and this explains the phenomenon illustrated by Fig. 11·3.

Formula (11·4) may be used for computing the reductions direct from the equivalent extra premium provided that certain limitations are borne in mind. First, the method does not depend in any way upon an equivalence of policy-values. The method of computing the reductions suggests, indeed, that some adjustment should be made to the surrender values and valuation reserves, though whether this is necessary would depend on the incidence of the extra risk. Secondly, since the reduction in sum assured is not arranged so as to limit the liability at the time the extra risk is incurred, it is probable that some margin for fluctuations should be included in the calculations. These limitations are of most importance when the extra risk is decreasing rapidly, and where that position obtains it would be better to use formula (11·3).

The student may also notice that a comparison of double endowment assurance with sinking fund assurance is instructive in the consideration of the effect of extra risk.]

11·6. The rating of proposals.

Let us now turn to the practical question of rating proposals, having regard to the medical evidence and bearing in mind the theoretical considerations which we have reviewed in the preceding section. The rating of proposals requires a practical outlook because it is only possible to deal with it on fairly broad lines though the theoretical considerations are helpful as a background to the subject.

We shall first briefly describe the numerical system of rating which is used in North America and in many other countries. Our description is based on *Life Insurance* by Joseph B. Maclean.

The numerical system of rating is a system of classifying risks. Its chief advantages are that a certain measure of consistency is achieved in dealing with a large number of proposals, and secondly, that the classification of risks facilitates and systematizes the knowledge of extra risks that can be gained from the statistics of life assurance companies.

In the numerical system, a numerical value is allotted to each of the principal elements involved. The system assumes that the total value of the 'risk' can be expressed numerically by adding or subtracting the numerical values of the component factors. There are objections to the addition and subtraction of the various numerical values, but the system may be regarded as sufficiently correct for practical purposes. It should be borne in mind, however, that certain impairments when present together need a higher rating than the sum of the separate values. A suitable allowance is made for this in the rating manual.

In applying the system, the first step is to determine the basic rating depending on the proposer's age, height and weight, and, possibly, on other factors. This basic rating is taken from a prepared table covering a wide range of heights and weights and is then increased by the numerical values allotted to the unfavourable factors and decreased by the numerical values of the favourable factors. The resulting figure is the numerical rating. The purpose of the rating is to enable the risk to be classified in one of various groups, each covering a range of the factors. The rating may be considered as an indication of the percentage addition to the normal mortality, but it can only be regarded as an index of the total amount and not of the incidence.

The rating schedule would include ratings for occupation and for the type of assurance as well as for the various medical factors we have discussed in § 11·4. The rating would be contained in a manual which would be compiled with the aid of such statistics as may be available, but the personal judgment of the actuary and medical officers responsible for the rating manual is bound to play a considerable part.

When the system is worked out in detail, the manual would deal with the various cases where the percentage system is not really applicable and would indicate how such cases should be dealt with.

We think that those who use the numerical rating system would agree that the numerical rating can only be regarded as a guide and that the selection of risks depends to a considerable degree on personal judgment. The use of the manual does not do away with the necessity for that personal judgment but it provides a ready means of handling large numbers of proposals by relatively unskilled staff with a considerable measure of consistency, and enables such statistics as are available to exert a direct influence on the selection of risks.

In North America extensive investigations have been made into the mortality of under-average lives but it may help the student who is interested to refer briefly to a small-scale investigation as giving a broader view of the problems.

A paper by Gunnar Trier deals with the Norwegian experience for 1917–45, during which period practically all under-average lives were assessed by a committee of the offices participating in the scheme. Originally the assessment was based on various tables allowing for the incidence of risk but since 1924 the assessments have been based on percentage additions to the normal mortality. A proposal is allocated to one of seven groups, which represent additions of 25, 50, 75, 100, 150, 200 and 300% respectively.

Where the main weight of the extra risk appears to be in the early years the extra premium is assessed according to the initial risk but the assured is given the right to be re-examined after, say, 5 years and possibly also the right to a second re-examination after, say, 10 years. The extra premium would be reduced on re-examination if the circumstances justify such a course.

The statistical investigation compares the actual mortality both with the current normal experience and with that experience adjusted to allow for the various percentage additions to mortality assumed in the premiums. The first comparison shows the percentage additional mortality actually experienced. The latter comparison is a measure of the success of the underwriting. The data were insufficient to give much indication of incidence of mortality.

The statistical investigation may be used to confirm or correct underwriting practice but care must be exercised in interpreting the results not only because the data are usually few but also because a change in underwriting practice may affect the mortality experience.

Summing up, we may say that the strength of the numerical rating system lies in its appeal to statistics as the foundation of underwriting and in the measure of consistency it achieves in its practical application. The weakness of the system lies in its reliance upon a percentage basis which can only reflect the expected amount and not the incidence of the extra risk.

In Great Britain the selection of risks is in the hands of the actuary and of the chief medical officer, who would usually be a consulting physician. The chief medical officer will have the background of clinical experience which is required for the assessment of the significance of the various factors. He will be familiar with the medical statistics that are available though he may not be able to put his impressions in the statistical form that would be required for the calculation of the extra premium. It is for the actuary to interpret those impressions as may be required for the particular proposal.

Where the medical examiner thinks that a proposal is not acceptable at normal rates he will usually express his impression of the proposed life by suggesting an addition to the age of, for example, 3, 5, 7, or 10 years. The medical examiner does not mean by this that he would expect a group of lives similar to the proposed life to experience mortality precisely equal to that of lives exactly 3, 5, 7, or 10 years older than the true age. He is giving his general impression of the amount of variation from the normal that might be expected. Thus, it would not necessarily be correct to add the recommended number of years to the age for the purpose of calculating the extra premium. This point need not be laboured: it is sufficiently illustrated by Table 11·1, taken from Wood.

Suppose that the extra premium for whole-life assurance has been computed by an addition to the age of the proposer and that the corresponding extra premium for endowment assurance is required. The chief medical officer would have given his impression of the incidence of the extra risk and we need some simple method of giving general effect to the incidence.

Where the extra risk is deferred it is probably sufficient to charge the premium for the endowment assurance with the same addition to the age as for the whole-life assurance. This, however, assumes a rather special type of extra risk: a simple and more general, though arbitrary method is as follows.

We can see from Table 11·1 that the endowment assurance extra premium for many types of extra risk lies between (*a*) the extra premium based on the rating in age, and (*b*) the corresponding extra premium for whole-life assurance. We may therefore mix (*a*) and (*b*) in suitable proportions, for example

$$2/3\ (a) + 1/3\ (b), \quad \text{or} \quad 1/2\ (a) + 1/2\ (b).$$

Taking the 10-year endowment assurance in Table 11·1 we have (*a*) = ·045 and (*b*) = ·347. Thus the 'two-thirds' rule would give an endowment assurance extra premium of ·146 and the 'half-way' rule ·196.

TABLE 11·1

Extra premiums per policy of 100. *Life aged* 30 *years*

	Number of premium payments	Type of extra risk		
		Extra mortality decreasing rapidly to zero	Constant addition of ·005 to q	Addition of 6 years to age
Endowment assurance	10	·785	·236	·045
	20	·516	·276	·077
	30	·413	·305	·132
	40	·369	·328	·221
Whole-life	—	·347	·349	·347
Whole-life by limited-premiums	40	·370	·357	·316
	30	·419	·380	·314
	20	·534	·447	·371
	10	·879	·679	·605

The problem does not always present itself in the simple form of a rating in age. For example, on one occasion the medical examiner diagnosed a condition of aortic valvular disease in a proposed life aged 40 years. The chief medical officer thought that about one-half of such lives would live about 15 years after diagnosis of the disease and only a small proportion would live 20 years. The evidence was interpreted by putting ${}_{15}p'_{40} = \cdot 5$ and trying one or two assumptions for the special mortality. Ordinary assurance would have required a heavy loading but a double endowment assurance for a term not exceeding 15 years was acceptable at normal rates.

It is not easy to give specific advice about the calculation of decreasing debts because practice varies considerably. The general principle should be, as stated in the preceding section, to arrange the decreases in the amount of the assurance so that the extra risk shall be met at about the time it is incurred. The amounts of the decreases may be computed by formula (11·3) and smoothed empirically.

The method is suitable for whole-life assurances only when the extra risk is of a decreasing or temporary character as has been referred to in the previous section.

The method is of more general application to endowment assurances because the sum at risk decreases rapidly. Except where the extra risk is of a rapidly decreasing character, the assumption as to incidence of the extra risk is of comparatively small importance. The method described in the next paragraph is an attempt to systematize the computation of decreasing debts but the student should be warned that this represents a personal opinion. There is considerable variation in the terms quoted in practice.

*[Suppose we assume that the extra mortality is a constant percentage, say K, of the normal rate of mortality during the period covered by the term of the endowment assurance. It follows from equation (11·3) that D will be a corresponding percentage, $K/(100+K)$, of the death strain at risk. For example:

Percentage extra mortality K	Corresponding deduction from death strain at risk $K/(100+K)$
50	1/3
100	1/2
200	2/3

We then reach the figures of Table 11·2. The suggested extra premiums include a margin for contingencies of 100%.

It will be observed that the extra premiums are very nearly proportionate to the assumed percentage extra mortality. We might as a practical measure tabulate the office extra premiums corresponding to 100% extra mortality, the sixth column of Table 11·2.

Then, where the extra premium is r times that extra premium for the given age and period of assurance, the corresponding reduction in the death strain at risk would be $r/(1+r)$.]

TABLE 11·2. ENDOWMENT ASSURANCE

Table showing the extra premium corresponding to certain decreases in the death strain at risk, on the basis of a percentage increase in mortality

Age at entry	Theoretical increase in $P_{x\overline{n}\rvert}$ corresponding to a deduction from the death strain at risk of			Suggested extra premiums per £1,000 corresponding to a deduction from the death strain at risk of		
	$\frac{1}{3}$	$\frac{1}{2}$	$\frac{2}{3}$	$\frac{1}{3}$	$\frac{1}{2}$	$\frac{2}{3}$
	Endowment assurances maturing at age 50					
				£ s.	£ s.	£ s.
20	·00078	·00156	·00313	1 10	3 0	6 0
30	·00084	·00168	·00341	1 15	3 10	7 0
40	·00099	·00198	·00405	2 0	4 0	8 0
	Endowment assurances maturing at age 60					
20	·00100	·00201	·00402	2 0	4 0	8 0
30	·00119	·00239	·00479	2 10	5 0	10 0
40	·00160	·00321	·00644	3 5	6 10	13 0
50	·00214	·00429	·00851	4 5	8 10	17 0
	Endowment assurances maturing at age 70					
20	·00135	·00271	·00529	2 10	5 0	10 0
30	·00172	·00344	·00674	3 10	7 0	14 0
40	·00248	·00496	·00977	5 0	10 0	20 0
50	·00383	·00766	·01527	7 10	15 0	30 0

Note. Practically identical results would have been obtained by the method of formula (11·4).

11·7. Types of extra risk.

So far, discussion has been limited to extra risks of a medical character because they give rise to some of the most intricate problems but the principles we have dealt with are applicable to all extra risks. We will now consider some of them.

Occupation

The attitude to occupational extra risks has changed considerably of recent years. There has been the desire that the normal rates class should comprise as wide a variety of risks as is possible without injustice. This desire has been supported by the measures for public health and prevention of accidents which have tended to reduce occupational mortality to a common level. Those industrial risks which affect workpeople are of less importance to the majority of offices transacting 'ordinary' assurance business because workpeople mostly take 'industrial' rather than 'ordinary' assurance policies.

Occupational hazards arise chiefly from exposure to dust, heat, the elements, unhealthy conditions, and to special risks of accident. Examples are butchers in the slaughter-house, bakers in the bakehouse, workers in metal and glass, sawmill workers, miners, waiters, seamen, jockeys, police, steeplejacks. The incidence of the extra risk varies according to circumstances but may generally be taken to be of a constant or slowly increasing character. For some of the extra risks it is suspected that the mortality in later life may be comparatively heavy and it is suitable in those cases to offer endowment assurance on appropriate terms. The extra risk may be set off to some extent by a high standard of physical fitness, as might, for example, be found among policemen.

Proposals on the lives of those who serve alcoholic drinks need to be underwritten carefully and habits are particularly important. The best type of risk is that of a manager of a good residential hotel who occasionally serves behind the bar and such a risk might well be accepted at normal rates. The other risks should be graded suitably according to the class of life and the quantity of alcohol consumed. The extra risk may be regarded as of an increasing character and it would be important to get a full report from the salaried representative of the office.

Modern advances in science and technology bring new occupational risks, such as aviation, which will be dealt with under that heading and atomic energy research. The extra risks in atomic energy research arise from the effects of radiation upon the human body. The types of radiation have been known for many years, for example with X-ray apparatus. The effects also are known and can be guarded against. The extra risk is probably minimal where the proposed life is engaged in purely scientific research such as with a cyclotron. Where, however, the atomic energy is applied to industrial and other uses as, for example, in an atomic pile the intensities of radiation are much greater. Special industrial precautions are taken which minimize the extra risk but there remains the question whether the high intensities of radiation in use will produce long-term effects which cannot at present be known. Some extra premium is probably justified for persons working in the presence of an atomic pile.

Service in the armed forces carries several different kinds of extra risk some of which may be set off by the high standard of physical fitness of the lives concerned. These are war risks, risks of civil commotion, of residence in unhealthy climates and of aviation. War risks are dealt with in Chapter 7. Except for members of air-crews who are dealt with later, the other risks may be lumped together and a 'service' extra premium charged either for the duration of service or for the whole duration of the policy. The amount of the extra premium would, we think, lie between 3*s.* and 6*s.* % per annum but some offices take officers of the Army and Navy at normal rates. Where the extra premium is charged for the whole duration of assurance we reach position (*b*) of § 11·5 and some adjustment should be made to surrender values.

Similar remarks apply to the mercantile marine but something would depend on the standing of the employer and the class of life proposed for assurance.

Residence

It is difficult to give any clear guidance at the present time because the statistics are few and have been made completely out of date by advances in medical science. The control of malaria by modern drugs has very substantially reduced the mortality from tropical diseases.

The risks of foreign residence do not arise only from tropical diseases. There is the possible lack of prompt medical attention and there are the risks of civil commotion and of aviation. Political and other similar risks need to be taken into account. Further, there may be a moral hazard because the individual is removed from the influence of the moral restraint which would be operative in his homeland. Owing to the lack of transport facilities it is more common for persons resident abroad to travel by air than it would be for similar persons living in Great Britain and though the risk is one which might not justify a special charge it is a risk which we think should be taken into account in considering the risks of foreign residence as a whole.

The definition of the 'free limits' quoted by Wood† (with slight modifications) is as follows:

All places (Asia excepted) north of 33° N. latitude or south of 30° S. latitude and also the United States, Australasia, The Union of South Africa, Southern Rhodesia, Egypt (North of 22° N. latitude), Palestine, Japan, Korea, Madeira, the Canary Islands, Ascension, Cape Verde Islands and St Helena.

These limits would have to be modified from time to time because of risks of civil commotion.

There are two general methods of charging for residential extra risks. Either a fixed extra premium may be charged for the whole duration of the policy (or what is the same thing, a special table of premiums may be quoted) or the extra premium may be payable during the period of residence only. With the latter type of extra premium, rebates may be allowed for periods of residence within the free limits and the extra premium may vary according to the actual place of residence from time to time; also there may be a maximum limit on the number of years' extra premiums. For example, the extra premium might cease when 5 or 10 years' extra premiums have been paid.

The former type of charge is suitable when a branch organization exists in the country to which the extra premiums are to be applied and is also helpful where simplicity of operation is regarded as important. Since the extra premium might be payable after the extra risks had ceased, there should probably be some adjustment to surrender values where this method is used. The provisions of the Fourth Schedule of the Assurance Companies Act, 1909, should be borne in mind where the extra premium, or the special table of premiums, is based upon a different table of mortality than that used for business in Great Britain.

† *The treatment of extra risk*, pp. 45–6.

The second type of charge has the advantage that the extra premium can be arranged to be collected before the extra risk is incurred. The method is, however, somewhat more complicated to operate and, from the point of view of the policyholder, this method has the disadvantage that the amount of premium payable is not definitely known and the policy might be invalidated should the policyholder inadvertently omit to notify a change in the extra risk.

It has been the custom to divide the world into groups of areas for the purpose of assessment of extra premiums. We feel that, with the advances in medical science, the time may have come to average all risks of foreign residence in all parts of the world outside the free limits and to charge one rate of extra premium for them all. However, it is doubtful whether this view would be generally shared by other actuaries. Probably it is sufficient to group the areas into the free limits and two other groups, for example:

Normal rates	Group 1	Group 2
Europe North America Union of South Africa and Southern Rhodesia Australasia	Asia Africa (except Union of South Africa and Southern Rhodesia and parts in Group 2) South and Central America (except parts in Group 2) West Indies East Indies (except New Guinea)	West coast of Africa Mombasa Zanzibar Madagascar North coast of South America New Guinea

The extra premium for Group 2 might be, say, double that for Group 1.

Race

The question of race needs to be considered in relation to the mortality table on which the normal premiums are based. There are considerable differences between the mortality of the various races and the possibility of residence in an unhealthy climate would also have to be considered.

Generally speaking, we think that those permanently resident in Great Britain would be acceptable at normal rates for endowment assurances up to, say, age 60 years whatever the racial origin of the proposed life. More care would be required for whole-life assurances.

The population of the Latin countries of Europe tends to experience a higher mortality than the population of Great Britain and an extra premium might be required for persons resident in those countries who are not of British origin.

Where a branch organization exists the premiums for each country would be based directly or approximately on the mortality appropriate to insured lives in that country and it might be necessary to differentiate between the different races within the country. Where no branch organization exists proposals might be dealt with on the basis of an arbitrary adjustment, e.g. in age, to allow for differences in race compared with that assumed in calculating premiums but great care would be necessary in the selection of such lives.

Aviation

The rapidity of development of aviation makes it extremely difficult to give in a text-book useful advice on the underwriting of aviation risks because much of what is said may soon become out of date. We propose to draw attention to some of the general questions arising and to avoid as far as possible the recommendation of specific extra premiums.

Method (iii) referred to in § 11·3 is especially appropriate for aviation risks because the extra risk can be fairly easily defined and excluded from the assurance. Further, the persons proposed for assurance who are interested in flying are often young men whose purpose in effecting an assurance is investment rather than protection of dependents. Such a proposer would prefer a limitation in the scope of the assurance to the relatively heavy cost of full aviation cover.

The aviation risk might be met by method (ii) of § 11·3. Where this method is used the reduction in sum assured must apply to all causes of death and not merely to aviation accidents because the assurance fund must set off the cost of the limited aviation cover against the saving on other causes of death by reason of the limitation in amount. The method is not generally useful because the necessary reduction in sum assured is rather large.

Where the assured has accepted a limitation of the scope of the assurance as suggested earlier, the aviation risk may be covered by means of an accident insurance effected with those who specialize in the business. Such an insurance would be on a year-to-year basis and the assured would pay each year according to the circumstances from time to time. In some ways this may suit the assured but the method has several disadvantages. First, the cost of the insurance is not known at the outset. Secondly, the accident insurance must be based on a careful definition of the risk to be covered and there may well be circumstances in which a claim may be outside that definition and yet be also excluded by the special condition applicable to the life assurance. The assured would, as it were, fall between two stools. Thirdly, the cost of insurance must be increased in the long run if the insurance is to be divided between two separate insurers. For all these reasons we think it is preferable that the life assurance should include the aviation cover rather than that the aviation risk should be insured separately.

Where the life assurance is to include aviation cover the extra premium has to allow not merely for the extra risk at the time of proposal but also for the possible extension of that risk by an increase in the flying activities of the proposer. The extra premium is fixed at the outset and may not be increased though it may be reduced should circumstances justify that course. For this reason the extra premiums for aviation cover may appear heavy compared with the corresponding premiums for aviation accident insurance.

Turning now to the assessment of the extra risk we may notice examples of co-operation in various countries. In 1928, the Actuarial Society of America appointed an Aviation Committee and, in 1932, the Committee began the compilation of the experience on insured lives exposed to the aviation hazard. The Aviation Committee is a fact-finding body and does not make recommendations about the extra premiums to be charged. The extra premiums are fixed by the individual offices. In Great Britain in 1936, the Life Offices' Association and the Associated Scottish Life Offices began an arrangement between a considerable number of their member offices by which (*a*) a minimum tariff was established for civil aviation risks, (*b*) recommendations were made for extra premiums for Service aviation risks, (*c*) the instructors of flying clubs were to supply reports on pilots they had instructed, and (*d*) an Aviation Joint Committee was set up to operate the scheme and to collect such data as might be available. Thus in Great Britain the extra premiums for civilian aviation risks are fixed in general by the Aviation Joint Committee.

When assessing aviation risk it is necessary to take account of the amount and type of flying but the precise basis of assessment is an open question. The major risk is generally considered to be at the time of take-off and of landing and thus the number of ascents is important. It may, however, be convenient to deal with the total flying and we have to decide whether to assess the amount of it on the basis of flying-hours or of flying-mileage. Time in the air is perhaps the more natural basis. With aircraft of slow average speed shorter flights are likely to be adopted than with high-speed aircraft and this would tend to suggest that a journey of 3,000 miles by air is likely to be a worse risk when made in slow aircraft than in high-speed aircraft. There are, however, other factors to be considered and, so far as the passenger risk is concerned, flying-mileage provides the more suitable basis of assessment because the proposer is usually able to give the necessary information most easily in that form.

A general conclusion that has emerged from the study of flying statistics is that the improvement in the safety of aviation has been most marked in those types of flying which are subject to the closest supervision. The scale of extra premiums would illustrate this conclusion and special attention to it should be paid in the underwriting of aviation risks.

A further conclusion is that pilots tend to be subject to a high rate of fatality in the period just after qualifying when, perhaps, confidence outruns ability. There is also evidence that pilots with a record of accident or of violation of air-regulations are subject to a higher rate of mortality for some time thereafter, especially perhaps young pilots. We think that flying-men would maintain that there is at least as much variation in aviation risk between pilots as there is known to be medically in lives proposed for assurance. It is important to have as full information as possible about the individual pilot. Where an aviation risk is to be assessed a special aviation proposal form would be required.

When aviation fatalities are being considered a little care in underwriting may be necessary because the unit of variation is the aircraft accident rather than the individual life. For example, in the 21 years 1926–46 the accident experience of regular air services flown by United Kingdom operators showed 55 aircraft accidents which resulted in the death or serious injury of 220 passengers and 144 air-crew. The deaths cannot necessarily be assumed to be independent: where a number of such risks are being considered, the average sum at risk per accident may be considerably larger than the average sum at risk per assured life. Such a consideration might influence the maximum sum that would be retained at risk on any individual life and possibly also the rate of extra premium.

Some of the aviation risks may be expected to be found to a greater extent amongst the wealthier classes whose assurances would, probably, also be larger than the average. The aviation risk should be underwritten with especial care for the larger assurances and since it is not possible to catch all such risks at the time of proposal it might be preferable to reconsider the very general practice of allowing a small reduction in the rate of premium for the larger assurances. The saving on expenses for the larger assurances might be set against the aviation and other extra risks which tend to be incurred to a greater extent amongst the wealthier classes.

We may deal with the various risks under four general heads.

Fare-paying passengers

It would not be practicable to charge an extra premium from time to time according to the actual flights and some attempt must be made to assess the risks at the outset.

We may distinguish between air travel by aircraft operating to a regular schedule and by charter aircraft. It might be thought that the first type ought to be covered at normal rates because most assured lives will travel by air at some time or another. However, statistics show that the risk is not negligible where the amount of such flying is large: there will therefore be a limit above which the amount of flying is too large to be ignored. The experience in North America shows considerably lighter mortality amongst fare-paying passengers than the experience in Great Britain and the maximum mileage permitted free would no doubt be affected by that experience. The expected yearly mileage has to be computed from the information in the proposal and, in Great Britain, where the expected yearly mileage does not exceed, say, 15,000 miles, full aviation cover for all flights would be given at the normal rate of premium. Where the expected yearly mileage exceeds 15,000 miles the extra premium would be charged in respect of the excess expected mileage. A lower limit might be required for temporary assurances particularly for short periods because the premium for this class of assurance is so much more sensitive to variations in the assumed mortality.

Flights as a fare-paying passenger by charter aircraft or for pleasure trips might be dealt with on a similar basis but the purpose of the flights would have to be considered because that might have a material bearing on the extra risk.

Other passenger flights

This is a very mixed group on which it is difficult to give general guidance.

Some flights are made under similar conditions to fare-paying passenger flights but without actual payment of a fare and these would be dealt with in a similar manner to those flights. This is probably also true of flights made in private aircraft maintained for business purposes by Government departments and by business corporations.

Some flights are purely pleasure flights made, for example, by members of flying clubs who are not themselves pilots. These carry a risk similar to the risk amongst the pilot-members of flying clubs. Also, such persons may become interested in gliding or may themselves become pilots.

Some flights may be undertaken for scientific observations or the testing of instruments and the risk would depend on the purpose of the flights, the abilities of the pilots and the weather and other conditions at the time.

Members of the armed forces may be required to fly for purposes of transport and in the ordinary way this is best regarded as included within the general charge for service risks. The special class of airborne troops and parachutists would be charged a further extra premium to cover the special risks of their occupation.

Spare-time pilots

The flying clubs have not been able to resume activities on a large scale since the 1939–45 war, but in normal times the ordinary pilot with a private pilot's licence who is a member of a flying club provides an example of a common risk which is a difficult one to assess for the purposes of life assurance. The amount of actual flying may be small but the risk per flight may be high and a good deal would depend on the experience and ability of the particular pilot. There is also the possibility that the flying activities may be greatly extended and some charge should be made for that possibility. The extra premium would be assessed according to the expected number and character of flights.

Flights in gliders are of comparatively short duration but the number of flights may be considerable. The experience of the gliding clubs has been good but the data are insufficient to provide a firm basis for the assessment of the risk. There is also the possibility that a person interested in gliding only at the time of proposal may later take up flying in powered aircraft.

Persons who own their own aircraft form a small and special group that have to be dealt with individually. The owner may employ a pilot with a commercial licence.

Air-crew

The pilots employed on regular air-transport are a select group but they average about 1,000 hours flying per annum and the amount of flying is very considerable. This type of employment may continue up to about age 50. The risk would vary according to the character of the routes flown and the standing of the employer. The extra premium might be only two or three times that for a pilot with a private pilot's licence though the amount of flying would be incomparably greater.

Transport aircraft now carry a large crew. These risks are not distinguishable from the corresponding risks for pilots except that the amount of flying may be less and the risks may continue to a later age.

The risks for other pilots with commercial licences would depend on the character and amount of the flying to be undertaken.

The risk for pilots in the armed forces has been found to decrease with advancing age. The older pilots have the advantage of greater flying experience and probably also fly less because more of their time is taken in administrative duties. In the Air Force this decrease with advancing age may be linked to the rank attained but in the Army and Navy rank is likely to have little to do with flying experience. As a rough guide we may put the extra premium at, say, age 25–30 years at about the same as for a pilot on a commercial air-line. The less experienced pilots might be charged more and the senior pilots less.

The risk for other members of the air-crew would not, of course, depend upon experience. It would vary with the amount and character of the flying to be undertaken. The risk per flight would correspond with that of the pilot risk for similar type aircraft but since the larger aircraft both carry larger crews and have a better accident record than the smaller aircraft, the average aviation risk for pilots as a whole would probably exceed the average aviation risk for other members of air-crew.

BIBLIOGRAPHY

A. Levine (1899). On extra risks in relation to double endowment assurances. *J.I.A.* vol. xxxiv, p. 514.

W. P. Elderton (1923). Notes on the treatment of extra risk. *J.I.A.* vol. liv, p. 24.

C. F. Wood (1939). *The treatment of extra risks.* Cambridge University Press.

J. B. Maclean (1945). *Life insurance* (6th ed.). McGraw Hill Publishing Co. Ltd.

J. A. RYLE (1949). The meaning of normal. *The Lancet*, 4 January 1947, p. 1.

INGER MOLTKE (1950). Insurance of under-average lives in Denmark. *Het. Verzekerings-Archief*, vol. XXVIII, p. 161.

This paper describes the attempt which has been made in Denmark to allow for the incidence of extra risk by the use of hypothetical tables. The 'normal' table, graduated by Makeham, is adjusted by varying the Makeham constant *A* and the age. The 'under-average' tables, though frankly hypothetical, seem to be a sufficient representation of the limited experience (1916–45).

The British experience with regard to various medical conditions is discussed from time to time in the papers submitted to the *Assurance Medical Society* and there have been several large-scale studies of the experience in North America with regard to various extra risks. Reference may also be made to the papers on this subject, submitted to the Eleventh International Congress of Actuaries, Paris, 1937.

Papers submitted to the Centenary Assembly of the Institute of Actuaries:

GUNNAR TRIER. Insurance of under-average lives in Norway. *Proceedings*, vol. II, p. 352.

J. E. HOSKINS. Aviation fatality statistics. *Proceedings*, vol. II, p. 333.

J. H. KITTON. Civil aviation risks in connexion with life assurance underwriting. *Proceedings*, vol. II, p. 338.

CHAPTER 12

METHODS OF VALUATION

In this chapter we consider the methods employed in valuing the liability in respect of the life assurance contracts in force at the valuation date. The subject may be considered under two heads, the assembling of the data and the grouping of the data.

12·1. The assembling of the data.

In early days, the data for valuation were assembled direct from the policy registers or other records each time the valuation was made. Where the number of contracts in force was comparatively small this could be done without excessive expense, and quite large numbers of policies could be dealt with in this way because of the simple nature of the majority of the contracts. As the contracts in force increased in number and in complexity the method became cumbersome, and continuous methods were adopted by which the data for valuation were obtained from the data at the previous valuation by a process of continuous adjustment. This development, of course, took place over a long period of time. We have, for example, the records of a continuous system which Arthur Morgan commenced from the totals of assurances in force at 31 December 1828 whereas McCormack, writing in 1917, could refer to the recent adoption of the continuous method of classification by an office which had not previously employed it.

For many years the assurances were classified in books with subsidiary books in which each of the various types of movement 'on' and 'off' were also classified. The use of cards was introduced for friendly society statistics by A. G. Finlaison in 1853 and for life assurance statistics by O. G. Downes in 1863. Later, the invention of loose-leaf books facilitated the tabulation of statistics. McCormack refers to the controversy whether it would be better to keep the valuation records on cards alone with only totals in the class-books or whether the assurances should be tabulated both on cards and in class-books.

Continuous processes of classification had the important advantage of making an annual valuation feasible, whether the results were to be published or were merely for internal purposes. An annual valuation is now the almost universal practice.

The invention of punched-card machinery in connexion with the 1890 census of the United States of America has led to a revolution in methods of handling life assurance statistics which is not yet complete. The installation of such machines may lead to a revolution in the processes of valuation because the machines make possible the use of processes which could not have been undertaken with the older systems. Where punched-card machinery is available an important part of the duties of the actuary may be to adapt as much as possible of the work of the office to the capabilities of the machines which have been installed.

As a consequence of the developments we have referred to, the methods of assembling the valuation data vary from office to office to a very considerable extent and, in this text-book, it is not proposed to advocate the use of any one method. We propose to consider the fundamental purposes of the continuous process leaving the student to link up those aims with the actual methods with which he may be familiar. Students who have no practical experience should try to obtain access to one or two systems in actual use and there are various papers on the subject to which they may refer, for example McCormack (1917).

Modern machinery might make it possible to assemble the data at each valuation direct from the primary records and if this should become the general practice the wheel will have turned full circle. We think, however, that a continuous process has sufficient advantages to justify its retention though, of course, the actual methods employed in the process may be modified from time to time.

12·2. The continuous process of classification.

The main purpose of the continuous process of classification is to enable the totals of the various items in each classification group at the valuation date to be accurately ascertained as soon as possible after the closing of the books, thus providing the data required for the valuation in groups of the assurances in force. To achieve this object it is necessary

(*a*) to tabulate the data in the simplest form consistent with legislative requirements and the methods of valuation and of distribution of surplus;

(*b*) to derive a process by which the particulars of assurances in force at any valuation date may be reconciled with those relating to the valuation a year earlier;

(*c*) to arrange that the various elements (for example, new assurances, claims, surrenders, etc.) leading up to this balance, shall be self-balancing so that errors may be easily traced;

(*d*) to make the process so straightforward that it may be operated by clerks who have no actuarial training;

(*e*) to link up the system with the records needed for general office purposes, such as dates of last premiums, of maturity of endowment assurances and of expiry of temporary assurances.

The information to be recorded in respect of each assurance may vary according to the type of assurance and valuation formula but it will normally comprise the following items:

Policy number and name of life assured.

Dates of birth, entry and maturity (and also, ultimately, date and mode of exit).

Sum assured.

Reversionary or other bonus.

Office tabular premium, renewal date and date of last premium.

Extra premium (if any).

Net premium, and proportion (if any) falling due after the valuation date.

Other valuation constants.

For valuation, we require totals of the recorded information for each subdivision of the data. The purpose of the continuous process is to produce the totals from those recorded at the previous valuation. Thus we have the following scheme:

Summary totals in respect of the..................class of assurance
Valuation group..................

	No. of assurances	Sum assured	Bonus	Tabular office premium	Extra premium	Net premium
In force on........................ (beginning of period)						
Add						
New assurances in period						
Adjustments 'on'						
Deduct						
Claims in period						
Surrenders in period						
Lapses in period						
Adjustments 'off'						
In force on........................ (end of period)						

A further column would be required for each additional valuation constant. The figures on each line for new business, adjustments 'on', claims and so on would be produced by classifying the movements separately and transferring the totals to the summary total sheets shown above. The classification for each of the movements would be subdivided into the appropriate valuation groups so that the totals could be readily obtained.

The student should notice that the 'surrenders' would normally be those actually paid during the period whereas the 'claims' would usually be those announced during the period. Claims which have been announced but which for various reasons remain unpaid at the date to which the accounts are made up should be treated as a liability in the balance sheet. They do not appear in the valuation liability.

The general form of the classification will be affected by the returns which have to be made to comply with legislative requirements. Thus, British valuation methods are very largely conditioned by the returns under the Fourth and Fifth Schedules of the Assurance Companies Act, 1909. These Schedules should be carefully studied at this stage.

12·3. Preliminaries to valuation.

Before proceeding to the valuation it is essential to check the accuracy of the data, an important question which does not always receive the attention that it deserves. The form of the checks that may be possible will depend upon the individual circumstances of the particular fund but we propose to consider some of the possible checks arising from the continuous process of classification.

Generally speaking, the movements 'on' and 'off' between any two valuations will be recorded in the office books or accounts, under the various headings of 'new business', 'claims', 'surrenders', etc., together with alterations 'on' and 'off'. Thus the totals from these books provide figures for the total movements between the two valuations. If, therefore, the totals of aggregate business in force at the earlier valuation be adjusted by the totals 'on' and 'off' from the office books in the intervening period, the result should represent and be capable of precise reconciliation with the totals of aggregate business in force at the later valuation.

Since, however, complete agreement at the first attempt is probably unusual it would be better to arrange the books so that the same type of check can be applied to sections of the business separately, or to each type of movement separately. Further, the work might be so arranged as to provide checks of the total movements 'on' and 'off' at convenient intervals, for example monthly, without waiting for the elapse of the whole valuation period.

The process we have described provides a check of the number of policies, the totals of sums assured and bonuses and, where necessary, the office premiums. The process would, of course, check the net premiums and the other valuation constants only if they were to be recorded in the office books for new business and cancellations. This may be practicable but it is often impossible because the departments which deal with the various movements may not have the necessary information.

An alternative check of the net premiums is provided by a comparison of the office and net premiums within each sub-group (e.g. year of birth or maturity) or by a comparison of the difference, i.e. the loadings, with the sums assured. Where the office and net premiums bear a simple relationship to each other it would be possible to base the check on this relationship but such a simple solution is not usually available since the business in force will have been written at different times at varying scales of premium and the office and net premiums will not be related to each other.

The continuous process we have described checks the totals in force but it does not necessarily pick up the error when a movement is posted to the wrong valuation sub-group. Thus an error in one valuation sub-group may be set off by a corresponding balancing error in another sub-group. From time to time it may be desirable to cast the data within each sub-group direct from the valuation cards. Such errors are usually, however, of minor effect and will disclose themselves with the efflux of time as the assurances in force in the particular sub-groups grow less.

The majority of the changes which affect the valuation data arise automatically from the movements in the office books. Some, however, may escape notice and enquiries about them should be made before the books are closed at the end of the valuation period. Such enquiries are principally required for unreported deaths which may occur where the death produces no claim under the assurance. The following are examples of deaths which may not be reported:

(*a*) earlier deaths under last survivor assurances;
(*b*) deaths of counter lives under contingent assurances;
(*c*) deaths of lives assured under issue and similar contracts;
(*d*) deaths of lives assured during the deferred period under endowments and deferred annuities without return of premiums.

Claimants may also be unaware of the existence of paid-up assurances for small amounts and these may be investigated when the life assured appears to have reached an abnormally advanced age.

Other enquiries may be necessary about certain types of assurance such as, for example, guarantees of assurances carrying other offices' rates of bonus where it is necessary to ascertain the amount of the vested bonus and of the accrued interim bonus at the valuation date.

We may conclude this section with a few general remarks on grouping. The grouping of assurances in force has the two advantages of systematizing the work and of facilitating the valuation. First, the grouping should be chosen to produce groups and sub-groups of a reasonable, but not unwieldly, size. This is a practical question which can only be determined in the light of the circumstances of the particular assurance fund.

Secondly, the groups will naturally be chosen to fit in with any returns which may have to be made to comply with legislative requirements.

Thirdly, the assurances within each sub-group should possess at the valuation date at least one common characteristic required for their valuation, for example, duration, attained age or unexpired term. This question will be discussed more fully in the next section.

It will be readily appreciated that the simplest classification from the point of view of office work is a classification primarily by year of entry. Each year's business is treated as an integral unit: the same scale of premiums usually applies to the whole year's business: the effects of withdrawals and of new business strain can be closely watched: and the computation of the 'in force' merely requires the deletion of movements 'off'.

The year of entry classification is not customarily adopted because it does not lend itself to a simple valuation formula nor to legislative requirements and the actual methods adopted must be studied against the background of the various formulae that are available for valuation. This is the subject of our next section, necessarily a long but an important one.

There is, of course, a very considerable variation between offices in the actual form of the summary sheets and the valuation schedules but to help those students who have no practical experience we include two specimens of forms which are used by a particular office (see pp. 242–3).

The summary sheet includes spaces for net premiums on two different bases so as to simplify the work should a change be necessary. It also provides for the totals of the Z constants and the mean age M is computed on the summary sheet. The last column is for the adjustment where a full 5 years' bonus will not be earned at the next quinquennial valuation.

The actual annual premium is the tabular annual premium *plus* the extra annual premium, if any, because the life is not acceptable at normal rates *minus* the reduction of premium, if any, by the application of bonus.

The valuation schedule includes spaces for the valuation factors and for the valuation results on two different bases, should these be required.

The particular office provides for the valuation of a whole-term loading which is a uniform percentage of the paid-up sum assured. That sum assured is tabulated in the column 'P.U.S.A.' and a loading of 1% is valued, the value of the actual loading being obtained by proportion.

The cost of a new bonus of 1% per annum for the quinquennium is equal to 5% of the values of sums assured and bonuses *minus* the value of the short-fall where the assurance has not been in force for the full 5 years. The latter is tabulated in the columns headed B_{5-n}. The cost of the actual new bonus is obtained by proportion.

The new assurances and the other adjustments 'on' would be classified in their appropriate groups and the totals transferred to the summary sheets. Similarly the claims, surrenders, lapses and other adjustments 'off' would be classified in their appropriate groups and the totals deducted from the totals 'in force' in the summary sheets.

12·4. The valuation formula.

The ingenuity of actuaries has produced a mass of formulae for the valuation of assurance contracts. The student will, we think, find it helpful to classify them into four main types according to the essential idea underlying the process of valuation.

Type (*a*) A valuation by groups in which a specific value is placed upon each individual assurance within the group.

Type (*b*) A valuation by groups in which the value of the group depends upon a *mean* age or other characteristic.

..................SERIES ....WITH PROFITS. Assumed Year of..............................1...............

No. of policies	Sum assured	Z	Bonus	M	Tabular annual premium	Extra annual premium	Reduction of premium	Net premium		B_{5-n}	
								O^{M} 3 %			

..................................SERIES CLASS.. 31 December 19..............

No. of policies	Sum assured	Bonuses	Age	No. of premiums remaining to be paid			Tabular premium	Extra premium	Re-duction of premium					P.U.S.A.	B_{5-n} on basis of 1 % per annum
					A	A				Net premium	$\bar{a}$	Net premium	$\bar{a}$		

.... VALUES 19.......................... ....

Value of sum assured	Value of bonuses	Value of tabular premium	Value of re-duction	Value of net premium	Value of 1 % per annum of P.U.S.A.	Liability	Value of B_{5-n} on basis of 1 % per annum	Value of sum assured	Value of bonuses	Value of tabular premium	Value of re-duction	Value of net premium	Value of 1 % per annum of P.U.S.A.	Liability	Value of B_{5-n} on basis of 1 % per annum

Type (*c*) A valuation by an accumulative process, no grouping being essential for the purpose.

Type (*d*) Methods suitable for making estimates of various kinds.

For some purposes a formula of the first type might be essential: this might happen where the contribution method of distribution of surplus is in use. A formula of the second type might be preferred where the data have to be produced in a particular form because, for example, of legislative requirements. Each method has been proposed to meet a special need and it is as important to know *when* to use a given formula as *how* to use it.

For the sake of clarity the following symbols will be used to denote the characteristics of assurances for valuation.

Age at entry x years: original period n years.
Age at valuation y years: duration t years.
Unexpired term r years: age at maturity M years.

Formulae of Type (*a*)

(i) *Prepared tables of policy-values*

The assurances in force may be classified and sub-classified according to all of the characteristics and the valuation may then proceed on the basis of tables of policy-values which may be prepared in advance. Whole-life assurances would be classified by year of entry and age at entry, a grouping which is both clear and simple. Endowment assurances and more complicated forms of assurance are not so easy to handle by this process because there are at least three different characteristics which would involve triple classification; but the method may be practicable where assurances may be effected only for periods of (say) 10, 15, 20, 25 and 30 years or to mature at (say) ages 40, 45, 50, 55, 60, 65 and 70 years.

Once the tables of policy-values have been prepared the method involves no actuarial knowledge and the valuation may be performed by unskilled labour. The data to be tabulated are reduced to a minimum since only the sum assured need be recorded though it may be convenient also to record the office premiums.

The method has the advantage that the valuation may be made as readily by a select table as by an aggregate or ultimate table and were this a live issue the method might be more popular.

The method has the disadvantage for British actuaries that separate calculation might be necessary for the values of sums assured and bonuses and of net premiums because the separate values are required for the Board of Trade returns. However, if whole-life assurances are grouped first by age at entry and subdivided by year of entry the values of sums assured could be obtained for each age at entry by the formula:

$$\Sigma_{(t)} S \times A_{x+t} = A_x \Sigma_{(t)} S + (1 - A_x)\, \Sigma_{(t)} S \times {}_tV_x. \qquad (12\cdot 1)$$

The values of net premiums could be obtained by subtraction but it would be necessary to calculate the value of declared bonuses separately and also to approximate to the value of office premiums.

(ii) *Classification by attained age*

To British eyes the most natural method of valuing whole-life assurances is in groups by attained age. The data for this purpose are grouped by the office year of birth which is the valuation year minus the valuation age. By this method the valuation is reduced to a comparatively few groups and the tabulation of the net premiums can be easily effected provided that the mortality and interest bases are not changed frequently.

At this point we may pause to consider the precise effects of the various methods of reckoning ages, durations, and so on. Since few of these will be integral at a valuation date it is necessary to make some assumptions and since $x+t=y$ the assumptions about any two of the characteristics x, t and y will determine the third.

The figures in Table 12·1 were extracted from those given by D. C. Fraser in respect of a particular distribution of business, the figures relating to (1) a new fund, (2) a medium fund, and (3) an old fund.

The duration is not, of course, produced directly by a classification by attained age. If the valuation assumptions define x and t it is necessary to classify the assurances by attained age in such a way as will produce the desired value for the duration t. If the valuation assumptions define y and t it is necessary to compute the net premiums at such an age at entry x as will produce the desired value for the duration t.

For example, suppose that x is the age next birthday at entry and that t is the curtate duration at the date of valuation which may be assumed to fall, as is customary, on 31 December in a given year. The valuation age at the end of the year of entry must be taken as x, at the end of the following year as $x+1$, and so on. The assumed valuation age, and thus the assumed duration, will be obtained by classifying the assurances in 'office years of birth' determined by subtracting the age next birthday at entry from the calendar year of entry.

TABLE 12·1

Age at entry	Duration	Valuation age	Comparative reserves by H^M 3%		
			(1)	(2)	(3)
Exact	Exact	Exact	10,000	10,000	10,000
Nearest	Exact	—	9,996	9,996	9,997
	Nearest	—	10,004	10,000	9,999
	—	Nearest	10,032	10,014	10,010
	Curtate + ½	—	10,240	10,115	10,083
Next birthday	Exact	—	10,104	10,093	10,084
	Nearest	—	10,112	10,096	10,086
	Curtate	—	9,403	9,751	9,834
	Curtate + ½	—	10,351	10,213	10,171
	Curtate + 1	—	11,298	10,675	10,508
	—	Next birthday	10,449	10,261	10,206
	—	Nearest	9,518	9,806	9,874
	—	Last birthday + ½	9,508	9,801	9,869
'Mean'	Curtate + ½	Last birthday + ½	10,202	10,081	10,053

The 'mean' age at entry is the calendar year of entry minus the calendar year of birth. The student should notice the wide disparity between the results of the various assumptions: and the effect of the age of the business in diminishing that disparity.

A similar process may be followed when x is the nearest age at entry and t is the curtate duration $+\frac{1}{2}$. The office year of birth is determined by subtracting the nearest age at entry from the calendar year of entry. This produces a valuation age which is equal to the nearest age at entry plus the curtate duration and the addition of $\frac{1}{2}$ is made at the final stage.

When x is the 'mean' age at entry and t the curtate duration $+\frac{1}{2}$, it will be seen that the classification is by calendar years of birth.

When t is the nearest duration the assurances effected in the first half of the calendar year must be assumed to enter on the previous 31 December and the assurances effected in the second half of the calendar year must be assumed to enter on 31 December in that year. For an assurance effected at assumed age x the valuation age at the end of the year of entry is $x+1$ if the assurance entered in the first half of the year and x if in the second half. This result may be achieved by classifying the assurances by office years of birth which are determined by subtracting the assumed age at entry x from the calendar year of entry for entrants in the second half of the year, and from the previous calendar year for entrants in the first half of the year. This process is a little complicated but, judging by Table 12·1, the assumptions of nearest age at entry and nearest duration seem to yield the closest approximation to a valuation by exact ages and durations.

(iii) *Karup's method*

The valuation formula for almost all kinds of assurance may be so arranged as to include only two kinds of factors, those dependent on the attained age from time to time and those dependent on characteristics which are invariant. The parts of the formula dependent on the latter type of factor may be tabulated in respect of each assurance for use at successive valuations, and are called 'valuation constants'.

The general valuation formula is then:

$$S \times V = S \times A_y - S \times P \times \ddot{a}_y + H/D_y. \tag{12·2}$$

The student will have studied the formula for earlier examinations: at this stage it is helpful to notice that the same formula is obtained whether the approach is retrospective or prospective. Taking, for example, endowment assurances, we find that:

$$H = S\,(P_{x\overline{n|}} + d)\,N_{x+n}.$$

Two valuation constants are required where the values of the sums assured and of the premiums have to be computed separately. The valuation of reversionary bonus would require the tabulation of a further constant, periodically adjusted for new bonus.

The same process is applicable to double endowment assurances for a sum S at death within n years or $2S$ on survival, but the constant H becomes:

$$H = S\,(P_{x\overline{n}|} + P^{\;1}_{x\overline{n}|} + d)\,N_{x+n} + S.D_{x+n}.$$

Thus we have a powerful method which facilitates the valuation of nearly all classes of assurance in groups by attained age. The price to be paid for this convenience is the tabulation of a sufficient number of valuation constants in respect of each assurance.

The method is conveniently applied to the valuation of whole-life assurances by limited premiums. For this class the valuation of the sum assured requires no correction and the valuation constant becomes

$$K = S \times {}_nP_x \times N_{x+n}.$$

The method of calculating the age $(x+n)$ for the valuation constants will determine the assumption with regard to unexpired duration. It is desirable to link this age with the valuation age at the time so that an explicit value will be put upon the unexpired duration. Where, for example, the valuation age is the nearest integral age and M is the valuation age at the end of the calendar year of maturity, the valuation constants would be

$$S \times dN_{M-\frac{1}{2}} \quad \text{and} \quad S \times P.N_{M-\frac{1}{2}}$$

respectively, 6 months being assumed from the valuation to the next premium.

In practice it is an advantage to reduce the number of figures in the constants by dividing by a suitable power of 10, say c. The valuation factor becomes $10^c/D_y$ and c may be so chosen that the factor is about unity near age 60. The valuation constants may then be tabulated to the nearest integer.

(iv) *Elderton's method*

W. P. Elderton suggested a method of valuing endowment assurances which is conveniently considered with Type (*a*) formulae (though the method is approximate, not exact) because a specific value is put upon each individual assurance.

The determination of an endowment assurance policy-value

depends principally on the characteristics of original period and duration or unexpired term. The characteristic of age is of comparatively little importance as may be seen from the following table.

TABLE 12·2

Policy values for endowment assurances for 100

Original period of years	Age at entry	Duration of assurance		
		5 years	10 years	20 years
15	20	28·94	62·08	—
	30	29·01	62·07	—
	40	28·87	61·81	—
	50	28·71	61·21	—
	60	28·05	59·32	—
25	20	15·03	32·25	74·30
	30	15·28	32·52	74·23
	40	15·53	32·83	73·94
	50	16·58	34·08	73·18
35	20	9·37	20·09	46·08
	30	9·91	20·97	46·92
	40	10·94	22·87	49·16

We may, therefore, value all the endowment assurances on the assumption of one fixed maturity age which may be selected arbitrarily (for example 55 or 60 years) as being suitable for the business in force *provided*, and the proviso is important, that the premium valued is also computed on the same assumption about the maturity age.

The method is not strictly applicable to single premium and minor classes of assurance but may be applied to certain of these classes, as a practical measure, because the error would not be appreciable.

The assumed maturity age would not necessarily be suitable for the valuation of bonuses and it may be necessary to assume a higher maturity age for the bonus than for the sum assured.

A minor objection to the method is that, though the value of the net liability is a good approximation, the values of sums assured and of premiums stated separately may contain appreciable errors. The method is not applicable to a gross premium valuation unless the corresponding gross premiums at the assumed maturity age are tabulated and valued.

The method distorts the analysis of surplus by transferring part of the mortality element to the loading element.

Notwithstanding the objections to which we have referred, we think that this method is of great utility and it has been successfully applied in practice for many years.

Formulae of Type (*b*)

There is not much place for formulae of Type (*b*) in the valuation of whole-life assurances because the normal solution is so simple. It may, however, be convenient to group the assurances in extended groups and this gives rise to a method suggested by A. E. King.

(v) *A. E. King's method*

Suppose that whole-life assurances within a range of h ages are valued together by mean values of the valuation factors. King demonstrates that we may use the valuation factor for the mean age with a second-difference correction appropriate, strictly, to the factor at the central age. Thus for a summation of valuation data $S(x)$ over a range of h ages, we have

$$\text{Mean age } w = \sum_{(h)} xS(x) / \sum_{(h)} S(x).$$

Where the valuation factor, F_x, is a function of the second degree Lidstone has shown that the true average valuation factor would be

$$F_w + \left[\sum_{(h)} x^2 S(x) / \sum_{(h)} S(x) - w^2\right] \frac{F''_w}{2!}.$$

This reduces to the form suggested by A. E. King if we assume that $S(x)$ is equal at each age for the purpose of the correction, thus producing the simple factor:

$$F_w + \left(\frac{h^2 - 1}{24}\right) \delta^2 F_w. \tag{12·3}$$

The method can be applied to valuation data which are tabulated for each integral age provided that the summation of the data is so arranged as to give the totals for the required groups of ages. The method is, perhaps, most effective when the work of tabulating the data is reduced by restricting the tabulations to groups of ages suitable for the method of valuation. In this way the method may secure a very real and substantial saving in arithmetical work but some process would be required for the calculation of the mean ages, for example valuation constants of the form $xS(x)$.

Turning to the valuation of endowment assurances we see that, since we have to deal with the three variables of age, duration and original term, some approximation is both more necessary than for whole-life assurances and more difficult because the whole range of ages and not a limited range has to be dealt with.

(vi) *Z method*

The student will have studied the Z method of valuation of endowment assurances for earlier examinations. Suffice it to say here that the differences by age of the temporary annuities for a given period of years (and of the endowment assurance A factors for the same period) may be represented with sufficient accuracy by a geometrical progression. Hence we may say:

$$\left.\begin{aligned} a_{y\overline{r-1}|} &\doteqdot \alpha - \beta\gamma^{y}, \\ A_{y\overline{r}|} &\doteqdot (v - d\alpha) + d\beta\,.\,\gamma^{y}. \end{aligned}\right\} \qquad (12\cdot4)$$

Where the mortality table follows Makeham's law γ has a value somewhat less than c and it is convenient, as a practical measure, to use c.

The method may be applied in a number of ways but the most usual method is to compute the weighted mean age from the geometrical progression and to make the valuation by the factor at that weighted mean age. The weighting is conveniently performed by the tabulation of a constant, called Z, giving the product of the sum assured and c^{M} where M is the age at maturity.

Strictly speaking, it is necessary that separate mean ages should be calculated for the valuation of sums assured, bonuses and premiums, but it is normally sufficient to base the factors for all three items on the same mean age. Within a group of assurances all of the same unexpired duration those assurances which have been longest on the books would have, proportionately to the sum assured, the largest reversionary bonuses and, of necessity, the smallest premiums. Thus the mean age based on the sums assured tends to lie between the corresponding mean ages based on bonuses and on premiums, being smaller than the one and larger than the other. The difference is, however, small.

The calculation of the valuation constant Z and of the weighted mean ages may be facilitated by various special devices and there is a considerable literature on the subject. It is generally considered sufficient for the weighted mean age to be computed to the nearest integer but practice differs on this question. It may be convenient to base Z on, say, c^{M-55} instead of c^M: this has the advantage that Z would equal the sum assured for all assurances maturing at age 55, a popular age at maturity for such assurances.

Since for assurances maturing in a particular year the Z method would yield the same mean age year by year if the distribution of business were to remain the same notwithstanding the reduction in the unexpired term, we might expect the Z method to give good results when the year's working is analysed. It is found in practice that the Z method does give a reasonable approximation to the expected death strain for the year. In general, the expected death strain is the product of the rate (or sometimes the force) of mortality and the death strain at risk and the Z mean age derived from the sums assured may be used for both these items.

The use of the Makeham constant c instead of the true value γ tends to overstate the weighted mean ages and produces a small overstatement of the liability in respect of endowment assurances. Where the assurance factor is of the pure endowment type, the overstatement of the weighted mean ages would lead to an understatement of the liability, a consideration which should be borne in mind when the method is applied to double endowment assurances and other contracts of that type.

Since the differences by age of the values of $(A_{y\overline{r|}} + A_{y\overline{r|}}^{\;\;1})$ for a given value of r are usually negative and necessarily decrease at a slower rate than the increase in the corresponding differences of $A_{y\overline{r|}}$ it follows (a) that a lower value of γ should be used for the weighted mean ages under double endowment assurances, and (*b*) that an overstatement in the weighted mean age *diminishes* the values both of the sums assured and of the premiums, the two errors tending to counterbalance each other. This value of γ would be considerably less than the normal value and it would be simpler, and sufficiently accurate, to use the arithmetic mean age.

The Z mean age provides a useful check on the net premiums for new business within each group. For example, all the 20-year endowment assurances in the new business for a given year must appear in the new assurances 'on' for the group of assurances which mature 20 years later. If the sums assured 'on' in this group be multiplied by the pure premium for 20-year endowment assurances at the mean age derived from the Z's for the group, the product will approximate closely to the aggregate of the tabulated net premiums. If the Z's and the net premiums have been calculated independently, the totals for the one provide a useful check on the totals for the other.

The idea of the preceding paragraph may be applied in another way. Suppose the assurances are classified in groups by original periods with sub-groups by years of entry—it is then not necessary to tabulate both the Z's and the net premiums. If the net premiums alone are tabulated, the mean net premium (the quotient of the aggregate net premiums and the aggregate sums assured) for a group of original period n may be used to determine the mean age at maturity for the group by inversely entering the table of pure premiums, $P_{x\overline{n}|}$, to find the entry age corresponding to the mean net premium and hence the mean age at maturity. All the sub-groups for original period n would be valued on the assumption of that mean maturity age.

Should the Z's alone be tabulated the mean age derived from the Z's may be used to calculate the net premiums for each original period as well as the valuation factors for the relative sub-groups. Effectively this means that endowment assurances can be brought within the simple process described in the last paragraph of § 12·4 (i) for whole-life assurances. Formula (12·1) would apply to each original period n with the mean age derived from the Z's for that period.

The basic idea underlying the Z method can be applied in several ways but we cannot pursue them in this book. Some of them are noted in the list of references so that those who are interested can follow up the various suggestions.

(vii) *n-point method*

So far the assurances have been assumed to be grouped according to unexpired duration. Where the assurances are grouped by year of entry the assurances within each group have a common duration but differing ages at entry. There are approximations available in these circumstances, for example founded on the representation of policy-values of duration t by a mathematical function of age.

Two interesting papers by W. Perks discuss experiments on these lines. First he assumes that whole-life assurances are grouped by years of entry and that the data for duration t are to be valued by the mean of the policy-values at two selected ages at entry. On the assumption that ${}_tV_x$ takes the form $a+bx+cx^2$, t being constant, he finds that the two ages required are $\bar{x}+\sigma$ and $\bar{x}-\sigma$. The value of the mean age $\bar{x}$ and the standard deviation σ can be found by tabulating $xS(x)$ and $x^2S(x)$ as valuation constants.

Endowment assurance policy-values do not take the same simple form but by assuming that all assurances mature at an appropriate fixed age (see § 12·4 (iv), Elderton) Perks was able to assume that ${}_tV_{M-n\overline{n}|}$ took the form $a/n+b+cn$ and on this basis he found that endowment assurances of duration t could be valued by the two original terms of $\bar{n}+\bar{n}\sqrt{(1-1/\bar{n}\underline{n})}$ and $\bar{n}-\bar{n}\sqrt{(1-1/\bar{n}\underline{n})}$.†

In his second paper Perks extended the method to the representation of two variables and he found that suitable formulae for whole-life assurances would be either

$$\cdot 25\,(1+r)\,{}_{t_1}V_{x_1}+\cdot 25\,(1+r)\,{}_{t_2}V_{x_2}+\cdot 25\,(1-r)\,{}_{t_1}V_{x_2}+\cdot 25\,(1-r)\,{}_{t_2}V_{x_1}, \qquad (12{\cdot}5)$$

where $x_1=\bar{x}+\sigma_x \quad t_1=\bar{t}+\sigma_t, \quad x_2=\bar{x}-\sigma_x \quad t_2=\bar{t}-\sigma_t,$

and r is the coefficient of correlation;

or
$$\cdot 25\,({}_{t_1}V_{x_1}+{}_{t_2}V_{x_2}+{}_{t_3}V_{x_3}+{}_{t_4}V_{x_4}), \qquad (12{\cdot}6)$$

† $\bar{n}$ is the mean duration and $\underline{n}$ the reciprocal of the harmonic mean.

where
$$x_1=\bar{x}+\sigma_x\sqrt{(1+r)} \quad t_1=\bar{t}+\sigma_t\sqrt{(1+r)},$$
$$x_2=\bar{x}-\sigma_x\sqrt{(1+r)} \quad t_2=\bar{t}-\sigma_t\sqrt{(1+r)},$$
$$x_3=\bar{x}+\sigma_x\sqrt{(1-r)} \quad t_3=\bar{t}-\sigma_t\sqrt{(1-r)},$$
$$x_4=\bar{x}-\sigma_x\sqrt{(1-r)} \quad t_4=\bar{t}+\sigma_t\sqrt{(1-r)},$$

and r is the coefficient of correlation. A two-variable formula for endowment assurances was also devised.

The principal advantages of the *n*-point method are (*a*) that it assumes a grouping by years of entry which is convenient for office routine and which gives an insight into the working of the business, e.g. lapse rates by durations, and (*b*) that the classification is independent of the valuation basis so that changes can be made in the basis as may be desired. The price to be paid for these advantages is the tabulation of two constants for each assurance. For whole-life assurances the constants xS and x^2S must be tabulated: for endowment assurances the constants nS and S/n are required.

The *n*-point method would facilitate a valuation on a select basis should this be desired. If an allowance for initial expenses were considered to be desirable in all the circumstances, the amount and nature of the allowance would be left until a late stage in the work. Blocks of business for different years of entry could be valued on different bases where this is appropriate.

The *n*-point method is essentially a rationalization of the empirical *n*-ages method [(x) on p. 261]; they may be usefully studied side by side.

Formulae of Type (*c*)

(viii) *Cumulative methods*

From time to time it is suggested that the reserves may be built up from year to year by a kind of accountancy from the elements which constitute the policy-value. This was, for example, suggested by Searle.

The usual formula which connects policy-values at successive durations was transposed by Searle into:

$$V(t+1)=\phi(t)-q_x/p_x[1-\phi(t)], \qquad (12\cdot 7)$$

where
$$\phi(t)=[V(t)+P](1+i).$$

The last item of the equation can be tabulated in advance for each assurance, or it can be computed at each valuation by grouping by attained age.

It would be necessary to devise a process which would take explicit account of the various types of movement. For example, withdrawals might be assumed to occur in the middle of the year and the valuation liability in respect of them might be computed at that time, thus providing for half-a-year's exposure. However, it would probably be simplest to treat all those in force at the beginning of the year as being exposed to risk for a full year. This would enable the valuation liability at the end of the year to be computed directly in respect of the 'in force' at the beginning of the year. For all movements 'on' or 'off' the valuation liability at the end of the year must be tabulated in respect of the individual movements or the valuation liability must be calculated in groups for each movement from time to time as may be convenient. At the end of the year we have:

Valuation liability computed from previous year's 'in force', *plus* valuation liability in respect of new business and other assurances 'on',
minus valuation liability in respect of claims, surrenders, and other assurances 'off'.

The treatment of surrenders with regard to the expected death strain may appear arbitrary. However, it is simple and follows the usual assumption in the calculation of surrender values, that the value is computed at the end of the policy-year and not at the actual time of surrender within the policy-year. Since the withdrawals are usually replaced by new business with a larger death strain at risk though at lower ages attained, the two errors tend to offset each other.

Where there is no life risk the last term of formula (12·7) disappears. Thus we have a simple process applicable to contracts of the accumulative type, such as sinking fund insurances, endowments with return of premiums, and children's deferred assurances during the deferred period. The process is commonly applied in practice to those types. It may even be extended to whole-life and endowment assurances by representing the true policy-values, empirically, as the sum of sinking fund accumulations at three rates of interest, for example 0, 4 and 8 %. The whole solution is very simple but tends to lose sight of the basic elements of which the reserve is composed.

FORMULAE OF TYPE (d)

The methods we have described so far have all been suitable for the main valuation but it often happens that it is necessary to make an approximate estimate for a limited purpose and we now propose to review some of the methods available.

(ix) *Henry's method*

Where the valuation factor, F_x, can be represented by a rational integral function of x the valuation can be performed by successive summations of the data. Thus if the factor is:

$$F_x = a + bx + cx^2$$

and $S(x)$ represents the valuation data the required valuation for a range of $(r+1)$ values is:

$$\sum_0^r F_x \times S(x) = a\sum_0^r S(x) + b\sum_0^r xS(x) + c\sum_0^r x^2 S(x),$$

and by a simple transformation analogous to that used for moments

$$= (a-b+c)\sum_0^r S(x) + (b-3c)\sum_0^r{}^2 S(x) + 2c\sum_0^r{}^3 S(x). \quad (12\cdot8)$$

It is not to be expected that the factor will take the precise form stated but good results may be obtained where the fit is only approximate if the constants a, b and c are derived from weights which roughly correspond with the data to be valued. The weighting is an integral part of the method which, by means of it, achieves a balance of errors.

For most purposes it would be sufficient to use the data from one of the model offices as weights. The successive assumed values of the factor are a, $(a+b+c)$, $(a+2b+4c)$ and so on. These assumed values are combined with the weights and compared with the products of the actual factors and the weights, in three groups of ages. This process yields three equations which are solved for the three unknowns a, b and c. In effect the factor is roughly regraduated by a formula of the required form.

In the form stated the long summations of data at individual ages make the process somewhat laborious, especially bearing in mind the third summation that is required. The arithmetical work can be curtailed without material loss of accuracy by dealing with the data in two or three sections for each of which the factor is assumed to be a straight line, and by summing in quinary groups instead of by individual ages or terms.

The theoretical error which arises from the use of quinary groups can be corrected through the weighting. Suppose the weights are valued by the factor at individual ages or terms but the total weight for each quinary group is combined with the assumed value of the factor

$$F_x = a + bx$$

for the central age of the group. If the values so found for the quinary groups are combined into two groups of ages or terms, there will be two equations from which a and b can be derived.

Now let the data for valuation in successive quinary groups be U_1, U_2, U_3 and so on. The corresponding factors at the central ages of the groups will be $(a+2b)$, $(a+7b)$, $(a+12b)$ and so on with the origin at the lowest age of the initial group. The required value will be

$$U_1(a+2b) + U_2(a+7b) + U_3(a+12b) + \dots$$
$$= (a-3b)\,\Sigma U_t + 5b\Sigma^2 U_t,$$

where ΣU_t and $\Sigma^2 U_t$ represent respectively the first and second sums of the quinary groups from the bottom upwards.

The example given on p. 259, Henry's Example 1, will make the process clear.

The method was devised as a rapid check on a large number of friendly society valuations all of which would be made on a standard basis for which the constants could be computed from suitable data and tabulated in advance. The method might also be useful where the life assurance fund consists of many small sections, for example in local agencies or currencies, which must be valued separately to comply with local legislation.

Office A. Whole-life with profits. Valuation of sums assured and bonuses. O^M 3%

The origin is taken at age 15 for ages 15–54 and at age 55 for higher ages. Any policies existing at ages under 15 must be included in the first age-group, and summation made up to and including that group.

Age group	Sums assured and bonuses	Sum from bottom upwards		
15–19	22	$11{,}514=\Sigma$		
20–24	162	11,492	$a-3b=$	·217252
25–29	624	11,330	$5b=$	·0449525
30–34	1,305	10,706	$(a-3b)\,\Sigma=$	2,501·4
35–39	2,022	9,401	$5b\Sigma^2=$	3,134·4
40–44	2,328	7,379	Total, ages 15–54	5,635·8
45–49	2,398	5,051		
50–54	2,653	2,653		
		$69{,}526=\Sigma^2$		
			$a-3b=$	·590640
55–59	2,363	$7{,}070=\Sigma$	$5b=$	·0491891
60–64	1,683	4,707		
65–69	1,755	3,024	$(a-3b)\,\Sigma=$	4,175·8
70–74	733	1,269	$5b\Sigma^2=$	834·5
75–79	294	536	Total, ages 55 and over	5,010·3
80–84	159	242	Add for ages 15–54, as above	5,635·8
85–89	57	83		
90–94	17	26	Total, all ages	10,646·1
95–	9	9		
		$16{,}966=\Sigma^2$	True value = 10,646	

The method has also been used to provide a rapid estimate of the liability by the use of constants derived from the previous year's figures. Where the full published valuation is made once only in each 5 years the method might be suitably used to test the progress of the fund in the intervening years.

The method has been applied by Kenchington to the valuation of limited age-groups without the use of weighting. In this form it has an affinity with A. E. King's method (p. 250) and should properly be included with FORMULAE OF TYPE (*b*) because it is suitable for the main valuation.

King's mean age w is found from $\Sigma S(x)$ and $\Sigma x.S(x)$: Kenchington uses these same statistics in a different way. Suppose that F_x can be represented by a linear expression $a+bx$. The valuation of a group of h ages becomes

$$a\sum_{(h)} S(x)+b\sum_{(h)} x.S(x).$$

Henry obtained a and b from the sum of two sets of the (weighted) valuation factors, and the corresponding (weighted) values of $a+bx$, but the weighting is unnecessary for a limited range of ages.

Kenchington found a and b by taking first and second summations over the whole group of h ages. The following comparison is based on King's example of a 10-year group valued by O^M 3%.

Calculation of King's mean age w, and of Henry's a and b

Age x	$S(x)$	$\Sigma S(x)$	A_x	$a+b(x-47)$	ΣA_x	$\Sigma\{a+b(x-47)\}$
57	192,702	192,702	·63596	$a+10b$	·63596	$a+10b$
56	180,889	373,591	·62516	$a+9b$	1·26112	$2a+19b$
55	206,423	580,014	·61440	$a+8b$	1·87552	$3a+27b$
54	129,708	709,722	·60368	$a+7b$	2·47920	$4a+34b$
53	147,563	857,285	·59302	$a+6b$	3·07222	$5a+40b$
			3·07222	$5a+40b$		
52	126,722	984,007	·58244	$a+5b$	3·65466	$6a+45b$
51	134,623	1,118,630	·57194	$a+4b$	4·22660	$7a+49b$
50	114,779	1,233,409	·56154	$a+3b$	4·78814	$8a+52b$
49	115,348	1,348,757	·55123	$a+2b$	5·33937	$9a+54b$
48	165,686	1,514,443	·54104	$a+b$	5·88041	$10a+55b$
Total	1,514,443	8,912,560	2·80819	$5a+15b$	33·21320	$55a+385b$

A. E. King	Henry (unweighted)	Kenchington
$w=47+\frac{8,912,560}{1,514,443}=52\cdot885$	$5a+40b=3\cdot07222$ $5a+15b=2\cdot80819$	$10a+55b=5\cdot88041$ $55a+385b=33\cdot21320$
$A_w+4\frac{1}{8}\delta^2A_w=\cdot59210$	$a=\cdot52995$ $b=\cdot010561$	$a=\cdot52998$ $b=\cdot010557$

		Value of $S(x)$	Error
True		896,755	—
A. E. King	1,514,443 × ·59210	896,702	−53
Henry (unweighted)	1,514,443 × ·52995 +8,912,560 × ·010561	896,705	−50
Kenchington	1,514,443 × ·52998 +8,912,560 × ·010557	896,714	−41

Henry's (unweighted) values and Kenchington's values of a and b can be tabulated in advance and if the same ranges of ages are grouped at each valuation the same values of a and b may be used year after year.

(x) *n-ages method*

Where it is necessary to make a quick estimate of the cost of changing from one valuation basis to another, the most serviceable method, and one which has been found to work well in practice is the n-ages method suggested by Elderton and Rowell.

Suppose the valuation data $S(x)$ have been valued by the factor F_x on basis α. The mean factor is $\Sigma F_x S(x)/\Sigma S(x)$ and this mean factor may be represented as the mean of n values of the factor, $[F_{x_1}+F_{x_2}+F_{x_3}+\ldots+F_{x_n}]/n$. The mean of these n values of the factor on a second basis β provides a simple solution to the problem of passing from one valuation basis to another.

The method may be used with any number, n, of the values of the factor but we have found that four terms are best for whole-life assurances and four or five terms for endowment assurances according to the spread of the business. The four values may be chosen in two pairs each of which gives the required mean approximately and so chosen that the four values are more or less evenly spaced over the range of the data. With the temporary annuity it may be necessary to use five terms, two short durations being included in order to obtain a third duration sufficiently long to represent the spread of the business, and the fourth and fifth terms being a pair comparatively near the mean.

The following table (taken from Elderton and Rowell, p. 275) relating to whole-life assurance will make the process clear.

The numerical work may be indicated as follows:

Whole-life with profits.

The facts were:

Sum assured	£7,410,896	
Bonus	1,245,716	$O^{M(5)}$ $2\frac{1}{2}$% value of total = 5,908,282.
Total	8,656,612	
Net premiums	200,512	
Reductions	16,517	$O^{M(5)}$ $2\frac{1}{2}$% value of difference
	183,995	= 2,197,570.

Hence, average value of £1 of SA and B

$$=5,908,282/8,656,612=\cdot 68252=A_{56\cdot 965}.$$

Hence, average value of net premium

$$=200,512/7,410,896=\cdot 02706=P_{40\cdot 183}.$$

Hence, average value of £1 of net premium less reduction

$$=2,197,570/183,995=11\cdot 944=\bar{a}_{58\cdot 385}.$$

TABLE 12·3

4-Ages method

OM(5) $2\frac{1}{2}\%$ $A_x=\cdot 68252$			OM(5) $2\frac{1}{2}\%$ $P=\cdot 02706$			OM(5) $2\frac{1}{2}\%$ $\bar{a}=11\cdot 944$		
Age	$2\frac{1}{2}\%$	3%	Age	$2\frac{1}{2}\%$	3%	Age	$2\frac{1}{2}\%$	3%
51	·62451	·57335	37	·02435	·02303	53	14·099	13·427
63	·74095	·70105	43	·02985	·02848	64	9·729	9·396
36	·49156	·43340	27	·01813	·01694	40	18·999	17·788
79	·87353	·85145	48	·03598	·03458	78	4·950	4·856
	4)2·73055	4)2·55925		4)·10831	4)·10303		4)47·777	4)45·467
	·68264	·63981		·02708	·02576		11·944	11·367
	−·00012	−·00011		−·00002	−·00002			
	·68252	·63970		·02706	·02574			

These functions gave at OM(5) 3%:

	Approximation	True Value
Value of sum assured and bonus	£5,537,634	£5,535,402
Value of net premiums *less* reductions	1,980,580	1,978,686
Value of net liability	£3,557,054	£3,556,716

The method has an obvious extension to policy-values and Elderton and Rowell found that, for example, King's 50-year model office could be expressed by the following eight policy-values which approximately reproduce the average values of A, $\ddot{a}$ and P on the tabulated bases.

$${}_4V_{35},\ {}_{12}V_{27};\quad {}_8V_{38},\ {}_{19}V_{27};\quad {}_{13}V_{42},\ {}_{27}V_{28};\quad {}_{27}V_{42},\ {}_{40}V_{29}.$$

(xi) *Model offices*

By way of concluding this review of methods of valuation we may refer briefly to model offices though, on the whole, these are more useful for illustrating theoretical questions than for dealing with actual practical problems of estimation.

The model office originated at a time when there was much discussion about the proper reserves that should be set up in relation to premium income. What reserve is proper would depend to a considerable extent on the age of the business and the model office was designed to show what the proper reserves would be assuming an even flow of business had been secured for various periods of time. Manly used policy-values at certain ages and durations but George King developed the idea on the basis of the H^M experience, using entrants at each fifth year of age and the 'in force' at every duration. Subsequent tests with O^M data showed that the results would not be sufficiently different to justify fresh calculations on that basis.

The original purpose was limited but the model office has changed its functions with the years and has become a useful standard of reference in all sorts of problems. Even for this purpose the model office has, perhaps, had its day because it is based on out-of-date data and other methods have been developed.

The figures for new entrants in the model offices were obtained by taking the entrants in the mortality experience for the central ages 20, 25, 30 and so on and for the two ages on either side of the central age. The model office was assumed to transact a uniform amount of new business in each year distributed in that way and the business was assumed to be subject to certain rates of mortality and discontinuance. The business in force after 5, 10, 15 years and so on up to 50 years constituted the 'model office' of the particular 'age' in years. The business in force was then valued on various bases and the comparative reserves worked out taking a particular basis as 10,000 to form a standard of comparison.

The following table shows the percentage age-distribution of new entrants in the two model offices which have been prepared for whole-life assurances. The O^M entrants were at somewhat earlier ages than the H^M entrants but the difference was small and comparative reserves have been based on the H^M figures. The growth of endowment assurance business has led to an increase in the average age at entry for whole-life assurances and by way of comparison the figures in the final column have been calculated approximately from the exposed-to-risk at duration 0 for medically examined whole-life assurances with profits in the A 1924–29 experience. The A 1924–29 figures are probably also affected by the inclusion of duplicates and by the greater willingness now shown to consider assurances at the older ages.

TABLE 12·4

Central age at entry	H^M Model office, no. 1 (%)	O^M Model office, no. 2 (%)	A 1924–29 Medically examined whole-life with profits (%)
15	—	—	2·2
20	6·97	7·30	6·7
25	17·75	20·45	10·8
30	21·04	23·11	11·8
35	18·41	18·40	11·4
40	13·82	13·05	10·8
45	9·45	8·44	10·8
50	6·23	5·07	11·5
55	3·51	2·58	10·9
60	1·97	1·20	8·1
65	·85	·40	4·0
70	—	—	1·0
All ages	100·00	100·00	100·0

Model offices have been constructed for endowment assurances from the 1863–93 experience (Buchanan, 1907): for annuities from the 1863–93 experience—by Ryan—and the 1900–20 experience (Elderton and Oakley, 1924). The usefulness of a model office largely depends on the extent to which the assumed distribution of new business represents a common experience among offices. If the distribution is merely the average of widely varying distributions of new business the model office must be of limited use. For example, there is reason to believe that the distribution of new endowment assurances by the original periods of assurance may vary to a much greater extent between the various offices than the distribution of whole-life assurances by age at entry. The endowment assurance model office might be expected to be of a less general application than the whole-life model office.

The assumption of a uniform new business is somewhat artificial but it is of little practical importance. Where the business has been increasing the model office must be taken at a correspondingly lower age. The character of the model office is largely determined by the assumption with regard to new business. The assumed experience with regard to mortality and discontinuance governs the building up of the 'in force' but variations in this experience, as also in the rate of increase of new business, may be allowed for by the choice of a suitable age of office to represent the actual business under consideration.

TABLE 12·5

Mortality table	Rate of interest (%)	Comparative reserves for whole-life assurances			Comparative reserves for endowment assurances		
		(1)	(2)	(3)	(1)	(2)	(3)
H^M	$2\frac{1}{2}$	10,545	10,368	10,277	10,041	10,008	10,006
	3	9,854	9,808	9,803	9,652	9,761	9,776
	$3\frac{1}{2}$	9,216	9,282	9,353	9,274	9,518	9,550
	4	8,627	8,789	8,928	—	—	—
O^M	$2\frac{1}{2}$	10,810	10,527	10,385	10,183	10,094	10,086
	3	10,113	9,964	9,908	9,791	9,846	9,855
	$3\frac{1}{2}$	9,464	9,432	9,455	9,413	9,603	9,630
	4	8,867	8,935	9,026	—	—	—
$O^{M(5)}$	$2\frac{1}{2}$	10,474	10,310	10,217	10,043	10,015	10,013
	3	9,782	9,748	9,740	9,649	9,766	9,781
	$3\frac{1}{2}$	9,143	9,221	9,290	9,274	9,524	9,557
	4	8,554	8,728	8,864	—	—	—
A 1924–29	$2\frac{1}{2}$	10,770	10,617	10,518	10,406	10,255	10,236
	3	10,000	10,000	10,000	10,000	10,000	10,000
	$3\frac{1}{2}$	9,301	9,425	9,512	9,609	9,751	9,769
	4	8,660	8,888	9,050	—	—	—

Table 12·5 (Bunney and Falconer, p. 434) gives comparative reserves for the model office by a few different bases of mortality and interest though it should be remembered that the figures are based on an old distribution of business which may be no longer applicable. The figures relate to (1) a new, (2) a medium, (3) an old distribution of business in force.

There are various ways of approximating to the results of the model office and some of the methods of approximate valuation that have been discussed earlier in this chapter may be of service in curtailing the arithmetical work. One of the simplest and most flexible methods is that mentioned in the preceding section on the *n*-ages method. A 'pocket model office' may be constructed by a suitable choice of ages at entry and durations combined with weights to represent the distribution of business between the various classes. The following is an example of a pocket model office which will illustrate the idea though it must not be assumed to be necessarily suitable in other circumstances (Elderton, 1931).

Whole-life with profits (*three of each*):

Age at entry	Duration	Existing bonus (%)	New quinquennial bonus (%)
28	5	1	6·06
	19	21	12·1
	27	30	13·0
	40	45	14·5
42	7	4	8·32
	13	11	11·1
	27	30	13·0
56	7	4	8·32

Endowment assurances at 60 with profits (*seven of each*):

Age at entry	Duration	Existing bonus (%)	New quinquennial bonus (%)
30	5	1	6·06
	12	12	11·2
	22	24	12·4
45	4	1	4·04
	11	9	10·9

Whole-life without profits (*two of each*):

Age at entry	Durations
28	5 and 19
42	2, 7 and 13
56	2 and 7

Endowment assurances at 60 without profits (*two of each*):

Age at entry	Durations
30	5 and 12
45	4 and 11
50	3

The average ages, periods and durations of the assumed business on the books are given in Table 12·6.

The durations and the number of cases at the ages at entry have been chosen to approximate to the distribution of an established business which has been augmented in recent years by non-profit assurances. The ages at entry of without profit life assurances are rather older than for with profits and the terms of endowment assurances average less for without profits than for with profits. The average age at entry of new business will usually exceed the average age at entry when calculated from business on the books because the younger entrants will be longer on the books than the older entrants; so that an age at entry calculated as, say, 42 from business on the books might mean an average age at entry for new business of over 45.

TABLE 12·6

Class	Age at entry	Duration	Percentage of total business	Proportion of existing bonus to sum assured before new quinquennial bonus
Life, without profits	42	7·9	·17	—
Life, with profits	37	18	·29	·183
	Original period			
Endowment assurance without profits	20	7	·12	—
Endowment assurance with profits	24	11	·42	·094

12·5. Notes on special types of assurance.

The valuation formulae we have discussed in § 12·4 are generally applicable to assurances of various types but there are certain special types which give rise to special considerations and we propose now to review some of these types.

Temporary assurances

While a valuation by one of the suggested formulae would be feasible, a full valuation of temporary assurances is not usually considered to be necessary. The temporary assurance policy-value, considered as a function of duration, rises to a maximum usually in the second half of the term and then declines rapidly to zero at the expiry of the period of assurance. The liability is small compared with the premium unless the assurance is for a long period of years. The following table illustrates the feature (Lochhead, 1932).

TABLE 12·7

Temporary assurances for 1,000 by annual premiums

O^{M} 3% *policy values*

Age at entry	Period of insurance	Office annual premium	Years in force				Mean† policy value
			3	8	12	18	
30	10	10·08	3·05	2·65	—	—	2·85
30	20	11·79	8·21	17·79	20·24	9·51	14·09
50	10	21·79	12·14	11·71	—	—	11·92
50	20	30·29	35·15	82·16	99·62	52·43	68·30

† Mean assuming an even distribution of business in force by duration.

Though the most important part of the liability is, probably, the unearned part of the premium, i.e. the part paid in respect of the fraction of the year of assurance which falls after the valuation date, the table shows that the effect on the liability of the distribution of business by original term cannot be ignored. An arbitrary figure might be put on the liability of, say, one or two annual premiums according to the distribution by original term.

Temporary assurances by single premiums may be valued by apportioning the single premiums over the durations of the respective contracts.

For office purposes it may be convenient to group temporary assurances according to the calendar year in which the period of assurance expires.

Where the temporary assurance premiums include a charge for the option of conversion into whole-life or endowment assurance, the value of the liability should be increased by the aggregate of the sums so paid in respect of this option on all assurances in force on the valuation date (possibly accumulated with interest and benefit of survivorship).

After conversion, such policies would be transferred to the appropriate groups and valued as normal policies effected at the age at date of conversion, the option premiums received and the reserve (if any) on the temporary assurance falling into surplus. Theoretically, the option premiums should be set against any increased mortality that may be incurred in the years following conversion but the normal practice is simple and the error is not of any serious consequence.

Family income benefits

The type of decreasing temporary assurance which is generally known as a 'family income benefit' gives rise to special valuation

TABLE 12·8

Duration	Reserve for 1,000 whole-life policy		Deduction from reserves for income of 150 gross, i.e. 115 net, for 20-year period			
			Premiums payable			
			For 20 years		Throughout life	
	Age at entry 30	Age at entry 45	Age 30	Age 45	Age 30	Age 45
Net premium			3·379	9·759	2·241	7·643
1	10·5	19·1	·5	−1·2	1·7	1·0
2	21·3	38·7	1·0	−2·2	3·4	2·3
3	32·6	58·6	1·6	−2·7	5·3	4·1
5	56·0	99·8	2·7	−3·3	9·0	8·6
10	120·0	208·1	5·4	1·0	19·5	28·0
15	192·2	321·1	6·8	10·5	30·2	57·3
19	256·0	411·2	2·6	6·5	35·2	75·3
20	272·8	433·5	—	—	35·2	75·6
25	360·3	540·2	—	—	31·0	61·3
30	451·6	632·8	—	—	26·5	49·0
35	542·3	709·6	—	—	22·2	38·7
40	628·5	770·2	—	—	18·0	30·7

problems because the premiums are not usually limited to such a period as will avoid the complication of negative reserves. The problem is illustrated by the above table taken from Raynes's paper. The calculations were made at A1924–29 $3\frac{1}{2}\%$ and should now be regarded as illustrative only.

It will be seen that the valuation liability on the 'basic contract' should be reduced by the negative value of the liability under the supplementary family income benefit. However, the figures of Table 12·8 have been calculated by A 1924–29 ultimate. For the purpose of valuing income benefits it is more appropriate to assume select mortality, and had select mortality been used the deductions—where premiums are limited to the income period—would have disappeared or have become sufficiently small to be ignored. A reserve should be made for unexpired risks.

Where the premiums for the supplementary benefit are payable throughout the duration of the basic contract some deduction must be made from the valuation liability for that contract.

There are two general methods for a full valuation of these supplementary benefits, Karup's method and Lidstone's Z method.

The income benefits can be grouped according to the year in which they expire though this may entail classification separately from the respective basic contracts. The income benefit for unexpired duration r would be valued by a factor of the form

$$\bar{a}_{\overline{r}|} - \bar{a}_{y\overline{r}|},$$

where y is the mean age obtained by applying Z to the amount of the income benefit. If the premiums are payable over the same unexpired duration they can be valued in the same way but if they are payable over the durations of the respective basic contracts they would need to be classified and valued with those contracts.

Should it be preferred to keep the income benefits and basic contracts together in the same groups, fair results can be obtained by using the same Z mean age for the basic contract and the supplementary benefit.

An alternative solution is to classify the income benefits by attained age and to tabulate two constants for the income benefit with a further constant for the premium should that be required. The general formula for income benefit I is:

$$I\,(1/\delta - \bar{a}_y) - (v^M . I/\delta)/v^y + (I . \bar{N}_M)/D_y - P . \ddot{a}_y,$$

with suitable modifications for the particular circumstances.

Children's deferred assurances

During the deferred period, children's deferred assurances essentially consist of the accumulation of money at interest, similar to sinking fund insurances and endowments with return of premiums. The valuation liability may be computed in the same way provided that the business in force has been written on comparable terms to those appropriate at time of valuation.

Such assurances may be suitably grouped in years of entry though the alternative grouping, by year of vesting, is sometimes preferred because it simplifies the extraction of the necessary particulars when the assurance vests.

After vesting, children's deferred assurances would be grouped with the ordinary assurances but a special net premium would be required. The assurance would consist, in fact, partly of an annual premium and partly of a single premium contract (see p. 277 regarding single and limited payments). The special net premium would be less than the net premium for the annual premium part of the contract because provision has to be made for loading on the single premium part.

One solution of the problem is to compute a special net premium such that the value of the liability is the same before and after the vesting of the assurance. An alternative solution is to reduce the net premium by the same amount as the office premium has been reduced compared with the normal premium at the vesting age.

The problem is especially difficult because it is often necessary to reconcile business effected on many different scales of premium with a valuation basis which is unrelated to any of them. The precise nature of the solution adopted in practice is not of major importance.

Assurances on more than one life

The only assurances likely to require grouping are joint-life assurances. Approximations are available based on Gompertz's and Makeham's laws. Where Gompertz's law holds the assurances may be valued at an equivalent single age and where Makeham's law holds the assurances may be valued at the equivalent equal ages. The latter method is the more useful as an approximation where neither law applies.

Joint-life endowment assurances may be valued by these methods and Ackland has shown that Lidstone's Z method is applicable to the computation of the mean maturity ages for such assurances. It is probable, however, that the value of the liability will be affected to only a small extent either by the age or the number of lives involved.

Contingent assurances may present a difficult problem because they may range from what is a nominal risk to one which approximates to whole-life assurance. However, this is not an important class of assurance and an arbitrary value may be placed on the majority of such assurances, as for temporary assurances. Where the risk approximates to a whole-life assurance the contracts should be valued individually: the liability might be assumed to be roughly that under a whole-life assurance or a proportion of it.

A simple transformation of the contingent-assurance policy-values shows that we may write

$$ {}_tV^1_{xy} = (A_{\overset{1}{x+t}:y+t} - A^1_{xy}) + A^1_{xy} \times {}_tV_{xy}. \qquad (12\cdot9)$$

The first part of this expression may be positive or negative: if it can be assumed to be zero on the average, the second part of the expression would give a simple but rather rough approximation.

Annuities

Perhaps the most difficult problem in the valuation of annuities arises from the mortality basis since it may be necessary to allow for the improved vitality of annuitants. This problem has been discussed in the appropriate chapter and we do not discuss it further here.

Where the instalments of the annuity may be payable on any day of the year it is usually sufficient to assume that they are evenly distributed. Since ${}_{\frac{1}{2m}|}\ddot{a}^{(m)} = a + \frac{1}{2}$ approximately, it is possible to value all the annuities in course of payment by the factor $(\frac{1}{2} + a)$. Where the annuity is apportionable to the date of death the value of the average proportion must be added to the liability.

Annuities payable for a minimum period in any event may be valued in two parts, an annuity-certain valued according to the unexpired period and a deferred annuity valued by a Karup constant tabulated with the other annuities. Where the excess (if any) of the consideration over the annuity payments is to be returned at death the contract may be valued in the same way though, strictly, provision should be made for the annuity-certain to be paid-up at once should the annuitant die during its course.

Normally, joint-life annuities are few and may be valued individually but last survivor annuities may be sufficiently numerous to constitute a real problem. Various approximate methods of valuation have been suggested but the best, we think, is due to Elphinstone and Lindsay. Under this method put:

$$a_{\overline{xy}} = \alpha \times a_{\overline{xx}} + \beta \times a_{\overline{yy}}. \qquad (12{\cdot}10)$$

Then α is valued by a last survivor annuity for two lives of the same age and sex as one of the lives and β is valued by a similar last survivor annuity for two lives of the same age and sex as the other life. The approximation is rather closer if $\alpha+\beta \neq 1$. It may, however, be convenient to assume $\alpha+\beta=1$ so that the parts may be used in obtaining a balance of the annuity movement. No doubt similar approximations would be available for annuities on more than two lives, were they sufficiently numerous, and the method could also be extended to last survivor assurances.

12·6. Adjustments to the crude liability.

So far we have assumed that premiums are payable annually and that the policy anniversary and the valuation date coincide. We must now consider the adjustments required for these and other items.

Incidence of premium income

Since the policy anniversary will rarely coincide with the valuation date some assumption must be made with regard to the period to the next policy anniversary unless an automatic adjustment is provided by the method of computing the ages, durations, etc. The problem is, in fact, closely linked to those methods and we will consider them briefly in turn.

In general, there are two methods of dealing with fractional durations: we may take either the nearest integral duration or the curtate duration. The first method gives an automatic allowance for the incidence of premium income whereas the second method requires some assumption with regard to the fractional period to the next policy anniversary. Since the new business is not evenly distributed over the calendar year but is usually heaped up towards the end of the year, it is found that the policy anniversary falls, on the average, rather more than half-way through the calendar year. Where the valuation date is the last day of the calendar year it is usually rather more accurate to assume a period of about two-thirds rather than one-half of a year to the next anniversary.

Where the nearest integral duration is taken we may tabulate those premiums falling due in the 6 months before the valuation date separately from those due in the 6 months after the valuation date. The former are valued by the factor a and the latter by the factor $1+a$. It will be seen that the method gives a close approximation to the true incidence and, where the method is applied to endowment assurances, the valuation factors for both sums assured and premiums will be for integral unexpired periods, enabling tabulated functions to be used.

Where the curtate duration is taken and the period to the next policy anniversary is k the endowment assurance policy-value takes the form ${}_{t+1-k}V_{x\overline{n}|}$ or approximately,

$$k\,({}_tV_{x\overline{n}|}+P_{x\overline{n}|})+(1-k)\times{}_{t+1}V_{x\overline{n}|}.$$

The normal grouping for endowment assurances gives the curtate unexpired period $r=n-t-1$ and the valuation age y must be assumed to approximate to $(x+t)+(1-k)$. Hence the valuation factors are $A_{y:\overline{r+k}|}$ and $1-k+a_{y\overline{r-1+k}|}$, i.e. where

$$k=\tfrac{1}{2},\quad A_{y\overline{r+\frac{1}{2}}|}\quad \tfrac{1}{2}+a_{y\overline{r-\frac{1}{2}}|},$$

$$k=\tfrac{2}{3},\quad A_{y\overline{r+\frac{2}{3}}|}\quad \tfrac{1}{3}+a_{y\overline{r-\frac{1}{3}}|}.$$

The assumption that the valuation age is an approximation to the entry age plus the exact duration is not always borne out in practice. For example, the office premiums may be computed at the age next birthday at entry or at the half or quarter-age and it may be convenient to compute the net premium at the same age.

On the other hand, it is both convenient and customary to take the nearest age at valuation. Clearly this combination will not produce the exact duration but other considerations may be of more importance.

Frequency of premium payments

Lidstone has investigated the adjustment for premiums payable more frequently than once a year and in the main we follow his work. There are two cases to consider: (*a*) the valuation of *m*thly premiums by annual factors, and (*b*) the valuation of the equivalent annual premiums.

Comparing contracts by annual and by *m*thly premiums it will be seen that under the former contract an aggregate of rP premiums remains to be paid whereas under the latter there will be payable rP plus a fraction of a year's premium which may be denoted by F. We may also notice that the average value of F will be $\frac{m-1}{2m}\times P$ with an even incidence of business.

The *m*thly premium may either be 'instalment' when the balance (if any) to make up the full year's premium will be deducted at death or 'true' when there will be no such deduction. The amount of this deduction also averages $\frac{m-1}{2m}\times P$ with an even distribution of deaths.

(*a*) *The valuation of* m*thly premiums by annual factors*

The addition to the value of *m*thly premiums by annual factors is

True *m*thly $\qquad F\times A_{y\overline{n}|}^{\;\;1}$.

Instalment *m*thly $\qquad F\times A_{y\overline{n}|}$.

The former vanishes for whole-life assurances and the latter becomes $F\times A_y$.

(*b*) *The valuation of equivalent annual premiums*

Where annual premiums have been valued F must be added to the value of the premiums. However, the *m*thly premiums payable contain a loading to provide for loss of interest and (where 'true') for an assurance of $\frac{m-1}{2m} \times P$ at death on the average. The former requires no reserve but the latter requires a reserve equivalent to an assurance of $\frac{m-1}{2m} \times P$ at death. This reserve reduces the addition F to the value of the premiums which becomes:

True $m$thly $\qquad F(1 - {}_tV^{1}_{x\overline{n}|})$.

Instalment $m$thly $\qquad F$.

The former would not be convenient for computation but it would be sufficient to ignore V for limited-premium assurances and to take an average value of ${}_tV_x$ for whole-life assurances.

Early payment of claims

It is the practice in some countries to calculate premiums and valuation factors on the basis of continuous functions and where this practice obtains no adjustment is, of course, required for early payment of claims. It has been customary in Great Britain and in many other countries to calculate valuation factors on the basis of the usual tabulated functions which provide for payment at the end of the year of death. Assuming that claims are evenly distributed over the year of death and that, on the average, they will be payable two months after death, an interest adjustment is required for an average period of four months.

For whole-life assurances valued by the gross premium method the factor $(1+i/3)$ must be applied to the value of the sums assured and bonuses. Where the net premium method is used the factor $(1+i/3)$ need only be applied to the value of the net liability because the net premiums bear the adjustment equally with the assurance factors and set off the cost. (The office premium presumably contains an appropriate provision.)

The adjustment is required only for claims by death. Endowment assurances and similar types of assurance may be regarded as consisting partly of temporary assurance and partly of the endowment payable on survival. The adjustment for early payment of claims is required on the first part only of the contract and since this is much the smaller part unless the period of assurance is exceptionally long the adjustment may usually be ignored.

Loading for expenses and profits after premiums have ceased

Single premiums and limited premiums will no doubt contain a provision for expenses throughout the duration of the contract, though possibly on a modified scale after premiums have ceased. A net premium valuation on the same basis as the premiums would release the whole of the loading during the premium-paying period and make no provision for the continuing expenses. The problem is often obscured, however, by the use of an arbitrarily low rate of interest in valuation and this may make an adjustment less necessary.

A further complication is the question of bonuses on participating assurances. If bonuses follow the contributions to surplus released by a net premium valuation there is an abrupt fall in the bonus when the premium period expires because the loading contribution to surplus comes to an end. By allocating rather smaller bonuses during the premium-paying period it is possible to permit limited-premium assurances to share in profits throughout on the same basis. This has become customary in Great Britain where single premium and limited-premium assurances often share throughout on the same basis as if premiums were payable for the whole period of assurance. This practice necessitates a special reserve to augment the loading fund.

The solution to this problem is best approached by way of a bonus reserve valuation on bases as near as possible to the estimated experience. (Compare A. Fraser whose approach is essentially similar.) Suppose that unaccented symbols represent the valuation basis, symbols with a single accent the office premium basis and symbols with a double accent the bonus reserve basis, including the reserve for future bonuses. The valuation liability where premiums are payable over the whole period of assurance may be written:

Bonus reserve $(S+B)\,A'' - (1-p'')\,P'\ddot{a}''.$

Net premium $(S+B)\,A - P\ddot{a}.$

Excess of bonus reserve over net premium

$$(S+B)\,(A''-A) - [(1-p'')\,P'\ddot{a}'' - P\ddot{a}].$$

Since the bonus reserve method and the net premium method often produce similar values for the net liability the 'excess' shown will be the algebraic excess. It may be positive or negative and should approximate to zero in the aggregate.

A similar expression holds for limited-premium assurances but the bonus reserve method should produce the larger values for the net liability because it makes a reserve for bonuses after premiums have ceased.

The excess of the limited-premium value of this expression over the whole-term value is the special reserve theoretically needed to place limited-premium assurances in the same profit-earning position as whole-term assurances. The first part of the expression which contains the reserve for future bonus is the same for both types of assurance and we are left with the following as the special reserve to be added to the net premium liability:

$$[(1-p'')P'_x\ddot{a}''_y - P_x\ddot{a}_y] - [(1-p'')\,{}_nP'_x\ddot{a}''_{y\overline{n}|} - {}_nP_x\ddot{a}_{y\overline{n}|}]. \quad (12{\cdot}11)$$

This is the theoretical additional reserve and to apply it in practice it would be necessary to tabulate both the office limited premium and the corresponding whole-term office and net premiums. (The net limited premium need not be tabulated because it is only a step in arriving at the final liability.)

Since the formula is hardly convenient to apply in practice it is sometimes simplified by taking all the annuity values on the valuation basis, and by putting $p''=0$. The valuation formula for limited-premium assurances including the special reserve, then becomes:

$$S \times A_y - {}_nP'_x\ddot{a}_{y\overline{n}|} + (P'_x - P_x)\,\ddot{a}_y. \quad (12{\cdot}12)$$

The loading $(P'_x - P_x)$ may be tabulated and valued with the sum assured. This formula is simple but it has the defect that the liability at the outset is not zero. Todhunter suggested that the true office premium should be replaced by such an 'office premium' as would produce the required value of zero for the reserve at the outset. This is obtained by commuting the whole-term office premium on the valuation basis, not the premium basis.

Where the limited-premium assurances are classified separately it may be possible to assume that the whole-term loading is a constant proportion of the sum assured whatever the age at entry. If this be assumed to be ϕ, say, its value $\phi\ (1+a)$ can clearly be put in the form $\phi/d\ (1-A)$, a simple form for calculation since the value of the sum assured is available.

The formulae we have given are suitable for either participating or non-participating assurances. The magnitude of the reserve is so much smaller for the latter class that a simple approximation is quite sufficient whereas for the former class one of the more refined methods may be necessary.

BIBLIOGRAPHY

R. K. LOCHHEAD (1932). *Valuation and surplus*. Cambridge University Press.

CLASSIFICATION AND GROUPING

D. C. FRASER (1904). A comparison of the various methods of grouping whole-life assurances for valuation. *J.I.A.* vol. XXXVIII, p. 385. (Reprints, 1935.)

P. H. MCCORMACK (1917). Continuous valuation machinery. *J.I.A.* vol. L, p. 231.

G. J. LIDSTONE (1945). The origins of the card system. *J.I.A.* vol. LXXII, p. 229.

N. E. COE, K. J. HEDLEY and L. H. LONGLEY-COOK (1948). Punched-card equipment. *J.I.A.* vol. LXXIV, p. 246.

FORMULAE OF TYPE (*a*)

G. KING (1905). On the valuation in groups of whole-life policies by select mortality tables. *J.I.A.* vol. XL, p. 1.

G. KING (1907). On the method of Dr Johannes Karup of valuing in groups endowment assurances, and policies for the whole of life by premiums limited in number. *J.I.A.* vol. XLII, p. 145. (Reprints, 1946.)

W. P. ELDERTON (1913). Approximate valuation of endowment assurances. *J.I.A.* vol. XLVIII, p. 1.

FORMULAE OF TYPE (*b*)—*Z* MEAN AGE

G. J. LIDSTONE (1903). Further remarks on the valuation of endowment assurances in groups. *J.I.A.* vol. XXXVIII, p. 1. (Reprints, 1935.) Further notes upon the application of Mr Lidstone's method to the case of joint endowment assurances, by T. G. Ackland. *Ibid.* p. 61.

H. VAUGHAN (1916). The valuation of double endowment assurances. *J.I.A.* vol. L, p. 1.

G. J. LIDSTONE (1921). A group-check for endowment assurance net premiums, by means of mean ages based on the *Z* method. *J.I.A.* vol. LII, p. 488.

G. J. LIDSTONE (1933). The application of the *Z*-method of valuing endowment assurances to valuations based on the new A1924–29 mortality table. *J.I.A.* vol. LXIV, p. 478.

O. DRAMINSKY (1921). Calculation of reserves by Lidstone's and Givskov's methods. *Skand. Akt.* vol. IV, p. 239.

Givskov's method was based on the same idea as Lidstone's but he allowed for the true value of γ for each duration instead of using the Makeham constant c. This enabled him to deal with the distribution of business as a whole instead of by each duration, and extending the formula to unexpired duration as well as maturity age he was able to value endowment assurances in one multiplication.

OTHER FORMULAE OF TYPE (*b*)

A. E. KING (1914). On the extension of existing valuation methods of grouping policies by the employment of a system of weights. *J.I.A.* vol. XLVIII, p. 121.

C. W. KENCHINGTON (1921). Modern developments in the methods of industrial assurance valuations. *J.I.A.* vol. LII, p. 453.

A. W. JOSEPH (1931). Formulae for approximate valuation: a comparison. *J.I.A.* vol. LXII, p. 119.

W. PERKS (1933). On a modification of the net premium method of valuation of participating assurances and on the application of the *n*-ages method to the valuation of assurances grouped by years of entry and to the approximate calculation of isolated values of actuarial functions. *J.I.A.* vol. LXIV, p. 264.

W. PERKS (1945). Two-variable developments of the *n*-ages method. *J.I.A.* vol. LXXII, p. 377.

FORMULAE OF TYPE (*c*)

T. J. SEARLE (1893). On the progress of profit in a life assurance fund. *J.I.A.* vol. XXX, p. 493.

H. J. TAPPENDEN (1929). A valuation of non-participating policies without classification. *J.I.A.* vol. LXI, p. 63.

FORMULAE OF TYPE (*d*)

A. HENRY (1918). On a method of approximate valuation. *J.I.A.* vol. LI, p. 118.

A. HENRY (1920). Some further suggestions on the subject of approximate valuations. *J.I.A.* vol. LII, p. 48.

H. L. TRACHTENBERG (1920). A new method of valuing policies in groups. *J.I.A.* vol. LII, pp. 38, 402.

W. P. ELDERTON and A. H. ROWELL (1925). Some approximations from valuation statistics. *J.I.A.* vol. LVI, p. 263.

A. W. JOSEPH (1933). A note on Henry's method. *J.I.A.* vol. LXIV, p. 313.

H. G. JONES (1933). A note on the *n*-ages method. *J.I.A.* vol. LXIV, p. 318.

Model Offices

G. King (1902). On the comparative reserves of life assurance companies according to various tables of mortality, at various rates of interest. *J.I.A.* vol. XXXVII, p. 453.

J. Buchanan (1907). Model office reserves for endowment assurances. *J.I.A.* vol. XLI, p. 18.

W. P. Elderton and H. J. P. Oakley (1924). Further notes on the annuity business of British offices and the valuation thereof. *J.I.A.* vol. LV, p. 211.

C. F. Trustam (1927). On a new method of calculating model office reserves. *J.I.A.* vol. LVIII, p. 195.

The average reserve in a fund which is replenished each year for an indefinite period by a uniformly increasing amount of new business is $-\dfrac{P^i-P^j}{d^i-d^j}$, where j is the rate of increase. Trustam applied this formula to the calculation of model office reserves.

W. P. Elderton (1931). Valuations in modern conditions. *J.I.A.* vol. LXII, p. 62.

This paper included an example of a 'pocket' model office.

I. J. Bunney and W. J. Falconer (1935). Model office reserves and the A1924–29 tables. *J.I.A.* vol. LXVI, p. 433.

Special Classes

H. E. Raynes (1934). Family income policies. *J.I.A.* vol. LXV, p. 122.

M. D. W. Elphinstone and W. G. P. Lindsay (1939). The valuation of joint life and last survivor annuities. *T.F.A.* vol. XVII, p. 39.

CHAPTER 13

ANALYSIS OF SURPLUS

13·1. The purpose of and requirements for analysis of surplus.

A life assurance valuation provides a test of the financial position of a fund on a certain date. It is obviously convenient to have some idea of the progress of the fund in the intervening periods between valuations and this is provided by the analysis of surplus. Such an analysis also places a check on the valuations and may give useful information in the distribution of surplus.

If the valuation assumptions were related either to those underlying the premium scale or to the estimated future experience of the fund, the analysis of surplus would reveal how profitable had been each of the principal sources of surplus and the analysis would have a real meaning with regard to the financial position of the fund. Where the valuation is made by the net premium method, the valuation bases are usually artificial, being chosen more for the purpose of maintaining the sources of surplus than for the purpose of revealing the true financial position of the fund. The various elements in the analysis of surplus are thereby distorted and the analysis has little real meaning though it may still be useful as a check.

It was formerly an axiom that a knowledge of the sources of surplus was necessary to the equitable distribution of surplus. Lochhead states that 'this idea has long since vanished' and if we understand by the axiom that an equitable distribution of surplus *must* be based on the individual contributions to surplus, the axiom is clearly false. Since surplus may be regarded as a function of the valuation basis (which itself may be the product of many extraneous considerations) the equitable distribution of surplus would also be tied to the valuation basis, to the exclusion of other and possibly more important considerations.

However, it is important for the student to appreciate that surplus arises primarily as a sum of money, being the difference between the values placed on the assets and on the liabilities. Surplus is thus partly the monetary expression of the difference between the assumed and actual experience with regard to the factors explicit in the valuation basis and partly the product of experience with regard to realization of assets, contingency funds, etc. It remains true in general, therefore, that a knowledge of the sources of surplus is necessary to the proper distribution of surplus.

The analysis of surplus first of all requires valuations on the same basis at the beginning and end of the period of the analysis which may, for convenience, be taken as one year. Normally, an annual valuation would be made, for internal purposes at least, and the analysis would relate to the intervening calendar year. Where the valuation basis is changed it is really necessary to have the second valuation on the original as well as on the altered basis, the difference being the 'cost of change of basis'. The analysis would then follow the assumptions of the original valuation and the 'cost of change of basis' would be brought in at the end.

It is important to appreciate that the analysis of surplus merely tests the working of the valuation basis and that the valuation assumptions must, therefore, be rigidly followed through in the analysis. Some of the results may appear to be absurd but that is beside the point for this purpose. The analysis must show the actual working out of the valuation assumptions.

The degree of accuracy which is possible in the analysis of surplus depends to a considerable extent on the precision with which the valuation is itself performed. Various approximations may be used for convenience to shorten the work of valuation and such approximations affect the analysis unless the resulting error happens to be the same at successive valuations. Generally speaking, the approximation should be followed through in the analysis but it may be necessary to bring in an item 'error of approximation'.

It is important to have a clear grasp of the process of analysis. We have, as it were, two aggregates, namely the 'fund' and the 'valuation liability', which are in a state of continual flux. The fund is being increased by premiums and interest and investment profits and diminished by claims and other outgo and expenses. The valuation liability is being increased by net premiums and by interest at the assumed rate and diminished by the expected death strain and by the valuation liability in respect of assurances going off the books. The valuation liability is also affected by any change there may be in the basis or method of computation and by any strain there may be in respect of new business.

Since the analysis of surplus is based on a comparison of the revenue account with the valuation assumptions we are concerned only with items which enter into the revenue account. Changes in the values of the assets are recorded in the analysis only to the extent that they are brought into the revenue account.

13·2. The analysis of the experience.

The analysis of the actual experience starts from the revenue account which shows the progress of the fund during the year. The excess of the fund over the valuation liability on the same date is the accumulated surplus at that date. The surplus earned in the year is the difference between the accumulated surplus at the beginning and end of the year.

The amount of the year's surplus so found must be adjusted for any special items in the revenue account, such as depreciation written off or transfer to contingency reserves. These items may be assumed to be debited at the end of the year so that if A is the fund at the beginning of the year and B the fund at the end of the year, B (and consequently the surplus) has to be increased by the amount of these deductions.

The item of interest which we may call I will probably be the part of the total interest earned which is apportioned to the assurance fund as distinct from other funds and contingency and other reserves. It may be regarded as consisting partly of interest on the valuation liability and partly of interest on the surplus. The mean yield is usually computed by Hardy's formula

$$i'' = \frac{2I}{A+B-I},$$

where I is net after deduction of income tax. The surplus interest consists of (a) the excess interest $(i''-i)$ in respect of the valuation liability, and (*b*) earned interest on the surplus. However, it is more convenient if we compute the excess interest $(i''-i)$ on the mean fund $(A+B-I)/2$ and add back interest at the assumed valuation rate on the surplus.

Hardy's formula assumes that all income and outgo is evenly distributed over the year. Since I includes 'interest on interest' the formula produces the effective rate of interest, but assuming simple interest within the year.† When an item of account is brought into the analysis of surplus it must be increased by half-a-year's interest at the *valuation* rate to bring it to the end of the year. The interest is added at the valuation rate, not the earned rate, since the excess has been included in interest surplus.

The revenue account shows the gross premium income and the expenses including commission. The loading is the difference between the gross and net valuation premium income and the surplus loading is the excess of the loading over the expenses. Hardy's formula assumes that the gross premium income and expenses are both increased by half-a-year's interest (at the *valuation* rate for this purpose) and the valuation may also assume that the net premium income is due in the middle of the year. Where this is so the adjustment of half-a-year's interest may be applied to the loading surplus, but other assumptions may require special treatment.

The amount of the valuation net premium income is usually known only for the 'in force' at the dates when the valuation is made and not for the year of account. Generally speaking, the premium income includes a full year's premiums for assurances in force throughout the year, and for new business (subject to the fractional premiums due after the end of the year where premiums are payable more frequently than once a year), but only half-a-year's premium on the average for claims by death and probably less than that for surrenders and other assurances 'off'. It is usually sufficient to estimate the net premium income for the year of account by proportion from the gross premium income taking for

† The formula for a continuous even flow of income and outgo is

$$B=A(1+i'')+(B-A-I)\,i''/\delta''.$$

Simple interest within the year leads to the substitution of $(1+i''/2)$ for i''/δ''.

this purpose the proportion between the corresponding items in force at the end of the year adjusted as may be necessary for such special classes as temporary assurances and for extra premiums.

The interest surplus and loading surplus may well comprise the bulk of the surplus and it is convenient at this stage to consider a check on the arithmetic. Suppose that we write down the Revenue Account as follows:

REVENUE ACCOUNT

Fund at beginning of year	A	Claims and other outgo excluding commission and expenses	C
Premiums received	P'	Commission and expenses	E
Interest, less tax	I	Fund at end of year $(=A+P'+I-C-E)$	B
	$A+P'+I$		$A+P'+I$

V_0 = Valuation liability at beginning of year at rate i.
V_1 = Valuation liability at end of year.
P = Valuation net premiums corresponding to P'.

Interest surplus

$$\{I \quad -(P'-E-C)\, i/2 - i\times V_0\}$$

Loading surplus

$$+\{(P'-E)+(P'-E)\, i/2 \quad -(1+i/2)\, P\}$$

Mortality and miscellaneous surplus

$$+\{-C \quad -C\times i/2+[V_0\,(1+i)+P\,(1+i/2)-V_1]\}$$

Total surplus for year

$$(B-A) \quad -(V_1-V_0)$$

which is evidently the surplus for the year. The third group, mortality and miscellaneous surplus, is a balancing item and is usually written

$$V_0(1+i)+(P-C)\,(1+i/2)-V_1. \qquad (13\cdot 1)$$

In this form it provides a useful arithmetical check on the other items but it does not, of course, check the valuation liability at the end of the year because this enters directly into the process. The next step is to analyse the third group.

13·3. The analysis of the mortality and miscellaneous group.

First of all, we may notice that the mortality and miscellaneous group will contain some items not provided for in the valuation basis, for example interim bonuses. The amount of interim bonus paid in the year, with half-a-year's interest at the valuation rate, should be added to the surplus to be analysed.

In the preceding analysis realized investment profits may have been added to I or deducted in C; in the latter case they now fall to be deducted from the mortality and miscellaneous surplus to be analysed.

The surplus from mortality is the excess of the expected over the actual death strain and the analysis of the remainder of surplus turns upon how the mortality item is dealt with. This is a question partly of taste and partly of what is practicable in all the circumstances. It is usually possible to compute the valuation liability individually for claims during the year and hence to arrive at the actual death strain, but the expected death strain must be computed by a formula such as those set out in the next section and the assumptions implicit in the formula with regard to new business and withdrawals must be followed out in the analysis of those items.

The mean death strain at risk is equal to:

(*a*) one-half of the death strain at risk in respect of the 'in force' at the beginning of the year, revalued as at the end of the year,

plus (*b*) one-half of the death strain at risk in respect of the 'in force' at the end of the year,

plus (*c*) one-half of the death strain at risk in respect of claims, valued as at the end of the year.

One half-year's net premium should be added to each item assuming that premiums are due in the middle of the year. This mean death strain at risk must be multiplied by q_y, where y is the age at the beginning of the year.

Where the expected death strain is effectively based upon the mean death strain at risk over the year, new business and surrenders must be treated as taking place in the middle of the year. The initial strain on new business would be computed as if the business were written at that time, and the valuation liability on surrenders, computed in the middle of the year, would be compared with the actual surrender values paid.

The process can be simplified, if it be thought worth the extra work, by closing the books in the middle of the year. By then, the 'in force' would have been increased by 6 months' new business and decreased by 6 months' surrenders and other 'offs', but the 6 months' claims should not be deducted. This 'in force' in the middle of the year, before deducting claims, would be valued as at the end of the year and the death strain at risk so found would be multiplied by q_y, where y is the age at the beginning of the year. Formula (13·4) would be a simple one for this purpose.

TABLE 13·1

Expected death strain related to	Contribution to the year's expected death strain		
	New business	Claims by death	Surrenders
Mean in force	$\frac{1}{2}$	1	$\frac{1}{2}$
In force at mid-point	(*a*) 1 (*b*) 0	1	(*a*) 0 (*b*) 1
In force at beginning of year	0	1	1
In force at end of year	1	1	0

(*a*) relates to first 6 months, and (*b*) to second 6 months.

Should this alternative process be adopted, the treatment of the year's movements would have to be varied appropriately. New business, surrenders and so on would be treated as occurring at the beginning of the year if within the first 6 months, and as at the end of the year if within the second half of the year.

It will be seen that the treatment of the movements within the year depends upon the contribution that the several movements make to the expected death strain according to the process adopted for the calculation. There are four general processes and the corresponding contributions to expected death strain are shown in Table 13·1.

Under each process claims are to be given a full year's exposure and the reserves on claims are calculated as at the end of the year.

With the other movements the reserve is to be calculated as at the beginning, the middle or the end of the year according to whether the exposure is for 0, ½ or 1 year.

Lapses would be treated in a similar way to surrenders but there would not be any surrender value, except possibly to repay any loan there may be on the assurance.

Alterations of various kinds may affect the analysis, for example alterations to other classes of assurance, conversion to paid-up assurances either by payment of a single premium or by a reduction in the sum assured, and deferred or optional annuities or assurances coming into force. The cost of the change must be computed either as at the middle of the year or other suitable date having regard to the method of computing the expected death strain.

The treatment of assurances subject to extra risk must follow the assumptions in the valuation. Where the normal reserve is held together with 1 year's extra premium it is simplest to add a year's extra premium (excluding first year's extras) to the expected death strain. Assurances subject to a debt would carry the normal reserve and would, therefore, be included for the full amount in the expected death strain, though the actual death strain would be reduced by the amount of the debt.

13·4. The expected death strain.

From what has been said it will be apparent that analysis of surplus requires (*a*) a process for computing the figures in respect of movements, and (*b*) a formula for calculating the expected death strain and that the two should be intimately linked.

The mathematical foundation of analysis of surplus is the differential equation (8·11) which shows the financial effect of the difference between the assumed and actual experience. However, it is probably best to begin the study of analysis of surplus by starting from simple formulae for the expected death strain and we propose to do this.

Very generally, we have for integral policy-years under annual premium assurances:

$$S\,[V(t)+P]\,(1+i)=S\,.\,q_{+t}+S\,.\,p_{+t}V(t+1). \qquad (13\cdot2)$$

This equation expresses the fact that the reserve and the premium accumulated with interest are just sufficient in total to pay the expected claims assumed due at the end of the year and to provide for the valuation liability in respect of the survivors. The right-hand side of the equation may be transposed in a number of ways to obtain a suitable formula for calculating the expected death strain.

The classic formula is:

$$S.V(t+1)=S[V(t)+P](1+i)-S.q_{+t}[1-V(t+1)]. \quad (13\cdot3)$$

The last term of this formula is the expected death strain. It is suitably applied to the mean business in force, before taking out claims, and assumes that this mean business is valued as at the end of the year, the resulting death strain at risk being multiplied by the rate of mortality at the beginning of the year.

It is not necessary to carry out this arithmetic in full. The work may be shortened by noticing that for many types of assurance (though not for limited-premium assurances) the final term of (13·3) may be written:

$$S(P+d)\times q_{+t}\ddot{a}_{+t+1}. \quad (13\cdot4)$$

If the values of $q_{+t}\ddot{a}_{+t+1}$ are tabulated as a special valuation factor the calculation of the expected death strain can be obtained direct from the mean business in force.

The mean business in force cannot, of course, be calculated until the end of the year figures are known, unless the office is willing to go to the extra work of closing its books in the middle of the year as suggested in § 13·3. This difficulty can be obviated by working from the business in force at the beginning of the year.

Now if formula (13·2) be divided throughout by p_{+t} and rearranged we find that

$$S.V(t+1)=S\phi(t)-Sq_{+t}/p_{+t}[1-\phi(t)], \quad (13\cdot5)$$

where $\phi(t)=[V(t)+P](1+i)$ (Searle, 1893). It is simple to calculate $\phi(t)$ from the previous year's valuation figures and the expected death strain for the year can thus be calculated at the beginning of the year. This is a great advantage, but it has consequences for the treatment of new business and surrenders which have been mentioned in § 13·3.

(It is interesting to compare (13·5) with the formula suggested by Carpmael. He worked on the figures in force at the end of the year, after deducting claims, and he suggested that the expected death strain should be taken as

$$S.q_{+t}/p_{+t}\,[1-V\,(t+1)].$$

The process is simple, but clearly it assumes that the actual survivors are equal to the expected survivors.)

As a numerical example, consider the eleventh policy-years of 10,000 whole-life assurances effected at age 60, assuming pure functions on A 1924–29 3% ultimate. We will assume that there are (*a*) no deaths, (*b*) actual deaths equal to expected deaths, and (*c*) actual deaths equal to twice the expected.

$10{,}000 . P_{60} = 520{\cdot}5$ $q_{70} = {\cdot}05327$ $q_{70}/p_{70} = {\cdot}05627$

$10{,}000 . {}_{10}V_{60} = 3{,}311$ $\mu_{70} = {\cdot}05195$

$10{,}000 . {}_{11}V_{60} = 3{,}606$ $\mu_{71} = {\cdot}05760$

By accumulation we find:

$$(3{,}311 + 520{\cdot}5)\,1{\cdot}03 = 3{,}946{\cdot}4 = \phi\,(10)$$
$$-3{,}606$$

Expected death strain $340{\cdot}4$

TABLE 13·2

	(*a*) No deaths in year	(*b*) Deaths equal to the expected	(*c*) Deaths twice the expected
Survivors of 11th year	10,000	9,467	8,935
Valuation liability in respect of survivors	3,606	3,414	3,222
Claims in respect of deaths	—	533	1,065
	3,606	3,947	4,287
Accumulated fund	3,946	3,946	3,946
Surplus or strain	+340	−1	−341
Expected death strain:			
Formula (13·2)	340·6	340·6	340·6
Searle (13·5)	340·7	340·7	340·7
Carpmael	359·8	340·6	321·5
Ryan (13·6)	349·6	339·6	329·7

Both Carpmael's formula and Ryan's (applied in this way) assume that the actual mortality is approximately equal to the expected mortality.

The type of formula we have been discussing is derived from (13·2). Ryan's formula is of a different character because it is derived from the corresponding continuous formula. For this we return to (8·11) and pick out the terms which relate to the actual and expected death strain. The surplus from mortality at the moment of time t to $t+dt$ is

$$S.l''(t)/l''(0)\{\mu''(t)[1-V(t)]-\mu(t)[1-V(t)]\}.$$

It will be recalled that symbols with a double accent represent the actual experience. The first part of this expression is the actual death strain and the second part is the expected death strain. If t be the duration at the beginning of the year and $(t+1)$ the duration at the end of the year, the expected death strain for the year is approximately equal to

$$\tfrac{1}{2}(1+i/2)\{S(t)\mu(t)[1-V(t)]+S(t+1)\mu(t+1)[1-V(t+1)]\}, \tag{13·6}$$

where $S(t)$ is written for $S.l''(t)/l''(0)$, that is to say, the sum assured in force after t years. The value of (13·6) is a simple calculation from the 'in force' at the beginning and end of the year with the corresponding valuation liability.

From the way in which the formula has been developed it will be seen that the formula proceeds from a consideration of the actual death strain at risk from time to time throughout the year. Claims are exposed up to the time of death only and not for the whole year.

Let us adjust the figures of Table 13·2 so that the claims are exposed up to the time of death only, that is to say, the reserves in respect of claims are calculated as at the middle of the year, and suppose also, for simplicity, that each item of reserve is increased by $1\frac{1}{2}\%$ for early payment of claims. The result is given in Table 13·3.

So far, we have dealt with policy-years and premiums have been assumed due at the beginning of the year. In practice we deal with calendar years and a convenient and usual assumption is that premiums are due in the middle of the calendar year. (Should King's nearest duration grouping be used the formulae we have given would be directly applicable.)

TABLE 13·3

	(a) No deaths in year	(b) Deaths equal to the expected	(c) Deaths twice the expected
Survivors of 11th year	10,000	9,467	8,935
$1{\cdot}015\phi\,(10)$	4,005·6	4,005·6	4,005·6
Claims, plus $1\frac{1}{2}$ % to end of year	—	541·0	1,081·0
Accumulated fund	4,005·6	3,464·6	2,924·6
Valuation liability	3,660·1	3,465·2	3,270·3
Surplus or strain	345·5	−·6	−345·7
Actual death strain	—	336·7	673·0
Expected death strain:			
(i) Calculated	345·5	336·1	327·3
(ii) By Ryan's formula	346·5	336·6	326·7

The problem is tackled by considering what happens when we pass from $(\frac{1}{2}+a_y)$ to $(\frac{1}{2}+a_{y+1})$. We have

$$(\tfrac{1}{2}+a_y)(1+i)=(\tfrac{1}{2}+a_{y+1})-q_y(\tfrac{1}{2}+a_{y+1})+(1+\tfrac{1}{2}i-\tfrac{1}{2}.q_y). \quad (13{\cdot}7)$$

The last item is the payment in respect of the survivors to the middle of the year, accumulated to the end of the year.

Looking back to (13·3) we see that under the new conditions only the valuation liability is to be multiplied by $(1+i)$ and that the credit for premium is $S.P(1+\frac{1}{2}i-\frac{1}{2}.q_y)$. The last part of this may be conveniently combined with the expression for the expected release by death which becomes

$$q_y(1+a_{y+1}).$$

Thus we see that in formulae (13·3), (13·4) and (13·5) the premium is to be valued by $(1+a)$ not $(\frac{1}{2}+a)$ so that, where the premium is assumed to fall due k of a year after the valuation date, the expected death strain will include the expected loss of k of a year's premiums on expected claims.

In those formulae we have assumed that claims are payable at the end of the year of death. Should the valuation liability $V(t)$ include the adjustment, $(1+i/3)$ say, for early payment of claims the expected death strain becomes

$$S.q_{+t}[1+i/3-V(t+1)]$$

in (13·3) with corresponding adjustments in the other formulae. Care must be taken to see that the corresponding adjustment in the net premium, and therefore in the loading, is made.

New business generally needs special treatment even in a net premium valuation because it is difficult to choose valuation assumptions about ages, etc., which ensure that the net premiums on the new business pass smoothly into the valuation liability at the end of the year. With most of the common assumptions there is an error of approximation which must be allowed for. It may be convenient for this purpose to keep the new business separate until the end of the year and to value it separately. The accumulated net premiums in respect of new business less the relevant claims and valuation liability at the end of the year will produce one omnibus item which may be called 'error of approximation for new business'.

With a bonus reserve valuation the value of the liability will include a provision for future bonuses and the assumption underlying this provision must be followed through in the analysis of surplus.

The bonus reserve at the beginning of the year together with interest and the reserve for future bonus expected to be released by death, after providing for the expected strain on bonus paid out, is sufficient to provide the bonus at rate b.

If we write F_y for the factor for valuing future bonus at rate b at age y, the general formula is

$$(1+i)F_y+[q_y\times F_{y+1}-q_y\times b(1-A_{y+1})]=b\times A_{y+1}+F_{y+1}. \tag{13·8}$$

In practice there might be adjustments to this formula, for example, because a full year's bonus may not be provided for all expected claims.

For a uniform simple reversionary bonus $F_y=b\times(IA)_y$. For an annual compound reversionary bonus $F_y = (A^j_y - A_y)$, where $(1+j) = (1+i)/(1+b)$.

Where the valuation depends upon an approximation, the actual assumption must be followed through in the analysis. Perhaps the most common example is the valuation of endowment assurances. Should endowment assurances be valued by Karup's method in groups according to attained age there would, of course, be no difficulty. Should, however, the endowment assurances be grouped according to unexpired duration, some approximation is required to the age.

Elderton's method is based on the assumption of a common maturity age for both net premiums and valuation factors. This assumption must also be followed in the calculation of the expected death strain though, of course, its value will not be an approximation to the true expected death strain. It will be distorted and the distortion will be matched by a corresponding error in the loading, which will approximately balance.

Lidstone's Z method requires the calculation of mean ages for each unexpired duration. Though these mean ages are very near the true values, there is a small error which may not, of course, be consistent from valuation to valuation. There is of necessity a small error of approximation. Since the mean age at maturity depends only on the distribution of business and not upon the duration, the same mean age can be used to calculate the expected death strain and this is found to give good results in practice. It depends, however, on the distribution of business being about the same throughout the year and where the distribution is changing rapidly, for example because of an extensive new business, special treatment might be required.

13·5. Special features of analysis with a bonus reserve valuation.

Since a certain rate of bonus is assumed in the valuation the analysis will, in general, relate to surplus in excess of the assumed rate of bonus. Where bonuses are not declared each year the interim valuations should allow for bonus at the assumed rate for the period since the last valuation. This assumed rate may not equal the interim rate of bonus in respect of claims, and should there be a declaration of bonus at the end of the year the declared bonus may be at a different rate from that assumed in the valuation. The following special considerations arise out of this situation:

(i) The reserve for future bonus may give rise to an interest surplus which is computed in the same way as the remainder of the interest surplus.

(ii) Claims by death lead to a release of the reserve for future bonus. At the beginning of the year the factor may be written, say F_y, but at the end of the year the reserve will include the year's bonus assumed to be declared, that is $F_{y+1}+bA_{y+1}$. This must be included in the reserve at the end of the year for the calculation of the expected death strain. The exact form of bA_{y+1} will depend on the valuation assumptions.

(iii) The valuation will assume a certain rate of bonus on claims which may differ from the interim bonus actually payable. The interim bonus paid on claims must be compared with the valuation provision, namely $b' \times q_y$, where b' is the *average* bonus assumed over the year. The factor for future bonus may assume a full year's bonus on claims, or only on claims after the renewal date. In the latter case it is the *average* bonus, probably one-half the assumed future rate, that must be allowed for on expected claims.

(iv) Claims by survival as well as claims by death must be looked at from this point of view. The bonus assumed on claims maturing by survival may differ from the actual interim bonus payable.

(v) Where a bonus is declared at the end of the year the rate may differ from that assumed in the valuation. Since, however, the analysis of surplus is usually made on the basis of the valuation *before* the declaration of bonus, the analysis for the previous year is not affected by the declaration. When commencing the analysis of the following year the valuation liability must be increased (and the surplus brought forward decreased) by the excess of the value of the bonus declared over that assumed in the valuation.

Since the gross premiums are valued in a bonus reserve valuation it is always necessary to investigate the position of new business. First of all the gross premiums include a provision for initial expenses which is usually released at the inception of the assurance, because the valuation only provides for renewal expenses thereafter. The 'loading' element thus consists of (*a*) the provision for initial expenses on new business, and (*b*) the provision for renewal expenses in the valuation. The sum of these items must be compared with the actual expenses which for this purpose may be treated as one sum though for other purposes it may be desired to analyse them also into initial and renewal expenses.

Secondly, the values of the gross premiums, less initial and renewal expenses, may differ from the values of the liabilities on the bonus reserve basis at the inception of the assurances. A deficiency would constitute a strain which must be taken into account. It is sometimes difficult to distinguish between such a strain and the opposite item of provision for initial expenses: as a matter of convenience the two might be combined and the provision for initial expenses might be taken as the excess of the value of the gross premiums, less renewal expenses, over the value of the liabilities on the bonus reserve basis at the inception of the assurances.

The question of a change of valuation basis is more important with bonus reserve valuations because such changes occur more frequently. No special principle is involved. The analysis should be on the old basis up to the end of the year and the cost of change of basis should be brought in at that time.

13·6. The analysis of surplus of an annuity fund.

Life assurance and annuity business is usually kept in one fund and we may first of all refer to problems of apportionment which strictly belong to accountancy rather than to analysis of surplus.

The accounts or office books will show separately the majority of the items for the two accounts, life assurance fund and annuity fund, but the items of interest *less* tax, and of expenses must be apportioned.

The gross interest and expenses would be apportioned on bases suitable to the circumstances which we need not discuss here. The gross interest would probably be apportioned on the basis of the mean funds excluding interest, though this may not always be a fair basis.

The apportionment of income tax calls for some comment because in the United Kingdom the two funds are taxed on different bases. Before apportionment the income tax stated in the accounts should be increased by the reliefs credited in respect of one or other of the accounts and these reliefs should be carried direct to the proper accounts. These items are rebates in respect of management expenses, income tax withheld on annuities and claims (if any) for under-deduction of tax on annuities. Further, the tax on annuity profit must be carried direct to that account.

In the result the annuity fund may be taxed on profit only or on 'interest less annuities', but in either case it seems best to analyse surplus on a gross basis and to bring in tax as a special item in surplus. Thus the interest surplus would be computed gross, i.e. before deduction of tax.

It is probable that the immediate annuities will all be valued by the factor $(\frac{1}{2}+a_y)$ whatever the frequency of payment. We then have

$$(\tfrac{1}{2}+a_{y+1})=(\tfrac{1}{2}+a_y)(1+i)-(1+i/2)+q_y(1+a_{y+1}). \quad (13\cdot 9)$$

We thus see that the expected release of reserve by death is just sufficient to bring the total reserve up to the required amount for the following year.

The only item which requires calculation is the final item of (13·9), and since there are few withdrawals we may compute this item from the 'in force' at the beginning of the year. The expected release must be compared with the sum of (*a*) the actual value of the liability at the end of the year in respect of annuities terminating by death, and (*b*) the instalments of annuity not payable by reason of the death of the annuitant.

New business is best dealt with separately. The considerations *minus* any instalments of annuity paid in the year and the provision for expenses, *plus* interest for half-a-year at the valuation rate, should be compared with the value of the liability at the end of the year in respect of the surviving new annuitants.

The new annuitants may include deferred annuities which have come into full force, the 'consideration' effectively being the reserve accumulated up to the time of transfer.

Where the valuation liability includes a provision for a proportion of the annuity or other payment at death the final item of (13·9) must be reduced by the expected strain on such payment, thus:

$$q_y\,(1+a_{y+1}-\tfrac{1}{2}m+\tfrac{1}{2}m\;A_{y+1}).$$

With last survivor annuities the final item of (13·9) is not susceptible of ready calculation. However, we may see from (13·9) that it is equivalent to

$$(1+i/2)+(\tfrac{1}{2}+a_{\overline{x+1:y+1}})-(1+i)\,(\tfrac{1}{2}+a_{\overline{xy}})$$
$$=1-(1+i)\,a_{\overline{xy}}+a_{\overline{x+1:y+1}}. \qquad (13{\cdot}10)$$

Deferred annuities do not raise any special problem though the benefit of survivorship must be allowed for, where necessary, by a term similar to the corresponding item for immediate annuities.

Survivorship annuities raise some difficult problems but they are usually comparatively few in number and may be dealt with on broad lines, following whatever assumptions, arbitrary or otherwise, are made in the valuation.

BIBLIOGRAPHY

G. H. Ryan (1892). I. On the method for determining the gain or loss from mortality in an annuity company. II. On a means of calculating the expected death-strain in a life office. *J.I.A.* vol. xxx, p. 189.

This paper and the discussion on it contain most of the ideas on which the analysis of surplus is based, though some of the ideas, of course, are of much older origin and some have since been further developed.

T. J. Searle (1893). On the progress of profit in a life assurance fund. *J.I.A.* vol. xxx, p. 493.

C. Carpmael (1923). The analysis of profits of a life office. *J.S.S.* vol. II, no. 2, p. 129.

R. Ll. Gwilt (1926). Analysis of surplus. *Act. Stud. Mag.* No. 2, p. 18.

R. K. Lochhead (1932). *Valuation and surplus.* Cambridge University Press.

D. D. Overy and G. B. Palmer (1945). Analysis of surplus with particular reference to a bonus reserve valuation. *J.S.S.* vol. v, no. 4, p. 197.

CHAPTER 14

METHODS OF DISTRIBUTION OF SURPLUS

14·1. Introduction.

The purpose of this chapter is to discuss the various methods of distribution of surplus. We assume that the valuation basis has been settled, the valuation made and the surplus determined as a lump sum £*x*. How should this sum be apportioned between those entitled to participate in it?

The surplus disclosed by the valuation is not necessarily wholly divisible and the first problem is to determine the amount of the divisible surplus. It may be felt desirable that some transfer should be made to contingency or other reserves and possibly also that some of the surplus should be applied to the strengthening of the valuation basis in certain respects. The approximate amount of surplus which it seems desirable to carry forward unappropriated should also be considered.

The decision about the amount of divisible surplus will be affected to some extent by the period over which the surplus has accrued. In Great Britain the results of a full valuation have to be published at intervals of not more than 5 years and it is natural to use these valuations for the distributions of surplus. The customary periods are annually, triennially and quinquennially. The period of 5 years gives a longer period for the averaging of surplus and it is consequently somewhat easier to maintain equity in the face of changing experience where surplus accrues for this period. The distribution of surplus annually has a popular appeal but it requires a rather more conservative attitude to the appropriation of surplus. The longer periods of distribution need to be supplemented by some form of interim bonus arrangement to make the plan fair as regards claims which occur between successive distributions.

In a mutual assurance society the whole of the surplus belongs to the participating policyholders whereas in a proprietary office the proprietors are also entitled to share. The respective rights of proprietors and participating policyholders would be laid down in the constitution of the company. The shareholders' capital, both called and uncalled, provides a guarantee for which they customarily receive interest on the paid-up capital and a small proportion of profits, for example 10%. The other 90% of profits would be divisible among the participating policyholders. An alternative type of arrangement is for the participating policyholders to take the whole of their own surplus and the proprietors to take the surplus on non-participating assurances; in modern conditions, this is probably the effective, if not the nominal position. The participating policyholders would take the bulk of their own surplus and we may thus treat the problem as one of dividing the surplus among them alone, though the proprietors' share should be remembered and provided for, where necessary.

14·2. General nature of the problem.

Maclean says that there are, in practice, only two essential qualifications for a good system of distribution of surplus: 'It should be *equitable* and it must be *practical*'. This may give us a starting-point for our discussion of the various methods of distribution.

A life assurance fund consists of long-term contracts whose future experience cannot be accurately estimated. For this reason the business of life assurance has been founded upon the basis of participating assurance, the policyholders being charged premiums sufficiently high to be adequate in all likely eventualities and being given by way of compensation a share in the emerging profits. It follows that the method of distribution should take some account of the relative overpayments of the various policyholders and this is the basis of the claim that the method should be 'equitable'.

It might be thought that there would be one and only one equitable system of distribution of surplus, that, in fact, the problem would be capable of a precise mathematical solution. That this is not so is a consequence of the practical conditions within whose framework the solution must be found.

In the first place, the problem is not solved once and for all. It recurs at each valuation with each division of surplus and the decisions made at one valuation are bound to affect the problems at later valuations. Too little or too much may prove to have been distributed or one class may prove to have been unduly favoured at the expense of another and the periodical valuations give an opportunity for the problem to be examined afresh each time in the light of the further information available, that justice may be done.

Secondly, a life assurance fund consists of a mass of contracts of varying types, amounts and durations effected at different ages and scales of premium. The assurances may be grouped with a view to reducing the magnitude of the problem but there can be no clear-cut division between the groups; one shades into the other with infinite degrees of variation.

In the third place, the practice with regard to earlier distributions of surplus will have been known to those who effected assurances and figures may have been quoted to illustrate the working of the bonus system on the basis of past experience. However carefully qualified such statements may have been they form part of the background to the solution of the problem of equitable distribution of surplus.

A dictionary definition of equity is 'recourse to principles of justice to correct or supplement law'. This definition illustrates the actuarial problem. We have a mass of contracts subject to certain 'laws', that is to say the premium scales and general terms and conditions on which the assurances have been granted. In course of time these premium scales and terms and conditions of assurance may prove to be unfair. We must then have recourse to principles of justice to correct or supplement the original 'laws'. These principles of justice may be given effect to in the working of the bonus system, though it should be remembered that only rough justice is possible in such a complicated problem.

Evidently the problem is not one which can be considered in isolation. The actuarial bases of the premium scales and of the valuation should be suitably chosen for the particular system of distribution of surplus in use, and, conversely, the system of distribution of surplus should be fitted to the premium scales and valuation bases.

A test of an equitable distribution which has been commended from time to time was given by R. W. Weeks,† more particularly with regard to initial expenses:

> If a given company experiences year after year uniform rates of initial expense, renewal expense, mortality and interest, then the dividends ought not to rise or fall according as the volume of new business is less or greater in one year than in another year.

The definition is capable of expansion to include other ideas than fluctuations in new business and it has the merit of placing the emphasis on the major difficulty, that of making a just analysis of experience.

There have been many attempts to define equity in the distribution of surplus but the definition is elusive and equity is only one consideration amongst many. We think it difficult to improve on William Morgan's statement of the aim of an equitable distribution.

> I hope that the time will never come when the annual profits shall entirely cease. It is necessary for (the Society's) credit and security that these should continue, and it is to be wished that all future measures, like those which have hitherto been pursued, may be directed no further, than to moderate those profits in such manner, as that the Members may derive a due share of advantage without endangering the expectation and property of those that shall succeed them.

14·3. Early analytic methods.

For many years there was a good deal of experiment with methods of distribution of surplus and the present position is the outcome of years of experience. The passage of time has seen the firm establishment of the uniform reversionary bonus systems in Great Britain and of the contribution method in America, and it is an interesting question why this should have been so. We must, however, confine this chapter to description rather than to interpretation.

Practice in Great Britain has, no doubt, been influenced by the

† *Trans. Act. Soc. of America*, vol. IX, p. 310.

fact that scientific life assurance was established by a mutual society which successfully practised a system of reversionary bonuses, though on a special plan. However, the question of the proper method for distribution of surplus began to claim the attention of actuaries at an early date and the idea soon gained currency that the distribution should be in some way linked to the sources of surplus. There are, for example, manuscripts of the elder Griffith Davies dating from the 1820's which advocate such an idea.

Some of the early suggestions were impracticable, such as the distribution of surplus in proportion to the excess of the accumulated premiums over the valuation liability, though this may have had some advantages in reserving the largest share of surplus for the oldest lives. This method was commonly displaced by a system under which surplus was divided in proportion to the premiums paid since the last distribution. With the growth of the business this method became inequitable because interest surplus came to play a larger part in the total surplus and a number of systems of distribution were developed out of it, which gave recognition to the relation of the interest surplus to the valuation liability. These are referred to as 'contribution methods' in British actuarial literature, though we have preferred to call them 'analytic methods' in order to distinguish them from the contribution method as practised in America at the present time.

T. B. Sprague in 1864 (following the practice of Sylvester in 1854) suggested the division of surplus into two sums. One, the interest surplus, was to be divided in proportion to the liability at the *previous* valuation and the other, the remainder of surplus, was to be divided in proportion to the premiums paid during the distribution period.

T. G. C. Browne subsequently suggested the division of surplus into three sums. The first, the interest surplus, was to be divided in proportion to the *current* valuation liability. The second, the loading surplus, was to be divided in proportion to the valuation loading. The third, comprising the mortality surplus and extraneous elements, such as investment profits and the lapse and surrender surplus, was to be divided rateably between the other two groups.

The methods give scope for considerable variation. For example, the interest surplus may be allocated in proportion to the 'initial', 'mean' or 'terminal' liability; and the loadings may be computed on a select or ultimate basis. The methods gave some recognition to the sources of surplus but they were, especially Browne's plan, tied to the valuation basis—which proved to be somewhat rigid and inconvenient in practice.

It will be seen that the methods do not accept the obligation to trace the individual contributions to surplus and hence they fall short of the contribution method as practised in America. It is for this reason that we have preferred to call them 'analytic' methods.

In modern times, the fall in the rate of interest has brought to the fore the question whether it is equitable to allot the same average earned rate of interest to recently effected assurances as to the older assurances. Single premium and short-term endowment assurances tend to take too large a share of surplus unless some adjustment is made. The fall in the rate of mortality, and the introduction of the A1924–29 table, has posed some difficult problems with regard to the division of surplus in proportion to valuation loadings. We need not concern ourselves here with the adjustments that have been made.

The share of surplus allotted to a particular assurance is determined primarily as a cash sum. However, the share of surplus is not necessarily paid as a cash sum but may be, and we think generally is, converted to reversion on the valuation basis so that it becomes a reversionary bonus attaching to the sum assured. The amount of the reversionary bonus would naturally vary with plan, age and duration, but Lidstone has shown that, with a suitable premium scale and a net premium valuation at a rate of interest sufficiently below the earned rate, the contribution plan produces reversionary bonuses similar to the uniform reversionary bonus plans (see p. 311).

14·4. The contribution method.

The contribution plan for the distribution of surplus was devised by Sheppard Homans and D. P. Fackler in 1863. The principle of the plan was that the divisible surplus should be allotted to the various assurances in proportion to the individual contribution of each assurance to the surplus. The words 'in proportion to' should be given their full weight. The individual contributions to surplus do not necessarily equal in total the amount of the divisible surplus: but whether the one exceeds or falls short of the other the individual shares of the divisible surplus are to be in proportion to the individual contributions.

The share of divisible surplus so computed is, in fact, usually paid in cash as a 'dividend' though this, of course, is not a necessary feature of the method. The surplus could be converted to a reversionary bonus.

In the original form of the method the individual contribution was determined as one sum which was not analysed into its components. Nowadays the individual share of divisible surplus is computed by a 'dividend formula' which expresses in mathematical form the relationship between the divisible surplus and the elements which make up the contributions to surplus. It will be understood that a certain degree of approximation is permissible in the interests of simplicity when the 'dividend formula' is fixed, and it reflects recent trends in experience rather than current fluctuations. This is important because it shows that the modern method must depend to some extent on the averaging of experience over a period of years, more especially with those elements which are of a fluctuating nature.

The contribution plan may seem to require the grouping of assurances primarily by year of issue. While this undoubtedly facilitates the work it is not essential and Marshall has used the plan with a Karup valuation with the assurances grouped by age attained.

The conventional formula given by Marshall (but in our notation) is

$$B(t)=[V(t-1)+P](i''-i)-(q''-q)[1-V(t)] \\ +[P'-P-e''(t)](1+i'').$$

Here $B(t)$ is the 'dividend' for year t and $e''(t)$ the assessed expenses for year t in respect of the particular plan and age at issue. The double accent denotes the assumed experience, the single accent the premium basis, and the unaccented symbols the valuation basis.

There is a very wide variation between the different methods of applying the contribution plan in practice and the formula is sometimes reduced to a 'two-factor' form which brings it close to the analytic methods previously described. The student should, however, note the difference particularly with regard to the assessed expenses.

It is not necessary to have the results of an analysis of surplus in order to fix the 'dividend formula'. The various elements of such an analysis would not equal the total of the respective individual contributions for various reasons, particularly since the fluctuating elements are averaged to reflect the trend rather than the experience of the particular year. The analysis of surplus, however, provides a useful check on the other work.

In general, the factors by which the contributions to surplus are determined are chosen in accordance with the general trend of experience so that the total contributions will equal the amount of divisible surplus. These factors may be adjusted from time to time as experience may suggest, particularly having regard to the amount of the divisible surplus from year to year. The equity of the 'dividend formula' may be tested by the computation of 'asset shares', which simply represent the net accumulated excess of actual receipts over payments (including dividends) based on the actual average experience with regard to mortality, interest, expense and withdrawal. The 'asset shares' for specimen ages and durations under the several plans are compared with the corresponding valuation liability and proposed dividend, and any considerable excess or deficiency will show that the 'dividend formula' requires adjustment.

An alternative approach is to compute for representative ages and durations for the several plans of insurance a network of theoretical 'contributions to surplus', starting from the previous year's valuation liability and allowing for the average experience of the year. The actuary is then in a position to compare (1) the maximum dividends indicated by the theoretical 'contributions to surplus', (2) the dividends according to the previous year's formula, (3) the corresponding dividends of other companies. This approach enables the actuary to give proper weight to both theoretical and practical considerations when fixing the 'dividend formula' for the current year.

Generally speaking, investment profits and losses are dealt with by means of contingency and investment reserve funds, but a loss on investments could be recouped by reducing the interest factor for some years. Withdrawal profits are used to finance new business and are usually credited against first-year expenses. The assessment of expenses by plan, age and duration varies in its details from office to office but it is based on a thorough study of the facts. The mortality factor is usually designed to reflect the excess of the assumed over the actual ultimate mortality and the gain from select mortality offsets initial expenses. The mortality factor is commonly expressed as a percentage of the expected death strain, the percentage varying with attained age.

The big fall in the rate of interest in recent years has resulted in a much flatter dividend scale than formerly. For some assurances the fall has brought the earned rate below the assumed rate of interest and a negative interest factor has been required in the dividend formula. Where the deficiency was too large for this treatment the valuation liability has had to be computed on a lower interest basis. Strictly the cost of this change should be charged as a negative item in the dividend formula, but it was sometimes possible to meet the cost out of contingency and other funds and other adjustments were made. The problems were tackled with the help of a gross premium valuation based on the assumed probable future experience to determine the 'reservoir' for future dividends taking the business in certain suitable groups.

The differences between the rate of interest earned on new and on existing investments, and also on short-term and on long-term investments, have made it necessary to treat specially such types of assurance as single premium assurances.

The fall in the rate of interest has brought the earned rate below the rate assumed in the interest, annuity and instalment options at maturity of certain assurances. In order to set up adequate reserves against these options, a negative factor has been included in the dividend formula for such assurances. The same has been necessary to meet losses in disability benefits included with certain life assurances.

Where the full net premium liability is set up, the strain of new business tends, in prosperous times, to divert surplus into reserves. The strain is, however, lessened in times of depression when the volume of business is reduced.

The general introduction of a new table of mortality, the C.S.O. table, in 1948 has given rise to considerable problems. The curve of the table was steeper, with higher policy-values and, consequently, a steeper dividend scale, but steps were taken to compensate for this tendency. An interesting innovation by some companies was an 'experience premium' formula. This was a return to a two-factor formula, but the second factor was the excess of the gross premium over the 'experience premium' which was computed (usually) on the valuation rate of interest with allowance for the actual mortality and expense rates and a margin for contingencies. The new method is simpler and there is perhaps less need for the third factor since the new table of mortality has been introduced. The three-factor formula is more adaptable to changing conditions and time will show whether the two-factor formula can be maintained.

If we may sum up the impressions of a British actuary after reading American literature on the contribution method, they would be

(i) that the strength of the method lies in the way in which it keeps clearly in view the premium actually payable and the changing sources of surplus;

(ii) that the numerical work, though extensive, is such as can be performed for the most part by unskilled labour with machines;

(iii) that the approximations and averaging involved in the method are very similar, in effect, to the approximations of the uniform reversionary bonus methods.

14·5. Uniform reversionary bonus systems.

We may open this discussion on the uniform reversionary bonus systems by first discussing why bonus should be declared as an addition to the sum assured rather than as a cash sum or a reduction in premium. The first bonus, in 1777, arose out of a reduction of one-tenth in the premium scale that had been decided upon: the excess paid in the past was allowed as a rebate from the next premium. Richard Price had advised that the right method of distributing surplus was 'either to increase the claims or sink the payments and not to enter upon the stock', that is to say, not to disperse the surplus, but William Morgan cautiously preferred to increase the claims rather than to reduce the payments because he saw that it was essential to put first the credit and stability of the assurance fund. The arguments for this course are perhaps still valid though they have less force in modern conditions when the stability of assurance societies is not in question.

Since the assured has paid his premiums to secure as much life assurance, presumably, as he can afford, having regard to the class of assurance appropriate to his circumstances, it seems only natural that the assurance should be increased by reversionary bonuses, should the experience prove more favourable than was assumed.

The classic defence of the uniform reversionary system would, we think, run on the following lines. If it were possible to make an accurate estimate of future experience the premiums for life assurance could be computed accordingly and such small surplus as might be disclosed from time to time would be incidental and due to random fluctuations. The surplus might be expected to average out at even amounts over the duration of the assurance and might be equitably distributed in proportion to the amounts assured or the premiums as might seem suitable.

Since, however, it is not possible to make an accurate estimate of future experience the surplus cannot be considered as merely incidental: it arises from definite margins in the estimates and tends to increase with duration because of the effect of the interest margin. Further, the amount of divisible surplus from time to time depends upon the decisions of the responsible boards of directors who naturally pursue a cautious policy in distribution of surplus. Thus it happens that surplus is held back and it is only reasonable that the older policies should receive a larger share of the surplus when it is distributed.

Now, if the bonus be declared as a reversionary addition to the sum assured its value at the time will depend upon the attained age of the life assured (and the unexpired duration). Thus the reversionary bonus system provides just the sort of increase with duration that is desired and, in suitable conditions, the margins in the loadings in the premium scale and the interest margin on the valuation liability will produce the surplus at about the rate of release required to provide the uniform reversionary bonuses.

Lidstone gave a numerical example of this feature, but it can be very easily proved from a simple transformation of the policy-value, though we do not remember having seen it before. We have

$$b.A_{x+t}=b.{}_tV_x(1-A_x)+b.A_x. \qquad (14\cdot 1)$$

Suppose that the earned rate of interest is i'' but that the premiums and the valuation liability have been calculated at a rate of interest i such that

$$i=i''-b(1-A_x^i).$$

It is clear that an interest surplus will emerge equal to $b(1-A_x)$ on the valuation liability. Should the premiums also be loaded by an amount equal to $b\times A_x$, which is the cost of the first year's bonus, equation (14·1) shows that the combined interest and loading surpluses will emerge in just the right amounts to provide the desired bonus. This throws light on the old rules (*a*) that the uniform reversionary bonus method requires a suitably calculated premium scale, and (*b*) that to maintain a simple reversionary bonus there should be an interest margin equal to about half the rate of bonus.

Strictly speaking, we should notice that the interest margin would also produce a surplus in respect of the value of the existing declared reversionary bonuses. Since this would be at the rate of $b(1-A_x)$ and not at the rate of b on the existing declared reversionary bonuses the actual bonus from (14·1) would be between a simple and a compound bonus.

It would, of course, be possible to continue this theoretical argument further but it is more profitable to consider some of the practical conditions which must be taken into account. The loading and interest surplus is only a part of surplus and we cannot ignore other items, such as mortality surplus, surplus from lapses and surrenders, profits from other classes of business and miscellaneous sources of surplus. There is no justification for dividing mortality surplus in the form of reversionary bonus, though as regards the other items it might be said that there is no theoretical reason for preferring one method to another. Such profits may be reserved for the older policyholders because that will make for the stability of the assurance fund and each generation of policyholders may hope in due time to share in the surplus so reserved.

There is, however, no justification for withholding mortality surplus in that way and it is necessary to use a mortality table which represents the experience as closely as possible so that mortality surplus may be kept to a minimum. This is a feature of the uniform reversionary bonus methods to which, perhaps, insufficient attention has been paid in the past.

It will be noticed that the justification for the uniform reversionary bonus methods lies elsewhere than in the fact that, in certain conditions, the bonuses approximate to those produced by the contribution method. In these circumstances we may ask what test can be applied to see whether the bonus system is working fairly? There is no simple solution to this problem as may be seen from the extent of the literature on the subject. One of the difficulties is that the problem may be looked at from so many different points of view. We may simplify the discussion by referring to three investigations that Elderton suggested should be made:

(i) What surplus may be divided in order that any bonus now declared may be maintained in future (in respect of existing business).

(ii) Whether all policies should receive the additions at the same rate.

(iii) Whether new entrants can be admitted at the current rates of premium.

The first investigation requires a bonus reserve valuation. It answers the question what uniform bonuses can be declared, assuming that such a system is equitable. Perhaps it is not essential for the rate of bonus declared to be the same as that assumed for the future, but it is a convenient assumption and any other course would be difficult of explanation.

The third investigation is a comparatively simple one for it follows from the assumptions made with regard to future experience and the rate of bonus which is shown by the bonus reserve valuation to be capable of being maintained for existing business.

The second investigation is much more difficult but attempts have been made from time to time, for example by Coutts. Effectively, we have to compute on the one hand the 'asset shares' which will show retrospectively the share of the funds in hand for representative ages and durations for the several classes of assurance, and on the other hand the prospective liability on the basis of the assumed future experience and including a provision for future bonus at certain rates. By interpolation, we find the appropriate rates of bonus for the representative assurances.

Relatively minor variations would be ignored in view of the approximate nature of the calculations but rough effect should be given to any major variations, for example between the various classes of assurance.

At this point we may take up the question whether the bonus should be allowed to fluctuate with profits or whether the bonus should be stabilized as far as possible. This is not only a question of equity but also of the stability of the assurance fund. No doubt a stabilized bonus is popular with both office staff and policyholders and the board of directors would naturally be cautious in the distribution of surplus. These practical considerations may be supported by the theoretical one that, could such fluctuations be foreseen, there would be no need for the fluctuations in experience to be reflected in corresponding fluctuations in bonus. A numerical example of this was provided by Lever.

The argument can, however, easily be carried too far. Where a temporary fluctuation in experience makes possible a higher bonus for a short period there seems no reason why those who are policyholders at the time should not have the benefit of the higher bonus. Suttie gave an illustration of this in discussing the effect of capital appreciation.

A related question is whether the premium scale should be adjusted from time to time with a view to the maintenance of about the same rate of bonus or whether the fluctuations in experience should be allowed to have their effect on the bonus in due course. Formerly, we think that the latter answer would have been given without hesitation and there is a good deal to be said for this view. Problems of equity are much more easily handled where the bulk of the assurances are on the same premium scale. Further, there is no particular sanctity in a particular rate of bonus and, assuming the premium scale provides an adequate safety margin, it seems more practical to allow experience to take its course through the operation of the bonus system.

In favour of a change in premium scales, it may be argued that it would be inequitable to allow the bonus to find its own level where a large amount of new business is admitted on terms which are inadequate to support the same bonus as could be maintained in respect of existing business. There is here a question of policy to be decided which is closely linked with new business policy.

When a change in premium scales is decided upon, a further question is whether the new assurances shall be entitled to the same participating rights as the existing assurances. This question can only be answered in the light of the particular circumstances and depends to some extent on the nature of the bonus system.

14·6. Characteristics of 'compound' systems.

It may be convenient here to refer to some of the special features of the compound system and other similar systems which involve the reservation of surplus for the older assurances.

One rather obvious feature of the compound system is that the element of deferment depends upon the rate of compounding which itself depends upon the rate of bonus. A compound bonus of 20*s.*% involves a much smaller element of deferment than a rate of 40*s.*%. This may not matter much but it should be borne in mind that a fall in bonus may alter the character of the system to some extent and, correspondingly, that an increase in bonus means an increase in the element of deferment which must be provided for.

Another and rather objectionable feature arises from the operation of bonus on bonus. Suppose that too much bonus proves to have been distributed so that a reduced bonus is declared next time. The older assurances which have already had too much bonus will get the benefit of bonus on that bonus! This is a feature which is not of much importance in normal times but which may be noticeable in times of sudden changes. The outbreak of war in 1939 and the sudden increase of income tax provided an example of this situation.

The net premium method of valuation may prove an untrustworthy guide for a compound bonus system, as was pointed out by Elderton, and this is especially true in a time of falling interest rates. The reason is that so large a part of surplus has to be held back to provide the 'bonus on bonus'. Personally, we feel that this feature should be definitely provided for by valuing the bonuses at a lower rate of interest than the sum assured and premiums but this adjustment is not usually made.

There are a number of special systems of reversionary bonuses which have a similar 'compound' effect without some of the objections to the usual compound system, but a discussion of them is outside the scope of this book.

Table 14·1 illustrates the importance of a properly graduated premium scale. The basis is A1924–29 $2\frac{1}{2}\%$ select but that is of less importance than the comparative magnitude of the figures.

Perhaps the simplest way of showing the element of deferment inherent in the various bonus systems is to plot for each type of bonus the ratio of the cost of the current bonus to the bonus loading for that type of bonus. These ratios are compared in Fig. 14·1.

The element of deferment in the bonus system may also be illustrated in the following manner. Suppose that we assume quinquennial valuations and that we compute (*a*) the cost of the quinquennial bonus from time to time, and (*b*) the cost of future bonus *minus* the value of future bonus loadings. It will be seen that (*b*) is the excess of the bonus reserve value over the net premium value of the liability on the same basis in the assumed conditions. The 'true' surplus will be $(a)+(b)$ of which (a) is divided and (b) is reserved for the maintenance of bonus. The proportion $(b)/[(a)+(b)]$ is the proportion of surplus which for a given age at entry, duration and bonus system must be reserved to provide for future bonus.

TABLE 14·1

Participating assurances for 100

Age at entry (1)	Pure premium (2)	Bonus loading for bonus at rate of 20*s*. % simple (3)	Bonus loading for bonus at rate of 20*s*. % compound (4)	Percentage of compound to simple bonus loading (5)
		Whole-life		
25	1·272	·517	·644	125
40	2·146	·623	·726	117
55	4·100	·734	·806	110
		Whole-life by premiums limited to age 60		
20	1·268	·560	·714	127
30	1·862	·686	·835	122
40	3·078	·893	1·041	117
45	4·272	1·076	1·228	114
50	6·610	1·418	1·586	112
		Endowment assurance at age 60		
20	1·649	·592	·704	119
30	2·461	·676	·766	113
40	4·137	·770	·831	108
45	5·810	·820	·864	105
50	9·132	·873	·898	103

Note. The last column in the table shows the effect of compounding where the rate of bonus is 20*s*. %.

The student should notice that this bonus reserve would not usually be shown explicitly but would be wrapped up in the valuation liability by making the valuation on a conservative basis.

Table 14·2 compares the proportions of surplus which must be reserved to provide for future bonus with simple and compound bonuses of 20*s*. % on a basis of A 1924–29 $2\frac{1}{2}$%. This proportion would, of course, be zero for a level cash bonus because the whole of the bonus loading would be distributed as surplus as it arose: and the proportion would be unity were the whole of the surplus to be reserved for the ultimate survivor. The proportions in the table thus give a kind of index of the element of deferment in the bonus system.

14·7. The floating bonus.

By way of contrast we may now study a form of participation which gives as large a benefit as possible to the early claims. By this system the premium scale is fixed upon a 'basis of the first

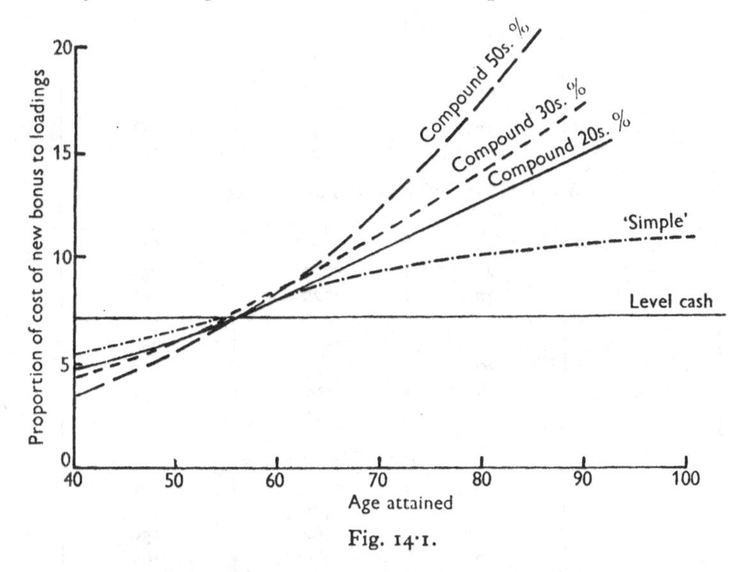

Fig. 14·1.

order' which is assumed to be adequate in all likely eventualities. From time to time the premiums are also computed on a 'basis of the second order' which is chosen to represent the actual experience as closely as possible. By proportion, we have the percentage additional assurance that could have been given had the basis of the second order applied throughout the period of the assurance. Thus had the premium been £100 on the basis of the first order and £90 on the basis of the second order the bonus would be 11%.

This system has been successfully applied in the Scandinavian countries and it is interesting to notice that one form of the system

TABLE 14·2

Proportion of reserved surplus to 'true' quinquennial surplus

Age at entry	Duration	20s. % simple bonus	20s. % compound bonus
		Whole-life	
25	10	·437	·571
	25	·524	·636
	40	·451	·553
	55	·310	·399
40	10	·313	·436
	25	·343	·458
	40	·244	·343
	55	·151	·232
55	10	·169	·268
	25	·158	·258
	40	·103	·188
		Whole-life by premiums limited to age 60	
20	5	·428	·548
	10	·574	·676
	20	·683	·752
	30	·720	·766
30	5	·426	·525
	10	·572	·654
	20	·687	·736
40	5	·460	·532
	10	·612	·665
		Endowment assurance at age 60	
20	5	·291	·401
	10	·406	·520
	20	·462	·559
	30	·380	·460
30	5	·225	·313
	10	·311	·409
	20	·300	·381
40	5	·148	·212
	10	·184	·252
45	5	·103	·152
	10	·102	·139
50	5	·058	·078

was adopted by an English office about 1840. After a period during which the system was wrongly applied, a new series of participating assurances was opened by H. W. Manly with a corrected form of the 'floating bonus' system. The system was not, however, successful in England and was discontinued in 1893.

From the point of view of the assured, the system gives the maximum protection at the point where it is most needed, that is to say at early death. This is an advantage where investment is not a prime consideration and the system certainly places the emphasis on the life-assurance part of the contract.

From the point of view of the assurance fund, the system enables the life assurances to be put from the outset on a basis which closely approximates to the estimated future experience. The effective amount of the assurance can be adjusted from time to time in the light of experience and, should the experience prove worse than was anticipated, not much harm will have been done because the bonus will only have been paid in respect of the early claims, which generally are comparatively few in number, and the bonuses for the survivors can be appropriately adjusted. It would seem, however, that in such an event there should be some distinction between old and new assurances since the former will have been assured for the higher bonuses.

The system has certain advantages during a period of general adverse experience such as may happen in war-time. During such a time there are many risks of diverse types and it is convenient, and in accordance with the trend of modern opinion, that the burden of these extra risks should be spread as widely as possible. Further, there are investment and other losses to be taken into account. By reducing or cancelling the bonus during the war the burden is spread over all war-time claims, and after the war the bonus assured on the lives of the survivors can be suitably adjusted.

The system has the disadvantage that the assured cannot rely on receiving more than the basic sum assured until the assurance actually becomes a claim. It is necessary that this feature of the system should be understood and accepted by the assured.

14·8. Miscellaneous bonus systems.

Many special systems of distribution have been tried, too numerous for us to mention them all. We may, however, refer briefly to a few of them.

Various forms of tontine bonuses have been arranged from time to time, under which the bonus is payable only on survival of a period of years or, sometimes, on survival of the period of assurance with policies of the endowment assurance type.

There is, of course, no objection to this system provided that it is accepted by the assured and that the bonus is properly provided for during the tontine period. Several forms of such a tontine bonus are being successfully used.

Tontine systems have a bad name because of the undesirable features of the system as it was applied in the United States of America towards the close of the nineteenth century. The system was then used as a competitive weapon by weaker companies and the bonus was not properly provided for during the tontine period. Further, no surrender values were paid at first, the benefit being theoretically accumulated for the survivors. These systems have disappeared long ago.

The idea of reserving surplus for those who survive longest has some advantages, especially because it is possible to combine such a system with a lower scale of premiums than would be possible with a normal system.

There are various forms of cash bonus under which the bonus is usually expressed as a percentage of the premiums paid or of the loadings during the distribution period. These have already been referred to in the section on 'analytic methods'. It would not be fair to allot the same percentage to all policies irrespective of duration, except in very special circumstances, and various devices may be adopted to provide for increases at the longer durations.

A cash bonus and a reduction of premium are essentially of the same basic character, but the latter bonus is contingent upon payment of the next premium and is given as a reduction of that premium whereas the former may be converted in fact to a reversionary bonus.

One of the oldest methods of distribution is the reduction of premium system though only one fund is now open for new business of this type in the United Kingdom. The system should not be confused with the option to apply a reversionary bonus towards the temporary or permanent reduction of premiums.

In theory the reductions of premium (expressed as a percentage of the full premium) are declared for one year only, but to avoid wide fluctuations the practice has been adopted for over 100 years of setting aside, in the valuation, the necessary reserve for the maintenance of the reduction at the rate last declared. In fairness, therefore, the reductions should increase with duration and this is effected by opening fresh series from time to time for which the rate of reduction is a fixed amount less than that for the preceding series.

14·9. The requirements of a good bonus system.

We may conclude our discussion by considering briefly a question which was touched upon in our opening remarks. How is it possible for such diverse systems as we have described each to be a proper and equitable system for the distribution of surplus?

Elderton suggested as a test of fairness:

> If we could foretell what would be the future mortality, interest, expenses, surrenders, bonus surrenders, and lapses, we could calculate the premium required to provide any bonus that we wish to pay. In fact, for any premium at any age there must be many different future bonuses which on this experience basis are fair, if *fairness* means that the present value of all the benefits to all the entrants at a given age, for a given kind of policy, will be equal to the present value of all their payments.

This argument should not be pressed too far because in the circumstances mentioned there would, of course, be no need for any system of participation in profits. However, it does suggest that an essential element in any system is the knowledge and consent of the assured; otherwise there would be no reason for preferring one system to another.

A second requirement of any bonus system is that it should be such as will contribute to the stability and good repute of the office. This is, perhaps, obvious since the element of participation in profits is itself designed for the safety and stability of the assurance fund.

A third requirement is that the system should be flexible and adaptable to changing circumstances, or it will not be possible to give effect to those 'principles of justice' which constitute equity.

Finally, the system should be simple to apply in practice and capable of ready explanation to the assured.

BIBLIOGRAPHY

WILLIAM MORGAN. Addresses delivered at the General Courts of the Equitable Society, 1793, 1795, 1800, 1809, 1816, 1819, 1825, 1829, 1830.

This remarkable series of addresses deals with practical problems of distribution of surplus and still reads freshly to the modern reader.

SHEPPARD HOMANS (1863). On the equitable distribution of surplus. *J.I.A.* vol. XI, p. 121.

This was the original paper advocating the contribution plan but it is now of historical interest only.

G. J. LIDSTONE (1895). On the distribution of the divisible surplus of a life assurance company, with special reference to the method originated by Dr Sprague and other methods derived therefrom. *J.I.A.* vol. XXXII, p. 73.

SIR GERALD RYAN (1900). Methods of valuation and distribution of profits in the United Kingdom. *J.I.A.* vol. XXXVIII, pp. 75–80, 87–8.

Reprinted from the *Transactions* of the Third Int. Congress, Paris, 1900. This paper provides a useful historical survey.

C. R. V. COUTTS (1926). On the distribution of life office profits. *J.I.A.* vol. LVII, p. 159.

G. H. RECKNELL (1926). On the bonus earning power of a new business fund. *J.I.A.* vol. LVII, p. 192.

Papers submitted to the Ninth Int. Congress, Stockholm, 1930, on subject A:

How far is it possible and suitable to determine the bonus distribution in conformity with the fluctuations of interest, mortality and expenses?
Is it necessary to take into account the effect caused by lapses, and, if so, how is the surplus to be divided?

We refer especially to the two following papers but many of the others were of considerable interest on this subject:

(*a*) W. P. ELDERTON. Fair distribution of bonus. *Trans.* vol. I, p. 158.
(*b*) E. H. LEVER. Fluctuations in life office profits. (Their origin and method of treatment.) *Trans.* vol. I, p. 181.

J. B. MACLEAN (1931). Notes on the practical application of the contribution method of distributing surplus. *J.I.A.* vol. LXII, p. 243.

W. P. ELDERTON (1932). Bonus distributions: a study in differences. *J.S.S.* vol. IV, no. 1, p. 71.

J. B. MACLEAN and E. W. MARSHALL (1937). *Distribution of surplus.* Actuarial Studies No. 6, Act. Soc. of America, New York.

K.-G. HAGSTROEM (1939). Notes on bonus and solvency valuations. *J.I.A.* vol. LXX, p. 119.

T. R. Suttie (1944). The treatment of appreciation or depreciation in the assets of a life assurance fund. *J.I.A.* vol. LXXII, p. 203.

E. W. Marshall (1948). Surplus distribution under ordinary insurance in the United States and Canada. *Proc. Cent. Assembly Inst. Act.* vol. II, p. 275.

J. B. Maclean (1948). Some recent actuarial developments in the United States of America. *T.F.A.* vol. XVIII, p. 281.

CHAPTER 15

SURRENDER AND PAID-UP-POLICY VALUES

In earlier chapters we have studied the methods of valuing assurances in groups with a view to placing a value upon the liability of the assurance fund as a whole. We now turn to the consideration of the problem of valuing individual assurances for the purpose of surrender and paid-up-policy values.

For this purpose a scale of surrender values will be devised which applies either to the whole or to a large section of the business so that individual calculations may be made without difficulty. It is obviously important that the scale should be simple and rapid in application and easily understood by unskilled staff.

The main difficulty that is met in the framing of such a scale is the number of different points of view that have to be reconciled. These points of view may be conflicting and the choice of a suitable basis in face of such contradictions is not an easy one.

15·1. The different points of view.

It is helpful first to consider the surrender of a life assurance policy as being analogous to the sale of the policy in the open market. A purchaser may be found who will buy the assurance as a well-secured reversion, subject to the continuance of the annual premium, if any, and the price the reversion will fetch is one of the considerations which have to be borne in mind in settling a scale of surrender values. The price in the open market is generally less than the surrender value offered by the life assurance office because, from the earliest days of life assurance, it has been recognized that the office should be able to 'buy back' its own assurances at a better price than could be paid by a third party. In special circumstances, for example where there are exceptional bonus rights, the price in the open market may be larger than would normally be paid on surrender.

Secondly, since suitable assumptions will presumably have been made in the premium scale, it is perhaps natural to follow out those assumptions in the calculation of surrender values. The procedure would have the advantage of relating the surrender values in the early years to the actual facts in so far as they are represented in the premium basis. This basis, however, would be chosen to represent the experience amongst those who continue their assurances and would not necessarily be a suitable basis for those who terminate their assurances. Further, the method would be equivalent to 'buying back' the assurances on the same terms as those on which the assurances were sold (unless some deduction for profit is made from the surrender values so found).

It must be remembered that there will have been many variations in the premium scale. Logically, this method would require a different scale of surrender values for each and that might not be either convenient or desirable. The fitting of a scale of surrender values to a mass of existing assurances is a most complicated problem.

A third point of view is provided by the value put upon the assurance in the periodic valuation of the liabilities. This is the amount that would be released should the assurance be surrendered and the excess over the surrender value is the contribution to surplus. Much the same remarks, however, apply to the valuation basis as we have made with regard to the premium basis. Further, the valuation basis is chosen with a view to placing a suitable value upon the group as a whole, but not necessarily on the individual assurance.

In the United States of America this method has been widely used, and has had statutory backing, but the tendency in recent times has been away from the method. The practice tends to introduce a rigidity which seems undesirable: for example, a proper and reasonable change in the valuation basis might be made difficult by the necessity of a corresponding alteration in the surrender-value basis.

The surrender-value basis should include an adjustment for the unrequited balance of initial expenses whereas this adjustment is not commonly made in the valuation basis. It might also be advisable to take a margin in the surrender values for possible depreciation in assets at the time of surrender and for profit for the benefit of continuing members.

Perhaps the best course from a theoretical point of view is to consider the value of the assurance on a basis as close to the experience as possible, but so that the profit (or loss) in the premium scale is not anticipated. Such a valuation would show the 'real' value of the assurance without any accumulation of surplus such as is usually contained in the valuation basis. Retrospectively, this 'real' value would represent the sum accumulated out of the premiums paid after deducting the surplus margin (if any) in the premiums. Prospectively, it represents, as nearly as may be estimated, the value of the assurance when the future surplus is not to be anticipated.

15·2. The basis.

Mortality

It has been suggested that the lives who surrender their policies probably experience a lighter mortality subsequently than the lives who continue their policies, because it is unlikely that policies on lives who are in bad health will be surrendered. There are no reliable statistics bearing on the question, and it is doubtful whether the contention is well founded in the ordinary way. In special circumstances it might become important. For example, there might be a ready market in policies on lives in poor health, so that only policies on lives in good health would actually be surrendered.

It is usual to base surrender values on the average mortality experience and to ignore the health of the individual life assured. An allowance for the considerations in the previous paragraph may be made by assuming that the life assured, at the time of surrender, is a select life. Thus the valuation factors would be the factors for duration 0 in the select life table. Such an allowance seems arbitrary because the selection exercised on surrender is not related to the medical selection exercised by the office at the inception of the assurance.

The financial effect of using select mortality is usually small and the general margin of profit in the scale of surrender values may be considered to be sufficient to cover any possible loss of this kind.

Since the mortality table is usually based on the experience of assured lives, that is upon those who continue their assurances, the premium scale will contain some allowance, though not necessarily an appropriate one, for the effect of discontinuances upon mortality.

Interest

The premium scale and the valuation liability will usually have been based upon a conservative rate of interest that seems likely to be well within the interest-earning capacity of the assets of the assurance fund. The quoting of a surrender value is, as it were, the reverse of the quoting of a premium and as we have suggested we think that it is appropriate to choose as interest basis a net rate of interest close to that actually earned, possibly a little higher than that to leave a margin. Since, however, the earned rate will usually be computed on the funds as written down, and so will be a little overstated, the margin may be thought to be unnecessary.

Expenses

Initial expenses, consisting of commission, medical fee, stamp, etc., are incurred in one sum at the inception of a policy. The office is recouped for the outlay by a constant annual loading in the premium, but if a policy does not run its full course there is still outstanding against that policy some of the initial expense. It follows that allowance for initial expenses must be made, either directly or indirectly, in the scale of surrender values.

Expenses will probably have been analysed for the purpose of calculating the scale of premiums, and it seems reasonable to have regard to the results of this analysis when calculating the surrender values of policies effected on that scale of premiums. Suppose the premium scale is computed by the formula

$$[P+I/(1+a)+c]/(1-p)$$

where, for example, I might be ·03,

c " ·0025,

p " ·04.

It would be natural in considering the theoretical scale of surrender values to value the office premiums less the renewal expenses and margin represented by c and p. This is equivalent to valuing the pure premium increased by $I/(1+a)$, the annual charge required to liquidate the initial expenses. The theoretical form for whole-life assurance would then be

$$ {}_tU_x=(1+I)\,{}_tV_x-I. \qquad (15\cdot 1)$$

At this point the student should refer to the discussion of the 'true net interest' and the 'effective net interest' methods in § 6·3. By the former method the interest and the expenses are both assumed to be reduced by income tax. Though such an assumption may be the logical outcome of British income tax law, it does not seem equitable that withdrawing policyholders should be charged less than the full costs of acquisition, and the procedure might be dangerous were the new business so large that full relief could not be obtained on the initial expenses.

On the other hand the interest assumption appropriate to the remaining period of the contract is clearly 'true net interest'. There is here a conflict of opinion which can only be resolved in the light of the particular circumstances.

A specific deduction may be made for expenses of surrender or this item may be assumed to be met by the margins in the basis.

Practical considerations

The scale of surrender values has to be considered in relation to the premium scales which have been in force from time to time. So many comparisons have to be made to ensure that the scale is reasonable that it is desirable to maintain the basis without alteration for as long as possible. A fall in the scale of surrender values should, if possible, be avoided because loans are often granted up to the amount—or a percentage of the amount—of the surrender value by the assurance office or by a bank or others. A decrease in the amount of the surrender value would be awkward in practice. Thus the basis should be one which the assurance office can reasonably expect to maintain over a considerable period of years.

A practical difficulty which needs a little care arises from the fact that premiums are usually payable yearly whereas the risk is continuous.

It is not convenient to have surrender values reducing during the policy year, and in practice when surrender values are based on a policy value formula the difficulty is overcome by taking the policy value at the end of the policy year, not the value allowing for the exact part of the year which has expired. If this rule is followed for all policy values there will be some values where $(V_{+1}-V_0)$ exceeds P', and the surrender value on the day the premium is paid will increase by more than the amount of the premium. It is, however, convenient to have one rule, even though it leads to illogical results, if the anomalies introduced are not of financial importance. The practice is not invariable: some offices interpolate between (V_0+P') and V_{+1} when V_{+1} is the greater.

If surrender values are guaranteed by the terms of the contract the scale should be lower than if it can be varied by the assurance office in the light of subsequent experience. Some period of notice of intention to surrender appears to be desirable in the case of large assurances if the scale of surrender values is guaranteed.

The considerations we have outlined with regard to the basis lead us to suggest that, when framing a scale of surrender values, it is, in principle, best to start from the policy value on a basis in accordance with the actual experience but with a margin in favour of the life assurance fund which represents the continuing members. Such a basis would normally lead to values smaller than the reserves on the basis of the premium scales and larger than the values on sale in the open market.

15·3. The conventional formulae.

Formulae based on policy values

The calculations of surrender values are generally made by unskilled operators and it is desirable to sacrifice theoretical considerations which have only a small effect on the final result so as to produce simple working formulae. The general procedure would be to fix a scale which takes into account the theoretical considerations that have been mentioned and then to find a simple working formula which gives values reasonably close to the theoretical values by the scale.

The expenses could be allowed for directly by valuing the office premiums less estimated future expenses, but it is generally better to use the pure premium on the surrender basis to avoid difficulties with policies of short duration.

The first year's expenses can be met by omitting the first year from the calculation (e.g. by taking ${}_{t-1}V_{x+1}$ instead of ${}_{t}V_{x}$, where x is the age at entry and t is the number of years' premiums paid). The provision thus made is usually rather too small in the case of whole-life assurances effected at young ages, and too large in the case of endowment assurances for short terms. It is probably better to make a specific allowance for the first year's expenses.

Taking the first year's expenses, for example, as 2% of the sum assured the deduction may be put in the form $S \times \cdot 02\,(1-V)$ for whole-life and endowment assurances. The formula would then be

$$S \times V - S \times \cdot 02\,(1-V) = S \times V \times 1 \cdot 02 - S \times \cdot 02.$$

This formula will give relatively low values at the younger ages at entry compared with the premiums paid (possibly even negative values) and the scale might need adjustment for practical reasons.

It is a common practice to make a deduction from the surrender value so found in order to provide a margin for contingencies and profits. The deduction of a flat percentage is not reasonable because the surrender values will be too low at the older ages, or near to maturity in the case of endowment assurances. Various artifices are used to get over this difficulty. Thus there might be a scale of percentage deduction, for example, which would vary with attained age (or unexpired duration in the case of endowment assurances) or the percentage deduction might depend upon V, the policy value per unit sum assured. The following is a simple method which has been used in practice.

If $\quad S$ is the sum assured

$\quad\quad V$ is the policy value per unit sum assured,

the surrender value is taken as

$$S \times V\left(1-\frac{1-V}{K}\right),$$

where K is a whole number which might be taken to be any number, say, between 5 and 10 according to circumstances. A simple table giving the values of

$$U = V\left(1-\frac{1-V}{K}\right)$$

may be constructed.

Formulae based on paid-up-policy values

It has been assumed in the foregoing that the value of the policy will be based on a pure-premium policy value. This is not essential and it is perhaps not the most common method in use. It is necessary as a matter of practical convenience to reduce to a minimum the number of rules for calculation of surrender values, and there are obvious advantages in a basis which gives the same surrender value immediately before and after conversion to some other form of policy, for example a paid-up policy.

Now paid-up-policy values for endowment assurances are fairly accurately reproduced by the proportionate rule, that is to say, if t premiums have been paid out of n originally payable, the paid-up policy is t/n per unit assured. This rule is often used for whole-life assurances by limited-premiums though it is less accurate for that class of business. The rule is popular with the public, and is so convenient for these classes that it is usual to base the surrender value on the proportionate paid-up policy rather than to base the paid-up policy on the surrender value. It should perhaps be said that paid-up-policy values are required very much less frequently than surrender values, and it seems a case of 'the tail wagging the dog' to base surrender values on paid-up-policy values.

The paid-up-policy value scale for whole-life assurances cannot be put into a simple form like the proportionate rule. Theoretically the value is $(1-P_x/P_{x+t})$. If pure premiums were used this formula would make no allowance for expenses. Initial expenses can be allowed for by taking P_{x+1} instead of P_x and a further margin will generally be obtained if office premiums are used instead of pure premiums. The formula for the paid-up-policy value becomes $(1 - P'_{x+1}/P'_{x+t})$ and the surrender value could be based on this value.

The values of P'_{x+1} and P'_{x+t} should normally be taken from the same table of rates of premium, but if there are or have been frequent changes in rates, there may be difficulty in applying the formula. Logically it would seem that P'_{x+1} should always be taken on the original scale of premiums and P'_{x+t} on the scale of premiums in force at the date of surrender, but the effect of such an arrangement would normally be to reduce the surrender value of existing policies when rates for new policies are reduced and, conversely, to increase the surrender values when rates for new policies are increased. Such a practice might be theoretically correct but would be hard to justify in practice. Similar arguments might be used whatever the formula for calculating surrender values, but in practice surrender values of existing policies are not usually altered to give immediate effect to the changed conditions implied in a revision of premium rates.

Similar considerations to those we have discussed must be taken into account in fixing the valuation factor for valuing the paid-up policies calculated by the methods described in this section. The unexpired term for the factor for endowment assurances would normally be taken as the original term less the curtate duration and the age would be taken as the age last birthday or some similar rule would be followed.

Paid-up policies

Certain formulae for paid-up-policy values have been discussed in the preceding section, and the use of the proportionate rule for endowment and limited-premium assurances is so general that no other methods need be considered here. The formula for whole-life assurances needs further consideration. It may be mentioned that a simple rule can generally be devised for obtaining the surrender values of whole-life assurances from the policy values tabulated in published tables. Because of this it is usual to calculate the surrender value first and to derive the paid-up-policy value from the surrender value. There is much to be said for the practice of converting the surrender value into reversion, using as the denominator for this purpose the factor on the basis used for the surrender value of the paid-up policy.

15·4. Participating assurances.

The general considerations are the same for participating as for non-participating assurances, but in addition the actuary has to take into account the equitable share of the assured in the profits of the fund. The amount of bonus declared to date of conversion will usually be added to the paid-up policy and its value will be included in the surrender value. An allowance may also be made for interim bonus. Even so, it may be that the scale of values brought out by the methods previously indicated does not make a reasonable allowance for the share of the assured in the undivided profits of the fund. By undivided profits we do not mean simply the accrued profit of an intervaluation period; that item is covered by the allowance for interim bonus. We mean rather, the surplus held up, directly or indirectly, for the purpose of maintaining uniform bonuses.

This problem is an intricate one and each fund must be considered separately bearing in mind the premium scales, the sources of profit and the methods of distribution of profit. To settle the question whether a surrendering policyholder is entitled to a share at all it is perhaps best to approach the problem retrospectively. From this point of view the question is: Does the bonus declared to date represent an equitable return, having regard, in particular, to the bonus loadings paid to date and, in general, to the profit earned during the currency of the policy?

Consider first the question of paid-up policies. In this connexion there is an obvious distinction between a surrender and a paid-up-policy value. In one case the policyholder severs his connexion with the office which has no further prospect of profit from the policy. In the other case there is still the prospect of some profit though on a reduced scale. From a practical point of view a considerable amount of work may be involved if paid-up policies for small amounts are allowed to participate. If the method of calculation were invariably a true actuarial one, this could, if considered advisable, be avoided by suitably allowing in the calculation for the paid-up policies to be non-participating.

In practice, however, the issue is clouded by the use of the proportionate method, which so far as the sum assured is concerned gives the same numerical result for a participating policy as for a similar non-participating policy. Since the method is quite arbitrary the question of participation must be decided on general grounds. Actually the proportionate method is generally favourable to policies of short duration and unfavourable to policies of long duration. British offices using the simple or compound reversionary bonus system are about evenly divided on the question whether paid-up policies should be allowed to participate in profits. A few giving non-participating paid-up policies allow the option of a participating paid-up policy provided the declared bonus is reduced in the same proportion as the sum assured.

Assuming that participation is granted the surrender value based on the paid-up policy may be obtained by using a lower rate of interest for the reversionary factor than for a non-participating policy. This correctly reproduces the value of a compound reversionary bonus. It is not correct for a simple reversionary bonus but is probably sufficiently accurate having regard to the somewhat arbitrary nature of the calculations.

If participation is not allowed there is a further question under the compound bonus system. It would not be fair to add the amount of the declared bonus to the paid-up policy but to take away the right of participation in respect of the declared bonus. Such a practice might involve difficulties with the surrender values because the value of the non-participating bonus added to the paid-up policy would be less than the corresponding value of the bonus just before conversion when the bonus carried the right to share in profits. As a practical measure in order to preserve the principle that the surrender value should not alter merely because of the conversion, the amount of the non-participating bonus to be added to the paid-up-policy value may be taken as the amount of the participating bonus increased in the ratio which the reversion factor on the surrender value basis (allowing for the right to participate in profits) bears to the non-participating reversion factor.

The issue is clearer where surrender values are based on the policy-value method. If after examination it is decided to give participating policyholders some share in the undivided profits, a simple expedient is to use a somewhat lower rate of interest for the policy value: rough justice will generally be done by this method.

If the paid-up policy is based on the surrender value, then the question of participation can be decided simply on the grounds of convenience and general policy. Division of the surrender value of the sum assured by a non-participating factor will result in a non-participating paid-up policy. Here again, under a compound bonus system, the declared bonus to be added should be increased in the ratio of the participating to the non-participating reversionary factor. Division of the basic surrender value by a participating factor (i.e. one based on a lower rate of interest) will give a participating paid-up policy.

15·5. Altered-class policies.

In practice frequently the class of a policy is altered, for example, from whole-life assurance without profits to endowment assurance with or without profits. In calculating the surrender value of the altered policy it is desirable to use a method which makes the surrender values immediately before and after conversion identical, and which is in harmony with the general office rules for calculating surrender values.

One method is to treat the converted policy as a new policy effected at the date of conversion. The surrender value of this portion would be obtained by the application of ordinary office rules. The surrender value, at date of conversion, of the original policy would be regarded as purchasing a reduction of premium and, at any subsequent date, the value of the outstanding reductions would be added to the basic surrender value. In symbols where the change is to an n-year endowment assurance, the surrender value of the converted policy is

$$S \times {}_tU_{x\overline{n}|} + C\,(1 - {}_tV_{x\overline{n}|}). \tag{15·2}$$

Since $C\,(1 - {}_tV_{x:\overline{n}|})$ is a function which increases with the rate of interest it may be considered preferable to spread over and value

C at a rate in keeping with the office premium rate of interest rather than the comparatively high rate used for surrender values.

The method is general and is suitable either for surrender values based on a policy-value method or on the paid-up policy, but since initial expenses are not incurred at conversion some adjustment to C may be considered desirable to meet the criticism that allowance has been made for initial expenses in both C and ${}_tU_{x\overline{n}|}$. If the original policy was participating, the value of C, if bonus is to be transferred, must also be adjusted to offset any increase in the value of the bonus. Thus for a whole-life assurance, if B is the amount of bonus per unit assured at date of conversion at age x and C is the surrender value excluding bonus, it would be necessary to take $C' = C - B\,(A_{x\overline{n}|} - A_x)$.

An alternative method is to treat the altered policy as (*a*) an investment equal to the surrender value at date of conversion, and (*b*) a policy for the sum assured less the amount invested, the annual premium on which is diminished by the interest on the investment. The surrender value *t* years after the date of conversion at age x to an n-year endowment assurance would be

$$C + (S - C)\,{}_tU_{x\overline{n}|}, \qquad (15\cdot3)$$

where $\begin{cases} S & = \text{sum assured}, \\ C & = \text{surrender value at date of conversion}, \\ {}_tU_{x\overline{n}|} & = \text{surrender value per unit assured}. \end{cases}$

If pure-premium functions are used it is easy to establish that this method and the first method give identical results, but it will be observed that the general reasoning on which it is founded is equally valid whether ${}_tU_{x\overline{n}|}$ is based on the policy-value method or the proportionate method, provided the investment falls in at the date when the premiums terminate, e.g. a whole-life or endowment assurance.

The formula for the surrender value of a policy converted to a whole-life limited-premium assurance becomes

$$S \times {}_t^nU_x + C\,(1 - {}_tV_{x:\overline{n}|}). \qquad (15\cdot4)$$

The addition in respect of C necessarily vanishes when premium payments under the converted policy are completed.

In recent years a non-participating whole-life assurance carrying guaranteed options to transfer to an endowment assurance has proved popular. This alteration and indeed any similar alteration where the duration of the original policy is not large can be conveniently dealt with by the following empirical method. Put

$$S\times V=S\times\frac{l}{n+l}\times A_{x:\overline{n}|}$$

and solve for l at date of conversion. At any subsequent date take the surrender value as

$$S\times\frac{t+l}{n+l}\times A_{x+t:\overline{n-t}|}.$$

This method is tantamount to converting V to reversion on the surrender-value basis.

Another type of policy is the whole-life policy with a special reduced premium during the first 5 years. The method to be used will, of course, depend on the nature of the reduced premium. If this approximates to a temporary assurance premium, no surrender value will be allowed during the first 5 years and, subsequently, the policy will be treated as entering at the date when the first increased premium becomes payable. If more than a temporary assurance premium is charged, then some quite arbitrary value such as 40% of reduced premiums paid, less the first, may be allowed. At the end of 5 years the position can be met by equating this value to ${}_mV_{x-m}$ where x is the attained age. If the policy was a participating one, some adjustment for bonus would be required since the arbitrary allowance would be regarded as including the value of any bonus attaching. In practice it would probably be found that m could be represented sufficiently accurately as a constant integer, say 2, for all ages at entry.

15·6. Double endowments, pure endowments without return.

Normally no surrender value is allowed on any policy which may never become a claim (e.g. temporary assurances, contingent assurances, etc.). A few offices do allow a value on pure endowments subject to evidence of good health. The value may be quite arbitrary such as half the premiums paid, or it may be based on the proportionate paid-up policy.

In the case of double endowment assurances, most offices will allow a value not exceeding the sum payable at death without evidence of health. When the surrender value exceeds the sum payable at death, the balance (if material) may be converted to a paid-up pure endowment or evidence of good health would be required. The normal surrender value would be allowed for the endowment assurance part and allowance on the lines indicated above made for the pure endowment part.

15·7. Pure endowments with return.

Surrender values are frequently guaranteed, and a common basis is a percentage of all premiums paid with interest at a rate lower than that assumed in calculating the premiums. Initial expenses are small. Some offices omit the first premium in calculating the return, but such a stipulation is usually accompanied in the case of short term policies by a guarantee that the deduction will not exceed the premium for, say, a 15 or 20-year term policy. As in the calculation of premiums, mortality is usually ignored and the policies in effect are treated as sinking fund policies.

In framing the basis, it is necessary to ensure that the surrender value does not exceed the sum payable in event of death and that both values run smoothly into the sum assured as the policy nears maturity.

Let us assume, as is customary, that mortality is ignored and that

i_0 is the rate of interest used for premium scale,
i_1 is the rate of interest guaranteed for surrender values.

The guaranteed surrender value would normally be the premiums paid or a part of them accumulated at rate of interest i_1. Since $i_1 < i_0$ the guaranteed surrender value will not approach the sum assured as the policy nears maturity, and in the last few years the position becomes so anomalous that most offices would ignore the guaranteed value and base the surrender value on the value of the sum assured discounted to date of surrender less the discounted value of any outstanding premiums. In principle this means that premiums would be accumulated at i_1 for l years and at i_2 thereafter. Strictly speaking l should be ascertained for each term, but it will be sufficiently accurate to determine l for a few quinquennial terms and hence convenient integral values for all terms, at which values discounting would commence.

In practice a proportionate paid-up policy is frequently guaranteed, but if the surrender value is also guaranteed on the lines discussed above, any attempt to link the one with the other will lead to inconsistencies. If the paid-up policy basis is not guaranteed it seems natural to derive the paid-up value from the surrender value. Assuming the adjustment described above is used, the same principle might be used for paid-up values: the premiums actually paid would be accumulated at i_1 for l years and at i_2 for the remainder of the term.

15·8. Children's deferred assurances.

Before vesting age

(*a*) *Surrender value.* The problem is very similar to that of pure endowments with return. Initial expenses are, however, larger, and in practice the first premium is customarily ignored in finding the cash option or surrender value. Sometimes the position is complicated by an educational option given at about age 14. If the option is given as instalments over a period of years any inconsistency might be ignored, but if the cash equivalent is also guaranteed, then to avoid anomalies it might be desirable to run the surrender value into the educational option at age 14: the surrender value between age 14 and the vesting age would be calculated on the cash option basis.

It should, perhaps, be said that both the surrender and cash option values should be less than for the corresponding pure endowment with return, but in practice owing to the keen competition for this class of business, this does not always obtain.

Frequently an additional premium is paid to provide that premiums falling due after the death of the parent and before the vesting age shall be waived. This is a decreasing risk met by a level annual premium, and the theoretical reserve for the benefit may be negative, but this is often ignored in practice and many offices allow full surrender values based on the normal premium.

If for any reason the surrender value should be required after the parent's death and before vesting age, it seems reasonable to discount the cash option to date of surrender at a rate of interest about that earned on the funds, though some offices pay the normal surrender value only.

(*b*) *Paid-up policy.* So far as the cash option is concerned, the problem is very similar to that of the pure endowment with return. The practice is not uncommon to guarantee paid-up cash options on the proportionate basis. The proportionate method has not here the same popular appeal which it has under other classes, and as it is not entirely satisfactory, it is better, we think, to derive the paid-up cash option directly from the surrender value.

The question of the treatment of the remaining options must to some extent be influenced by the general policy of the office and the circumstances surrounding the case.

If the original proposer has died it may be considered desirable to include the option of resuming premiums at vesting age. On the other hand, if the proposer is not dead many offices would prefer to withdraw the option of resuming premiums because of the possibility of adverse selection and would only quote the paid-up whole-life or endowment assurance if the amount were material, say, £50 or more. The policy may have to be rewritten at the vesting age, and if the sum involved is small the trouble is not worth while.

Assuming that paid-up assurance is allowed it can be found by multiplying the original paid-up option at the vesting age by the ratio of the reduced cash option to the full cash option. The sum assured secured by the annual premiums from the vesting age should be added if the option to resume premiums is to be allowed.

After attainment of vesting age

It is instructive first to consider the problem using pure premiums and policy values.

Let Cash option

$= C,$

Sum Assured

$=S$ (whole-life) or $S(n)$ (n-year endowment assurance),

Portion of Sum Assured paid up at vesting age

$=W$ (whole-life) or $W(n)$ (n-year endowment assurance),

Premium corresponding to portion of Sum Assured paid up

$=R$ (whole-life) or $R(n)$ (n-year endowment assurance).

If net functions are used throughout it follows that

$$C=W\times A_x=R(1+a_x)$$
$$=W(n)\times A_{x:\overline{n}|}=R(n)(1+a_{x:\overline{n-1}|}).$$

Considering first the paid-up-policy value, it seems natural to use the formula

$$W(n)+[S(n)-W(n)]_t W_{x:\overline{n}|}, \qquad (15\cdot5)$$

where x is age at vesting and t the subsequent duration. We have, however, to consider the relationship between the paid-up-policy value and the surrender value. The theoretical surrender value may be put into any of the following forms:

(i) $S(n)\times {}_tV_{x:\overline{n}|}+C\times \ddot{a}_{x+t\overline{n-t}|}/\ddot{a}_{x\overline{n}|}$,

(ii) $S(n)\times {}_tV_{x:\overline{n}|}+R(n)\times \ddot{a}_{x+t\overline{n-t}|}$,

(iii) $[S(n)-W(n)]\ {}_tV_{x:\overline{n}|}+W(n)\times A_{x+t:\overline{n-t}|}$,

(iv) $[S(n)-C]\ {}_tV_{x:\overline{n}|}+C$.

In the first two expressions the policy is regarded as entering at the deferred age with a reduced premium. In expression (iii) the policy is divided into two parts, one secured by a single premium of C and the other by the annual premium. In expression (iv) the contract is regarded as the investment of a single premium C and the purchase of an assurance for $S(n)-C$ by the interest on the investment and the annual premium that is payable.

The formula for the surrender value can be based on any of these forms, but the difficulty is to interpret the theoretical form in the conditions of practice. In the first place, the surrender value must start at C and increase therefrom in an orderly fashion. The relationship between C, W, and R given above will depend upon an office premium basis which may be obsolete at the time when the surrender basis is used. The pure-premium policy value, ${}_tV_x$ or ${}_tV_{x:\overline{n}|}$ as the case may be, must be replaced by the office surrender value, which may be either a proportionate value or actually based on the policy value.

If the cash option is to be reproduced at the vesting age, expressions (i) and (ii) become identical since $R(n)$ and C must be related by

$$R(n) = C/\ddot{a}_{x\overline{n}|}.$$

In effect the actual reduction in the premium would be ignored for surrender purposes and replaced by a hypothetical figure.

The simple formula (iv) is derived from formula (i) if the surrender basis of mortality and interest is used in both parts of the formula.

If the proportionate method is in use the formula (i) becomes for an endowment assurance

$$S(n) \times \frac{t}{n} \times A_{x+t\,\overline{n-t}|} + C \times \ddot{a}_{x+t\,\overline{n-t}|}/\ddot{a}_{x\overline{n}|},$$

where t is the number of premiums paid since the vesting age. The formula for a whole-life assurance by limited premiums would be on similar lines.

One difficulty about these methods is that the surrender value is not based directly on the simple expression for the paid-up-policy value. The paid-up value might be obtained by converting the surrender value into reversion on the surrender basis, but this procedure would probably result in anomalous values as compared with W the paid-up option.

Expression (iii) looks clumsy but it gives rise to what is probably the most satisfactory solution of the problem. Treat $(S-W)$ as a normal policy entering at age x and the balance W as a single premium policy with a commencing value of C. The value of the single premium part may be written as $C+(W-C)\,{}_tV_{x:\overline{n}|}$ where ${}_tV_{x:\overline{n}|}$ is the pure-premium policy value on the surrender basis. This solution has the advantage that the surrender value is based on C and the paid-up policy on W and the two are always related (though not in the normal manner) even if the proportionate method is used for surrender values. The disadvantage is that the formula is rather cumbersome and the empirical extension (iv) would give similar results in a much simpler way. The formula reduces to formula (iv) if the actual surrender value is used instead of the pure-premium value.

It will be seen that there is really no ideal solution and none of the formulae suggested preserve the normal relationship between the surrender and paid-up-policy values. If the option $W(n)$ is guaranteed in the policy or elsewhere, expression (iii) probably gives the most suitable working method. If $W(n)$ is not guaranteed the simpler form (iv) could be used. Alternatively, any of the formulae can be used and the paid-up value, if required, calculated independently. In that event if the value of a policy which had been made paid-up was required, care would be necessary to ensure that the surrender value harmonized with the value before conversion.

If the policy participates in profits the value of bonus would have to be added to the values found as above.

15·9. Family income benefits.

We referred in § 12·5 to the special problems which arise from the inclusion of supplementary decreasing temporary assurance, known as 'family income benefits' in the basic contracts of whole-life and endowment assurance. The problem is of special importance in connexion with surrender values.

When the premiums for the supplementary benefit are limited to the income period the deduction required from the surrender value of the basic contract is comparatively small. It was suggested that the deduction from the valuation liability might be ignored but it seems that the deduction from the surrender value ought not to be ignored, in fairness to other policyholders.

The deductions shown in Table 12·8 are those that would be required on the pure basis of the A 1924–29 table. They represent the net cost of the supplementary life assurance over and above the net premiums paid for the supplementary contract. If the view be held that the normal surrender value for the basic contract contains sufficient margin of itself, it might be considered appropriate to reduce the normal surrender value merely by the net mortality cost of the supplementary benefit to which we have referred.

This course is open to two objections. It assumes that the additional expenses consequent upon the granting of the supplementary benefit are equal at all durations. Admittedly, it was suggested in § 10·3 that the premium loading should be calculated upon the mean sum at risk during the income period. That was a convenient method of calculation but it should be recognized that the true loading would probably show a tendency to reduce with the amount at risk. Secondly, some charge should be made on surrender because the assured is exercising an option. When a whole-life or endowment assurance is surrendered the charge is made either explicitly in the basis of calculation or by keeping a margin in the values allowed. When an income benefit is discontinued it seems that some further charge than the net mortality cost of the supplementary life assurance should be made.

There is no agreed solution to this problem but a simple method of making some allowance is to increase the rate of mortality by a small constant, for example ·0025, when calculating the deductions on account of the supplementary benefit. This can be easily effected by using the normal mortality for the temporary life annuity with a corresponding increase in the rate of interest.

From a practical point of view the deduction is comparatively small and does not justify a complicated calculation for each surrender value. A sufficient approximation can usually be devised by choosing suitable percentage deductions varying with the age and duration and also with the type of assurance represented by the basic contract. In practice, we believe that it is customary to make no deduction where the premium for the supplementary contract is limited to the income period or less.

15·10. Loans and non-forfeiture schemes.

Loans are granted by the offices on security of their policies up to 90 or 95 % of the surrender value. From an office point of view a policy loan is an excellent investment. The rate of interest is good, the security is absolute and the asset is realized when the policy becomes a claim.

Sometimes a paid-up policy free of debt is required for a policy carrying a loan. This would be calculated by simple proportion. The full normal surrender and paid-up values would be ascertained, and from the surrender value there would be deducted the loan with accrued interest. The paid-up policy free of debt would bear the same ratio to the full paid-up value as the reduced surrender does to the full surrender value.

Most policies carry some form of automatic non-forfeiture privilege which comes into play when a premium is not paid within the days of grace. The following are the most common varieties.

(i) Provided the net surrender value after deducting any existing loan and interest is sufficient the premium is advanced as a loan for one year. At the end of the year, if no settlement has been made the policy is converted to a paid-up policy free of debt. Thereafter revival would only be considered within a limited period and evidence of health would be necessary.

(ii) In this form the advances are continued until the surrender value, which is increased from year to year, will no longer meet the outstanding premium. The policy is then lapsed. During the period when the policy is held in force, payments on account of arrears are usually permitted, but if the policy is finally lapsed it can only be revived subject to evidence of good health.

(iii) The policy is converted to a temporary assurance for the full sum assured for such term as the surrender value will permit. Since no commission, stamp, medical fee, etc., are involved the temporary assurance single premium used for the conversion might be

$$A' = 1{\cdot}1\,(A^{1}_{x\overline{n}|} + {\cdot}00125\,\ddot{a}_{x\overline{n}|})$$

on the surrender basis. Once converted a policy can only be brought back into full force, subject to evidence of good health.

In the case of an endowment assurance, if the surrender value is more than sufficient to carry the policy to maturity, the balance would be converted on the surrender basis to a pure endowment payable on survival.

The first form gives ample time to rectify an accidental omission, and in the case of real inability to pay the premium the position can be met by a bond. One disadvantage of the method is that it results in numerous small paid-up policies which are a nuisance to handle, but it does preserve the balance of the surrender value intact. The second form entails a great deal of book-keeping. Normally this method is inclined to pamper the policyholder, but during the war when signatures to bonds could not always be obtained it proved extremely useful. The third form has been widely used in America but has never been very popular in this country. In some respects this is unfortunate because the method does give the maximum possible death cover, but again the surrender value would be eaten away.

15·11. Policies subject to extra premiums.

Some consideration must be given to the surrender values to be allowed for policies accepted on special terms because of extra risk.

The practical considerations are: (*a*) the type and amount of extra risk, (*b*) the class of policy, and (*c*) the method of charging for the extra risk. The values brought out by various theoretical assumptions as to extra risk are useful as a guide but should be used with caution. A particular life assured may be classified as one subject to (say) increasing extra risk, but it may subsequently be found that the condition has improved and the life assured has become a normal life. This could happen, for example, if a proposer is accepted on special terms but takes care of himself and is subsequently accepted for a further assurance at normal rates.

If a level extra premium is charged for an extra risk of the increasing type we think that no adjustment in surrender values is necessary either for whole-life or endowment assurances. Theoretically increased values should usually be allowed for whole-life assurances, but against this may be set the possibility that the extra risk has altered and has proved in the event to be only temporary.

If a level extra premium is charged for an extra risk of the constant type the surrender values should theoretically be reduced, but we think that it is probably sufficient to allow normal surrender values having regard to the fact that cases of this type will be few in number.

It is usual to allow normal surrender values for policies subject to debts, the assumption being that the debt is matched to the risk.

15·12. General considerations.

The practice of offices varies in regard to the number of annual premiums to be paid before a surrender value is allowed. Most offices stipulate two, but a few allow a value after one annual premium has been paid, subject in some cases to the condition that a certain percentage (say 3%) of the sum assured shall have been paid. Some offices require three under whole-life policies. There is a question of practice involved here. When, for example, the policy condition requires two annual premiums, it may nevertheless be advisable to allow a surrender value when, say, one-and-a-half has been paid under a half-yearly policy. This arises because sometimes the life could change to yearly premiums and then receive on surrender more than a half-yearly premium. To avoid the anomaly in practice, the policy condition is sometimes interpreted as providing for a surrender value if possible at the first anniversary. For half-yearly, quarterly or monthly cases the value allowed would assume two yearly premiums, and from this the outstanding instalments would be deducted.

When the basis and formulae for a scale of surrender values are being fixed, it is necessary to examine sample results carefully for anomalies, but it should be recognized that it is not always possible to eliminate them. For example, for certain ages at entry and durations the surrender value of a whole-life policy might exceed the surrender value of a long-term whole-life limited-premium policy. Speaking generally there should be consistency within each class and between different classes.

Surrender values should always be compared with the premiums paid. At the shorter durations in particular where the majority of surrenders take place, it is useful to consider the value retrospectively. The value should compare reasonably with the premiums paid less the cost of term insurance and initial expenses.

When an endowment assurance is nearing maturity or when an old life is involved, it is sometimes advisable to stipulate that the quotation is subject to proof of age if age has not been admitted.

Though it is hardly germane to the actuarial aspect of surrender values it may be mentioned that many enquiries do not come from the policyholder. A quotation should not be made unless it is clear that the enquirer has a legal right to the information. Moreover, sometimes enquiries are made in such a form that they could be construed as informal notice of assignment. If there is any suspicion of this the enquiry should be considered by the legal department.

BIBLIOGRAPHY

W. E. H. Hickox (1936). Surrender values and paid-up policy amounts. *J.I.A.* vol. LXVII, p. 222.

C. F. B. Richardson (1938). Guaranteed cash surrender values under modern conditions. *Trans. Act. Soc. of America*, vol. XXXIX, p. 237.

H. N. Freeman, G. F. Menzies and M. E. Ogborn (1946). *Surrender and paid-up policy values*. T. and A. Constable, Edinburgh.

The subject of the 'terms to be granted on withdrawal' was included in the subjects for discussion at the Twelfth International Congress, Lucerne, 1940. *Transactions*, vol. II.

CHAPTER 16

PENSION SCHEMES, DISABILITY INSURANCE AND OPTIONS

A. Disability Benefits combined with Life Assurance

16·1. Types of benefit.

With the discussion of disability benefits we enter upon a wide field which touches the fringe of subjects studied more fully in other parts of the examination. Here we can only give a brief outline of the problems involved in the inclusion of these benefits in life assurance contracts. Most of the experience of this type of business is American and Canadian though it has been successfully practised to a limited extent in the United Kingdom and elsewhere.

Various forms of disability insurance are provided by (*a*) friendly societies, (*b*) social insurance schemes, (*c*) pension schemes, (*d*) accident insurances, (*e*) continuous disability insurances as well as (*f*) by disability benefits combined with life assurance. Though we are concerned only with the last-named, the practices of this type of business are naturally affected by those of the other types.

The following are examples of the types of benefit that have been offered when combined with life assurance.

(i) Waiver of premium benefit.

(ii) Payment of sum assured on disablement.

(iii) Payment of sum assured by instalments over say 10 years, commencing on disablement (sometimes continuing as an income after the sum assured has been exhausted).

(iv) Purchase of an annuity-certain with the sum assured on disablement.

(v) Payment of an income or annuity on permanent and total disablement, the amount of the life assurance being unaffected.

The waiver of premium benefit is a means of providing for the continuance of the assurance when circumstances might put the assurance in jeopardy. The transaction of this type does not raise many special problems and it is the form in which disability insurance is most widely applied to life assurance. The benefit may be included automatically in all assurances accepted at normal rates or it may be included only on request when a suitable additional premium is paid for the benefit. These two practices raise rather different problems.

Payment of the sum assured on an event such as disablement is to be deprecated because the event is difficult to define. There is not the same objection to payment by instalments because a mistake can be rectified and the assurance restored, in part at least, should that be necessary.

Payment of an income commencing on disablement affords the most complete protection to the assured but it raises many problems which are different in character from those arising in life assurance and it is questionable whether it is wise to mix such different contracts.

There are obvious advantages when benefits of this type can be combined with pension schemes and the fourth type is commonly included in group life and pensions schemes. Even here, however, there is the difficulty that 'retirement on account of ill health' is not necessarily the same as disablement within the terms of the disability insurance, and disappointment may be caused when a member who retires on account of ill health finds that he is not eligible for benefit under the insurance.

16·2. Definition of incapacity.

The definition of incapacity varies widely from office to office and also according to the class of business. We may commence our remarks on this subject with a definition quoted by Heath in connexion with permanent sickness insurance:

> Such total and complete incapacity by reason of sickness or accident that the assured is able to perform no part whatever of his own or any other occupation.

Such a definition may seem harsh but experience has shown that a strict definition is necessary and the assured must trust the office to be reasonable in the interpretation of the definition. Where a dispute arises the condition will probably be interpreted by the Courts and this may lead to an undesirable extension of the insurance into fields not intended to be included within the definition.

The words 'or any other' are usually included but they need some interpretation. The general intention is that the assured should be unable to perform the duties either of his own occupation or of any alternative occupation in which he might reasonably be expected to make his livelihood.

Only total disability is provided for. In some countries partial disability has also been included in the assurance but it is not the practice in the United Kingdom. With partial disability, the settlement of claims may raise many difficulties and the contract becomes more in the nature of an indemnity than an assurance contract.

The definition of incapacity contains within it the conception of a loss of income which is replaced or mitigated by insurance. This raises the question whether the insurance should not be based directly on the loss of income and thus become a contract of indemnity. Rhodes strongly advocated that form of contract but practice in the United Kingdom has not followed the suggestion. The contracts are contracts of assurance, not indemnities. We may stress, however, that the maximum amount of insurance should bear a reasonable relation to the income of the assured.

Provision is usually made for the benefit to cease upon the recovery of the assured and the payment of benefit is conditional upon proof of the continuance of the disability.

Particularly where disability benefits are combined with life assurances it has been customary to use the expression 'total and permanent' disablement and the question whether the disability is permanent has given rise to a good deal of difficulty. It is often not possible to say at the time whether the disability will prove to be permanent and the use of that word seems anomalous in a contract which also provides for recovery! The cover has sometimes been extended to include all disability which lasts more than a certain time, for example 3 or 6 months. With this extension many claims may be paid which in no sense relate to permanent disability and the cost of the extension of cover should be carefully considered.

16·3. The practical requirements of the business.

Disability insurance needs to be conducted in a manner appropriate to the special nature of the insured risks. It ought not to be regarded merely as an adjunct to the life assurance but as an insurance which needs just as much attention as other risks.

It is necessary that the insurance, including any benefit that may be payable, should cease when the life assured attains age 65 and possibly at an earlier age for female lives. For this reason disability benefits are most suitably combined with endowment assurances maturing not later than age 65 or with pension schemes where the age-pension may be drawn at that or an earlier age. The waiver of premium benefit can also be combined with limited-premium life assurances where the premiums cease before age 65.

The selection of lives for disability insurance is different from that for life assurance. Occupation is especially important and accident risks must be treated with caution. The heaviest claims are for mental and nervous complaints which may lead to incapacity of long duration. Certain impairments must be dealt with more severely than for life assurance: these would include, for example, gastric ulcers, asthma, affections of the eyes and ears, and sinusitis. It is desirable for the examining doctor to be informed that the proposal is for disability insurance.

Prompt notification of claims is essential so that the insurance office may be able to obtain any medical evidence that it requires. Claims must also be carefully supervised preferably by the doctor and the actuary in collaboration as for the underwriting of risks.

The total amount of insurance of all forms must be disclosed and should not exceed, say, three-quarters of the total income of the life assured. Though the contract is not one of indemnity it is helpful to remember that the insurance is intended to provide for the pecuniary loss that may result from disease or accident.

The requirements we have outlined are more severe than could be adopted for group insurance. Here the unit is the group but careful attention may be paid to certain features, for example the occupations of the assured lives and the relationship of the benefit to income when other forms of insurance such as National Insurance are taken into account.

16·4. The actuarial technique.

The actuarial technique depends to some extent on the form of the available statistics and there are three general processes.

(i) The mortality table for all lives may be considered to be composed of two parts, *active* and *disabled* lives, and this subdivision may be used as a basis for disability benefits.

(ii) The cost of disability benefits may be based upon (*a*) the chance of becoming disabled, and (*b*) the cost of the benefit for an incapacitated life.

(iii) The claims for benefit may be spread over all lives and treated as sickness on a collective basis.

The first method has been customary in America and Canada whereas in the United Kingdom the second method has been used for pension funds and the third method for friendly societies and also for disability insurances—in so far as the charges for this have been based directly on tables and not expressed as more or less arbitrary percentages of the life assurance premiums.

A full discussion of these techniques is outside the scope of this book but we may add a few remarks on them.

The first process is based on the idea that the mortality table for all lives may be considered to be composed of two parts, active and disabled lives, and that the assumptions with regard to the parts should be consistent with the table as a whole. The l_x of the life table is thus divided into l_x^{aa} active lives and l_x^{ii} disabled lives and similarly with the deaths. Given the probability at every age of an active life becoming disabled within a year and the mortality experience of either active or disabled lives, the other is uniquely determined (recovery being ignored). Normally the mortality experience of disabled lives is given and that of active lives is computed accordingly. This technique has not, generally speaking, appealed to British actuaries, partly because it seems rather artificial, and they have preferred to base their calculations so far as possible directly on experience.

With the second process the first step is to obtain the cost of the disability benefit at the time of disablement based on the experience amongst disabled lives. This is then regarded effectively as an insurance for a varying sum payable on disablement and may be combined with the appropriate commutation function based on an *active life* table for a benefit payable on that event. This technique has been largely developed in connexion with pension funds.

The special feature of the third process is that claimants are not separated from active lives and the ordinary mortality table only is used. However, the average number of weeks of benefit at each age is also computed and this enables the disability insurance to be valued collectively.

The different techniques have some interesting consequences in valuation. The first method entails the separation of the active and disabled but both are dealt with on an aggregate basis. The incapacitated lives are not dealt with individually but according to the one aggregate table. The method seems somewhat rigid because of the interlocking of the separate *active* and *disabled* experiences with the total experience for all lives.

The second method also entails a separate valuation of active and disabled but the latter may be dealt with on a 'select' table which seems more suitable in the circumstances. The 'select' table would show a high mortality immediately after disablement but the mortality would rapidly reduce to a more normal level with increasing duration of disability. Claims may be valued individually on their merits according to circumstances should this course be preferred.

In the third method the lives are dealt with collectively and factors provide for the average duration of benefit amongst all lives. Thus the factors provide both for future claims and for the continuance of the existing claims, provided that the existing claims are about what would have been expected by the table. Should the claims experience be heavy a special additional reserve might be required.

A further question that has to be considered is whether the assurances carrying disability benefits should be entitled to the same participating rights as other assurances or whether the experience in respect of the disability benefits should be taken into account. Originally no different treatment seems to have been intended but the experience of disability benefits in America and Canada was so adverse that lower dividends (bonuses) had to be paid on assurances carrying those benefits, that is to say the losses on disability insurance were spread over the life assurances combined with disability insurance rather than over all assurances.

Whether assurances under which there are claims for disability benefit in course of payment should be treated differently in respect of bonus depends to some extent on the circumstances but normally no differentiation is made. This practice assumes that the disability insurance forms, as it were, a separate fund out of which claims are paid, whether these claims are for income benefit or for the redemption of the life assurance premiums which are to be waived during disability.

B. OPTIONS

16·5. Mortality options in life assurance.

At this stage it is convenient to pick up the threads of a subject upon which we have touched in earlier chapters in different contexts. This subject is the treatment of options which may affect the mortality to be assumed in the actuarial basis. Such options may arise in many different ways but we propose to confine our remarks to life assurance with the option of conversion to another class of assurance.

Sometimes a whole-life assurance, for example, contains the option of conversion to endowment assurance within a certain period of years. This option needs no special consideration from the point of view of mortality because the total mortality of both classes of assurance combined is unlikely to be affected by the proportion of conversions actually experienced. The whole-life class normally experiences a fair proportion of conversions to endowment assurance apart from any special contractual option and the effect on mortality can be considered as being included in the mortality table.

Very different problems are raised by the option of effecting at some later date whole-life or endowment assurance at the then current tabular premium without evidence of health, whether the option is given alone or in conjunction with a temporary assurance during the option period. The mortality experience of the opted assurances cannot be assumed to be represented by the mortality table derived from the experience of assured lives generally. Strictly speaking, it is necessary to investigate the mortality experience of opted assurances and since that experience is likely to be affected by the nature of the option, and the proportion exercising it, the experience must be based on options which are similar in all respects. This ideal is usually unattainable in practice and we have to consider what may be learnt from our existing tables.

In the early papers on options which were written when select tables first came into use, the view was taken that the ultimate l_x could be considered as consisting of $l_{[x]}$ select and $l_x - l_{[x]}$ damaged lives. The select $l_{[x]}$ was regarded as a homogeneous group which experienced a rate of mortality increasing from the select rate at x to the ultimate rate at the junction with the ultimate table. The damaged lives were all assumed to die before that point was reached. On this foundation a theory of options was erected which tied the calculated value of an option to the value and period of selection in the particular mortality table. This view of the select table is untenable and a sounder view of it may, we think be obtained by considering an aggregate table in conjunction with two analysed tables of 'selected' and 'rejected' lives respectively (Courcouf, 1934). For our purpose, however, it is sufficient to consider the range of mortality implied by an ultimate mortality table.

The lives subject to ultimate mortality are a heterogeneous group of lives subject to a wide range of rates of mortality. The ultimate rate of mortality is the mean rate of the group but we have little information about the dispersion. At one end of the range there will be those who are assurable at ordinary rates and who may be regarded as a sub-group subject to the select rate of mortality. Then there are those who are subject to varying degrees of impairment and finally those at the other extremity of the range who are uninsurable. Clearly the ultimate rate is an average of widely diverse rates.

Suppose that the 'ultimate' lives at attained age y are separated into a few groups, one group comprising those assurable at normal rates who may therefore be regarded as being subject to select mortality and the other comprising the remainder subject to various excess rates of mortality. We have, of course, no information on which we can make this separation but we may assume that it has been effected for the purposes of the argument. We will consider an option exercisable at age y by a select life of age x where $(y-x)$ is greater than the duration of selection.

TABLE 16·1

Excess mortality group	Rate of mortality	Excess rate	Percentage numbers in group	Product of percentage and excess rate
0	·00690	Nil	90	Nil
1	·01190	·005	6	·03
2	·01690	·010	2	·02
3	·05690	·050	1	·050
4	·40690	·400	1	·400
			100	·500

Now the cost of an option exercisable at age y by a select life x depends upon (i) the proportion of select lives aged x who survive to age y and exercise the option, and (ii) the mortality experience of the opted assurances. This may be illustrated by a somewhat artificial but a simple numerical example. Consider an option to (50) to effect at age 55 a temporary assurance for one year without evidence of health, and suppose that interest and expenses are both ignored. The premium for the 1 year temporary assurance may be assumed to be the select $q = ·00690$ by the A 1924–29 table. The average mortality among the survivors to age 55 is given by the ultimate $q = ·01190$, an average excess of ·005. This excess might be distributed as in Table 16·1, the figures being chosen merely as an illustration.

It will be seen that the groups have been chosen to reproduce the average excess mortality of ·005. On the traditional basis for option premiums the pure premium for the option would be the equivalent of an endowment of ·005 at age 55 which is the excess cost of ultimate as compared with select mortality. Clearly this assumes conversion in respect of all lives subject to excess mortality at age 55. Contrary to what is sometimes stated, however, it does not depend upon the proportion of conversions among those who are select at age 55, which proportion does not affect the calculation in any way.

The method assumes that the option premium is collected in respect of all those who enter assurance as select lives at 50 and who survive to the option age of 55. This assumption is justified if a single premium is charged at 50 equivalent to an endowment of ·005 at 55 but the assumption may not be justified if an annual premium is charged because some of the assurances may lapse within the 5-year period. The force of this objection is lessened when the option is combined with a temporary assurance during the option period.

It is sometimes suggested that the option premium should be returned to those who do not exercise the option. This is unsound because they are likely to be amongst those who are still select at the option age. For example, if 50% did not opt and these were all select lives, the charge on the remainder would be doubled, ·01 in the illustration instead of ·005.

So far we have ignored the incidence of expenses. There is commonly a saving of expenses on opted assurances because initial commission is not usually payable when the option is exercised. This saving will only be realized in respect of those who opt and the value of the saving depends upon how many do so. If a considerable proportion of all lives do, in fact, exercise the option the saving in expenses may make a material reduction in the cost of the option in respect of the few who are not select lives.

The successful transaction of options thus depends upon a number of special considerations. (i) Options should be granted only on lives who are undoubtedly select when the contract is made. Options should not be granted on lives who are 'borderline' but who might be acceptable for ordinary forms of assurance. (ii) The option premium should be collected in respect of all entrants who survive to the option date. This normally entails the quotation of a single premium. (iii) No refund of any kind should be made to those who do not exercise the option. (iv) The cost of the option should be based on the mortality for the appropriate duration of assurance at which the option is to be exercised. Since the usual construction of select tables does not admit of an exact analysis by duration consideration must be given to the question whether the standard table used for assurances generally is appropriate for estimating the costs of options.

The pure single premium for an option to (x) exercisable after n years may be written

$$(P_{[x]+n} - P_{[x+n]})\, N_{[x]+n}/D_{[x]}, \qquad (16{\cdot}1)$$

with a suitable modification where the option is to effect other forms of assurance than whole-life assurance. If the option is continuously exercisable during a period of years the value of the option might be taken as the mean of the values of (16·1), allowing for the proportions exercising the option from time to time. There may, however, be some selection against the office with regard to the time at which the option is exercised and this might necessitate some special allowance.

Though (16·1) is the theoretical formula for the value of the option it is rarely used in practice because practical considerations outweigh the somewhat abstruse theory on which the formula is based. The practical methods of dealing with options were discussed in § 10·4. The pure premium in (16·1) would require a substantial loading for fluctuations as well as an appropriate loading for expenses.

16·6. Comparison of options with disability insurance.

The reality underlying the somewhat abstruse theory of options is, we think, illuminated by a comparison with disability insurance which was discussed in the earlier sections of this chapter. Disability insurance is founded on the concept of an active-life table, which shows the mortality of actives and the proportions becoming disabled, together with an invalid-life table, which shows the after-history of those who become disabled. The active-life table is a double decrement table and the numbers of the actives at successive ages are connected by the forces of mortality and disability. In a somewhat similar way the force of mortality for successive ages at duration 0 could be regarded as providing the mortality basis for a table of lives who remain assurable at ordinary rates; but this would differ from the $l_{[x]}$ of the select table because there is no direct relationship between the successive values of $l_{[x]}$, and the select table does not trace the after-history of those who cease to be select.

The various forces of the active-life and invalid-life tables could be combined to produce the mortality at successive durations of a life known to be active at age x. The rates of mortality at successive durations would be derived from a mixture of lives including a proportion who would have become disabled since age x. The rates of mortality in such a table would be found to increase with duration in much the same way as the usual select rates of mortality: and after a period of years the analysed rates by duration could, with sufficient accuracy, be run into an 'ultimate' table in much the same way that select rates are made to run into the ultimate after a period called the duration of selection. The spread of the mortality in the ultimate table, illustrated by Table 16·1, corresponds to the spread of the mortality between the actives and the invalid lives that we have been discussing.

From the active-life and invalid-life tables it would be possible to compute the value to (x), known to be active at that age, of the option on becoming disabled to effect a life assurance at the current tabular annual premium for his then age, without evidence of health. In this calculation it would be necessary to assume that the option would be exercised. The form of the calculation would be similar to the usual calculation of an option premium but the character of the option itself would be rather different. This is because the disability calculation would assume the option to be exercised at the moment of disablement when the force of the option would be at its greatest whereas the usual option calculation assumes the option to be exercised at the end of a period of years. It is for this reason that the cost of an option which is exercisable at any time within a given period may be understated by (16·1) which is for an option exercisable at the end of the period.

C. Pension Schemes

16·7. The adaptation of assurances to pension schemes.

Since before the end of the nineteenth century assurances have been granted on groups of lives with a view to the provision of pensions at retirement. The pensions may be assured either by means of deferred annuities with or without return of premiums at early death or by means of endowment assurances which include an option to convert the proceeds of the assurance to an annuity at a guaranteed rate according to the age at the time (the assurance being arranged to mature at about the normal retirement date) or by means of special types of assurance which combine life assurance with a deferred annuity.

There are two ways of arranging the pensions. One, a *pension scheme*, is a tripartite agreement between the employer, the members and the assurance office. The respective rights and obligations of the employer and the members are governed either by a simple set of rules or by a trust deed. The contractual liability for the pensions is accepted by the assurance office in accordance with the rules of the scheme and the obligation of the employer in this respect is usually limited to the payment of the premiums to the assurance office.

The other, a *pension fund*, constitutes a trust fund set up by the employer and consisting of the contributions by the employer and, if contributory, by the members. The powers of investment of the trustees may include the power to effect annuity contracts for the purposes of the trust but such a contract is made solely between the trustees and the assurance office. The members must look to the fund for the due payment of their pensions and not to the assurance office.

The approval of the Revenue authorities has to be sought—for schemes under the Income Tax Act, 1918, s. 32, and the Finance Act, 1947, ss. 19–23, and for funds under the Finance Act, 1921, s. 32. The conditions of this approval and the consequences that flow from it cannot be discussed in this book.

There is probably a saving in expenses in handling a group of contracts as compared with the transaction of individual assurances and this saving may receive recognition in the premium scale. Against this saving must be set the cost of the somewhat lower standards of medical selection which might be appropriate for a group of contracts. There is also a tendency to maintain a given scale of premiums for a group scheme (by reason of a guarantee of rates or otherwise) for a longer period in the face of changing conditions than would be the case with individual assurances.

Assurances and deferred annuities effected in connexion with pension schemes and funds do not involve any special valuation problem. They may be grouped and valued with the corresponding individual assurances and annuities. There are, however, a number of objections to this type of arrangement from the point of view of the employer which have proved difficult to meet.

New assurances are required for each increase of pay beyond a certain amount and where increases of pay are frequent the method may be clumsy. A desirable simplification has been obtained by the issue of group contracts covering such assurances on groups of lives. Further, since premiums have to be paid within the period of assurance it is usually impracticable to include employees who are near to retirement when the scheme is started because the period of assurance would be too short and the premiums relatively heavy. As against these objections, the method is flexible because either the premiums or the benefits may be fixed by suitable rules chosen to fit the particular circumstances.

16·8. Group life and pension schemes.

The objections have been overcome by the issue of 'group life and pension schemes'. These schemes are an adaptation of group-life assurance and in principle, with certain exceptions, they are founded on the idea of providing each year merely the cost of the pension earned in the year. The unit becomes the group rather than the individual. One policy only is issued and the benefits of individual members are indicated merely by a card record, usually supplemented by a certificate held by the member.

Fundamentally, these schemes produce pensions which are related to average pay during service, not to the pay at the time of retirement. The members are divided into groups depending upon pay and to each pay-group an appropriate unit of pension is allotted. The member's total pension is the sum of the individual pensions purchased year by year as the member passes through the various groups. The following is a typical schedule showing the groups.

Category	Range of pay to which the category relates	Unit of pension for each year's membership in category	Member's weekly contribution	Amount of life assurance
1				
2				
3				
4				
(etc.)				

The scheme may be varied in a number of ways. For example, the categories may not be dependent upon pay, or the pensions—and possibly also the life assurance—may be paid for by level annual premiums not by the single premium cost from year to year. Further, the pensions may be specially adjusted to relate to final salary and years of service.

The cost is computed by a 'balance table' which shows for each attained age and for unit pension:

(*a*) the pension purchased by the member's contributions for the year, with return of premium with or without interest at death;

(*b*) the balance of the year's unit pension to be provided by the employer;

(*c*) the cost of the balance (*b*) without return of premium at death;

(*d*) the cost of the year's life assurance.

Since the figures in each category are usually proportionate to the unit of pension for the category, only one 'balance table' is required for the group and the cost is readily computed by tabulating the number of 'units' at each attained age.

Service before the scheme commenced should rank according to the categories previously passed through but the information would be difficult to obtain and the usual course is to provide pensions in respect of eligible past service at half the rate of pension for the category in which the member is placed at the start of the scheme. The employer pays the whole cost of past-service pensions, usually by an annual charge computed to suffice for the purchase of the required pensions from time to time starting with those members who are nearest to retirement. An alternative plan arranges for the 'definite funding' of the liability for past service.

Group-life assurance is usually included for an amount approximating to one year's pay. The assurance may also provide for payment of the sum assured by instalments on total and permanent disablement and for the option on withdrawal to effect ordinary life assurance up to the same amount without evidence of health.

Provision is made for temporary absences from work (even though the member may, technically, be discharged) and for early and late retirements, the allotment of part of a pension to a widow, and so on.

16·9. Premiums and valuation of group schemes.

So far it has proved possible to transact group-life and pension schemes on a simple actuarial basis. The rate of interest has been a suitable gross rate of interest without the complications of income tax referred to in § 9·5. Standard tables of mortality have been assumed to be appropriate, usually A 1924–29 during service and *a* (*f*) and *a* (*m*) after retirement. The loading has usually been a simple percentage (for example 5%) of the pure premium. Though such a basis seems to ignore all the problems mentioned in § 9·5, it may be found to strike a reasonable balance between many confusing and conflicting tendencies.

When group-life assurance and group pensions are transacted together they should be considered as one business. However, the group pensions may be included in a separate annuity fund whereas the group-life assurance is carried in the life assurance fund. A light mortality during service might lead to a profit on the group-life part, which would emerge in the life fund, and to a loss on the deferred annuities without return at death in the group pensions part of the business, which loss would emerge in the annuity fund.

The same scale of premiums may be guaranteed throughout the service of members who enter within a certain period, for example 5 years. Since increases in pay may be received at a time when the rates of premium that have been guaranteed are unremunerative, the practice makes the liability of the assurance office dependent to some extent upon the course of salaries and wages. It is probably more usual to limit the guarantee to increments arranged within the period.

The premium formula involves no special actuarial problem because it is possible to deal separately with the 'with-return' and the 'without-return' parts of the pension. This is not possible at the valuation but a sufficient approximation is usually available. The formulae are comparatively simple and the worst complications arise from changes in rates of premium with the virtual commencement of a new series.

The following information will usually be recorded in respect of each member of each scheme:

Names of employer and of member.
Dates of birth, entry to service, and entry to scheme.
Pension age or normal retirement date.
Member's weekly contribution.
Pension per year of future service in current category.
Total future-service pension if member remains in current category to pension age.
Amount of group-life assurance.
Past-service pension and single premium cost of it.

For valuation we also require to know the total member's contributions if the member remains in the current category to pension age.

Let y be the valuation age and r the period to the normal retirement date;
a and A be the pension per year of future service and the total to the normal retirement date respectively;
c and C be the member's contribution per annum and the total to the normal retirement date respectively.

The pension may be assumed to be payable for a minimum period of 5 years, for example. The general valuation formula is then

$$(A-ra)\times {}_rE_y\,(\bar{a}_{\overline{5}|}+{}_5|\bar{a}_{y+r})+(C-rc)\,\bar{A}^{1}_{y\overline{r}|}. \qquad (16{\cdot}2)$$

Where the member's contribution is returnable with interest, C must allow for this so that the accumulation to date can be obtained, and $\bar{A}^{1}_{y\overline{r}|}$ must be taken at a suitably lower rate of interest.

The formula (16·2) is not suitable at the younger ages where the member's contributions by themselves provide more than the scale pension. Such cases need separate treatment and various approximations may be devised to produce the member's accumulated contributions at the valuation date.

The age assumptions depend upon whether the valuation is to be made on the customary valuation date or upon the anniversary of the scheme, with an adjustment subsequently to the customary valuation date. This might depend upon whether each scheme is valued as a separate unit or whether similar schemes are aggregated.

The formula (16·2) relates only to the valuation of the pensions purchased before the date of valuation. It implicitly assumes that the terms for later premiums either are not guaranteed or are guaranteed on such terms as will not involve a strain compared with the valuation basis. Should these assumptions be incorrect some further reserve may be necessary. The additional reserve could be computed by means of suitable factors depending upon the age attained and making a rough allowance for the probable strain to be expected in respect of later premiums. The reserve must necessarily be approximate because it would depend amongst other things upon the course of future pay. Such factors would probably be required for a small part only of the business.

Should the scheme be founded on level annual premiums it is also necessary to record

d, the employer's contribution per annum.

The valuation formula then becomes

$$A\times {}_rE_y\,(\bar{a}_{\overline{5}|}+{}_5|\bar{a}_{y+r})-(c+d)\,\bar{a}_{y\overline{r}|}$$
$$+(C-rc)\,\bar{A}^{1}_{y\overline{r}|}+c.(\bar{I}\bar{A})^{1}_{y\overline{r}|}. \qquad (16{\cdot}3)$$

Where the member's contribution is returnable with interest at the valuation rate, the value of the member's future contributions less the relative return at death is

$$c \times {}_r p_y \bar{a}_{\overline{r}|}$$

instead of

$$c\,[\bar{a}_{y\overline{r}|} - (\bar{I}\bar{A})^{1}_{y\overline{r}|}].$$

Possibly that expression might also serve as a sufficient approximation where the return is at a lower rate of interest. The last term of (16·3) would then disappear and the accumulation of the member's contributions to date of valuation would be valued by $(1 - {}_r p_y)$ or by $\bar{A}^{1}_{y\overline{r}|}$ at a suitably lower rate of interest according as whether the return was to be at the valuation rate of interest or at a lower rate.

D. Group-life Assurance

16·10. Group-life assurance.

Group-life assurance consists of one-year renewable temporary assurance and presents no special actuarial problems though there are a number of practical problems which arise from the special features of the plan.

The plan is mainly confined to groups of employees, whether the scheme is contributory or non-contributory, but the plan has also been extended to certain other groups. However, it is difficult to ensure a proper average of risks with other groups than those of employees.

All employees or all within certain classes of employee must normally be insured. The amount of the assurance is computed by a process which precludes individual selection, for example in proportion to pay or in amounts varying with the occupational class, and there would usually be a maximum and a minimum amount of assurance. The plan would apply only to groups with a certain minimum membership.

With contributory schemes, the member's contribution is a fixed percentage of the amount of assurance and the whole cost of the age-distribution of the members would be borne by the employer. Membership would have to be voluntary for existing employees at the start of the scheme and a minimum proportion, for example three-quarters, of all eligible employees would be required to join the scheme.

No medical examination is required because the unit is the group. The underwriting of group-life assurance depends upon a classification of the various types of employment, extra premiums being charged for the more hazardous kinds of employment. Full particulars would be required of any special risks and it might be necessary to inspect the conditions under which the members are working in the particular factories. In some industries there may be a catastrophe risk. These remarks apply more especially to group-life assurance when transacted by itself. When group-life assurance and group pensions are combined in one scheme there is less need for these special enquiries.

An interesting analysis of claims under group-life assurance (Cammack, 1927) showed that about one-tenth only of the claims were due to accidents.

The lives insured under group-life assurance represent a cross-section of the population which includes many lives who would never appear in an 'assured life' mortality experience. The premiums should be based on population mortality. If an assured life table is adopted there should be a suitable loading. The insured lives are in active employment and population rates of mortality show a margin of profit which may be recognized by making only a small loading to cover the expenses of the business. The loading is commonly charged partly as a percentage of the sum assured and partly as a percentage of the premium.

The total premium payable under the policy is the sum of the premiums for the individuals insured under it. The total premium may be expressed as an average rate per cent of the total amount of assurance and the average rate could, if desired, be applied throughout the following year so as to save small and unimportant adjustments.

Group-life assurances used to provide for payment of the sum assured in the event of total and permanent disablement before the attainment of age 60. The analysis of claims we have mentioned showed that one-sixth only of the claims were for disability benefit. The rising cost of all types of such benefits led to a reconsideration of the practice and in the United States of America disability benefits were discontinued in group-life assurances in 1932. The benefit has been replaced by a provision for payment of the sum assured (now without limit of time) should the employee become totally disabled before age 60 and such disability continue without interruption from the date of termination of employment to the date of death, provided that evidence of the continuance of the total disability is presented to the insurance company once a year for the entire period of the disability. The original form of disability benefit has been continued in the United Kingdom though it is now confined to male lives.

The individual's insurance under the group-life assurance ceases with employment unless it is terminated because of illness when the insurance may be and usually is continued. The insurance may also be continued by the employer while the member is temporarily laid-off and pensioners may be insured if all are included.

Should the individual's insurance cease on termination of employment it may be replaced by whole-life or endowment assurance at the tabular rate of premium without evidence of health up to the same amount. A small proportion only exercise this option. The heavy mortality experience under such opted assurances must be provided for by a suitable charge in the group-life premiums.

Group-life assurance may participate in profits or may be non-participating. The distinction between the two kinds of assurance is somewhat blurred because the same scale of premiums is usually charged for both types of contract and the practical effect is much the same. With a participating contract cash bonuses are paid and there may be provision for reducing the premiums under an 'experience rating' plan. With a non-participating contract the premiums may be subject to reduction, possibly retrospectively, under the 'experience rating' plan. The bonuses and rate reductions may take account of the mortality experience of the specific group, and of the group business as a whole, or, in part, according to the particular industrial classification. True participation in profits would require the contracts to share in the profits of the business as a whole.

BIBLIOGRAPHY

A. Disability Benefits combined with Life Assurance

The subject of disability benefits has been discussed at various International Congresses of Actuaries, in particular at the Eighth, London (1927) and the Tenth, Rome (1934).

ARTHUR HUNTER and J. T. PHILLIPS (2nd ed. 1932). *Disability benefits in life insurance policies.* Actuarial Studies No. 5, Actuarial Society of America.

This book provides a complete review of the subject and includes an extensive bibliography.

E. E. RHODES (1932). Is disability insurance practicable? *J.I.A.* vol. LXIII, p. 115.

W. A. ROBERTSON (1932). Continuous disability insurance. *T.F.A.* vol. XIV, p. 21.

A. PEDOE (1934). Disability benefits in connexion with life insurance. *Trans. Tenth Int. Congress*, Rome, vol. I, p. 274.

E. A. J. HEATH (1939). Permanent sickness insurance. *J.I.A.* vol. LXX, p. 271.

H. F. PURCHASE (1948). Disability benefits in conjunction with life assurance policies. *J.S.S.* vol. VIII, pt. 3, p. 121.

The papers by Pedoe and Purchase provide a good introduction to the subject for the student who is interested in this class of business.

B. Options

P. H. McCORMACK (1923). Damaged lives and options. *J.I.A.* vol. LIV, p. 123.

W. J. COURCOUF (1934). Options in theory and practice. *J.S.S.* vol. IV, no. 3, p. 178.

F. L. GRIFFIN, jun. (1942). A new approach to the problem of term-insurance conversion costs. *Record Amer. Inst. of Act.* vol. XXXII, p. 131.

W. P. ELDERTON (1945). Mortality options in life assurance. *T.F.A.* vol. XVIII, pt. 1, p. 12.

C, D. Group Life and Pensions

A. G. SIMONS (1942). Group life and pension schemes. *J.I.A.* vol. LXXI, p. 375.

WILMER A. JENKINS (1948). The problem of annuity premium rates in the United States. *Proc. Cent. Assembly Inst. Act.* vol. II, p. 254.

E. E. CAMMACK (1927). Group life insurance in the United States. *Trans. Eighth Int. Congress*, London, vol. I, p. 125.

J. B. MACLEAN (1945). *Life insurance.* (Ch. XV on Group Insurance). McGraw-Hill Publishing Company, Ltd. 6th ed.

W. J. GRAHAM (1948). Development of group insurance. *Proc. Cent. Assembly Inst. Act.* vol. III, p. 35.

PART III

INDUSTRIAL ASSURANCE

CHAPTER 17

SPECIAL FEATURES OF INDUSTRIAL ASSURANCE

In Part III of this book we shall deal with the application of the general principles discussed in Part I to the special problems of industrial assurance. Before doing so, however, we propose, in this chapter, to give a brief description of the special features which distinguish the business of industrial assurance from that of ordinary life assurance.

GENERAL DESCRIPTION

17·1. Legal definition.

The Industrial Assurance Act, 1923, defines industrial assurance as the 'business of effecting assurances upon human life premiums in respect of which are received by means of collectors'. There are certain exceptions to this definition, the most important of which is the exclusion of assurances 'the premiums in respect of which are payable at intervals of two months or more'. Assurances on which premiums are payable not more frequently than monthly are also excluded in the case of companies or societies established before the passing of the Act and having no business on which premiums are payable more frequently; and in any case where the sum assured is £25 or more and the business is not treated as part of the industrial branch. In the latter case the terms must be certified by the Commissioner as not less favourable than those imposed by the Act. This last exclusion enables monthly ordinary branch business to be transacted, but if premiums are not collected by agents, as for instance under a banker's order scheme, the Commissioner is not brought into the matter and no certificate is required.

17·2. Collection of premiums.

From the foregoing definition it is seen that the essential feature of industrial assurance is the receipt of premiums by means of collectors. Premiums are collected, usually at weekly or monthly

(4-weekly) intervals, from the homes of the policyholders by collectors or agents. The receipt of premiums by the office is recorded in a premium receipt book which is retained by the policyholder, normally until a claim arises. More than one policy may be entered in a single book, but under the 1948 Act a separate book must be used for each proposer. However, policies effected by the proposer, and by his or her spouse and children under 16 years of age, may all be entered in the same book. There is a further restriction that policies free of arrears must not be entered in a book containing arrears, nor a policy in arrear in a book free of arrears. If the office takes possession of a premium receipt book or other document issued in connexion with a policy, a receipt must be given and the book or document returned within 21 days unless all claims have been satisfied. Certain provisions of the Acts of 1923–48 relating to the rights of policyholders must be printed in each premium receipt book.

For record and accounting purposes the agent also enters the premiums received in a collecting book or agents' register, and renders a weekly account to his head office, setting out the totals of collections, deductions for commissions, claims paid and so on.

In view of the frequency with which premiums are collected, rigid insistence on the payment of premiums on the dates when they are due is not practicable. Non-payment may result from temporary inability to find the money or merely because no one is at home when the collector calls. No action is taken, therefore, until premiums are overdue for a stated period (usually 8 or 9 weeks), and during that period the policy is kept in force, subject only to the deduction of arrears in the event of a claim. At the end of the period, if no further premiums have been paid, a notice before forfeiture is issued in accordance with Section 23 of the Industrial Assurance Act, 1923. But such notices must allow a further 4 weeks' grace before the policy may be finally lapsed, so that the effective period of grace is 12 or 13 weeks.

17·3. Types of assurance.

Industrial policies are mainly for smaller sums assured than those issued in the ordinary branch, and very large numbers of policies are involved. The average sum assured by industrial policies now being issued is between £30 and £40, while for ordinary policies it is more than ten times as great. It is thus desirable to restrict the types of policy issued to a few relatively straightforward tables. Most of the policies issued are whole-life assurances and endowment assurances for, say, 10, 15, 20, 25 and 30 years, the premiums being payable weekly or monthly. In some offices the whole-life tables are weekly only, and the endowment tables monthly only. Endowment assurances are also frequently issued to mature at fixed ages, usually 55, 60 or 65. Joint-life versions of the single-life tables are granted by some offices but the number issued is not large.

In addition an office may have one or two 'special' tables, but for the reasons we have stated they are kept to a minimum. Probably the most popular of such tables is the 'periodic endowment' table, which consists of a whole-life assurance for a fixed sum at death and in addition the payment of a fixed cash amount every 5 or 10 years that the life assured survives. For a given premium the endowment sum is the same for all ages at entry, only the sum assured at death varying with the age.

An appreciable number of assurances have been issued under 'infantile' tables on the lives of children, the sums assured up to age 10 being the amounts permitted by law. Sometimes such tables may contain provision for cessation of premiums on the death of the parent or proposer before the child attains a certain age. Under the 1948 Act, however, policies on the lives of children must now be issued in 'own life' form, for the absolute benefit of the child. Further, it is illegal to pay a death benefit (other than return of premiums) at the death before the attainment of age 10 of a child born on or after 5 July 1948.

In the great majority of tables the unit is the premium and not the sum assured, a variable sum assured being quoted for a fixed weekly or monthly premium. For weekly whole-life assurances the unit is commonly 1*d.* a week, but for weekly endowment assurances and other weekly tables it is often more, say 3*d.*, 6*d.* or even 1*s.* per week. For monthly tables the unit is usually greater, sometimes being as high as 10*s.* per month. Units of 2*s.* or 4*s.* per month are, however, more common. Average premiums are in the neighbourhood of 6*d*. per week for weekly tables and 5*s*. to 6*s*. per month for monthly tables.

Some offices also quote in their prospectuses variable premiums for a fixed sum assured of £50 or £100. This is usually, but not always, confined to monthly tables. Where weekly tables are quoted in this way it may be necessary to quote the premiums in halfpence in order to make them as consistent as possible with the tables based on unit weekly premiums.

Administration

17·4. Organization of field staff.

The collection of premiums from the homes of the policyholders necessitates the employment of collectors or agents. These agents are also concerned with securing new business and, if the office transacts ordinary or general business, they may be encouraged to secure these classes as well as industrial business. The amount of weekly premiums collectable by an agent, usually referred to as his debit, varies considerably but the average is probably between £30 and £50 per week. In addition to the collectors, canvassers may be employed who are not concerned with the collection of premiums but solely with the procuration of new business. The number of such canvassers is usually small in relation to the number of agents and they may not be confined to any particular area, but may move from place to place on instructions from the management.

The area over which an office operates is divided into districts, each district being under the control of a district manager. Sometimes a number of districts are grouped to form a division, under the supervision of a divisional manager or inspector. A division may comprise from three or four up to twenty or thirty districts. An office is maintained in each district and this forms the headquarters of the district manager who normally recruits and trains his own agents and supervises their activities. In large districts the manager may have the services of an assistant manager to help with these duties. A company operating over the whole country may maintain several hundred of such local offices. Among the larger companies the number varies from about 200 to 600.

This type of organization has been considered necessary (*a*) to stimulate the flow of new business, (*b*) to provide adequate control over the activities of agents, and (*c*) to facilitate service to policyholders. Since no up-to-date records of premium payments are available at head office it has seemed desirable to have a trustworthy official in close contact with the agents who can keep a watchful eye on their cash transactions and generally superintend their activities. The expense of maintaining the local offices and of paying the district manager has added, of course, to the running costs of the business, but it has been felt to be well justified. One small office has recently centralized the control of its business at its head office, dispensing with the local offices and managers and dealing direct with its agents.

The 'block' system is a device which has been introduced to cut down expenses. Prior to the introduction of this system, although the district boundaries may have been clearly defined, the boundaries of the agencies within a district were not. Thus the position often arose of two agents of the same office collecting in the same street and even in the same house. This added considerably to the cost of collecting premiums. To avoid it, the block system was introduced, by which each district was divided into clearly defined areas or 'blocks', one agent being allocated to each block. To facilitate reference, the districts and blocks are given code numbers which remain unchanged when the agent changes. This system has now been in use for many years among the larger companies; it has enabled the system of payment by commission to be replaced by a system of salaries in the offices using it, and this has resulted in a lower cost per cent of the premiums collected.

We have so far considered the organization of the field staff in relation to the office. The number employed as industrial assurance agents is very considerable, however, and it is not surprising that they have followed the example of other large bodies of workers and organized themselves into trade unions. There are several such unions in existence, some of them confined to employees of particular offices. They are capable of exerting considerable pressure where matters concerning the welfare and working conditions of their members are involved. Such matters may not be confined to those directly affecting the agents, such as remuneration or hours of work, but may extend to questions of office policy, such as the tables to be issued, which may indirectly have a considerable influence on the agents' conditions.

17·5. Remuneration of field staff.

Methods of payment of agents differ considerably among offices and it is not proposed here to give a detailed account of such methods. Basically it may be said that the payment depends (*a*) on the amount of premium collected, and (*b*) on the amount of new business introduced.

In the collecting societies and the smaller companies payment is made directly in this form—the agent is paid a percentage of his collections plus procuration fees in respect of new business he introduces. The percentage is usually about 20 to 25% for the weekly business and from 10 to 20% for the monthly business. The lower figure for monthly business is justified on the ground that it entails only one visit a month instead of four. In practice, however, a proportion of premiums under monthly tables are collected weekly. Since, however, the average premium is generally larger under monthly than under weekly tables, and larger sums would be collected, the lower rates of commission remain justified. The maximum collecting commission may be paid only on the first £*x* of debit, a lower percentage being paid on amounts in excess of £*x*. In some offices several different rates may be used in this way. The procuration fees are normally a fixed number of times the weekly premium, say up to twenty times for weekly business with corresponding figures for monthly business, but it is customary to set off against the new business the business going off the books, so as to discourage the agent from entering business which is unlikely to remain in force. The procuration fees are thus based on a 'net increase' figure. In determining this figure claims may or may not be taken into account.

It will be apparent that payment on a commission and new business basis can result in considerable fluctuations in an agent's weekly earnings. To mitigate this all the larger companies have adopted a modified system by which the agent is paid a weekly salary which may or may not be related to the size of his debit but which anyway does not vary directly with it. Where the salary is related to the debit, a 'notional' weekly debit is obtained which includes a proportion of the monthly debit, sometimes one-quarter, sometimes less, say one-eighth. The weekly salary is based on a sliding scale of such 'notional' debits, being constant for a given range of the debit. New business fees are paid in addition, based on the new business procured or on the net increase. Such schemes usually provide for a minimum salary to be paid in any one week. Where the scale figure is less than the minimum, the difference is set off as a charge against future new business earnings which are paid on a reduced scale until the charge is liquidated. Alternatively, the salary is fixed, irrespective of the size of debit, but increases in salary are based on net increase. Sometimes a reserve of new business fees is built up on which the agent may draw so as to equalize his weekly earnings over a period.

District managers are paid on the basis of a fixed salary, depending on the size of the district, plus a variable figure related to the net increase for the district.

17·6. Chief office organization.

The nature of the chief office organization of an industrial office is determined by two main considerations, namely (1) the very large number of small units which must be handled, and (2) the dependence on the agent for supplying information concerning the movement of policies and, in particular, the fact that the primary record of premium payments remains with him. Thus the office is in the position of having to maintain records which are adequate for the purposes of valuation, accounts and payment of claims while at the same time it has no complete and immediate control over the accuracy of some of the information from which these records are compiled.

It is not practicable, in the space here available, to give a detailed account of the various systems used and the student should endeavour, if possible, to study carefully the methods of one or other of the industrial offices or collecting societies. Here we will content ourselves with a broad outline of the subject.

We have already seen how the premium payments are recorded, first in a premium receipt book which is held by the policyholder, then in a collecting book held by the agent, and finally summarized for each group of tables bearing the same rate of commission in a weekly account rendered by the agent to his chief office. This weekly account will also show particulars of the total debit and the arrears as well as details of any outgoings, such as claims paid or expenses. At the chief office the accounts are analysed and summarized in a form suitable for building up the yearly revenue accounts and other records.

The primary record of an individual policy is the proposal, which is filed at the chief office. Where punched-card machinery is not employed the proposal usually takes the form of a card which is itself used as a record card. The cards are filed in, say, district and policy number or alphabetical order and details of the movement on and off are obtained by hand-sorting and scheduling, thus providing the valuation data and any other statistical records which may be required. Where punched-card machinery is used a card is punched from the proposal which is then filed and referred to only in exceptional circumstances. The punched cards are used for compiling the various records and valuation data, and a policy register may be constructed from them. This matter is dealt with in more detail in Chapter 20.

Particulars of movement off are derived from various sources. Death claims, maturities and surrenders are normally obtained from the chief office claim records. Lapses, on the other hand, are compiled from information supplied, in the first instance, by the agent. A policy cannot be lapsed until 4 weeks after the issue of the statutory notice before forfeiture. In some offices these notices are issued from head office, and in these circumstances the lapse records can be linked with the issue of the notice. The information leading to the issue of the notice must, however, be supplied by the agent. In other offices the agent himself issues the notice and subsequently informs head office when the policy has lapsed. On the lapsing of a policy, the card is extracted from the 'in force' file. The card may sometimes be extracted when the notice is issued, in which event it is convenient to retain it for a while in a 'suspense' file.

A number of different methods are used for ensuring the accuracy of the accounts and records. The basis of all returns made to head office is the agent's collecting book, which usually covers a period of a year. At the end of the period it is sent to head office and can be checked against the various returns made during its currency. The books in current use are also inspected periodically by local officials or by inspectors from head office. Policyholders are visited and the entries in their premium receipt books are compared with those in the collecting book. Periodic census returns may be made from the collecting books by local officials and submitted to head office for comparison with the agent's own returns.

In addition to these periodic inspections and returns a general watch, both locally and at head office, is kept on the agent's accounts and returns. In particular, the arrears are closely watched and any abnormal movements or trends are at once investigated. If any irregularity is suspected, a detailed investigation into the agent's book is made without delay.

By such methods, the majority of errors, whether deliberate or accidental, are detected within a reasonably short time of their occurrence. Of the few that do slip through the net, many are picked up at a subsequent stage, for example when the agent's collecting book is checked after being rewritten. A few, of course, will remain undetected, possibly until the policy becomes a claim, but it can be said that the percentage of such undetected errors is so small as to have no significant effect.

17·7. Payment of claims.

Detailed consideration of methods used in paying industrial branch claims is outside the scope of this book, but in order to complete the picture it may be as well to mention briefly a few salient features.

With the great majority of death claims under industrial policies, the money is required urgently. Prompt settlement of claims is, therefore, essential and the procedure followed is directed mainly towards this end. The first step is the completion of a claim form, the principal object of which is to obtain the information necessary to ensure that the claimant is the person legally entitled to payment. Proof of title in industrial claims is not always easy, and offices normally have to exercise a certain amount of discretion in the matter. There is a small number of difficult cases which may be referred to the Commissioner for a ruling. Where the total amount of the estate, after paying funeral expenses, is less than £100, the claim is usually paid without waiting for probate or letters of administration, though a declaration from the claimant regarding the solvency and size of the estate may be required unless the amount of the claim is very small. In some offices the local manager is authorized to pay such claims before reference to head office, the documents being subsequently sent to head office for approval of the claim. The claim will not be paid, of course, without production of the policy, premium receipt book and a death certificate. Even where all claims are paid from head office the need for prompt settlement often requires that payment shall be made without reference to the head office records, such reference being made subsequently as in the case of claims paid by the local office.

The payment of industrial branch claims is affected in a number of ways by insurance legislation. There are, for example, the laws limiting the amount that may be paid on the death of a child and those governing the relationships for which life-of-another policies may be issued.

In this connexion special reference may be made to the provisions of the 1948 Act. This Act limits to £20 the amount for which any person may insure his parent, step-parent or grandparent; and in assessing the amount for which a new policy may be issued it is necessary to take into account all policies with all offices proposed by the same person on the same assured life. Constituent items which need not be taken into account are bonuses (other than guaranteed bonuses), repayments of premium, free policies issued before the passing of the Act and any policies issued prior to 1924. To ensure compliance with these provisions the Act provides that claims on such policies may be paid only on production of a special death certificate and that the Registrar shall issue only one such certificate for each proposer. When paying the claim the office must endorse the certificate with the name of the office, the amount paid and the date of the contract.

All these requirements need to be carefully watched and add considerably to the difficulties of effecting prompt payment.

17·8. Special legal requirements.

In Chapter 3 we discussed the legislation governing industrial assurance, and the law affecting particular aspects of the business is discussed in the appropriate chapters, but for the sake of completeness we will conclude this chapter by drawing the student's attention to the three major features of insurance legislation which are peculiar to industrial assurance. They are:

(1) The power to issue life-of-another policies without insurable interest (granted by the Acts of 1896 and 1909, extended by the 1923 Act and considerably curtailed by the 1948 Act).

(2) The powers of the Commissioner to supervise the conduct of the business and to issue regulations controlling it (initiated in the 1923 Act and extended in the 1948 Act).

(3) The obligation to grant various statutory rights to policyholders and, in particular, to allow certain minimum benefits on withdrawal (initiated in the 1923 Act and extended in the 1929 Act).

BIBLIOGRAPHY

1. Acts

Industrial Assurance Acts, 1923 to 1948

2. Other References

R. B. Walker and D. R. Woodgate (1933). *Principles and practice of industrial assurance.* Pitman, London.

R. Dinnage and T. Hills (1934). *Industrial assurance organization and routine.* Pitman, London.

B. A. J. Bone (1938). Some aspects of industrial assurance. *J.S.S.* vol. v, no. 2, p. 70.

K. J. Britt (1948). The development of industrial assurance in Great Britain since 1928. *Proc. Cent. Assembly Inst. Act.* vol. iii, p. 3.

Reference may also be made to the Parmoor, Cohen and Beveridge reports.

CHAPTER 18

UNDERWRITING

On the average, there are more than two industrial life policies in force for each person in Great Britain. This is accounted for by the practice of effecting successive policies as a proposer's financial resources improve, and also to some extent by the fact that funeral expense policies have been effected by several different relatives on the same life, though in recent years the proportion of funeral policies has greatly decreased. But it is obvious that a considerable proportion of the population must be covered by at least one policy and it follows that a wide basis of selection of lives must be adopted.

18·1. Selection of lives.

For the smaller sums assured the basis of selection is very wide indeed. There is, in general, no medical examination, though there are certain exceptions to this which are discussed later. The questions asked in the proposal form relating to health and family history are far less comprehensive than in an ordinary branch non-medical proposal, and they do little more than give an indication that the life proposed is not actually suffering from illness or an obvious disease at the time the proposal is made. In addition to the proposal form the offices and societies rely on the personal contact of their agents with the lives proposed, but the value of this is probably weakened by the natural desire of the agent to secure new business. All proposals may be scrutinized by local officials, whose duty it is to report personally on any doubtful cases. The proposals are also subject to further scrutiny at head office, and may be referred back to the local manager for his report or for medical examination.

18·2. Medical examination.

Medical examination is called for not only in cases of doubtful health but also where the age of the life proposed is greater than a given age, or where the sum assured is in excess of a certain figure, the non-medical limits varying between the different offices. For ages at entry up to, say, 50 the figure is between £100 and £500 with lower limits for older ages at entry. Since these limits are much above the average size of policies it follows that a medical test is applied only to those who appear to be selecting against the office by insuring for relatively large amounts or at exceptionally old ages.

18·3. Extra risks.

Sub-standard lives and occupational hazards can be accepted on special terms, though the normal standard of selection is so wide that very few fall outside it. Generally speaking, where a rating is necessary, it is only practicable to deal with it by means of a level deduction from the sum assured. From the actuarial point of view this is, of course, equivalent to a level extra premium but practical considerations make it essential to insist on the policyholder's taking a reduced benefit for the original premium, rather than paying an additional premium for the full benefit. Certain extra risks of a temporary nature can sometimes be met by varying the period of reduced benefit which it is customary to include in industrial life policies (see § 18·5). The applications of this method are, however, limited.

18·4. Other forms of selection.

Apart from medical selection, there are certain other types of selection which can have a considerable influence on the mortality of the lives assured by an industrial office. For example, the office may operate mainly or solely in certain limited geographical areas. Again, the lives assured may be restricted to members of certain occupations, though this probably applies only to some of the smaller collecting societies. Any such restrictions on the selection of lives will, of course, have its effect on the mortality experience. Another form of selection which is common to all industrial business is that imposed by the social class of the lives assured. The members of the higher income groups do not normally effect industrial policies so that any differences in mortality between the various income groups will be reflected in the experience of industrial lives assured.

Finally, there is the self-selection exercised by the public in deciding which of the several lives in the home to insure. This operates against the office and tends to offset the selection exercised by the office.

18·5. Deferred full benefits.

In view of the lack of stringency in the initial selection where medical examination is not obtained, it has been found necessary to introduce some safeguard against premature claims. This takes the form of a period of reduced benefit, during which only a proportion of the full sum assured is payable on death other than by accident. These deferred benefit provisions vary among offices and in a particular office may vary according to the table, age or sum assured. Typical provisions provide quarter-benefit on death during the first 3 months, half-benefit on death during the second 3 months and full benefit thereafter, or half-benefit in the first 6 months and full benefit thereafter. When a satisfactory medical examination has been undergone it is usual to allow full benefit from the outset. Following on the 1948 Act, some of the larger offices have introduced immediate full benefits on all policies.

18·6. War conditions.

Although it is not strictly relevant to the subject of underwriting it is convenient to conclude this chapter with a brief mention of war conditions in industrial branch policies. During the 1914–18 war, war conditions excluding active service risks were inserted in the policies and this practice continued between the two wars. By general agreement, however, the war conditions on policies existing at the outbreak of the 1939–45 war were not enforced.

For new whole-life policies a standard condition has been agreed providing that if the death of the assured were to occur as a result of war or aviation the amount payable should be limited to:

(1) (*a*) £1 for each penny of the weekly premium, or
(*b*) half the sum assured current at the time of death, whichever is the smaller;

plus (2) the premiums paid. For new endowment assurances a similar condition is used with 10*s*. substituted for £1 in (*a*). The condition excludes civilian as well as active service risks.

BIBLIOGRAPHY

R. B. WALKER and D. R. WOODGATE (1933). *Principles and practice of industrial assurance.* Pitman, London.

C. F. WOOD (1939). *The treatment of extra risks*, pp. 64–6. Cambridge University Press.

K. J. BRITT (1948). The development of industrial assurance in Great Britain since 1928. *Proc. Cent. Assembly Inst. Act.* vol. III, p. 3.

CHAPTER 19

OFFICE PREMIUMS

19·1. General considerations.

The general principles discussed in Part I of this book apply equally to industrial and to ordinary branch business. In assessing office premiums the various basic elements must be considered in the light of the particular circumstances of the office. In some respects, e.g. expenses, there is probably more variation between industrial than between ordinary offices, yet the variations in premium scales do not seem to be greater among the former than among the latter. The explanation lies in the fact that most industrial offices have schemes whereby the policyholders participate in profits, and differences in experience are reflected in the bonuses rather than in the basic benefits. This is discussed in more detail later in this chapter.

19·2. Mortality.

There has been no collective investigation into the mortality of industrial branch lives assured. This is presumably due to the obvious difficulties of making such an investigation and to the fact that it would be of limited use in practice. All the large offices however, have adequate data with which to investigate their own experience, and the results of some of these investigations have been published. As might be expected from a consideration of the way in which the lives are selected, the mortality curve is broadly similar in shape to that of a population table. It tends, however, to be somewhat higher than the mortality of the general population measured at the same time, for the 'ordinary' lives assured are excluded, and there are the preponderance of urban dwellers among industrial lives assured and the adverse selective influence of withdrawals. There is also a certain degree of variation between the different types and classes of assurance. Monthly endowment assurances, for instance, show appreciably lighter mortality than whole-life assurances. It has also been suggested that life-of-another policies experience heavier mortality than own-life assurances, but the evidence is not conclusive.

The effect of the selection exercised by the office also needs to be considered. This is far less powerful in operation than in ordinary branch business and any effect it has tends to be offset by the adverse influence of withdrawals, the net result of the two opposing factors being to produce an over-all aggregate mortality approximating to a population table.

This does not mean, of course, that an aggregate table is necessarily the correct one to use, but from purely practical considerations, if for no other reason, it is customary to employ a population table. For the foregoing reasons, the most up-to-date population mortality would probably be too light, and it is necessary to use a table relating to an earlier period. Owing to the steady improvement which has taken place gradually in population mortality, this should normally provide an adequate margin. A further margin is provided by the practice of using a male table throughout, although a considerable number of policies are issued on female lives who experience lighter mortality than males.

For an average office E.L.T. No. 10 (1931) might be suitable at the present time, though the improvement in population mortality has been so continuous that something lighter could probably be used. In any particular office weight must be given to possible variations due to geographical or occupational selection.

19·3. Interest.

In applying the principles discussed in Part I to the question of the rate of interest to be used in calculating industrial branch premiums, the only special factor which needs to be taken into account is the basis of taxation. The interest income of most industrial assurance funds is less than the outgo on expenses or exceeds it by less than the proprietors' profit. The usual basis of taxation is therefore proprietors' profits. Even if the 'interest less expenses' basis applies the effective net rate of interest earned is much closer to the gross rate than in an ordinary branch fund, since the expense relief is so much greater proportionately in the industrial fund. The difference in the net yields of ordinary and industrial funds, similarly constituted as regards investments, can be as much as one-half of 1%.

There is no legal obligation to maintain separate assets for ordinary and industrial funds, but some offices may nevertheless make an internal separation. It is not likely, in such circumstances, that the constitution of the two groups of assets will be materially different, but the adoption of a separate investment policy for each group could lead to appreciable differences. Any significant difference must, of course, be taken into account in fixing the premium bases for the two funds.

As in the case of ordinary business, it would be possible to use rates of interest varying with the term of the contract. From the nature of the business, however, it is much more difficult to achieve strict equity between different classes of policyholder in industrial assurance than in ordinary assurance. Apart from differences in the interest yield there may be variations in mortality and expenses which it is not always practicable to reflect in the premium bases. For this reason, perhaps, such refinements have not been common practice.

19·4. Loadings.

It is not possible in the case of industrial assurance business to relate the expense loadings to the various items of expenditure so closely as in ordinary assurance business. Consequently industrial branch premium formulae are often more simple than the relatively complex formulae sometimes employed for the ordinary branch. The most important item of expenditure is the agent's remuneration and this has therefore tended to dictate the form of the loadings. As we have seen, the agent receives remuneration equivalent to a procuration fee of a fixed number of times the weekly premium and a collecting commission of a percentage of the premiums collected. This is equivalent to a percentage of the first year's premiums and a smaller percentage of subsequent premiums, and the loadings in the premium basis normally take this form.

Most of the existing offices are quoting premiums based on

formulae in which the loadings are probably higher than are justified by their present level of expenses. This arises because the basic benefits have sometimes remained unaltered while there has been a steady reduction in expenses, offset to a greater or less extent by a reduction in the rate of interest earned. At the same time schemes for distributing profits to policyholders have been introduced, so that a proportion of the excess loadings can be regarded as bonus loadings.

If an existing office should decide to revise its basic scales of benefits, great care is necessary in the choice of bases. If full effect is given to improvements in mortality and reductions in expenses, while at the same time the policies are still issued on a non-profit basis, the resultant benefit scales will probably be higher than the existing scales even after allowing for reductions in the interest yield. Holders of existing whole-life policies of short duration would find that it would pay them to discontinue their policies, to take a paid-up policy if one is available and to re-enter on the new scale at their attained ages. This might simply increase the amount of new business fees paid without bringing any corresponding advantage to the office. Moreover, the net result of the change would be a considerable reduction in the surplus earning power of the business, so that it might prove impossible to maintain bonuses at anything like the level which had previously been declared.

One solution of this difficulty is to increase the sums assured under existing policies so that it is no longer profitable to the policyholder to withdraw and re-enter. The way in which the increase is made may make a material difference. If the increase be held to be a bonus it must be added in full to the statutory values of free policies under the 1923 Act. It is sometimes possible to arrange otherwise but a retrospective increase in sums assured is now difficult because of the £20 limit under the 1948 Act.

An alternative solution is to issue the new policies on a with-profit basis and to include bonus loadings in the premium formulae. If this is done, even if full effect is given to changes in experience, the discrepancies between the old and new scales will be greatly reduced and no increase in sums assured under existing policies may be necessary. Existing policies should, of course, be given the right to participate in profits and it would be necessary to consider whether differential bonuses should be granted to old and new policies.

For a new office commencing to transact industrial business the expenses would inevitably be high for many years and it would not be possible for such an office to quote basic benefits comparable with those quoted by the existing offices and at the same time to grant bonuses to policyholders. The choice would probably lie between competitive basic benefits with no bonuses and lower basic benefits with bonuses. The loadings employed in the premium formulae would need to reflect this choice. The full expenses would, of course, have to be covered, but if it were decided to grant bonuses a further loading should be included to provide them.

It is not customary to include a specific loading for profit to proprietors. This is normally provided by allowing adequate margins in the other basic elements.

19·5. Withdrawals.

It would be possible in theory to incorporate in the calculation of office premiums a withdrawal rate combined with an average benefit payable (if any). Such a procedure would be complicated and cumbersome, and it is never adopted in practice, but the effect of withdrawals on the finances of the fund must be kept in mind when considering the other basic elements.

There is some evidence that withdrawal is a selective force; where there are several policies in force in one family, and they cannot all be maintained, those on lives in poor health are unlikely to be discontinued. Thus, those remaining in the fund will experience somewhat heavier mortality than if there had been no withdrawals and this must be taken into account in fixing the mortality table to be used.

Again, the bulk of withdrawals occurs at the early durations and, as we shall see in Chapter 22, it is at these durations that the statutory withdrawal benefits are most favourable to the policyholder. The extent to which withdrawals represent a profit or loss to the office must be borne in mind. Since the heaviest expenses are incurred early in a policy's duration, withdrawals at those durations will tend to inflate the over-all expense ratio of the business remaining on the books.

19·6. Participation in profits.

The question of bonuses to policyholders has already been mentioned, but in this section and in Chapter 21 we will discuss the matter in greater detail. The present position of industrial assurance as regards bonuses to policyholders is comparable to that of ordinary branch business in the earlier stages of its development. The bases on which premiums have been calculated have not allowed for the improvements in mortality and expenses which have taken place, and consequently much larger profits have emerged than were originally expected. Part of these profits has been passed back to the policyholders in the form of bonuses of one kind or another but policyholders in the proprietary companies, with one exception, have no contractual right to share in profits; the extent to which they are permitted to do so remains at the discretion of the directors and shareholders of the office. The exception is the Prudential, which, in 1907, inaugurated a scheme whereby the industrial policyholders receive a part of the industrial branch profits, a right which is incorporated in the articles of association of the Company. The societies are, of course, mutual bodies and their members have the right to dispose of profits as they wish. One of the smaller societies was granting bonuses to members nearly 100 years ago.

In industrial assurance there is no separate 'with profits' class paying a higher premium than the 'without profits' class for the right to share in profits, although profits may be allocated to certain classes of policy and not to others. For instance, bonuses may be granted on whole-life policies but not on endowment assurances, or the rates of bonus for the two classes may differ. Where such differentiation is made it is usually an attempt to achieve equity, having regard to the sources from which the profit has emerged. It must be appreciated, however, that only very rough justice is possible and that refinements would be impracticable.

A number of different systems are used for distributing profits to policyholders and the principal ones are listed below:

(*a*) Increase in basic sum assured.
(*b*) Mortuary bonuses.
(*c*) Reversionary bonuses.
(*d*) Cash bonuses.
(*e*) Limitation of premiums.

These are discussed in detail in Chapter 21.

19·7. Competition.

The element of competition does not operate in quite the same way in industrial as in ordinary assurance. There is not the same tendency on the part of proposers to compare the terms of several offices. The question is not so much which office but rather whether to insure at all. Consequently variations in benefits do not play so great a part in industrial as in ordinary assurance. Such variations do of course exist, but other considerations tend to have a greater influence on the total amount of new business secured by an individual office.

A much more important factor than the scale of benefits is the nature and efficiency of the selling organization and it is here that the element of competition exerts its greatest effect on the basic elements in the premium scale, because, clearly, the efficiency of the organization will have a considerable effect both on the amount of business written and on the cost of procuring it.

The competitive pressure of the more efficient offices will compel others, less efficient, to try to improve their sales methods and this compulsion, of course, will have its repercussions on the expense ratio and possibly, to a lesser extent, on the mortality experience.

19·8. Formulae.

Having discussed the various basic elements involved in the premium scale, we are now in a position to indicate the kinds of formulae employed for the various types of policy. As we have seen, however, the elements tend to be allowed for by implication rather than directly. The formulae given must not be taken, therefore, as being of general application. They merely serve to indicate the general nature of the formulae commonly employed and they would need modifying to meet the circumstances of any particular office.

Adult whole-life assurances

(i) Sum assured in pounds by a weekly premium of 1*d.*:

$$\cdot 70 \times \cdot 21741\,(\bar{a}_x - \cdot 5)/\bar{A}_x. \tag{19·1}$$

If premiums cease at a fixed advanced age, M, this formula becomes

$$\cdot 70 \times \cdot 21741\,(\bar{a}_{x\overline{M-x}|} - \cdot 5)/\bar{A}_x.$$

These formulae allow for expenses of the whole of the premiums for the first 6 months and 30% of subsequent premiums.

The factor ·21741 equals $365\frac{1}{4}/(7 \times 240)$.

If a reversionary bonus loading is to be included, $\bar{A}_x$ must be replaced by $\bar{A}_x + b.\dfrac{\bar{R}_{x+t+\frac{1}{2}}}{D_x}$ where b is the rate of bonus to be charged for and t is the waiting period. The $\frac{1}{2}$ addition to the age allows for the average period before the next valuation.

Alternative forms of these formulae are

$$\cdot 70 \times \cdot 21741/\bar{P}\,(\bar{A}_{x+1}), \tag{19·2}$$

and

$$\cdot 70 \times \cdot 21741/{}_{M-x-1}\bar{P}\,(\bar{A}_{x+1}).$$

These formulae allow the whole of the premiums for the first 12 months for the cost of the risk and expenses, and 30% of subsequent premiums for expenses.

If a reversionary bonus loading is to be included $\bar{P}\,(\bar{A}_{x+1})$ must be replaced by

$$\bar{P}\,(\bar{A}_{x+1}) + b.\frac{\bar{R}_{x+t+\frac{1}{2}}}{\bar{N}_{x+1}}.$$

The bonus loadings assume that bonuses commence to accrue from the $(t+1)$th valuation after entry, that is to say the formula allows for a waiting period of t years and an average of $\frac{1}{2}$ year to the next valuation. If it is hoped eventually to reduce or abolish the waiting period the premium formula should be suitably adjusted.

(ii) Sum assured in pounds by a premium of 2*s.* every 4 weeks:

$$\cdot 80 \times 1\cdot 30446\,(\bar{a}_x - \cdot 3)/\bar{A}_x. \tag{19·3}$$

This formula corresponds in form to formula (19·1), but allows for expenses of approximately the first four monthly premiums and 20% of subsequent premiums, the reduced loadings being justified by the monthly collection of premiums. The factor

$$1{\cdot}30446 = \frac{365\frac{1}{4}}{28} \times {\cdot}1.$$

If a bonus loading is to be included the adjustment is the same as for formula (19·1).

A formula similar to (19·2) is hardly appropriate in view of the fractional proportion of the premiums allowed for initial expenses.

Juvenile whole-life assurances

Under the Industrial Assurance and Friendly Societies Act, 1948, policies on the lives of children must be issued in own-life or 'donor' form. In the case of children born on or after 5 July 1948, the Act prohibits the payment of a death benefit (other than the return of premiums) before attainment of age 10. For children born before 5 July 1948 it is still possible to issue policies in own-life or 'donor' form providing the maximum statutory death benefits laid down in the 1923 Act, namely £6, £10 and £15 for children aged less than 3, 6 and 10 years respectively. The formulae for these policies are similar to those for adult assurances and the limitations on the death benefit could be taken account of in the formula. It must, of course, be assumed that the full statutory amount will be payable on death under each policy; no allowance can be made for possible reduction on account of the existence of other policies on the same life. However, the theoretical sums assured which can be granted for a weekly premium of 1*d*. approximate to the statutory limits and it has been, therefore, a common practice to ignore refinements and to grant for ages at entry up to age 10 next birthday a sum assured of £15 throughout life with the reduced statutory amounts payable on death before age 6, care being taken to secure a satisfactory junction with the benefits granted at age 11 next birthday. But since the passing of the 1948 Act many offices have discontinued issuing such policies.

Since the statutory limits apply irrespective of the amount payable on death after age 10 it is not possible to grant proportionate benefits for premiums greater than 1*d.*; the sum assured payable after age 10 in respect of the additional premiums should be appropriately greater than the amount proportionate to that secured by the 1*d.* premium. Because of this difficulty it has been common practice to refuse to grant assurances securing more than the 1*d.* premium benefits.

For children born on or after 5 July 1948 it is only possible to issue deferred whole-life or endowment assurances in own-life or 'donor' form. Such policies must only provide for return of premiums in the event of death before age 10 or preferably some later age, say 16 or 21. For a deferred whole-life assurance with return of premiums at death prior to age 21, the formula corresponding to formula (19·1) would be

$$\cdot 21741\,\{\cdot 70\,(\bar{a}_x - \cdot 5) - (\bar{I}\bar{A})^{1}_{x:\overline{21-x|}}\}\,D_x/\bar{M}_{21}.$$

Endowment assurances

The formulae for endowment assurances take the same form as for whole-life assurances, endowment-assurance functions being substituted for whole-life functions. Form (19·1) is more suitable than form (19·2) and the actual loadings in (19·1) might be suitable for weekly policies. For monthly policies slightly lower loadings would be justified. The percentage loading tends to bear heavily on the shorter terms and to avoid this the agents' commissions are sometimes reduced for the shorter term endowment assurances, a corresponding reduction being made in the percentage loadings.

The practice of paying salaries instead of commissions has made it more difficult, however, to allocate the cost of collection between the various tables.

Other types of assurance

It is not practicable to give here the formulae for all the various miscellaneous tables which are issued. In general they follow the same pattern as for the main tables. It should be borne in mind that the commission for 'odd' tables is often lower than for the principal tables and this should be reflected in the loadings.

BIBLIOGRAPHY

C. G. Marshall (1932). Industrial assurance: Valuations, office premiums and bonus systems. *J.S.S.* vol. IV, no. 1, p. 55.

W. J. Fulford (1937). Classification and valuation of industrial assurance policies. *J.I.A.* vol. LXVIII, pp. 384–410.

J. H. Gunlake (1939). *Premiums for life assurances and annuities*, Ch. VII. Cambridge University Press.

CHAPTER 20

VALUATION

The purpose of an industrial assurance valuation is precisely the same as in the ordinary branch, namely to determine what sums must be set aside out of current revenue to ensure that claims can be met when they arise. The principles discussed in Part I of this book apply equally to industrial assurance, but the special features of the business have led to modifications of the methods and bases used for ordinary life assurance. The legal requirements must be borne in mind in considering all aspects of an industrial valuation and it will therefore be convenient to consider them first.

20·1. Legal requirements.

The Industrial Assurance Act, 1923, requires in Section 18 that 'The basis of valuation adopted shall be such as to place a proper value upon the liabilities', regard being had to the mortality experienced, the interest earned and the expenses incurred. It further provides that the basis 'shall be such as to secure that no policy shall be treated as an asset'.

The requirement leaves the actuary free to exercise his judgment and it is unlikely that any basis adopted by an actuary in the exercise of his professional duties would fail to comply with this section. However, it is important to note that the Commissioner may reject any valuation if he is satisfied that Section 18 has not been complied with, and may direct the office 'to make such alteration therein as may be necessary to secure compliance with those provisions'. If he does so, the office must comply—or appeal to the High Court.

To enable the Commissioner to satisfy himself that a valuation is satisfactory, he may call for the additional particulars mentioned in the Second Schedule† to the 1923 Act and such explanations as he considers necessary. In making a valuation the actuary must bear these particulars in mind and must arrange the work

† See p. 59.

in a form which will enable him to furnish them if required to do so.

The provision requiring that no policy shall be treated as an asset, in other words requiring the exclusion of negative values, has an indirect as well as a direct effect on the valuation basis. It is more difficult to comply with it in the case of a gross premium valuation, where negative values may occur quite frequently, than in the case of a net premium valuation where they occur only at infantile ages of short duration. For this reason net premium valuations are more popular than gross premium valuations despite certain practical advantages which the latter valuations possess. This question will be discussed in more detail later.

Finally, published valuations must be in the form prescribed by the Fourth Schedule of the 1909 Act. This means that the values of sums assured, office premiums and net premiums must be shown as well as the net liability. If it were not for this, the method of grouping used for industrial business would often make it simpler to obtain the net liability direct.

For Societies—which come under the 1896 Act—the published valuations have to be in the form (C. 28) prescribed by the Registrar of Friendly Societies.

Bases

20·2. General considerations.

The considerations affecting the office premium bases apply also to the valuation basis, bearing in mind that the latter applies to the whole body of assured lives while the former applies only to new entrants. The basis must match the bonus system employed, so that if a level reversionary bonus is granted the basis must defer the emergence of surplus to facilitate maintenance of the bonus. As we have seen, there is usually no special participating class of policies, though in practice participation in profits may be limited to particular tables. There is not, therefore, the same justification as in the ordinary branch for the use of a different basis for non-participating policies.

There is no reason in theory why a bonus reserve valuation should not be made, valuing as a liability the rate of bonus which it is hoped to maintain. We have shown, however, that the surplus is influenced by withdrawals, and a bonus reserve valuation on a strictly experience basis would need to take account of withdrawals. As in the case of office premiums, this is not a practical proposition.

The suggestion has been made from time to time, in particular in the Onslow Bill which was based on the Parmoor Report, that a uniform valuation basis be adopted for all industrial offices and societies. At the present time the suggestion is perhaps of historical interest only, but it is one which has had a certain appeal outside actuarial circles and which may well be raised again in the future. The student will therefore be well advised to consider its implications.

If it can be assumed that the experiences of all industrial assurance offices are similar except for the rate of expense at which the business is conducted, it might be thought that the imposition of a statutory basis of valuation would make for a lower level of expenses because it would compel offices which were extravagant to restrict their expenses to a level consonant with the statutory basis. In fact, it is likely to have the opposite effect since those offices which could adopt a stronger basis than the statutory one would find it difficult to do so in face of the considerable pressure towards a higher expenditure. The assumption that the experiences of different offices are similar to each other is wide of the mark and the actual experience should be given due weight whether the valuation is for solvency or for any other purpose. The choice of a valuation basis is coloured by the purpose for which the valuation is made. It is probable that the imposition of a statutory basis would tend to weaken the authority of the responsible actuary in advising his board of directors and for that reason alone the proposal cannot be too strongly condemned. These arguments are sufficient to show how unsound such a proposal would be.

Another matter to which the actuary must direct his attention in fixing the valuation basis is the question of the free policy and surrender values provided by the Acts of 1923 and 1929. The basis should be such that the reserves are adequate to provide these statutory values. It may be deemed sufficient if the reserves are not less than the statutory surrender values but it is clearly desirable that they should be at least equal to the value on the valuation basis of the statutory free policy values; otherwise a valuation strain will be created on conversion of a policy to a paid-up policy. There are varying opinions as to whether the reserves should cover the statutory values in each individual case or whether it is sufficient if the total reserves cover the total statutory values. If the former opinion is held, any adjustment to the normal basis will probably need to vary with the duration, since it is at the short durations that the statutory values are most onerous. In considering this matter it must be borne in mind that it is holders of policies of short duration who most frequently avail themselves of the statutory concessions. On the strong valuation bases now being used by the larger companies and societies, the question is not material.

Bearing in mind these general considerations we can now proceed to discuss the various basic elements in detail.

20·3. Mortality.

No matter whether a gross premium or a net premium valuation basis is employed, the mortality table used should be such as to represent the anticipated future experience. As in the case of office premiums, a population table will generally be found to be suitable, due allowance being made for any marked geographical or occupational selection. Allowance must also be made for the lag behind current population mortality which was discussed in the previous chapter, but since the valuation basis applies not only to new entrants but to the whole body of assured lives an appropriate table may need to relate to an earlier period than would be suitable for an office premium basis. However, at the time of writing the latest published population table is English Life No. 10 based on the 1931 census. There has been a very considerable improvement in population mortality since then and the table may therefore be considered as suitable for industrial office valuations at the present time. It is in fact being used by practically all the larger offices, but further improvements in population mortality may soon render it out of date. The use of the 'male' table for female lives provides a further margin of safety.

The use of different tables for whole-life and endowment assurances could be justified in theory on two counts. The first is that endowment assurances tend to experience rather lighter mortality than whole-life assurances. The second is that endowment assurances, being of more recent origin, will benefit more than whole-life assurances from the improvement in mortality to the extent that such improvement is a generation effect. However, we have previously mentioned that refinements are both unpractical and unnecessary in industrial assurance and it is probably for this reason that such differentiation in the mortality table is seldom made.

20·4. Interest.

The choice of the rate of interest to be used needs to be considered under two main headings, namely:

(*a*) the net rate which it is expected will be earned by the fund in the future, and

(*b*) any modifications of this rate which may be required on account of the bonus system.

So far as (*a*) is concerned, the considerations in the discussion of the office premium basis apply equally to the valuation basis and there is no need to repeat them here. Once again, however, it must be remembered that in the valuation basis we are concerned with the whole fund and not only with new investments.

Having decided on the probable net rate which will be earned by the fund, the actuary must then consider whether a valuation at this rate would be appropriate. Generally speaking, used in conjunction with a fairly recent population table and true net premiums, it would produce too low reserves and would thus release surplus more quickly than is desirable. This is particularly true where a reversionary bonus system is employed. A somewhat lower rate would normally be used, but the precise rate would be influenced by the financial position of the office. It has been the policy of offices in this country to strengthen the position of their business by progressively reducing the valuation rate of interest whenever it has been possible to do so. At the present time all the larger offices and societies are valuing at rates of interest which are some 1% to $1\frac{1}{2}$% below the actual rates being earned on the funds. This margin is an important source of surplus which has contributed to the development of profit-sharing schemes.

20·5. Expenses.

In the customary net premium valuation the amount reserved for expenses is the difference between the office premiums and the valuation net premiums. This is generally less than the loading in the office premiums because the valuation net premiums are based on a lower rate of interest (though this effect may be modified or even reversed by the use of a lighter mortality table). The amount reserved may be more than or less than the expenses actually being incurred, but as in other net premium valuations the basis must be looked at as a whole; the individual items may be meaningless. For example, such a position can arise where the office is writing a proportionately large volume of new business. The heavy initial expenses will then inflate the apparent expense ratio, expressed as a level percentage of premiums, while the valuation basis, which relates to the whole existing business, takes no account of the incidence of expenses. In such circumstances the office may find it impossible to set up full net premium reserves and some allowance in the valuation for spreading the initial expenses may have to be made. The nature of an industrial valuation makes it desirable that such an allowance should be on simple lines. A convenient method for whole-life assurances is to value the net premium for an age one year or half a year greater than the valuation age at entry. This allows for initial expenses and cost of risk the whole or one-half of the first year's premiums. The increased net premium can be valued throughout the duration of the policy, or it can be gradually reduced until the true net premium is valued for policies more than a certain number of years in force. Where such a method is used, care must be taken to exclude negative values.

In a gross premium valuation the percentage of the office premiums thrown off for expenses could be varied with duration so as to allow for the incidence of initial expenses. It will be apparent from later sections of this chapter, however, that the advantages of a gross premium valuation are mainly practical and they are largely lost unless a fixed percentage is used for policies of all durations, at any rate under the same table. Admittedly such a percentage can be found at any given time which will produce the same result as a net premium valuation, but subsequent changes in the constitution of the business in force might render this percentage invalid. Moreover, the use of a fixed percentage may produce considerable negative values which have to be excluded. Not only does this mean holding reserves which are higher than those required by the valuation basis, but the task of ascertaining where the negative values occur and of excluding them tends to complicate the valuation procedure. For these reasons gross premium valuations are not popular with industrial assurance actuaries.

METHODS

20·6. Collection of data.

The method employed in the collection of the valuation data depends very much on the internal and external organization of the office. Methods vary considerably among offices and it is therefore possible to deal with the matter here on broad lines only. The student should endeavour to make himself familiar with the system of one or other of the offices if he can.

The first fact to bear in mind is that we are dealing with very large numbers of small policies. A continuous method is therefore essential, by which the 'in force' at the end of the year is obtained by adjusting the previous year's figures for the movement on and off which has occurred during the year. A periodical tabulation of the whole business in force is quite impracticable in view of the numbers involved and for most offices it is a very difficult undertaking to do it even once.

We are therefore concerned with obtaining in a form suitable for valuation, particulars of the policies issued during the year and of those discontinued by death, maturity, surrender and lapse. As we have seen, the basic records of the policies are contained in the agents' collecting books or the district register. A record may also be maintained at head office, but even where this is done it will not show the position regarding payment of premiums. In order, therefore, to obtain particulars of lapsed policies it is necessary to rely on returns furnished by the district offices. In some offices this is true also of policies becoming claims by death, maturity or surrender. In the great majority of offices, however, this information can be supplied direct to the valuation department by the claims department.

Particulars of policies issued are usually obtained from the proposals. Where proposal cards are employed they may be used to build up an 'in force' record file and to serve as valuation cards from which the valuation data can be obtained by hand sorting and scheduling, the exits being obtained by extracting the appropriate cards from the 'in force' file. Otherwise, some form of hand-written schedules or registers will be necessary unless a mechanized system of punched cards is in use. In the latter system a card may be punched showing full details of each policy and a file of such cards maintained as a permanent record from which the valuation data can be built up. Alternatively cards may be punched giving only such particulars as are required for the valuation, these cards being destroyed once the valuation is completed. In either system, particulars of new policies will be punched from the proposals while details of exits will be obtained from information supplied by head office departments or district offices.

The fact that some of the information at least must be obtained from returns supplied by the agents means that complete accuracy cannot be relied on. To safeguard against errors, the returns are checked, either completely or by sample, against the collecting books when they are returned to head office. If an 'in force' file is maintained sample checks may also be made with the collecting books from time to time. Errors may also come to light from policy inspections, audits and so on. Generally speaking a remarkably high degree of accuracy is secured, having regard to the nature of the business involved.

20·7. Grouping.

Although methods of obtaining the valuation data vary considerably, there are certain features which are common to them all and which affect the system of grouping to be employed. Whatever method is used, net premiums will not be available in respect of individual policies. This is true even where mechanized methods are employed, for though it would be possible to have the net premium punched into the individual record card in the first instance it would be quite impracticable to re-punch all the cards on a change of basis. In many offices the sum assured also is not recorded for individual policies, but in a mechanized system there is no great difficulty in doing this. Thus, since the net premium and the sum assured depend on the age at entry while the valuation factors depend on the attained age, we require a system of grouping which will give an analysis by both these ages.

To deal with this problem two broad systems of grouping have been employed. In one, the policies are grouped by age at entry subdivided according to year of entry; in the other by year of entry subdivided according to age at entry. In either method the valuation age is age at entry *plus* (valuation year *minus* year of entry). The policies coming on and going off the books are grouped by age and year, or year and age, according to which system is employed, and the particulars for each group are entered in class books or movement registers showing, for each group, totals of the business in force at the beginning of the year and the movement on and off during the year. The balance in force at the end of the year is then obtained by addition and subtraction. In a modern mechanized system the class books showing the group totals may be replaced by cards from which the new group totals can be obtained mechanically.

As we shall see, it is often the practice to value each age at entry or year of entry separately. The age/year grouping slightly facilitates the calculation of the sums assured and net premiums but where a reversionary bonus system is in operation the year/age grouping enables the amount and value of the bonus to be obtained in total for each year of entry; it also permits variations in the rate of bonus according to the duration to be dealt with without difficulty. For this reason the year/age grouping is now more generally used and our subsequent remarks will relate to this method.

A system of valuation which has been widely used is known as the 'unit' method. For each year of entry and age at entry there is recorded only the number of policies in force and the weekly premium or, more correctly, the equivalent number of unit premiums, the unit being usually 1*d.* per week or, say, 1*s.* per month. Thus a policy for 1*s.* 6*d.* per week would be recorded as one policy and 18 penny units of premium. Factor cards are prepared in advance of the valuation, giving for each year of duration and attained age complete valuation particulars in respect of a unit policy, i.e. amount and value of sum assured, amount and value of net premium, value of office premium and net liability. At the valuation the figures on the factor cards are simply multiplied by the number of unit premiums in force. The net liability figure could be omitted and obtained in total by taking the difference between the value of the sums assured and the value of the net premiums. It is usually included, however, for it provides a valuable check on the arithmetic. The reversionary bonus accrued for a policy of given duration will normally be K% of the sum assured, irrespective of the age at entry. To obtain the total accrued bonus for a given year of entry all we need do is take K% of the total sum assured for that year. Similarly the value of the bonus will be K% of the total value of sums assured for that year. The amount and value of new bonus can be obtained likewise.

The separate valuation of each year of entry is not essential, particularly where mechanized methods are used and the sums assured are recorded on the cards. Tabulations by year and age are first made as described above. The net premiums and accrued bonuses (where applicable) are then inserted by hand on each line of the tabulations together with the valuation ages. These additional items are punched into the summary cards from which the tabulations were made and the cards sorted and tabulated according to valuation age. The procedure is then exactly as for an ordinary branch valuation.

It is a matter of opinion which is the best method to use. The 'unit' method enables useful checks to be placed on the calculations because the average factors in respect of a given year of entry should progress fairly steadily from year to year. In the attained age method small errors are more difficult to detect owing to the aggregation of business by valuation age. Again, the unit method enables bonuses to be dealt with in total for each year of entry, whereas they must be recorded separately for each age at entry under the attained age method. On the other hand the unit method involves a great deal of arithmetic, even where the factor cards are already prepared, and the initial preparation of the factor cards is a very heavy task. The attained age method eliminates some of the arithmetic and dispenses with the need for factor cards. We do not think any hard-and-fast rules can be laid down. It depends very much on the circumstances of the office, on the number and nature of the staff available and in particular on whether punched-card machinery is employed.

To assist the student a specimen schedule is given at the end of this chapter. It must be understood that this schedule is given for the purpose of example only, and its form is not necessarily appropriate to the circumstances of every office.

We have so far discussed the problem in general terms, without reference to particular classes of policy. The procedure given is directly applicable to whole-life assurances but the student will doubtless have realized that something further is required for endowment assurances. If they are grouped by term, year of entry and age at entry the foregoing procedure can be adopted and produces exact results; each term is dealt with separately. This may be satisfactory when endowment assurances are issued for a few terms only or for a few maturity ages, the grouping in the latter case being by age at maturity, year of entry, and entry age. Where, however, endowment assurances are issued for all terms it involves a prohibitive amount of work and it becomes necessary to devise a method of simplifying the procedure. One such method is to tabulate a Z constant, as is done for ordinary branch assurances. This means recording an additional valuation constant, a practice which is to be avoided if possible on account of the additional labour which it involves.

An alternative which has been used with some success is to find for each term an average entry age for each year's endowment assurances and to value them at the attained age obtained by adding the curtate duration to this average entry age. The mean age can be found by dividing the total sum assured in force by the total premium in force and entering the result in the table of sums assured per unit premium. This gives good results for the sums assured but is not quite so accurate for the net premiums. Somewhat better results are obtained if the mean entry age is calculated from the net premiums instead of the sums assured.†

This method, of course, involves initial scheduling by age at entry as well as term so that the sums assured and net premiums can be obtained. Where the sums assured are not available in respect of individual policies such scheduling is unavoidable. Where, however, the sums assured are available it can be avoided if the net premiums can be obtained in some other way. This can be done by employing a fixed maturity age for all endowment assurances in the manner described in Part II of this book for ordinary assurances. The net premiums then depend simply on the term and the initial grouping is by year of entry and term only. Moreover, once the net premiums have been calculated, the business can be regrouped by unexpired term in the same way as whole-life assurances are regrouped by attained age, as previously described. This is particularly convenient where mechanized methods are employed. If reversionary bonuses are involved it may be desirable to use a somewhat higher maturity age for the valuation of the bonuses.

Apart from whole-life and endowment assurances, which represent the main body of the business, most offices will have a few other tables which may need special treatment. Whole-life assurances with periodic endowments can be treated in the same way as normal whole-life assurances, the net premiums and valuation factors taking account of the periodic endowment sums. Steps must be taken, of course, to write off the endowment sums as they are paid. Whole-life assurances with limited-premiums may present some difficulties. They can be dealt with by introducing a $P \times N$ constant, but this can sometimes be avoided by using a suitable average age at entry, at any rate for the shorter terms of premium payment. In many offices the whole body of whole-life policies is subject to the provision that premiums cease at a certain fairly advanced age, say 75, 80 or 85. In general all that is necessary

† See p. 253.

is to adjust the net premiums and valuation factors to allow for this. There may, however, be a further provision that a minimum number of years' premiums must be paid, so that for policies of advanced ages at entry premium payments will continue after the given age. Where the business of each year of entry is valued separately this presents no difficulties. The policies are scheduled by age at entry and the appropriate net premiums and valuation factors, allowing for the proper period of premium payment, are used. But if it is desired to pass to an attained-age grouping something more is necessary. All cases with premiums ceasing at the fixed age can be treated as one group, but for the others, though the correct net premiums can be inserted, an adjustment is required to allow for the right unexpired term of payment. Probably the best way to deal with this is to insert a suitable $P \times N$ factor for these policies.

We have so far considered net premium valuations only. In a gross premium valuation separate calculation of the net premiums is unnecessary since they can be obtained in total from the office premiums. Thus, if the sum assured is available for individual policies, there is no need to schedule by year and age, and we can proceed direct to an attained age or unexpired term grouping. Where the individual sums assured are not recorded we first need an age at entry grouping to give the sums assured and bonuses (if any), but, since gross premium valuations are generally confined to offices whose reserves are not so strong as those making net premium valuations, the bonus problem may not arise. We can then proceed to an attained-age grouping for purposes of valuation. This may be influenced, however, by the need for excluding negative values, to which reference has already been made.

Calculation and Formulae

20·8. General considerations.

Premiums are payable either weekly or 4-weekly and claims are paid promptly on notification. For valuation purposes it is therefore customary to employ continuous functions, $\bar{a}$ for premiums and $\bar{A}$ for sums assured. It is usual to assume $365\frac{1}{4}$ days in a year, allowing for leap years, so that a premium of 1*d*. per week is equivalent to $(365\frac{1}{4} \div 7)/240$ or £·21741 per annum.

It is usually assumed that all policies enter in the middle of the year, i.e. that the new business is evenly spread over the year. There are, in fact, seasonal fluctuations in the spread of new business but sample investigations have shown that the assumption is reasonably accurate. Its practical advantages outweigh any slight inaccuracy involved.

The age at entry is invariably the age next birthday. It is assumed that entries are spread evenly over the year of age, so that for policies entering at age x next birthday the average age at entry is $x-\frac{1}{2}$ and exact age x is attained on average at the end of the year, i.e. on the first valuation date. This assumption is reasonably accurate except for policies effected at age one next birthday, which are usually issued soon after birth. It enables the $\bar{a}$ and $\bar{A}$ factors used in the valuation to be calculated at integral ages. For endowment assurances the unexpired term is taken as the curtate unexpired duration plus one-half.

Strictly speaking, net premiums should be calculated at age $x-\frac{1}{2}$ so as to produce a zero reserve at entry. (If a reduced death benefit is payable in the first year it is often ignored, both the net premium and the sum assured factor allowing for the full sum assured throughout.) This would produce a reserve of between one-quarter and one-third of a year's net premium at the first valuation. In view of the heavy initial expenses the net premium for exact age x is often used—producing a zero reserve at the first valuation under whole-life assurances except for infantile ages at entry where it may give small negative values owing to the decreasing rate of mortality at these ages. It should be noted, however, that if credit is taken in the balance sheet for the full amount of arrears outstanding, some of these arrears will relate to policies less than one year in force, for which the reserve at the first valuation is zero. Thus negative values would be introduced indirectly and, to avoid this, some scaling down of the arrears is necessary. As we have seen, it may be necessary to obtain some relief in respect of new business expenses and the net premiums can then be calculated at age $x+\frac{1}{2}$ or age $x+1$. The use of net premiums at age $x+1$ produces zero reserves at the second valuation and negative reserves at the first. At infantile ages the negative values may continue for several years of duration. All negative values must, of course, be excluded. Where the net premium is calculated at an age greater than $x-\frac{1}{2}$ it may be necessary to set up a special reserve in respect of policies which are entitled under the 1929 Act to a surrender value or free-policy value after payment of 1 year's premiums.

20·9. Formulae.

The formulae used are as follow:

(*a*) Whole-life assurances:

Net premium $\bar{P}(\bar{A}_{x-\frac{1}{2}})$, $\bar{P}(\bar{A}_x)$ or $\bar{P}(\bar{A}_{x+1})$.

Reserve per £1 sum assured: $\bar{A}_{x+t}-\bar{P}(\bar{A}).\bar{a}_{x+t}$, where t is the curtate duration in force.

(*b*) Endowment assurances:

Net premium $\bar{P}(\bar{A}_{x-\frac{1}{2}\overline{n}|})$ or $\bar{P}(\bar{A}_{x\overline{n}|})$.

In the case of endowment assurances the use of age x instead of age $x-\frac{1}{2}$ makes very little difference. To correspond with the use of $\bar{P}(\bar{A}_{x+1})$ for whole-life policies it would be necessary to use $\bar{P}(\bar{A}_{x+1\,\overline{n-1}|})$ but this would be far too drastic except, perhaps, for the longest terms. However, owing to the basis of remuneration of the field staff for endowment assurances and the relatively large premiums which are received in respect of them, the incidence of new business expenses falls less heavily than for whole-life assurances and it is unlikely that any adjustment of this sort would be made.

Reserve per £1 sum assured $\bar{A}_{x+t\,\overline{n-t-\frac{1}{2}}|}-\bar{P}(\bar{A}).\bar{a}_{x+t\,\overline{n-t-\frac{1}{2}}|}$.

(*c*) Whole-life assurances with limited-premiums:

Net premium ${}_k\bar{P}(\bar{A}_{x-\frac{1}{2}})$, ${}_k\bar{P}(\bar{A}_x)$ or ${}_{k-1}\bar{P}(\bar{A}_{x+1})$ where k is the premium paying term. The third form would be used only for premiums ceasing at a fairly advanced fixed age.

Reserve per £1 sum assured $\bar{A}_{x+t}-{}_k\bar{P}(\bar{A}).\bar{a}_{x+t\,\overline{k-t-\frac{1}{2}}|}$.

This formula would apply to all policies under the 'unit' method and, also, under the attained age method where premiums cease at a given attained age. Under the latter method, for policies where premiums are payable for a fixed term of years, say *r* years, irrespective of the age at entry, the formula would need modifying along the following lines:

$$\bar{A}_{x+t}-\bar{P}(\bar{A}).\bar{a}_{x+t}+\bar{P}(\bar{A}).\bar{N}_{x+r-\frac{1}{2}}/D_{x+t}.$$

$\bar{P}(\bar{A}).\bar{N}_{x+r-\frac{1}{2}}$ would be recorded as a valuation constant.

For other tables the formulae would be on similar lines.

20·10. Checks.

The student will by now have realized that an industrial assurance valuation involves the manipulation of a large body of data and a very considerable amount of calculation. Errors can occur at any stage of the work and since a continuous system of classification is used, errors in the data will be perpetuated. It is therefore vital to impose adequate checks at each stage.

We have already discussed the checks which can be placed on the data supplied by the district offices. We must ensure, however, not only that each individual item is correct but also that in compiling the valuation data, all the movement is included. Without adequate checks it would be possible for a block of data to be omitted entirely. There is, in fact, a danger of 'not seeing the wood for the trees' and this must be guarded against. The totals of policies going on and off the books should be checked, wherever possible, against other office records of movement and the total valuation 'in force' reconciled with the previous year's figures adjusted by the movement totals. These checks should be made not only on the grand total but also separately on various sub-totals, e.g. separately for each table. This proves not only that the movement is included but that it is included in the right place.

A valuable check, where it is possible, is to reconcile the valuation premium income in force with that obtained from other sources such as accounts and agency records. This requires, however, a highly integrated system of records and it is not always possible to do so.

For over-all checks on the calculations we rely mainly on average factors and reserves. Where the unit method is used these are

SPECIMEN SCHEDULE FOR THE VALUATION OF WHOLE-LIFE ASSURANCES

VALUATION YEAR 1949 YEAR OF ISSUE 1944 YEAR OF ASSURANCE 5

Age at entry	Number of policies	Weekly office premium	Sum assured	Annual net premium	Accrued bonus	Valuation age	Present value of sum assured	Present value of weekly office premium	Present value of annual net premium	Net liability
(1)	(2)	(3)	(4)	(5)	(6)	(7)	(8)	(9)	(10)	(11)
1						6				
2						7				
3						8				
⋮						⋮				
75						80				
Total										
Present value of accrued bonus										

Unit method (non-mechanized):

Cols. (1), (2) and (3) are entered from the class books.

Cols. (4), (5), (8), (9), (10) and (11) are calculated from the factor card for year of assurance 5.

Col. (6) is obtained in total only, the amount and value of bonus being $K\%$ of the totals of cols. (4) and (8) respectively.

Unit method (mechanized):

Cols. (1), (2), (3) and (4) are printed direct from the group summary cards. The procedure is then as before.

Attained age method (mechanized):

Cols. (1) to (4) are printed from the group summary cards.

Cols. (5), (6) and (7) are inserted by hand for each line and the information is then punched into the group summary cards. The cards for all years of entry are sorted together into valuation age and printed on a suitable valuation schedule.

calculated for each year of entry and they should progress steadily from one valuation to the next. Errors of any importance would be readily disclosed. Under the attained age method the average factors, and more particularly the average reserves, are more liable to fluctuation than under the unit method but the averages would certainly disclose any major errors. A useful device is to employ the conversion table relationship. From the formula $\bar{A} = 1 - \delta\bar{a}$ we see that $\delta = (1 - \bar{A})/\bar{a}$. If we calculate the mean $\bar{A}$ and $\bar{a}$ and substitute them in this formula the result should be practically constant from year to year, even when the average factors are moving quite rapidly.

A further useful check is provided by a rough analysis of the surplus. This is discussed in the next chapter.

BIBLIOGRAPHY

1. Acts

Assurance Companies Acts, 1909 to 1946.
Industrial Assurances Acts, 1923 to 1948.

2. Other references

Actuarial aspects of industrial assurance, with special reference to the Report of the Departmental Committee on the business of industrial assurance companies and collecting societies (1920). *J.I.A.* vol. LII, p. 141.

J. Murray Laing (1923). Notes on the Industrial Assurance Act, 1923. *J.I.A.* vol. LV, p. 27.

J. Murray Laing (1926). Valuations under the Industrial Assurance Act, 1923. *J.S.S.* vol. II, no. 5, p. 279.

R. K. Lochhead (1932). *Valuation and surplus*, Ch. III. Cambridge University Press.

C. G. Marshall (1932). Industrial assurance: valuations, office premiums and bonus systems. *J.S.S.* vol. IV, no. 1, p. 55.

W. J. Fulford (1937). Classification and valuation of industrial assurance policies. *J.I.A.* vol. LXVIII, p. 369.

N. E. Coe, K. J. Hedley and L. H. Longley-Cook (1948). Punched-card equipment. *J.I.A.* vol. LXXIV, p. 246.

CHAPTER 21

SURPLUS

A. Distribution of Surplus

21·1. Benefits to policyholders.

In Chapter 19 we discussed the origins of industrial assurance bonuses and mentioned the principal methods of distributing surplus which are in use. We will now discuss these methods in more detail.

(*a*) *Increase in basic sums assured*

This system is often employed in conjunction with an improvement in the scale of benefits for new policies. When an improved scale has been introduced, it might pay existing policyholders to withdraw and re-enter on the new scale at their attained ages. To avoid this, surplus may be used to increase the sums assured under existing policies so as to bring them into line with the new scale.

Care must be taken to ensure that the increases in benefits do not rank as bonuses for the purposes of the Industrial Assurance Acts. Where the surplus is sufficient, all existing policies may be brought into the scheme, but the increase may be limited to policies of certain types or durations. Considerations of equity seem to require that the first policies to benefit should be those of long duration which have probably contributed most to the surplus in hand. These, however, are not the policies which can benefit by withdrawal and re-entry and practical considerations often result in the increases being given first to policies of short duration, though they may be extended subsequently by progressive stages to policies of all durations. In considering what bonuses should be granted in respect of periods several decades ago, it must be remembered that expense ratios were higher and mortality was heavier than to-day. It was difficult then to accumulate proper reserves and adequate reserves had to be accumulated before the distribution of surplus could be considered.

(*b*) *Mortuary bonuses*

These consist of payments by way of bonus on claims arising during a specified period. They do not constitute permanent additions to the benefits payable under a policy; if a policy does not become a claim during the period specified, its right to the bonus ceases. Such bonuses are usually declared each year in respect of the ensuing 12 months, and are so adjusted that the amount of bonus increases progressively with the duration of the policy.

A system of mortuary bonuses, if maintained indefinitely, has much the same practical effect as one of reversionary bonuses, the only differences being that at any particular moment the office is not committed beyond the period covered by the mortuary bonuses and that consequently they do not acquire paid-up-policy or surrender values. The system is, therefore, useful as the first step towards a reversionary bonus scheme and may be introduced before a reversionary bonus can be provided, the necessary surplus being gradually built up by allocations to policyholders. Even if an office has enough surplus in hand to declare a reversionary bonus it may feel that it would prefer to consolidate its position a little further before embarking on a system of reversionary bonuses. In such circumstances a mortuary bonus may be declared as a temporary expedient, the surplus necessary to declare a reversionary bonus being carried forward until such time as it is felt safe to grant reversionary bonuses. These can then be made retrospective to the date when the mortuary bonuses were commenced, so that the surviving policies are in the same position as those which became claims earlier.

(*c*) *Reversionary bonuses*

This is the most popular method of distributing profits to policyholders. The amount of the bonus depends, of course, on the amount of surplus available and at the outset of a bonus system offices usually find it necessary to limit participation to policies which have been a certain number of years in force. The waiting period can then be gradually reduced, policies of shorter duration being progressively brought into the scheme. Sometimes the waiting period is an essential feature of the bonus system in order to equalize the bonuses with the loadings in the premium scale. The loadings must be accumulated during the waiting period and the valuation process must give effect to this.

The bonus is normally expressed as a percentage of the sum assured. In at least two large offices, however, the bonus is based on the premium, being expressed as a fixed amount in respect of each 1*d*. weekly premium or as so many times the weekly premium. The type of bonus must be borne in mind, of course, in fixing the tables of benefits and valuation bases.

The rate of bonus may vary for policies of different types and durations but in view of the methods of classification used for industrial branch valuations it is a great convenience if the bonus can be made the same for all policies of the same duration, at any rate for each table. The same considerations make it necessary to prohibit the surrender of bonuses apart from the main contract.

(*d*) *Cash bonuses*

From the nature of industrial assurance it might be thought that a system of cash bonuses would be both appropriate and popular. Great numbers of industrial assurance policyholders are people living near the subsistence level, for whom insurance premiums constitute a serious item in the weekly budget. In such circumstances it might be supposed that if any share of the profits is to be given to them, it would be most acceptable in the form of cash or at least as a remission of premiums. Such a system of distributing profits has not, however, been widely adopted in this country. No doubt it entails certain administrative problems and there does not appear to have been any public demand for it. Whatever the reason, the fact remains that it has not been extensively used.

There is one possible exception to the foregoing statement. We have already referred to the 'periodic endowment' tables which provide cash sums at regular intervals, usually every 5 years. Surplus can be, and has been, used to increase the amount of the periodic payments, thus providing what is, in effect, a cash bonus.

Such increases would be made, however, at infrequent intervals and the method is really more analogous to method (*a*), viz. an increase in basic benefits.

(*e*) *Limitation of premiums*

This method consists in applying surplus to limit the number of premiums payable on whole-life policies. It is quite extensively used and has the merit of providing relief to the policyholder when it is most needed, namely in old age. Here again, it is not customary to apply the method every year but rather to use accumulated surplus to provide for cessation of premiums at a fixed age, say 75, 80 or 85. Once this has been done, new policies will probably be issued with premiums similarly limited, and any further surplus used to provide bonuses in some other form.

21·2. Other uses of surplus.

Although, generally speaking, a major part of the surplus is allocated for the benefit of policyholders, some of it may be utilized in other ways. In the proprietary offices some will be required to provide proprietors' dividends. Surplus may be used indirectly for the benefit of policyholders in the form of health propaganda, though such schemes are more popular on the American continent than here. Allocations may be made from surplus to the staff or to staff funds, such as sports funds and so on. Contributions may also be made to superannuation funds. In this connexion the student should bear in mind the argument of Chapter 8, that surplus arises primarily as a sum of money, being the difference between the assurance fund and the liabilities. Consequently it makes no difference in the end whether such sums are treated as expense items in the revenue account, or are allocated directly out of surplus. In the former case the fund will be reduced by the amount involved and the surplus will be that much less. The advantage of allocations out of surplus is that they can be made to depend on the amount of surplus available.

Surplus may also be utilized to strengthen the valuation basis, and, as we have seen, offices have tended to do this rather than to release large amounts of surplus immediately in the form of increased bonuses which it might not be possible to maintain. To the extent that the valuation basis is stronger than subsequent experience may show to have been necessary, surplus used in this way will emerge again in the future, but spread over a period instead of in one sum.

B. Analysis of Surplus

21·3. General principles.

The principles involved in analysing industrial branch surplus are the same as those given in Chapter 13 for ordinary business. Since premiums are treated as payable continuously, there is no difficulty in connexion with outstanding instalments and reserves will increase continuously over the year. Formula 13·6 therefore seems to be the most appropriate for the calculation of the expected death strain. It may be advisable to deal with new business separately, particularly if the valuation basis produces negative values at the first valuation date. The premiums received in respect of new business plus interest to the end of the year, less claims and expenses also with interest to the end of the year, should be compared with the reserves (if any) set up at the end of the year in respect of the new business then remaining in force. Care must be taken to include the premiums received on new business which lapses or becomes a claim before the valuation date.

The reserves in respect of death claims should be calculated at the middle of the year and deducted from the amounts actually paid. On claims at early durations only a proportion of the sum assured may be payable, although the valuation may not take account of this, the full sum assured being valued from the outset. If this is so, in calculating the actual death strain $(S-V)$ only the amount actually paid must be included in S but the reserves for the full sum assured must be included in V.

Similarly the reserves in respect of lapses should be calculated as at the middle of the year and compared with the cash surrender values paid plus the cost (on the valuation basis) of free policies granted.

The analyses of the interest and loading surpluses follow the lines indicated in Chapter 13.

21·4. Practical difficulties.

In theory, when all the sources of surplus are known, it should be possible to obtain a complete reconciliation. In practice it may not be possible to trace exactly some of the minor sources of surplus, such as policy alterations, and even in an ordinary branch fund some small untraced balance is to be expected.

In an industrial fund some of these practical difficulties are greatly accentuated. Owing to the very large number of policies involved, details of individual policies may not be readily accessible and consequently surplus arising from policy alterations, extra risks and so on may not be traceable without an excessive amount of work. The amount of such surplus, however, is not likely to be great.

A more serious practical problem arises in connexion with the valuation of the claims and lapses. Since large numbers are involved, these are likely to occur at the majority of ages and durations and their valuation may entail a considerable amount of work. This is particularly true where the unit method of valuation is used, each year of entry being valued separately. Only the reserves are required, of course, so that the work can be reduced by omitting the separate calculation of the values of sums assured, net premiums and office premiums. Where an attained age method is used, combined with mechanized methods of sorting, the difficulty is not so great, it being a fairly simple matter to sort the exit cards into valuation groups.

Although the large number of policies involved presents difficulties in one direction, it has advantages in another, because it usually results in the surplus from the various sources being fairly steady from year to year. Consequently, if a reasonably exact analysis of the mortality and miscellaneous group has once been made, it is often possible to make an approximate analysis in subsequent years, sufficiently accurate to place a reasonable check on the valuation.

BIBLIOGRAPHY

K. J. BRITT (1930). Industrial assurance profit sharing in Great Britain. *Trans. Ninth Int. Congress*, Stockholm, vol. I, p. 141.

R. K. LOCHHEAD (1932). *Valuation and surplus*, pp. 92–3. Cambridge University Press.

C. G. MARSHALL (1932). Industrial assurance: valuations, office premiums and bonus systems. *J.S.S.* vol. IV, no. 1, pp. 68–70.

F. H. SPRATLING (1935). Industrial assurance profit sharing. *J.S.S.* vol. IV, no. 4, p. 234.

W. J. FULFORD (1937). Classification and valuation of industrial assurance policies. *J.I.A.* vol. LXVIII, pp. 395–8.

J. H. GUNLAKE (1939). *Premiums for life assurances and annuities*, pp. 111–113. Cambridge University Press.

K. J. BRITT (1948). The development of industrial assurance in Great Britain since 1928. *Proc. Cent. Assembly Inst. Act.* vol. III, p. 3.

CHAPTER 22

PAID-UP POLICIES AND SURRENDER VALUES

22·1. Legal provisions.

Industrial assurance paid-up policies and surrender values are governed strictly by statute. The statutes governing the matter are the Acts of 1923 and 1929. These Acts not only make it obligatory to allow benefits on discontinuance after certain qualifying periods but also lay down minimum bases for the calculation of the benefits. Generally speaking, offices are now going beyond their statutory obligations either by reducing the qualifying periods, or by making benefits automatic instead of granting them only on application, or by increasing the actual amounts.

In an earlier chapter we discussed the question of a uniform valuation basis for all offices and many of the arguments there set forth apply equally to the idea of a uniform basis for paid-up policies and surrender values. But a recommendation for such a uniform basis was contained in the Report of the Parmoor Committee and this recommendation was adopted in the Industrial Assurance Act, 1923. The provisions of the Act relating to this matter did not come into operation, however, until June 1928. Endowment assurances and pure endowments on the lives of children under age 10, and similar life-of-another assurances effected for funeral expenses, have special rights under the Industrial Assurance and Friendly Societies Act, 1929, which was passed to remove a doubt that had been cast upon certain of such assurances by the decision of a magistrates' court. Thus the assurances to which the 1929 Act applies have alternative rights; they are entitled to the benefit of whichever Act, the 1923 Act or the 1929 Act, affords the more generous treatment in the particular circumstances.

The 1923 Act, alone, applies to own-life assurances and also to life-of-another whole-life assurances.

It will be convenient to give here a brief summary of the bases under the two Acts.

1923 ACT

Qualifying period: 5 years for whole-life assurances, and for endowment assurances and pure endowments for terms of 25 years or more; 3 years for shorter term endowments and endowment assurances.

Value of policy: E.L.T. No. 6 (Persons) 4% reserve, the values of bonuses being added in full. Allowance is made for initial expenses by assuming the policy to have been effected 1 year later than the actual date and for a term 1 year less than the actual term. For whole-life assurances on children less than 10 years old, no account need be taken of the period in force prior to the policy anniversary immediately following the attainment of age 10.

Durations: Curtate.

Surrender values: 75% of the value of the policy.

Paid-up policy: The reversionary equivalent of the surrender value on the basis of E.L.T. No. 6 (Persons) 4%.

When granted: Paid-up policy on application within 1 year from the date of service of the forfeiture notice. Surrender value if the life assured has disappeared or if the owner of the policy is, or intends to be, permanently resident abroad.

1929 ACT

Qualifying period: 1 year.

Durations: Exact, in weeks or months as the case may be.

Paid-up policy: That proportion of the sum assured and bonus additions that the premiums actually paid bear to those originally payable.

Surrender value: 90% of the value of the paid-up policy on the basis of E.L.T. No. 6 (Persons) 4%.

When granted: Both surrender value and paid-up policy on application within 1 year from the date of payment of the last premium.

It should be noted that the 1929 Act did not repeal any of the provisions of the 1923 Act. For policies to which the former Act applies it is therefore necessary to use whichever basis produces the higher value, or the terms set out in the contract if they are more favourable. Except for long-term assurances, the 1929-Act values will be the greater, but since bonuses are added in full under the 1923 Act, and only proportionately under the 1929 Act, cases can arise to which the 1929 Act applies at the earlier durations and the 1923 Act at later durations. Also, it is possible for the value to revert to the 1929-Act basis at the longest durations.

The student should also note the provision in the 1923 Act which limits the paid-up policy to the difference between the sum assured and bonuses under the discontinued policy and the sum which would be assured by the same premium under a new policy effected at the attained age. This enables offices to avoid widespread lapsing and re-entry by policyholders who could otherwise take advantage of the Act to secure, without any increase in premium, a greater total assurance than they originally held.

22·2. Bases.

It is apparent, we think, that the bases laid down in the two Acts are of an arbitrary nature and are not likely to be appropriate to the circumstances of all offices. It will be instructive, perhaps, to take each element of the bases in turn, and to consider briefly its appropriateness in present circumstances.

(*a*) *Mortality*. It has been suggested that withdrawal is a selective force and that the mortality of those who withdraw will be lighter than that of those remaining in the fund. Evidence on this question is not conclusive, but from consideration of the nature of industrial assurance it seems reasonable to expect some such effect. It is usual for several policies to be held by one family and if circumstances make it necessary to discontinue one of them it is not likely to be one on a life in bad health. In a paper in 1932, Tayler suggested that a deduction of one-half a year from the age would be a reasonable allowance for this. But whatever the proper allowance may be, it is apparent that the basis used in the Acts is not appropriate, for the use of E.L.T. No. 6 assumes withdrawals to be subject to much heavier mortality than the continuing policies, for which E.L.T. No. 10 might be more suitable.

(*b*) *Interest.* A fixed interest basis is even less likely to be appropriate to all offices than a fixed mortality basis. Moreover, a given rate may not be suitable for the same office at all times over a period of years. The variations that have occurred in the market rate of interest during the past 25 years can hardly have made the 4% basis laid down in the Acts appropriate to any office throughout the whole of that period. At the present time, having regard to the yield on new investments and the average yield on industrial branch funds, it may perhaps be said that a rate of 4% is not inappropriate.

(*c*) *Expenses.* The 1923 Act makes specific allowance for initial expenses by excluding the first year's premiums. Such an allowance is certainly too great for the short-term endowment assurances but may well be insufficient for whole-life assurances and long-term policies. The position is mitigated in the case of these long-term contracts, however, by the qualifying period of 5 years. There is also an over-all deduction of 25% of the policy value. But this 25% cannot be regarded as being entirely available for expenses, since some, if not all, of it is necessary to make good deficiencies in the basis in other respects; and a flat percentage, applied at all durations, cannot correctly allow for the incidence of expenses.

The use of a net premium in calculating the policy value automatically allows for total expenses if the net premium corresponds to that used in the office premium basis. All that is further required is an adjustment to allow for the incidence of initial expenses and perhaps a small deduction of, say, 5% to cover the expenses of withdrawal. The 25% deduction in the 1923 Act provides a safety margin which is useful because the net premium is not appropriate.

Under the 1929 Act the position is still less satisfactory. The proportionate basis used for paid-up policies gives excessive values at the early durations and inadequate values at later durations, particularly for long-term contracts; it makes no specific allowance for expenses. For surrender values there is a flat deduction of 10%, but as we have seen, a level deduction of this kind does not make proper allowance for the incidence of expenses. It should be further noted that the Acts apply the same basis to weekly and monthly policies in spite of the considerable differences between the two types.

(*d*) *Bonuses*. As we have seen in earlier chapters, practical considerations make it essential that any industrial branch system of bonuses should be simple and straightforward in operation. For this reason reversionary bonuses at a flat rate, irrespective of age or duration, have been widely used. Such bonuses may be granted from issue or after a qualifying period of one or more years. It cannot usually be claimed that the contribution made by a particular policy towards the cost of its bonus exactly equals the value of the bonus granted each year. In the early years it may well be inadequate particularly if bonuses are added from the outset. If this results in the payment of rather more bonus on early claims than they have strictly earned, no great harm is done. The position is very different, however, when we are considering what bonuses, if any, should be allowed to those policyholders who exercise their right to withdraw at a time convenient to themselves. It is obviously undesirable that they should benefit at the expense of the continuing policyholders by receiving more by way of bonuses than their premiums have earned. Yet under the 1923 Act bonuses are added in full to the sum assured in calculating the value of the policy and are subject only to the over-all deduction of 25 % from the value.

Under the 1929 Act the position is taken to the opposite extreme by reducing bonuses in the same proportion as the sum assured. Under a 30-year endowment assurance with 1 year's premiums paid, only one-thirtieth of the accrued bonus is added.

Clearly, neither of the two bases is correct in all circumstances and equally clearly, it would be impossible to devise such a basis. On the other hand, seeing that a substantial proportion of industrial policies in force are entitled to bonuses of one kind or another, a statutory minimum basis which made no provision for bonuses would hardly be satisfactory. No matter what basis is used, it will be open to criticism, and it may well result in forcing the bonus policies of the offices into channels which they would not otherwise follow.

22·3. Desirability of statutory values.

Apart from defects in the bases themselves, it is necessary to consider whether a statutory obligation to pay a cash surrender value on demand is advisable in any circumstances. There have been times in the history of life assurance, though fortunately not in the history of British life assurance, when offices have been compelled to suspend payment of surrender values during periods of crisis owing to excessive demand by the public because of lack of confidence. In such circumstances an obligation to pay statutory minimum values might well strain the resources of offices beyond their limits unless the statutory values were well within the amounts normally available on withdrawal. But in that event the statutory minima become meaningless.

22·4. Values in excess of statutory minima.

At the beginning of this chapter we mentioned the possibility of granting values in excess of the statutory minima. The extent to which this can be done depends on the circumstances of individual offices and no hard-and-fast rules can be laid down. However, in the paper previously referred to on p. 426, H. Hosking Tayler suggested a basis which he considered would be more appropriate for most offices than the bases in the Acts. We do not propose to discuss this basis in detail, but it may help the student to mention broadly how the suggested paid-up policies compare with those under the Acts. Bonuses are not taken account of in the comparison.

For whole-life assurances the values were less than those on the 1923-Act basis for durations up to 3 or 4 years and greater thereafter, the excess being as much as 30% at duration 30 years. It must be remembered, however, that the 1923 Act does not normally impose any value for durations under 5 years, so that where paid-up policies are in fact granted at the shorter durations they need not be on the 1923-Act basis.

For endowment assurances, Hosking Tayler's values were in excess of the 1923-Act values for all terms and durations, the percentage excess being greatest at the short durations. They were less than the 1929-Act values except for terms 20 and over at young entry ages where they slightly exceeded those values. The student should note that the 1929 Act does not apply to own-life assurances (nor to certain assurances on the spouse of the proposer), to which the 1923 Act only is applicable. It seems anomalous that two identical policies with the same office should be entitled to such widely different values merely because one is, say, on the life of the proposer's wife and the other on the life of his mother. Yet where the 1929-Act values are excessive, an office could not be expected to pay these values unless it is obliged to do so; but the anomaly can at any rate be lessened by quoting values in excess of the 1923-Act values, but less than those of the 1929 Act, for endowment assurances to which only the 1923 Act applies.

The foregoing comparison relates to paid-up policies. Surrender values on Hosking Tayler's basis would compare less favourably with the values under the Acts because in both Acts the surrender value represents the paid-up policy discounted by E.L.T. No. 6 (Persons) 4% whereas his basis was E.L.T. No. 9 (Males) 4%. Under the 1923 Act, however, it is not obligatory to grant surrender values save in special circumstances though the majority of offices now go well beyond their statutory obligations in this respect.

22·5. Automatic paid-up policies.

We will close this chapter with a few words on the subject of automatic paid-up policies to which reference has been made in earlier chapters. These paid-up policies are granted automatically on the lapsing of a policy, whether requested by the policyholder or not. The statutory paid-up policies are relevant but most offices are now granting them at earlier durations than the 5 years laid down in the 1923 Act, the necessary qualification being payment of not less than 2 years' premiums and, in several of the larger offices, 1 year's premiums. The values at the early durations are not necessarily the 1923-Act values (for policies not governed by the 1929 Act); several offices in fact allow the 1923-Act values at these durations or—on endowment assurances—the proportionate paid-up policy where this is greater.

Since a paid-up policy is granted to every withdrawal more than a certain period in force, it is important to ensure that the valuation basis is such as to avoid any valuation strain on conversion to a paid-up policy. It is also necessary to bear in mind the yearly statement of movement which has to be made to the Commissioner under the 1948 Act, and to ensure that the records are kept in such a form as to enable this return to be completed. In this connexion it is pertinent to note a particular difficulty which has been introduced by the 1948 Act. The Act requires that paid-up policies granted after the passing of the Act shall be taken into account in assessing the amount (if any) for which a new policy may be issued on the life of a parent, step-parent or grandparent of the proposer. The agent will normally be aware of the existing policies with the same office on which premiums are being paid, as they will be recorded in his collecting book. Paid-up policies, however, are not usually so recorded and unless they are of recent origin the agent may well be unaware of their existence. On the other hand the office could hardly plead ignorance of policies on its own books, so some means must be found of ensuring that the £20 limit is not exceeded because of existing paid-up policies. This is a problem to which each office must find its own solution, but there seem to be two main lines of approach. One is to set up a card index of paid-up policies for the relationships concerned, to which all new proposals for those relationships can be referred. The other is to pay a surrender value instead of granting a paid-up policy wherever possible.

BIBLIOGRAPHY

1. Acts

Industrial Assurance Acts, 1923–48.

2. Other References

J. Murray Laing (1923). Notes on the Industrial Assurance Act, 1923. *J.I.A.* vol. LV, p. 27.

H. Hosking Tayler (1932). On paid-up policies and surrender values under the Industrial Assurance Acts. *J.I.A.* vol. LXIII, p. 271.

POSTSCRIPT

CAPITAL REDEMPTION ASSURANCES

Since capital redemption assurances are not dependent on human life they are strictly outside the scope of the title of this book but such business is of the same character as life assurance and reference has been made to it in various chapters. It has been decided to include capital redemption assurances in Part IVA of the Examinations and this postscript attempts a brief sketch of the subject.

Capital redemption insurance business is not one of the defined classes of assurance business within the scope of the Assurance Companies Act, 1909 (see § 3·5) and, consequently, capital redemption assurances and life assurances—though similar in fact—are subject to different laws and to different bases of taxation (see § 5·1).

[Bond investment business, which is substantially the same as capital redemption insurance business with premiums at intervals of two months or less, is one of the defined classes within the scope of the 1909 Act but there is no space to discuss the subject in this book.]

The calculation of premiums for capital redemption assurances is affected by three main features of the business, namely (*a*) the very long periods—for example 99 years—for which such assurances may be arranged, (*b*) the very large sums assured that may be required, and (*c*) the 'savings bank' character of the business.

The rate of interest assumed should be a conservative one, normally less than would be assumed for life assurances, and should have regard to the period for which the assurance is to endure.

Commission is less than for life assurance, perhaps a percentage of the first year's premium varying with the period of the contract. The office may make a specific charge for expenses by way of loading in the premium scale or it may rely upon meeting its expenses out of a margin in the assumed rate of interest. The adequacy of such a margin should be tested on the lines discussed in § 10·6 on pure endowments with return.

For post-1937 capital redemption assurances, provision has to be made for income tax on the investment income, and for profits tax on the provision for income tax. Thus, if the rates of income tax and profits tax—at the 'undistributed' rate—be t_1 and t_2 respectively, the effective rate of tax, t, is given by

$$t = t_1 + t \, . \, t_2 \, (1 - t_1),$$

whence
$$t = t_1 / \{1 - t_2 \, (1 - t_1)\}.$$

The heavy and uncertain incidence of taxation makes it scarcely possible to transact this class of business.

It is customary to guarantee at surrender the return of the whole or almost the whole of the premiums paid with interest, but excluding the first year's premium. The right to surrender involves a 'financial' option which is liable to be exercised against the office and which cannot be offset by a margin in the cost of life assurance cover, such as might be available on surrender of a life assurance contract. The percentage deduction from the premiums returned on surrender should, perhaps, have more regard to this possibility of loss than to the deduction for expenses which is the usual justification of the practice.

The consideration for an annuity-certain can be based upon a gross rate of interest and a percentage is usually added by way of loading for expenses (see § 10·14).

The contracts effected before 1 January 1938, and the contracts effected after 31 December 1937, have to be valued separately for purposes of income tax. The valuations should allow for the different bases of taxation applicable to such contracts.

A gross rate of interest can be assumed for pre-1938 contracts. The valuation may be made by a prospective or a retrospective method. The former method is preferable where all the pre-1938 contracts are valued at a single suitable rate of interest. The latter method may be preferred where each group of contracts is valued at the rate of interest originally assumed in the premium scale.

The post-1937 fund presents an interesting situation. The annuities-certain can be valued at a gross rate of interest but the capital redemption assurances have to be valued at the corresponding net rate after deduction of income tax at the standard rate and of profits tax on the provision for income tax, in the manner discussed above. The variations that have occurred in the rates of income tax and profits tax make it desirable to value the capital redemption assurances by the prospective method at a suitable net rate of interest.

The subject of profits tax is regarded as being outside the scope of Part IV A of the Examinations and there are many complications which are not mentioned in this book.

INDEX

Printed in the United States
By Bookmasters